Sustainability of Young Companies

Sustainability of Young Companies: Contemporary Trends and Challenges

Special Issue Editor

Marek Jabłoński

MDPI • Basel • Beijing • Wuhan • Barcelona • Belgrade

MDPI

Special Issue Editor
Marek Jabłoński
WSB University
Poland

Editorial Office
MDPI
St. Alban-Anlage 66
4052 Basel, Switzerland

This is a reprint of articles from the Special Issue published online in the open access journal *Sustainability* (ISSN 2071-1050) from 2018 to 2019 (available at: https://www.mdpi.com/journal/sustainability/special_issues/sustainability_young_companies)

For citation purposes, cite each article independently as indicated on the article page online and as indicated below:

LastName, A.A.; LastName, B.B.; LastName, C.C. Article Title. *Journal Name* **Year**, *Article Number*, Page Range.

ISBN 978-3-03921-185-2 (Pbk)
ISBN 978-3-03921-186-9 (PDF)

Contents

About the Special Issue Editor

Marek Jabłoński is an Associate Professor at WSB University in Poznan, Faculty in Chorzow, Poland, e-mail: marek.jablonski@ottima-plus.com.pl. He is the Head of the Scientific Institute of Entrepreneurship and Innovation. He is also the Vice President of the Board of "OTTIMA Plus" Ltd. of Katowice, a reputable management consulting company, and President of the "Southern Railway Cluster" Association in Katowice, which supports development in railway transport and the transfer of innovation, as well as cooperation with European railway clusters (as a member of the European Railway Cluster Initiative). He holds a postdoctoral degree in Economic Science, specializing in Management Science in the following range of topics: value-based management, performance management, and business models. Having worked as a management consultant since 1997, he is the author of a variety of studies and business analyses on business models, creating shareholder value, the balanced scorecard, and implementing the high-performance organization concept. He has also written and co-written several monographs and over 100 scientific articles in the fields of strategic management, performance management, and business models. Marek's academic interests focus on the issues of strategic value, innovative business models, measurement systems of results, including companies listed on the stock exchange and the principles of creating shareholder value, and new trends in this area.

Preface to "Sustainability of Young Companies–Contemporary Trends and Challenges"

Ensuring the sustainability of early stage companies and increasing awareness of the need for balancing targets against different stakeholder groups among young companies are not well developed. Young companies, in the first place, want to achieve financial success very often without regard for aspects such as the environment, positive relationships with employees, suppliers or other stakeholder groups, fulfilling requirements of labor law, etc. Another issue is that of companies whose business models are based on actuarially-preferred concepts, such as sharing economy, sustainable development, e-comers, e-commerce, renewable energy, social media, and others. A key issue is the resignation of companies from an approach to business, based on the foundations of classical economics to the sharing economy. Theory and practice seek new solutions in the sphere of value sharing in these new areas of sharing, and innovative forms of its implementation. Intriguing is the relationship of these business models with sustainability issues, as well as wondering how technology can influence sustainability. A contemporary approach to consumer value fits in with the assumption of a shared economy. It is interesting how it affects the assumptions of sustainability of business. The ongoing changes in the value system of potential consumers create new conditions for the design of sustainability business models and creation of innovation. On the basis of the abovementioned assumptions, the key issue is to answer the following questions:

1. What is the problem of sustainability when it comes to young companies?
2. How can we design a sustainable business model?
3. What are the features of sustainable business models of companies in early stages of development
4. How can we create sustainable start-ups?
5. Why are the business models of young companies unstable?
6. Is there a connection among agility, flexibility, scalability, and sustainability of business models in the context of small and young companies?
7. How can we design a method for creating sustainable business models?
8. What are the differences between sustainability for big companies and small companies?
9. What are the roles of stakeholders in shaping sustainability for young companies?

Marek Jabłoński
Special Issue Editor

sustainability

MDPI

Article

Social Factors as a Basic Driver of the Digitalization of the Business Models of Railway Companies

Marek Jabłoński [1,*] **and Adam Jabłoński** [2,*]

1   Scientific Institute of Entrepreneurship and Innovation, Faculty in Chorzów, WSB University in Poznań, Sportowa 29, 41-506 Chorzów, Poland
2   Scientific Institute of Management, Faculty in Chorzów, WSB University in Poznań, Sportowa 29, 41-506 Chorzów, Poland
*   Correspondence: marek.jablonski@ottima-plus.com.pl (M.J.); adam.jablonski@ottima-plus.com.pl (A.J.)

Received: 22 May 2019; Accepted: 14 June 2019; Published: 18 June 2019

Abstract: The aim of the paper is to present the results of research into the assessment of social factors resulting from the digitalization of railway companies' business models and building, by means of the AHP method, a ranking of the significance of these criteria in the process of their digital transformation. The results focused on identifying the components of the business models of railway companies that are most affected by social factors and the creation of such factors. Railway companies do not operate within the business environment alone. In the context of processes, they form one common technical and service ecosystem. Digitalization should increase opportunities to create positive social effects which influence the quality of services provided and the safety of rail traffic as well as the increased efficiency of business models.

Keywords: digitalization; business model; social aspects; railway companies

1. Introduction

The aim of the paper is to present the results of research into the assessment of social factors resulting from the digitalization of railway companies' business models and building, by means of the AHP method, a ranking of the significance of these criteria in the process of their digital transformation. The results focused on identifying the components of the business models of railway companies that are most affected by social factors and create such factors. Railway companies do not operate within the business environment alone. In the context of processes, they form one common technical and service ecosystem. Digitalization should increase opportunities for creating positive social effects which influence the quality of services provided and the safety of rail traffic as well as the increased efficiency of business models. Digitalization has been recognized as one of the main trends which are changing society and business. Digitalization brings about changes for companies due to the adoption of digital technologies in an organization or in an operational environment [1]. The dynamics of global market development are based on the development of the digital economy. Traditional value chains are subject to digitalization. Business models based on classical solutions (traditional construct of the value chain) are also subject to digitalization, in part or in whole, and thus achieve new opportunities to increase their efficiency and effectiveness. The Internet economy is essentially characterized by its considerable dynamics and the speed of change. The rapid digitalization of numerous areas of life has resulted in a shift towards today's Information Society [2]. An innovative business model may be subject to changes in the individual components of business models, the extension of the existing business model, or the introduction of parallel business models bringing about the disorganization of the business model, which may potentially involve replacing the existing model with a completely different one [3]. Therefore, the concept of the business model refers to a more transformational approach, which uses the concept as a tool to make changes and innovations in the organization or change the model itself [4]. A positive effect of the dynamic development of the digital economy is the creation of social effects. Building a community focused on achieving common goals based on innovative technological solutions allows for the development of modern and conscious human behaviour and positive patterns. Traditional sectors of the economy also follow new trends and opportunities resulting from the development of the digital economy. The wider use of digital social innovations in transformation processes is used to fully exploit the potential of business models, designed not only in economic terms but also for the benefit of society [5]. The social nature of business activity is also apparent in the rail transport sector. This is influenced, in particular, by criteria related to railway traffic safety and the complex value-added chain based on cooperation between many entities. In Poland, as throughout Europe, the rail market is highly liberalized. The rules governing the operation of the railway market are based on directives regarding unrestricted access to the rail market, interoperability and safety. This legal arrangement ensures the transport of goods and services by rail across Europe while maintaining a standardized level of quality, safety and technical compatibility. There are several infrastructure managers in Poland and about 100 railway undertakings. In addition, in terms of market characteristics, it is possible to identify about 100 entities in charge of maintenance, as well as inspection bodies, notified bodies, and the market regulator and the National Safety Authority, which is important for the maintenance of railway vehicles. This arrangement of relationships builds an important ecosystem of the rail business where exogenous factors are the key to its effectiveness. The organizational and legal system means that railway companies' business models are strongly limited by legal regulations. The configuration of the value chain and the proposal to supply value to the customer depend on the solution adopted by entrepreneurs that meets stringent legal requirements in terms of interoperability, regulated accounting and security. At the same time, it should be noted that the railway undertaking market is very competitive while most of the transport processes are carried out on the railway network of the national infrastructure manager. The digitalization of railway companies in such a system is, on the one hand, building the potential to compete, and on the other hand, facilitating the development of social factors that can be achieved through digitalization. As already mentioned, rail transport operators, i.e., infrastructure managers and railway undertakings, are obliged to provide high quality services and the highest level of railway traffic safety. The digital economy creates new opportunities for achieving social effects, building communities, and improving the efficiency of railway companies. The aim of the paper is to present the results of research into the assessment of social factors resulting from the digitalization of railway companies' business models and building, by means of the AHP method, a ranking of the significance of these criteria in the process of their digital transformation. The research results focused, in particular, on identifying such components of the business models of railway companies that are most affected by social factors and create such factors. Railway companies do not operate within the business environment alone. In the context of processes, they form one common technical and service ecosystem. Digitalization should increase opportunities for creating positive social effects which influence the quality of services provided and the safety of rail traffic as well as the increased efficiency of business models. The social aspect in digital business models has two dimensions. The first one is built into the idea of building a community created by using, in whole or in part, the scope of activity of multifaceted technological platforms that are distinctive compared to other business models, while the other refers to the social impact of the value delivered by the business model. Both shape a pro-social approach, which is expressed in delivering social value to business model stakeholders. Both of these approaches are complementary and create the image of socially acceptable business models, where this social aspect is a condition for adapting such business models to the expectations of the contemporary global market. The issue of rail transport is strategic in terms of the place and role of this sector in the economy as well as the effectiveness of railway companies. The digitalization of the economy significantly determines changes in the configuration of business models, which also affects changes in the social ecosystem shaped by these enterprises. Research does not refer to political solutions from the sphere of regional development in the context of rail transport. It is focused on the study of the economic and social determinants of the digital transformation of the rail business. The research described in this paper is devoted to this issue. This paper is structured as follows: Section 2 presents the theoretical background of Digital Transformation—key approaches and definitions. Section 3 presents the main idea of digital business models and the genesis and direction of the evolution of business model concept. Section 4 presents the problems of digitalization through Service Management and Industry 4.0 concepts in the context of the specificity of the rail transport sector. Section 5 analyzed the theoretical aspects of social factors of the digital transformation of business models. In Section 6, research methodology based on the AHP method was presented. Section 7 described the results of research into the social results of digital transformation on the business models of railway companies. The subsequent sections present a discussion and conclusion—in addition, Section 9 presents limitations and includes suggestions for future research. At the end the references used were indicated.

2. Digital Transformation—Key Approaches and Definitions

Digitalization is now a dynamic process covering all sectors of the economy. Traditional solutions in the sphere of the value chain are subject to the process of digital transformation [6].

Contemporary business models are the subject of digital transformation. W. Smith, A. Binns, and M. Tushman define the business model as a "configuration" by which the company chooses the options of strategies that can create value, and then uses the organizational architecture to create and retain value [7]. The business model is "the architecture for products, service and information flow, with a description of the various business actors and their roles; a description of the potential benefits for various business actors and a description of the sources of revenue" [8]. The individual components of business models in the company's life cycle change so that enterprises are able to survive and develop in many situations. Digitalization is a factor which stimulates changes in business models. Digitalization forms a part of Industry 4.0 and constitutes both a threat and opportunity to transform business as we know it; and can make entire business models redundant [9]. The definitions of digital transformation include different approaches to this issue. Digital Transformation is defined as the use of technology to radically improve the performance or reach of enterprises [10]. Digital Transformation is the changes that digital technology causes or influences in all aspects of human life [11]. In turn, the level of digital maturity of companies is assessed in terms of numerous criteria such as strategy, leadership, products, operations, culture, people, governance, and technology [12,13]. The different definitions for Digital Transformation (DT) may be categorized in three distinct elements: (1) Technological—DT is based on the use of new digital technologies such as social media, mobile, analytics or embedded devices; (2) Organizational—DT requires a change of organizational processes or the creation of new business models; (3) Social—DT is a phenomenon that influences all aspects of human life by, e.g., enhancing customers' experience [14]. Digitalization has an influence on many areas of activities of an organization such as new and emerging customer segments, cultural diversity in a global marketplace, market volatility, heightened customer expectations in terms of the quality of products and services, and the impact of the internet on an organization's core business [15]. Digital transformation is the subject of research in many contexts: in the field of entrepreneurship [16], in the field of Digital Learning [17], in terms of the dynamic capabilities concept [18] as well as in the context of the sectoral approach [19,20], and also in the context of small and medium-sized enterprises [21]. Digital transformation processes are also studied in terms of changes in the labor market [22,23]. Digitalization plays a key role in the context of changes in business models, the configuration of which is shaped using innovative technologies. The problems resolved are related, among others, to the structured approach to the digital transformation of business models, the activities and results of digitalization of business models, and the role of enablers and best practice in the digitalization of business models [24]. Optimization solutions in the field of the effectiveness of digital business models are proposed, taking into account areas such as content, experience and platform [25]. In the context of business models, as research results reveal, the digital transformation involves the transformation of subsequent areas of business model configuration. The process of the digital transformation of the business model includes the preparation phases, value proposition, value creation, and value capture [26].

A broad approach to this issue results from the common digitalization of many aspects, not only of company activity, but in particular of modern life.

3. Digital Business Models—Key Aspects

The concept of digital business models is developing dynamically in the context of conditions for the development of new technologies. The very concept of traditional business models is widely recognized in the relevant literature. In general, the concept of business models is based on the development of three key research trends: the development of generic concepts and the search for optimal definitions, shaping effective business model structures, and the management of the business model [27].

The development of the concept of business models can be divided into several stages. The definition of a business model emerged in the 1950s. From 1975 to 2000 a technological approach was observed, leading to the initial phase of the development of online models. From 2000 to 2010 a strategic approach developed. Finally, from 2010 until today, solutions based on an integrated approach have been developed [28]. In the context of technology development resulting from the digital economy, the business model is a coherent link between products, services, information flow and the description of various roles of business actors [8]. The use of technology allows the business model to transform resources into economic results through the activation of customers and the use of markets [29]. This approach, based on the evolution of the approach to shaping business models, migrates the processes of business model design towards fully exploiting the potential of the digital economy. The digital economy creates many opportunities through the creation of many innovative approaches to transform traditional business models into partially or completely digital models. There is a distinction between innovative digital and non-digital undertakings. Combining practical management tools with the principles of network theory as well as the theory of organizational learning creates new possibilities for creating business models [30]. The specialist skills that change the existing balance of power in global markets are important for the development of digital business models [31], whereas digital ecosystems should provide companies based on innovative business models with attractive value sources that create new ways to grow [32]. Consequently, digitalization should affect the economic success of enterprises based on the potential of the digital economy [33]. This new approach to the dynamic search for attractive business models is in line with new trends based on the assumptions of consistent and interdependent development of management aspects and innovative technological solutions that support them.

4. Digitalization by Service Management and Industry 4.0 Concepts and the Specificity of the Rail Transport Sector

Industry 4.0 as a concept is a great challenge for many sectors of the world's economies. Despite many publications on the subject, there is no single model of its implementation in theory and practice. However, in the relevant literature there are descriptions of the positive effects of implementing the digital transformation of business models. In the context of the Industry 4.0 concept, the authors of the research indicate four areas of digitalization: changes in value creation and value offered, organizational aspects, and technical aspects [34]. In particular, it is based on intelligent solutions which combine aspects such as vertical integration, virtualization, automation, traceability, flexibility, and energy management [35]. The role of an employee as the operator of complex technical systems changes in the sense that the proportion of working time spent on decision-making processes declines [36]. Industry 4.0 and Internet-operated technologies are very useful for the creation of added value for organizations and society [37]. This is in line with the specificity of the rail transport sector, which belongs to the services sector as part of the transport of goods and people and infrastructure management. In this model of action, smart networks connect machines, processes, systems, products, customers and suppliers. The digitalization of the business models of railway companies is of key importance in this approach to improve the efficiency of their operation. In this context, an important role is played primarily by the service approach to the challenges in question, which is the Service Management 4.0 concept. Value can be offered as a physical product, a real or virtual service, or as a combination of products and services [38]. The business objective of Service Management 4.0 is dedicated to outlining a system of the future that drives the service organization and its information closer to the customer as a means of developing a deeper customer relationship [39]. The implementation of dynamic quality models and tailor-designed software solutions for transport companies was clearly beneficial on the basis of the findings. The benefits of implementation are a shortened response time during extraordinary circumstances; the transparency of transactions and responsibilities; the company's approach to customers in terms of taking into account their wishes and maintaining or increasing the number of passengers as a result; creating a positive image of the company; but ultimately also reducing the costs incurred in removing weaknesses and errors [40]. The required data capture and intelligence is an integrated part of the offering, which reflects a technology-driven business development strategy [38]. The use of Industry 4.0 and Service Management 4.0 concepts may include the following areas specific to the rail transport sector:

- Modern and innovative methods for ensuring the efficiency of companies by collecting and processing information in real time.
- Creating a Smart Factory in the rail transport industry.
- Machine support for modern companies.
- Using the Internet of Things (IoT) and Cyber-Physical Systems (CPS).
- The Connected Enterprise—a new cooperation model and a new value creation chain, expanded to include business partners and customers.
- Application of Lean Management.
- Supporting the automatization of technologies through innovative methods of optimization, configuration, self-control and intelligent employee support.

Therefore, the digitalization of the business models of railway companies is part of the conceptual assumptions which constitute a significant challenge for building theoretical and practical solutions due to the specific conditions for the functioning of this sector within the liberal rail transport market in Europe. The specificity of the rail transport sector is based on different models. The classic solution in the sphere of rail transport processes is the legal separation of the activity of railway undertakings from the activity of infrastructure managers. Both of these entities operate within one complex technical and organizational railway system, but based on two different business models. Digitalization plays a key role as part of their process integration. It provides a platform for improving customer service processes and the use of full automatization of processes, which improves transport safety and passenger satisfaction. Achieving social effects through the use of digitalization in the rail transport sector is becoming a priority challenge obtained through the implementation of innovative and complex technical and organizational solutions that are a key strategic goal for the dynamically developing rail transport sector. The dynamics of changes in the railway sector in the legal dimension determines the development of new organizational, operational and technical solutions, which must be systemic and multidimensional [41]. The key milestone of this assessment is to verify the accuracy of the description of the rail system undergoing change with regard to its scope, functions and associated interfaces [42]. Hence, the basic criterion for assessing the efficiency of railway companies is accessibility and safety. Both of these factors depend on the digitalization of the business model and the digital integration of operational processes. They are supported by formalized systems of safety management, which are used to integrate many processes, including the processes of mutual communication between railway system operators between which interfaces occur while creating technical and social relations [43]. In this way, the social factors of the digitalization of railway companies are created.

5. Social Factors of the Digital Transformation of Business Models

In terms of shaping business models, digitalization is also social in nature. Through innovative technological solutions, it is possible to develop social attitudes and behaviours and achieve social effects. The development of innovative ways of doing business that are oriented towards balancing the goal of making profit and achieving the assumptions of sustainable development is a key challenge for corporate managers and business strategists in the twenty-first century [44]. Research in this area is not extensive. This topic is just beginning to be the subject of scientific analysis.

A classical approach to sustainable development based on the new triple bottom line concept [45] can also be used to create sustainable solutions in the context of digital economics. It should be considered in the context of the life cycle of business models [46]. The Industrial Internet of Things (IIoT) is also influential in terms of economic, ecological, and social aspects referring to the Triple Bottom Line (TBL) of sustainable value creation. In recent years, digitalization and related social aspects have been the subject of research. A number of key articles have been published in this research area. Sustainable Industrial Value Creation in the context of Industry 4.0 was the subject of research by a team of scientists from Germany, as well as the influence of the Industrial Internet of Things (IIoT), and also in terms of economic, ecological, and social aspects referring to the Triple Bottom Line (TBL) of sustainable value creation. In [47] the authors included a triple bottom line concept in the logic of IIoT. From a broad perspective, the impact limit of IIoT is based on three pillars, namely Technical Integration, Data & Information, and the Public Context. The social aspect includes Resource Efficiency and mainly refers to human resources, while the economic factor includes issues such as competitiveness, finance, overall equipment effectiveness (OEE), novel business models, time and individualization. A research challenge in terms of Industry 4.0 is to identify the place and role of the concept of sustainability. The opportunities include elements such as strategy, operations and environment and people, while challenges include competitiveness and future viability, organizational and production fit and employee qualification and acceptance [48]. The aspect of sustainability in terms of the concept of the Internet of Things can be considered in the micro context in terms of the shape of the ecosystem of contemporary global economies and in the micro context in terms of changes in the construction of value chains [49]. Research into the social innovation perspective for the application of the fourth industrial revolution (Industry 4.0) has already been undertaken. Readiness for such revolutionary conversion requires coupling the forces of technological innovation and social innovation under the sustainability umbrella [50]. The target for the economic sustainability of digital information services is to ensure cheaper, easier and better access to information. The target for the social sustainability of digital information services is to ensure equitable access in order to build a better (well informed) and healthy society, whereas the target for the environmental sustainability of digital information services is to ensure reductions in the environmental impact of digital information [51]. In terms of digital business models, the sustainability aspects have an impact on the migration of value, as confirmed by research [52]. They are important in the context of fledgling enterprises [53]. The development of a new approach to stakeholder theory in the context of the digital age is also required. In this respect, the new approach to this theory includes stakeholder theory, sustainability as a transformative concept and Big Data and digitalization [54]. It also refers to hybrid organizations [55]. The acceleration of interest and the search for a scientific gap in the issue of creating social drivers through digital business models results from the dynamic development of the Circular Economy concept, the conceptualization and operationalization of which is more efficient thanks to the use of modern technologies. In this respect, the factor that dynamizes processes is the circulation of values [25]. In addition, in the context of the development of the digital economy, as highlighted by researchers, attention should be paid to the fact that social media is one of the major drivers in the change of public perceptions, as it has facilitated the spread of information and misinformation about sustainability issues [16]. Previous research also covers the principles underlying social trade [56]. The issues of creating social aspects in digital business models cover many research areas. The main assumptions are based on two issues. The first includes the aspect based on the traditional triple bottom line concept and the increased potential of this idea through innovative digital solutions, as in the case of Circular Economy assumptions, while the second one results from the specificity of technological solutions particular to the digital economy—building community and focused on socially acceptable ideas in its activities, trying to achieve positive social effects. Both of these approaches are built into the modern solutions of digital business models. The space for researching the digital transformation of business models may include many organizational and technological aspects that shape the effective configurations of business models. In this respect, social factors are the basic driver of business model value.

6. Research Methodology

The research procedure involved collecting the relevant literature on the digital transformation of business models, social aspects of the digital economy and the railway transport sector, and analyzing the evolution of the concept of a digital business model and its key trends. The authors defined the key attributes of digital business models and their development trends, taking strategic reflection into account. Factors that affect the digital transformation of the business models of railway companies were identified. The AHP method was applied to build a ranking of social criteria related to the digital transformation process of the business models of railway companies.

The AHP method was chosen as a research method because it is a general hierarchical approach to making multi-criteria decisions. It involves deconstructing the problem into simpler components and processing the ratings obtained on the basis of pairwise comparisons. The AHP method has numerous applications in terms of supporting economic, technical or social decisions. This allows for the arrangement of the elements of the decision-making problem, described in the form of the hierarchy of factors. This way, the best factor was selected. In this article, the following steps were taken using the AHP method to obtain a hierarchy of individual factors analyzed:

- The deconstruction and presentation of the problem in hierarchical form—defining the general objective to be achieved as regards the problem under consideration, attributes detailing the general objective and decision options considered,
- the specification of decision options and the final graphical representation of the hierarchy,
- the creation of a pairwise comparison matrix to compare all the elements of the lower level with the successive elements of the higher level,
- the calculation of local priorities—calculation of the largest eigenvalue and the eigenvector corresponding to this eigenvalue,
- the calculation of global priorities.

The results obtained by means of the AHP method give an image of how experts from the railway industry perceive the issues raised by the authors of the article related to the subject of the article. As a result, a ranking of individual criteria and sub-criteria was received, taking into account experience, strategies in the railway industry, and—most importantly—the value systems that individual enterprises follow. This means that making a decision involves identifying and defining the problem and objective, options and criteria. Subsequently, the decision-making problem is analyzed by evaluating the options/solutions and then the option/solution is chosen. Thus, the questionnaire was composed and sent to the companies surveyed. For the purpose of considering all possible sources of errors which the study could have been exposed to, a pilot study was conducted, which was a miniature of the main study. It aimed to provide data that was omitted by the researchers while planning the study. As a consequence, it could also have an impact on the final results. The pilot study, as part of testing research questionnaires, was conducted on a much smaller sample, i.e., 3%. After collecting the responses from the surveys, conclusions were inferred based on the research results.

As part of the research process, railway undertakings and infrastructure managers were taken into account. In Poland, 16 managers provide infrastructure to railway undertakings and 110 railway undertakings operate. The responses obtained through surveys were examined using the AHP method. Nineteen responses were received from the companies surveyed. This accounts for 15% of the companies to which questionnaires were sent—the entire population of all railway companies operating on the Polish market. All of the completed surveys were filled in correctly.

The aim of the analysis was to examine the problem of the digital transformation of railway companies in the context of building a ranking of factors which create social effects. The respondents were asked to give answers to key issues arising from the review of the relevant literature on company digitalization, including the following social factors:

- The digital transformation of the business models of railway companies.
- Opportunities for the development of social factors through digital transformation.
- The mutual process integration of railway companies through digital transformation.
- The servitization of railway companies.
- The socialization of the business models of railway companies.

The responses to the survey allowed for the presentation of the results in this article. Experts were consulted for their opinions on their activity, meaning the railway industry. This was the basis for the assessment of the criteria and provided the opportunity to build an initial matrix of preferences.

7. The Results of Research into Social Factors for the Digital Transformation of Business Models of Railway Companies

In the context of studying the issue of the digital transformation of railway companies, a ranking of factors which create social effects was developed. To this end, the AHP (Analytic Hierarchy Process) method proposed by Thomas L. Saaty [57] was used. This method is used in solving decision-making problems that contain more than one criterion. The algorithm of the AHP method consists of four phases: creating a hierarchical structure of the decision-making process, defining the decision-maker's preferences and calculating significance ratings for all elements of the hierarchy, examining the consistency of the preference matrix, and creating the final ranking. The following scheme of the hierarchical model was used in the study (Figure 1):

Decision options, which are at the lowest level of the hierarchy of the model, were subject to comparative analysis by means of the AHP method. These options are railway undertakings and railway infrastructure managers. The five areas adopted in which survey questions (in the form of statements) were defined are as follows:

1. The digital transformation of the business models of the railway companies.

   ○ Statement 1.1. The business model of our company is strongly supported by digital economy solutions.
   ○ Statement 1.2. Our operational processes are essentially based on the use of digital communication.
   ○ Statement 1.3. The strategy of our company assumes the digitalization of the key areas of our activity in the next three years
   ○ Statement 1.4. Guaranteeing cybersecurity is a priority in our company's activity.
   ○ Statement 1.5. The digital solutions used in our company improve railway traffic safety.

2. Opportunities for the development of social factors through digital transformation:

   ○ Statement 2.1. The implementation of digital solutions increases the chances of improving relationships with our stakeholders.
   ○ Statement 2.2. The digital solutions used in our company improve the quality of human-human, human-machine and machine-machine interfaces.
   ○ Statement 2.3. The digital solutions in our company generate positive relationships with suppliers/partners.

    ○   Statement 2.4. We build social capital with rail market actors through digital solutions.

    ○   Statement 2.5. The digital solutions used in our company foster the implementation of social effects—ecology, ethics, and economics.

3.   The mutual process integration of railway companies through digital transformation:

    ○   Statement 3.1. The digital solutions in our company improve process efficiency.

    ○   Statement 3.2. The digitalization of our technological processes helps us improve integration with other railway traffic participants.

    ○   Statement 3.3. The digital solutions in our company help improve the ability to cooperate within the organizational and technical solutions of the railway ecosystem.

    ○   Statement 3.4. We build cooperation platforms with other railway companies using digital technologies.

    ○   Statement 3.5. The digital solutions used are fully compatible with the solutions of other enterprises within the railway ecosystem.

4.   The servitization of railway companies:

    ○   Statement 4.1. We apply solutions based on the transition from a product/service- oriented model to a service-oriented business model and its logic.

    ○   Statement 4.2. We notice the potential of the effective management of the business model of our company.

    ○   Statement 4.3. We constantly monitor and adjust our business model in every case, in a bottom-up, emergent and iterative way.

    ○   Statement 4.4. We try to design a business model to co-create value with customers.

    ○   Statement 4.5. We pay attention to the creation of a value network with all rail market actors.

5.   The socialization of the business models of railway companies:

    ○   Statement 5.1. In our business model, the aspect of positive social impact plays an important role.

    ○   Statement 5.2. Employees in our company are treated with respect and are an important voice in the decision-making process.

    ○   Statement 5.3. We pay attention to positive relationships with communities gathered around the railway ecosystem.

    ○   Statement 5.4. Our business model is based on an effective dialogue with stakeholders.

    ○   Statement 5.5. Building trust with business partners is an important component of our business model.

The individual criteria (areas) were compared and the degree of their fulfillment was examined. Survey questions form sub-criteria in this study. The above criteria and sub-criteria were prepared in order to check to what extent social factors influence the process of the digitalization of business models of railway undertakings. They were constructed by the authors based on their knowledge of the railway market and railway company management. The above five criteria were compared in pairs using the following scale (Table 1):

Table 1. Saaty scale used to compare the pairs of criteria.

Significance Scale	Explanation
1	No criterion has an advantage over the other in achieving the goal.
3	Criterion A has a moderate advantage over option B.
5	Criterion A has a strong advantage over option B.

Source: Own study based on [59].

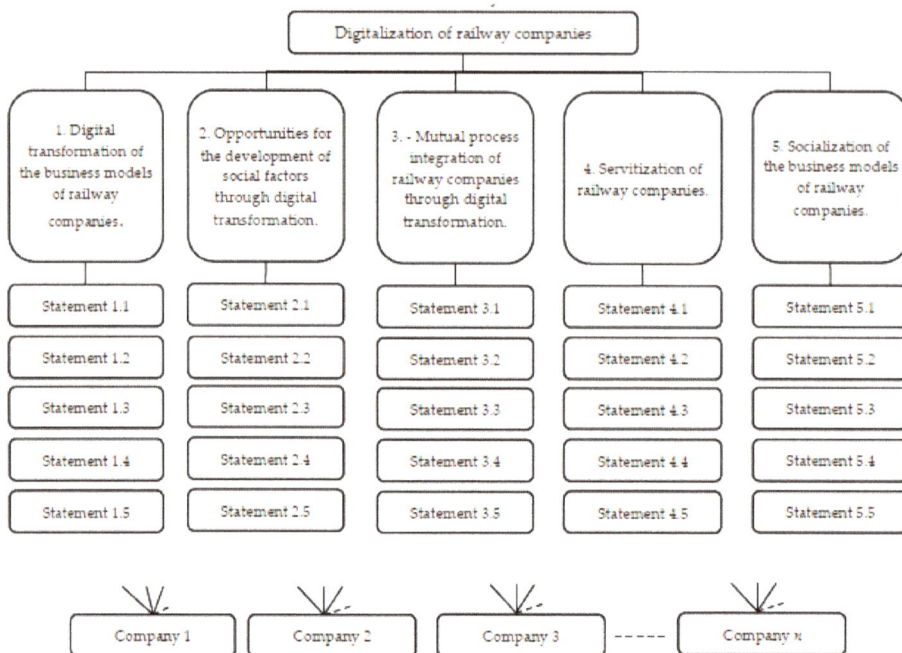

Figure 1. Scheme of the hierarchical model adopted for the study. Source: Own study based on [58].

7.1. Calculation of Global Weights for Adopted Criteria

Using the Saaty scale, a matrix was obtained that shows the advantage of a given criterion over another, in order to finally have them ranked by means of global weights.

In addition to the pairwise comparison of criteria, sub-criteria were also compared. This resulted in obtaining the weight values for all sub-criteria in order to assess the degree of the digitalization of railway companies.

After comparing the pairs of criteria, the matrix n x n was made, where n is the number of criteria. In this case n = 5, because five criteria were adopted. In the AHP method, there are inverse ratings, which means that the matrix is consistent in pairs, i.e.,

$$w_{ij} \cdot \frac{1}{w_{ji}} = 1$$

The data which was necessary to obtain a matrix of comparisons, i.e., the assessments of the significance of criteria and the superiority of one over the other, was obtained thanks to the participation of experts in the railway industry. Their necessary participation results from obtaining opinions on a different perception of reality and the processes occurring therein. Their approaches are built on experience, different priorities, value systems and other factors. Using the comparison scale, the AHP method directs the person expressing opinions to two types of questions. They refer to the strength of the advantage of the elements compared over a given criterion by selecting:

-       Which of the two criteria has a greater advantage over the other,
-       which of the two sub-criteria has a greater impact on the third main criterion.

As a result, the matrix showing the pairwise comparison of criteria is as follows (Table 2):

Table 2. Matrix showing pairwise comparisons for particular groups of criteria.

Criteria	1. Digital Transformation of the Business Models of Railway Companies	2. Opportunities for the Development of Social Factors through Digital Transformation	3. Mutual Process Integration of Railway Companies through Digital Transformation	4. Servitization of Railway Companies	5. Socialization of the Business Models of Railway Companies
1. Digital transformation of the business models of railway companies	1.00	1.00	1.00	0.33	0.20
2. Opportunities for the development of social factors through digital transformation	1.00	1.00	1.00	3.00	0.33
3. Mutual process integration of railway companies through digital transformation	1.00	1.00	1.00	1.00	0.20
4. Servitization of railway companies	3.00	0.33	1.00	1.00	1.00
5. Socialization of the business models of railway companies	5.00	3.00	5.00	1.00	1.00
Total	11.00	6.33	9.00	6.33	2.73

Source: Own study.

Subsequently the matrix of normalized W ratings was obtained by dividing the individual ratings in the criteria columns by the sum of the ratings of a given column and saving the results in a given matrix cell:

$$W = \begin{bmatrix} 0.09 & 0.16 & 0.11 & 0.05 & 0.07 \\ 0.09 & 0.16 & 0.11 & 0.47 & 0.12 \\ 0.09 & 0.16 & 0.11 & 0.16 & 0.07 \\ 0.27 & 0.05 & 0.11 & 0.16 & 0.37 \\ 0.45 & 0.47 & 0.56 & 0.16 & 0.37 \end{bmatrix}$$

The following criteria description is used in the tables so that the notation in the table is clear:

-       Criterion 1—The digital transformation of the business models of railway companies,
-       Criterion 2—Opportunities for the development of social factors through digital transformation,
-       Criterion 3—The mutual process integration of railway companies through digital transformation,
-       Criterion 4—The servitization of railway companies,
-       Criterion 5—The socialization of the business models of railway companies.

To obtain weights for each criterion, values from individual rows/lines were added up and then divided by the number of the criteria (i.e., number 5). Table 3 presents normalized matrix calculated for criteria and global weights obtained.

Table 3. Normalized matrix calculated for criteria and global weights obtained.

Criteria	Criterion1	Criterion2	Criterion3	Criterion4	Criterion5	Global Weight
Criterion1	0.0909	0.1579	0.1111	0.0526	0.0732	0.0971
Criterion2	0.0909	0.1579	0.1111	0.4737	0.1220	0.1911
Criterion3	0.0909	0.1579	0.1111	0.1579	0.0732	0.1182
Criterion4	0.2727	0.0526	0.1111	0.1579	0.3659	0.1920
Criterion5	0.4545	0.4737	0.5556	0.1579	0.3659	0.4015
						$\sum weight = 1$

Source: Own study.

The above weights are ranked from highest to lowest. As a result, the following ranking of criteria was obtained (Table 4):

Table 4. Ranking of adopted criteria together with global weights.

Ranking	Criterion	Criterion name	Global Weight
1	Criterion5	The socialization of the business models of railway companies.	0.4015
2	Criterion4	The servitization of railway companies	0.1920
3	Criterion2	Opportunities for the development of social factors through digital transformation	0.1911
4	Criterion3	The mutual process integration of railway companies through digital transformation	0.1182
5	Criterion1	The digital transformation of the business models of railway companies	0.0971

Source: Own study.

The above ranking shows that "the socialization of the business models of railway companies" is most important, achieving a global weight of 40.15%, followed by "the servitization of railway companies" with a global weight of 19.20% and the equally significant" opportunities for the development of social factors through digital transformation"—at 19.11%, "the mutual process integration of railway companies through digital transformation", and "the digital transformation of the railway companies", which gained 9.71% significance.

Subsequently, the correctness of the results was checked by calculating the inconsistency index λmax (i.e., the average of the matrix's own value). The value of λmax is a measure of the consistency of comparisons reflecting the proportionality of preferences. Pairwise comparisons are all the more consistent the closer λmax is to n (the number of elements in the matrix = the number of rows = the number of columns). In the case of total consistency, $\lambda max = n$ (Table 5).

Table 5. Inconsistency index λmax for criteria.

Criteria	Total rating of Individual Criteria (Columns)	Obtained Weights	Values in Relation to the Inconsistency Index
Criterion1	11.00	0.10	1.07
Criterion2	6.33	0.19	1.21
Criterion3	9.00	0.12	1.06
Criterion4	6.33	0.19	1.22
Criterion5	2.73	0.40	1.10
	5.66		

Study: Own study

The value of λmax is equal to 5.66, which means that it is close to 5, i.e., the number of criteria studied (Table 5).

The next step was to calculate the Consistency Index (CI) of the comparison matrix, which talks about the deviation from consistency. It was calculated using the following formula:

$$CI = \frac{\lambda_{max} - n}{n - 1}$$

However, the interpretation of CI is difficult. Thus, the CR (Consistency Ratio) was determined. The CR determines the degree of inconsistency of the comparison of the significance of the descriptions, which can be expressed as a number or percentage. It is determined by the following formula:

$$CR = \frac{CI}{RI} \times 100\%$$

To calculate the Consistency Ratio, you need the RI value—a Random Consistency Index which is unchanged, and which was presented in the book "Fundamentals of decision making and the priority theory with the Analytic Hierarchy Process" by T.L. Saaty. The value of the RI for the 5×5 matrix is RI = 1.12. The random consistency index was calculated from a randomly generated matrix with the dimensions $n \times n$ and the values of R.I. were generated from several thousand such matrices and presented by T.L. Saaty in his publication.

For such a matrix dimension, the CR value should not exceed 10% (CR $\leq$ 0.10), because then the CR is accepted and the comparisons are consistent. In this case, the CR value is 15%, which means that it slightly exceeds the recommended threshold. There is a risk that the comparisons are inconsistent. If the comparisons were fully consistent, the values of coefficients would be: $\lambda max = n$, CI = 0 and CR = 0.

7.2. Calculation of Local Weights for Sub-Criteria

In accordance with the previously presented steps to obtain weights for individual criteria, the same was done for sub-criteria to obtain local weights. Thus, five separate calculation sheets were developed. The matrices with the results obtained by testing pairs of sub-criteria are presented below (Tables 6–10).

Sustainability **2019**, *11*, 3367

Table 6. Pairwise comparison matrix for Criterion 1—digital transformation of business models of railway companies.

Digital Transformation of the Business Models of Railway Companies	Statement 1.1. The Business Model of our Company is strongly Supported by Digital Economy Solutions	Statement 1.2. Our Operational Processes are essentially based on the Use of Digital Communication	Statement 1.3. The Strategy of our Company Assumes the Digitalization of the Key Areas of our Activity in the next Three years	Statement 1.4. Guaranteeing Cybersecurity is a Priority in our Company's Activity	Statement 1.5. The Digital Solutions used in our Company Improve Railway Traffic Safety
Statement 1.1. The business model of our company is strongly supported by digital economy solutions	1.00	1.00	3.00	3.00	3.00
Statement 1.2. Our operational processes are essentially based on the use of digital communication.	1.00	1.00	5.00	3.00	3.00
Statement 1.3. The strategy of our company assumes the digitalization of the key areas of our activity in the next three years.	0.33	0.20	1.00	0.33	3.00
Statement 1.4. Guaranteeing cybersecurity is a priority in our company's activity	0.33	0.33	3.00	1.00	3.00
Statement 1.5. The digital solutions used in our company improve railway traffic safety	0.33	0.33	0.33	0.33	1.00

Source: own study.

14

Table 7. Pairwise comparison matrix for Criterion 2—opportunities for the development of social factors through digital transformation.

Opportunities for the Development of Social Factors through Digital Transformation	Statement 2.1. The Implementation of Digital Solutions Increases the Chances of Improving Relationships with our Stakeholders.	Statement 2.2. The Digital Solutions used in our Company Improve the Quality of Human-Human, Human-Machine and Machine-Machine Interfaces.	Statement 2.3. The Digital Solutions in our Company Generate Positive Relationships with Suppliers/Partners.	Statement 2.4. We Build Social Capital with Rail Market Actors through Digital Solutions.	Statement 2.5. The Digital Solutions used in our Company Foster the Implementation of Social Effects—Ecology, Ethics, and Economics
Statement 2.1. The implementation of digital solutions increases the chances of improving relationships with our stakeholders.	1.00	0.20	0.33	0.33	0.33
Statement 2.2. The digital solutions used in our company improve the quality of human–human, human-machine and machine-machine interfaces.	5.00	1.00	3.00	1.00	0.33
Statement 2.3. The digital solutions in our company generate positive relationships with suppliers/partners.	3.00	0.33	1.00	0.33	0.33
Statement 2.4. We build social capital with rail market actors through digital solutions.	3.00	1.00	3.00	1.00	0.33
Statement 2.5. The digital solutions used in our company foster the implementation of social effects—ecology, ethics, and economics	3.00	3.00	3.00	3.00	1.00

Source: Own study.

Table 8. Pairwise comparison matrix for Criterion 3—the mutual process integration of railway companies through digital transformation.

The Mutual Process Integration of Railway Companies through Digital Transformation.	Statement 3.1. The Digital Solutions in our Company Improve Process Efficiency	Statement 3.2. The Digitalization of our Technological Processes Helps us Improve Integration with other Railway Traffic Participants.	Statement 3.3. The Digital Solutions in our Company help Improve the Ability to Cooperate within the Organizational and Technical Solutions of the Railway Ecosystem.	Statement 3.4. We Build Cooperation Platforms with other Railway Companies using Digital Technologies.	Statement 3.5. The Digital Solutions used are fully Compatible with the Solutions of other Enterprises within the Railway Ecosystem.
Statement 3.1. The digital solutions in our company improve process efficiency	1.00	0.33	0.33	0.33	0.20
Statement 3.2. The digitalization of our technological processes helps us improve integration with other railway traffic participants.	3.00	1.00	3.00	3.00	0.20
Statement 3.3. The digital solutions in our company help improve the ability to cooperate within the organizational and technical solutions of the railway ecosystem.	3.00	0.33	1.00	0.33	0.33
Statement 3.4. We build cooperation platforms with other railway companies using digital technologies.	3.00	0.33	3.00	1.00	0.33
Statement 3.5. The digital solutions used are fully compatible with the solutions of other enterprises within the railway ecosystem.	5.00	5.00	3.00	3.00	1.00

Source: Own study.

Table 9. Pairwise comparison matrix for Criterion 4—the servitization of railway companies.

The Servitization of Railway Companies.	Statement 4.1. We Apply Solutions based on the Transition from a Product/Service-Oriented Model to a Service-Oriented Business Model and its Logic.	Statement 4.2. We Notice the Potential of the Effective Management of the Business Model of our Company.	Statement 4.3. We constantly Monitor and Adjust our Business Model in every Case, in a Bottom-Up, Emergent and Iterative way.	Statement 4.4. We try to Design a Business Model to Co-Create Value with Customers.	Statement 4.5. We pay Attention to the Creation of a Value Network with all Rail Market Actors.
Statement 4.1. We apply solutions based on the transition from a product/service- oriented model to a service-oriented business model and its logic.	1.00	3.00	0.33	3.00	0.33
Statement 4.2. We notice the potential of the effective management of the business model of our company.	0.33	1.00	0.33	0.33	0.20
Statement 4.3. We constantly monitor and adjust our business model in every case, in a bottom-up, emergent and iterative way.	3.00	3.00	1.00	3.00	0.33
Statement 4.4. We try to design a business model to co-create value with customers.	0.33	3.00	0.33	1.00	0.33
Statement 4.5. We pay attention to the creation of a value network with all rail market actors.	3.00	5.00	3.00	3.00	1.00

Source: Own study.

Table 10. Pairwise comparison matrix for Criterion 5—the socialization of the business models of railway companies.

The Socialization of the Business Models of Railway Companies.	Statement 5.1. In our Business Model, the Aspect of Positive Social Impact Plays an Important Role.	Statement 5.2. Employees in our Company are Treated with Respect and are an Important Voice in the Decision-Making Process.	Statement 5.3. We Pay Attention to Positive Relationships with Communities Gathered around the Railway Ecosystem.	Statement 5.4. Our Business Model is based on an Effective Dialogue with Stakeholders.	Statement 5.5. Building Trust with Business Partners is an Important Component of our Business Model.
Statement 5.1. In our business model, the aspect of positive social impact plays an important role.	1.00	0.33	0.33	0.33	0.33
Statement 5.2. Employees in our company are treated with respect and are an important voice in the decision-making process.	3.00	1.00	3.00	3.00	3.00
Statement 5.3. We pay attention to positive relationships with communities gathered around the railway ecosystem.	3.00	0.33	1.00	3.00	1.00
Statement 5.4. Our business model is based on an effective dialogue with stakeholders.	3.00	0.33	0.33	1.00	1.00
Statement 5.5. Building trust with business partners is an important component of our business model.	3.00	0.33	1.00	1.00	1.00

Source: Own study.

Subsequently the above data in the tables was normalized, thus obtaining matrices as below. They allowed us to obtain the values of weights, and subsequently the ranking inside the criterion studied (Table 11):

Table 11. Normalized sub-criterion matrix for Criterion 1.

Normalized W-Matrix	Statement 1.1	Statement 1.2	Statement 1.3	Statement 1.4	Statement 1.5	Weights = Local Priorities	RANKING
Statement 1.1	0.33	0.35	0.24	0.39	0.23	0.31	2
Statement 1.2	0.33	0.35	0.41	0.39	0.23	0.34	1
Statement 1.3	0.11	0.07	0.08	0.04	0.23	0.11	4
Statement 1.4	0.11	0.12	0.24	0.13	0.23	0.17	3
Statement 1.5	0.11	0.12	0.03	0.04	0.08	0.07	5

Source: Own study.

Among the five defined sub-criteria for Criterion 1 (Table 11), i.e., the digital transformation of the business models of railway companies, Statement 1.2—"Our operational processes are fundamentally based on the use of digital communication" was the most important, receiving a weight of 0.34. Statement 1.1 that "The business model of our company is strongly supported by digital economy solutions" was slightly less important—a local weight at the level of 0.31. The other three statements obtained local weights below 0.20. Statement 1.5 "The digital solutions used in our company improve railway traffic safety" was the least important, gaining a weight equal to 0.07.

Taking into account Criterion 2 (Opportunities for the development of social factors through digital transformation), the highest rated was Statement 2.5 "The digital solutions used in our company support the implementation of social effects—ecology, ethics, economics". It obtained a local weight of 0.40. It was followed by Statement 2.2 "The digital solutions used in our company improve the quality of human-human, human-machine and machine-machine interfaces", with a local weight of 0.22. Statement 2.1 "The implementation of digital solutions increases the chances of improving relations with our stakeholders" was at the bottom of the ranking with a weight of 0.07 (Table 12).

Table 12. Normalized sub-criterion matrix for Criterion 2.

Normalized W-Matrix	Statement 2.1	Statement 2.2	Statement 2.3	Statement 2.4	Statement 2.5	Weights = Local Priorities	RANKING
Statement 2.1	0.07	0.04	0.03	0.06	0.14	0.07	5
Statement 2.2	0.33	0.18	0.29	0.18	0.14	0.22	2
Statement 2.3	0.20	0.06	0.10	0.06	0.14	0.11	4
Statement 2.4	0.20	0.18	0.29	0.18	0.14	0.20	3
Statement 2.5	0.20	0.54	0.29	0.53	0.43	0.40	1

Source: Own study

In the case of Criterion 3 "The mutual process integration of railway enterprises through digital transformation" (Table 13), the overarching sub-criterion turned out to be Statement 3.5 "The digital solutions used are fully compatible with the solutions of other enterprises within the railway ecosystem", obtaining a local weight of as much as 0.44. Statement 3.2 "The digitalization of our technological processes helps us improve integration with other railway traffic participants" was ranked second, with the local weight being lower by half at 0.22. Statement 3.1 "Digital solutions in our company improve process efficiency", with a local weight of 0.06, was at the bottom of the ranking.

Table 13. Normalized sub-criterion matrix for Criterion 3.

Normalized W-Matrix	Statement 3.1	Statement 3.2	Statement 3.3	Statement 3.4	Statement 3.5	Weights = Local Priorities	RANKING
Statement 3.1	0.07	0.05	0.03	0.04	0.10	0.06	5
Statement 3.2	0.20	0.14	0.29	0.39	0.10	0.22	2
Statement 3.3	0.20	0.05	0.10	0.04	0.16	0.11	4
Statement 3.4	0.20	0.05	0.29	0.13	0.16	0.17	3
Statement 3.5	0.33	0.71	0.29	0.39	0.48	0.44	1

Source: Own study

When analyzing Criterion 4 "The servitization of railway companies" (Table 14), the highest local weight of 0.41 was for Statement 4.5 "We pay attention to the creation of a value network with all rail market actors". Statement 4.3 "We constantly monitor and adjust our business model in every case, in a bottom-up, emergent and iterative way" was ranked second with a local weight of 0.25. The fifth and last place was occupied by Statement 4.2 "We notice the potential of the effective management of the business model of our company", which obtained a local weight equal to only 0.06.

Table 14. Normalized sub-criterion matrix for Criterion 4.

Normalized W-Matrix	Statement 4.1	Statement 4.2	Statement 4.3	Statement 4.4	Statement 4.5	Weights = Local Priorities	RANKING
Statement 4.1	0.13	0.20	0.07	0.29	0.15	0.17	3
Statement 4.2	0.04	0.07	0.07	0.03	0.09	0.06	5
Statement 4.3	0.39	0.20	0.20	0.29	0.15	0.25	2
Statement 4.4	0.04	0.20	0.07	0.10	0.15	0.11	4
Statement 4.5	0.39	0.33	0.60	0.29	0.45	0.41	1

Source: Own study

When examining Criterion 5 (Table 15), Statement 5.2 "Employees in our company are treated with respect and are an important voice in the decision-making process" was the most important with a local weight of 0.40. It was followed by Statement 5.3 "We pay attention to positive relationships with communities gathered around the railway ecosystem" with a local weight of 0.21. Statement 5.1 "In our business model, the aspect of positive social impact plays an important role", which gained a local weight of 0.07, ranked last.

Table 15. Normalized sub-criterion matrix for Criterion 5.

Normalized W-Matrix	Statement 5.1	Statement 5.2	Statement 5.3	Statement 5.4	Statement 5.5	Weights = Local Priorities	RANKING
Statement 5.1	0.08	0.14	0.06	0.04	0.05	0.07	5
Statement 5.2	0.23	0.43	0.53	0.36	0.47	0.40	1
Statement 5.3	0.23	0.14	0.18	0.36	0.16	0.21	2
Statement 5.4	0.23	0.14	0.06	0.12	0.16	0.14	4
Statement 5.5	0.23	0.14	0.18	0.12	0.16	0.17	3

Source: Own study.

For each criterion matrix, the values of the inconsistency index λmax, the consistency ratio CR and the values of the random consistency index RI were calculated (Table 16).

Table 16. Values of the inconsistency index λmax, the consistency ratio (CR) and the values of the random consistency index (RI) for each criterion.

Criterion	Criterion1	Criterion2	Criterion3	Criterion4	Criterion5
λ_{max}	5.48	5.46	5.28	5.48	5.35
n	5	5	5	5	5
RI	1.12	1.12	1.12	1.12	1.12
CR	0.11	0.10	0.06	0.11	0.08

Source: Own study.

The previously obtained weight values for each criterion and the local weights for sub-criteria are as follows (Table 17):

The above-mentioned local weights of the sub-criteria multiplied by the global weights of the criteria gave the global weights of sub-criteria. It was assumed that the above percentage values represent the ideal state, where the digitalization of railway companies is at a very high level. Among all 25 sub-criteria, the most important statements in the global sense included:

- Statement 2.5—"The digital solutions used in our company foster the implementation of social effects—ecology, ethics, and economics." with a global weight of 0.09.
- Statement 5.2—"Employees in our company are treated with respect and are an important voice in the decision-making process", with a global weight of 0,09.
- Statement 3.5— "The digital solutions used are fully compatible with solutions of other enterprises within the railway ecosystem", with a global weight of 0.08.
- Statement 4.5—"We pay attention to the creation of a value network with all rail market actors", with a global weight of 0.08.

Table 17. Matrix of local and global weights for criteria and sub-criteria for the issue of the digitalization of railway companies.

1. The Digital Transformation of the Business Models of Railway Companies 0.18	Share in the group	Share in total	2. Opportunities for the Development of Social Factors through Digital Transformation 0.22	Share in the group	Share in total	3. The Mutual Process Integration of Railway Companies through Digital Transformation 0.17	Share in the group	Share in total	4. The Servitization of Railway Companies 0.20	Share in the group	Share in total	5. The Socialization of the Business Models of Railway Companies 0.22	Share in the group	Share in total
Statement 1.1	0.31	0.06	Statement 2.1	0.07	0.01	Statement 3.1	0.06	0.01	Statement 4.1	0.17	0.03	Statement 5.1	0.07	0.02
Statement 1.2	0.34	0.06	Statement 2.2	0.22	0.05	Statement 3.2	0.22	0.04	Statement 4.2	0.06	0.01	Statement 5.2	0.40	0.09
Statement 1.3	0.11	0.02	Statement 2.3	0.11	0.02	Statement 3.3	0.11	0.02	Statement 4.3	0.25	0.05	Statement 5.3	0.21	0.05
Statement 1.4	0.17	0.03	Statement 2.4	0.20	0.04	Statement 3.4	0.17	0.03	Statement 4.4	0.11	0.02	Statement 5.4	0.14	0.03
Statement 1.5	0.07	0.01	Statement 2.5	0.40	0.09	Statement 3.5	0.44	0.08	Statement 4.5	0.41	0.08	Statement 5.5	0.17	0.04

Source: Own study.

7.3. Analysis of Responses from Surveys Sent to Railway Companies

After creating the surveys which take into account the above criteria and sub-criteria in the form of statements, they were sent to railway undertakings and infrastructure managers. They were asked to evaluate the criteria set in relation to the functioning of their company and meeting the issues set using the following scale (Table 18):

Table 18. The scale used to assess the company in terms of sub-criteria.

Scale	Statement
1	I strongly disagree
2	I somewhat disagree
3	I have no opinion
4	I somewhat agree
5	I definitely agree

Source: Own study.

After collecting a certain sample from the data set, namely railway undertakings and infrastructure managers, calculations were made taking into account the accumulated ratings from questionnaires and percentage result calculated for the ideal company. The total score for each criterion for a given company was calculated. The maximum result in a given cell for a criterion are values of global weights calculated for six groups of criteria. At the end, the results obtained were ranked and the ranking of railway companies was obtained in terms of their digitalization. Below is a table with individual results in each area examined, together with the total result obtained and the final ranking from the above study. The total result obtained for each company studied by means of the AHP analysis, which took into account all five criteria, indicated the level of the railway company's digitalization in relation to the given statements. Obtaining the value of 1.0 characterizes an ideal company in terms of digitalization. The highest total value of ratings was obtained for Company 16—0.92, followed by Company 10 with a result of 0.89, and third place was occupied by Company 11—0.85. Company 7 was ranked last, with only a 0.62 rating.

The maximum ratings were achieved in Criterion 5. In this way, Company 6, Company 9, Company 10, Company 15 and Company 16 were evaluated. Company 3 dominated only in the case of Criterion 1. In other cases, it did not appear at all. An interesting case is Company 12, which ranked first in the rating in terms of Criterion 2 and Criterion 3, and it ranked third for Criterion 1. However, in the overall ranking, it occupied sixth place. This results from its low position for Criterion 4 (16th place out of 19) and Criterion 5 (17th place). Company 3, despite being in first place in Criterion 1, was ranked below 10th for the remaining criteria, so in the final analysis it ranked 17th. To sum up, the highest rated companies were Company 16, Company 10 and Company 11.

The values obtained within each criterion indicated that the highest mean is obtained in the results of Criterion5, amounting to 4.3. This mainly results from the assessment of individual statements such as "I have no opinion", "I somewhat agree" and "I definitely agree". The lowest ranked statements are from the Criterion 1 range—the average rating was 3.6. Other average values are also shown in the table below. The responses to particular groups of criteria indicated a 'somewhat agree' level.

Highly rated statements are:

- "Statement 3.1. The digital solutions in our company improve process efficiency",
- "Statement 5.4. Our business model is based on an effective dialogue with stakeholders".
- This means that such areas predominate in the functioning of railway companies. The lowest average was obtained for the following statements:
- "Statement 1.4. Guaranteeing cybersecurity is a priority in our company's activity",
- "Statement 1.5. The digital solutions used in our company improve railway traffic safety",

- "Statement 3.4. We build cooperation platforms with other railway companies using digital technologies",
- "Statement 4.1. We apply solutions based on the transition from a product/ service-oriented model to a service-oriented business model and its logic".

All four of the above statements received an average of 3.5. This means that this issue should be corrected by improving the business models of railway companies.

On the basis of the above, it can be concluded that the purpose of the article was achieved, because the study conducted showed that social factors are the fundamental factor in the digitalization of the business models of railway companies. In addition, the answer to the question of which of the given factors are the most important aspects in the activity of the railway companies studied was obtained. Due to the lack of significant deviations in the results obtained, it can be safely stated that the research is a reliable sample which gives an image of the hierarchy of basic social factors in building the digitalization of business models.

The homogeneity of the scale was verified by means of Cronbach's alpha. This coefficient takes values between [0; 1]. When $\alpha > 0.7$, the high reliability of the scale is demonstrated. This coefficient indicates to what extent a set of variables is consistent. If all positions were perfectly reliable and measured the same thing, the coefficient $\alpha = 1$. Cronbach's alpha was estimated using the following formula:

$$\alpha = \frac{K}{K-1}\left(1 - \frac{\sum_{i=1}^{K} \sigma^2_{\text{Statement } i}}{\sigma^2_{\text{Group}}}\right)$$

where:

K—number of statements,

Statement—answers obtained for individual questions given by all companies

$\sigma^2_{\text{Statement } i}$ —variance for the answers obtained to a given question, and

σ^2_{Group}—variance from the sum of answers to all questions for individual companies.

Hence the value of Cronbach's alpha was 0.90. The higher the value of the coefficient, the greater the reliability of the scale, therefore the reliability in this study is very high. This means that there was a large similarity between the individual responses, and the way of answering individual questions was similar. Therefore, the questions are similar to each other and examine similar phenomena.

8. Conclusions

As part of the research model adopted in the scope of the digitalization of railway companies, five key criteria were adopted: the digital transformation of the business models of railway companies, opportunities for the development of social factors through digital transformation, the mutual process integration of railway companies through digital transformation, the servitization of railway companies, the socialization of the business models of railway companies, and the process integration of railway companies. The research results showed that the ranking of the significance of the adopted criteria is as follows: the most important criterion is "The socialization of the business models of railway companies", which obtained a global weight of 40.15%. "The servitization of railway companies" ranks second with a global weight of 19.20% and "Opportunities for the development of social factors through digital transformation" is equally significant at 19.11%. The next place in the ranking was occupied by "The mutual process integration of railway companies through digital transformation", followed by "The digital transformation of the business models of railway companies", with a global weight of 9.71%. For each criterion, the results confirm that the defined criteria show the key factors responsible for the effectiveness of implementing the digital transformation of business models of railway companies. The above-mentioned local weights of the sub-criteria multiplied by the global weights of the criteria gave the global weights of the sub-criteria, assuming that percentages represent the ideal state, where the digitalization of railway companies is at a very high level. Among all 25 sub-criteria, four research areas which describe factors influencing the digitalization of the business models of railway companies were the most significant in the global sense. First of all, digital solutions foster the implementation of social effects—ecology, ethics, and economics. The companies surveyed pay attention to the role of employees in creating social attitudes. Moreover, employees should be treated with respect and be an important voice in the decision-making process, and digital solutions should be fully compatible with the solutions of other enterprises within the railway ecosystem. Finally, the creation of a value network with all rail market players is important within the socialization of the business models of railway enterprises. The research results are adequate for the specificity of the railway companies' operations and their business models.

The social factors of the business models of railway companies cannot be examined in terms of their digitalization without taking into account the complex value chain based on cooperation between infrastructure managers and railway undertakings that have an organizational and technical nature. The digitalization of one group of railway companies (infrastructure managers) should be compatible with the second group (railway undertakings). The implementation of digital solutions at the technical level facilitates the better integration of operational processes and building better mutual relations, which should affect the quality of services provided and the level of railway traffic safety.

The process of the digitalization of the business models of railway companies is important for the development of social factors. The search for social aspects in the field of digitalization is important for improving the efficiency of these business models as well as finding new spaces that have an impact on building relationships between enterprises as part of shaping a complex organizational and technical business ecosystem.

Constructing the configuration of social factors influencing the process of the digitalization of the business models of railway companies was used to identify several important conclusions.

1. The business models of railway companies are increasingly supported by digital economy solutions.

2. The operational processes are essentially based on the use of digital communication.

3. The strategies of railway companies assume the digitalization of key areas of activity in the next three years.

4. The issue of cyber security is a priority in the context of railway companies' operations.

5. Digital solutions built in the business models of railway companies significantly improve railway traffic safety.

6. The implementation of digital solutions increases the chances of improving relationships with stakeholders.

7. Digital solutions improve the quality of human-human, human-machine and machine-machine interfaces.

8. Digital solutions generate positive relationships with suppliers/partners.

9. Social capital is built with rail market actors through social solutions.

10. Digital solutions foster the implementation of social effects—ecology, ethics, and economics. Railway companies are subject to the process of digital transformation much like other companies in traditional sectors. The digitalization of business models is dynamic and results from technological progress as well as the need to improve the efficiency of these companies. Due to the strategic role of the rail transport sector in the economy, the social aspect plays a key role and the process of digitalization studied is conducive to it. The research results confirm that there are still many issues to be clarified in this respect. Research into the digitalization processes of the business models of railway companies requires further research and analysis, which results from the complexity of this sector and the dynamics of changes in the area of designing digital economy solutions. The socialization of business through digitalization is also the subject of further research projects by the authors. The social perspective demonstrates that technical innovations are likely to positively affect the diffusion of social innovation, and vice versa. The technological revolution that accompanies Industry 4.0 achieves its

true potential in combination with social innovation. It should be noted that, referring to other research into social aspects of digital business models, the results achieved are in line with other results in this area. The social perspective demonstrates that technical innovations are likely to positively affect the diffusion of social innovation, and vice versa.

Hence, businesses that succeed in Industry 4.0 will be those that offer both social progress and economic benefits. It should be noted that, referring to other scientific studies in the field of social aspects in digital business models, the results achieved are in line with other results in this area. The social perspective demonstrates that the development of social innovation and digital solutions influence digital process of business model transformation. Research by R. Morrar, H. Arman, and S. Mousa confirms the course of thinking and defines the scope of research and scientific argument adopted in this article [50]. Obviously, the specificity of the railway sector is quite different, but it is part of current research into the digitalization of the business models of technology companies. This subject seems to be very interesting in terms of the impact of research on the level of the perception of the digital transformation of companies which hitherto had poorly implemented the latest technological innovations while changing their business models evolutionally or sometimes revolutionarily.

9. Limitations and Suggestions for Future Research

The key limitations of the research process should include sector conditions typical of the complexity of the rail transport sector. Due to legal conditions, the description of rail transport business models is set in specific market realities. On the one hand, it has the character of a natural monopoly—some infrastructure managers, on the other hand, companies such as railway undertakings operate in a very competitive market. This means that research into this sector and the attempt to expand this research for other sectors is not always effective. Another limitation of the research conducted is the selection of criteria for evaluation. In the relevant literature, research into the digital transformation of business models is in its infancy. As regards research in this area, there are many issues which require clarification. The paper is a step towards a better understanding of the processes of the digitalization of business models which have operated in the traditional way so far.

The specificity of railway companies can also be a limitation. As those whose business models largely depend on legal requirements must create digital solutions on their own, believing that in a liberalized and very competitive market the readiness to create an ecosystem of the digital economy may help the company gain a competitive advantage over its competitors in future. Certainly, the national infrastructure manager may have a different opinion, with a safe and monopolistic position in this respect, but looking at the experience of Polish and other European companies, these entities can set standards in the use of digital solutions.

As regards the need to explore the subject presented in the context of future research, it is reasonable to study the processes of the digital transformation of business models in other sectors of the economy and services. It is worth examining the differences between digital transformation processes in sectors considered to be traditional, such as rail transport, heavy industry and the digital transformation of services. Differences between these areas in the context of universal digitalization can give results that allow for a better understanding of changes that are taking place in the dynamically developing digital economy and their impact on the business models of companies. These issues are important not only in terms of theory, but also in the utilitarian sense. Understanding digital transformation processes in terms of the development of social aspects is of key importance because, due to the development of social aspects, business models have a wider scope and can not only increase economic efficiency but also affect the added value of digitalization, namely social profit. The social aspect is also related to the issue of trust, which is the leading criterion for the development of digitalization. In addition, the influence and role of the mutual process integration of railway companies through digital transformation should be indicated as a research gap and thus the subject of future research. These issues are the subject of further research by the authors.

Sustainability **2019**, *11*, 3367

Author Contributions: Conceptualization, A.J. and M.J.; Methodology, M.J.; Formal Analysis, A.J.; Investigation, A.J. and M.J.; Data Curation, A.J. and M.J.; Writing—Original Draft Preparation, M.J.; Writing—Review & Editing, A.J.; Visualization, A.J. and M.J.

Funding: This research received no external funding.

Conflicts of Interest: The authors declare no conflict of interest.

References

1. Parviainen, P.; Kääriäinen, J.; Tihinen, M.; Teppola, S. Tackling the digitalization challenge: How to benefit from digitalization in practice. *Int. J. Inf. Syst. Proj. Manag.* **2017**, *5*, 63–77.
2. Wirtz, B.W. *Digital Business Models, Concepts, Models and the Alphabet Case Study*; Springer: Basel, Switzerland, 2019.
3. Khanagha, S.; Volberda, H.; Oshri, I. Business model renewal and ambidexterity: Structural alteration and strategy formation process during transition to a Cloud business model. *R&D Manag.* **2014**, *44*. [CrossRef]
4. Demil, B.; Lecocq, X. Business model evolution: In search of dynamic consistency. *Long Range Plan.* **2010**, *43*, 227–246. [CrossRef]
5. Eckhardt, J.; Kaletka, C.; Pelka, B. Inclusion through Digital Social Innovations: Modelling an Ecosystem of Drivers and Barriers. In Proceedings of the 2017 11th UAHCI International Conference, Vancouver, BC, Canada, 9–14 July 2017.
6. Reinartz, W.; Wiegand, N.; Imschloss, M. The impact of digital transformation on the retailing value Chain. *Int. J. Res. Mark.* **2019**. [CrossRef]
7. Smith, W.; Binns, A.; Tushman, M. Complex Business Models: Managing Strategic Paradoxes Simultaneously. *Long Range Plan.* **2010**, *43*, 448–461. [CrossRef]
8. Timmers, P. Business models for electronic markets. *Electron. Mark.* **1998**, *8*, 3–8. [CrossRef]
9. Von Leipzig, T.; Gamp, M.; Manz, D.; Schöttle, K.; Ohlhausen, P.; Oosthuizen, G.; Palm, D.; von Leipzig, K. Initialising customer-orientated digital transformation in enterprises. *Proc. Manuf.* **2017**, *8*, 517–524. [CrossRef]
10. Westerman, G.; Calméjane, C.; Bonnet, D.; Ferraris, P.; McAfee, A. Digital Transformation: A Roadmap for Billion-Dollar Organizations. *MIT Sloan Manag.* **2011**, *1*, 1–68.
11. Stolterman, E.; Fors, A. Information technology and the good life. In *Information Systems Research*; Springer: Berlin, Germany, 2004; pp. 687–692.
12. Azhari, P.; Faraby, N.; Rossmann, A.; Steimel, B.; Wichmann, K.S. *Digital Transformation Report*; Neuland GmbH & Co.: Köln, Germany, 2014.
13. Issa, A.; Hatiboglu, B.; Bildstein, A.; Bauerhansl, T. Industry 4.0 roadmap: Framework for digital transformation based on the concepts of capability, maturity and alignment. *Procedia CIRP* **2018**, *72*, 973–978. [CrossRef]
14. Reis, J.; Amorim, M.; Melão, N.; Matos, P. Digital Transformation: A Literature Review and Guidelines for Future Research. In *Trends and Advances in Information Systems and Technologies*; Rocha, Á., Adeli, H., Reis, L.P., Costanzo, S., Eds.; Springer: Cham, Switzerland, 2018; p. 745.
15. Markowitsch, J.; Kollinger, I.; Warmerdam, J.; Moerel, H.; Konrad, J.; Burel, C.; Guile, D. *Competence and Human Resource Development in Multinational Companies in Three European Union Member States: A Comparative Analysis between Austria, the Netherlands and the UK*; CEDEFOP: Thessaloniki, Greece, 2001.
16. Dovleac, L. The role of new communication technologies in companies' sustainability. *Bull. Transilv. Univ. Braşov Ser. V Econ. Sci.* **2015**, *8*, 33–40.
17. Sousa, M.J.; Rocha, Á. Digital learning: Developing skills for digital transformation of organizations. *Future Gener. Comput. Syst.* **2019**, *91*, 327–334. [CrossRef]
18. Warner, K.S.R.; Wäger, M. Building dynamic capabilities for digital transformation: An ongoing process of strategic renewal. *Long Range Plan.* **2018**, *52*, 326–349. [CrossRef]
19. Lam, C.; Law, R. Readiness of upscale and luxury-branded hotels for digital transformation. *Int. J. Hosp. Manag.* **2019**, *79*, 60–69. [CrossRef]
20. Zaharia, S.E.; Pietreanu, C.V. Challenges in airport digital transformation. *Transp. Res. Proc.* **2018**, *35*, 90–99. [CrossRef]

21. Goerziga, D.; Bauernhansl, T. Enterprise architectures for the digital transformation in small and medium-sized enterprises. *Procedia CIRP* **2018**, *67*, 540–545. [CrossRef]

22. Dengler, K.; Matthes, B. The impacts of digital transformation on the labour market: Substitution potentials of occupations in Germany. *Technol. Forecast. Soc. Chang.* **2018**, *137*, 304–316. [CrossRef]

23. Troshani, I.; Janssen, M.; Lymer, A.; Lee, D. Digital transformation of business-to-government reporting: An institutional work perspective. *Int. J. Account. Inf. Syst.* **2018**, *31*, 17–36. [CrossRef]

24. Schallmo, D.; Williams, C.A. Digital Transformation of Business Models—Best Practices and Roadmap. *Int. J. Innov. Manag.* **2017**, *21*, 1740014. [CrossRef]

25. Uusitalo, T.; Antikainen, M. The concept of value in circular economy business models. In Proceedings of the ISPIM Innovation Forum, Boston, MA, USA, 25–28 March 2018.

26. Klos, C.; Klusmann, C.; Clauss, T.; Spieth, P. Digital transformation of the business model: A qualitative empirical analysis. In Proceedings of the R&D Management Conference, Leuven, Belgium, 1–5 June 2017.

27. Wirtz, B.W.; Pistoia, A.; Ullrich, S.; Goottel, V. Business Models: Origin, Development and Future Research Perspectives. *Long Range Plan.* **2016**, *49*, 36–54. [CrossRef]

28. Wirtz, B.W. *Business Model Management Design—Instrumente—Erfolgsfaktoren von Geschaftsmodellen*, 1st ed.; Gabler: Wiesbaden, Germany, 2018.

29. Chesbrough, H.; Rosenbloom, R. The role of the business model in capturing value from innovation: Evidence from Xerox Corporation's technology spin-off companies. *Ind. Corp. Chang.* **2002**, *11*, 529–555. [CrossRef]

30. König, M.; Ungerer, C.; Baltes, G.; Terzi, O. Different patterns in the evolution of digital and non-digital ventures' business models. *Technol. Forecast. Soc. Chang.* **2018**. [CrossRef]

31. Sousa, M.J.; Rocha, Á. Skills for disruptive digital business. *J. Bus. Res.* **2019**, *94*, 257–263. [CrossRef]

32. Subramaniam, M.; Iyer, B.; Venkatraman, V. Competing in digital ecosystems. *Bus. Horiz.* **2018**, *62*, 83–94. [CrossRef]

33. Bleicher, J.; Stanley, H. Digitization as a catalyst for business model innovation a three-step approach to facilitating economic success. *J. Bus. Manag.* **2016**, *12*, 62–71.

34. Müller, J.M.; Traub, J.; Gantner, P.; Veile, J.W.; Voigt, K.-I. Managing Digital Disruption of Business Models in Industry 4.0. In Proceedings of the 29th International Society for Professional Innovation Management (ISPIM) Conference, Stockholm, Sweden, 17–20 June 2018.

35. Frank, A.G.; Dalenogare, L.S.; Ayala, N.F. Industry 4.0 technologies: Implementation patterns in manufacturing companies. *Int. J. Prod. Econ.* **2019**, *210*, 15–26. [CrossRef]

36. Rauch, E.; Linder, C.; Dallasega, P. Anthropocentric perspective of production before and within Industry 4.0. *Comput. Ind. Eng.* **2019**. [CrossRef]

37. Roblek, V.; Meško, M.; Krapež, A. A Complex View of Industry 4.0. *SAGE Open* **2016**. [CrossRef]

38. Kans, M.; Ingwald, A. Business Model Development towards Service Management 4.0. *Procedia CIRP* **2016**, *47*, 489–494. [CrossRef]

39. Service Management 4.0. *The Future Service Management Platform*; A Jolt Consulting Group White Paper; Jolt Consulting Group: Saratoga Springs, NY, USA, December 2012.

40. Štefancová, V.; Nedeliaková, E.; López-Escolano, C. Connection of dynamic quality modeling and Total Service Management in railway transport operation. *Proc. Eng.* **2017**, *192*, 834–839. [CrossRef]

41. Jabłoński, A. The efficient management of railway sidings in terms of a safety criterion—Selected aspects. *Arch. Transp. Syst. Telematics.* **2017**, *10*, 28–32.

42. Jabłoński, M. Assessment of the correctness of the application of the explicit risk estimation methods in making an independent assessment of a rail transport risk management process. *Arch. Transp. Syst. Telemat.* **2017**, *10*, 14–18.

43. Lia, Y.; Guldenmund, F.W. Safety management systems: A broad overview of the literature. *Saf. Sci.* **2018**, *103*, 94–123. [CrossRef]

44. Alberti, F.G.; Varon Garrido, M.A. Can profit and sustainability goals co-exist? New business models for hybrid firms. *J. Bus. Strategy* **2017**, *38*, 3–13. [CrossRef]

45. Elkington, J. *Cannibals with Forks: The Triple Bottom Line of 21st Century Business*; Capstone: Oxford, UK, 1999.

46. Jabłoński, A.; Jabłoński, M. Research on Business Models in their Life Cycle. *Sustainability* **2016**, *8*, 430. [CrossRef]

47. Kiel, D.; Müller, J.; Arnold, C.; Voigt, K. Sustainable Industrial Value Creation: Benefits and Challenges of Industry 4.0. In Proceedings of the XXVIII ISPIM Innovation Conference—Composing the Innovation Symphony, Vienna, Austria, 18–21 June 2017.
48. Müller, J.M.; Kiel, D.; Voigt, K. What Drives the Implementation of Industry 4.0? The Role of Opportunities and Challenges in the Context of Sustainability. *Sustainability* **2018**, *10*, 247. [CrossRef]
49. Stock, T.; Seliger, G. Opportunities of Sustainable Manufacturing in Industry 4.0. *Procedia CIRP* **2016**, *40*, 536–541. [CrossRef]
50. Morrar, R.; Arman, H.; Mousa, S. The Fourth Industrial Revolution (Industry 4.0): A Social Innovation Perspective. *Technol. Innov. Manag. Rev.* **2017**, *7*. [CrossRef]
51. Chowdhury, G. Sustainability of digital information services. *J. Doc.* **2013**, *69*, 602–622. [CrossRef]
52. Jabłoński, M. Value Migration to the Sustainable Business Models of Digital Economy Companies on the Capital Market. *Sustainability* **2018**, *10*, 3113. [CrossRef]
53. Jabłoński, M. Determinants of Sustainable Business Model of Companies Early Stage of Development. In *Sustainable Business, Management, and Economics*; Berger, L., Bergman, M.M., Eds.; MDPI: Basel, Switzerland, 2017.
54. Lock, I.; Seele, P. Theorizing stakeholders of sustainability in the digital age. *Sustain. Sci.* **2017**, *12*, 235–245. [CrossRef]
55. Jabłoński, A. Scalability of Sustainable Business Models in Hybrid Organizations. *Sustainability* **2016**, *8*, 194. [CrossRef]
56. Sukrat, S.; Papasraton, B. A maturity model for C2C Social commerce business model. *Int. J. Electron. Commer. Stud.* **2018**, *9*, 27–54. [CrossRef]
57. Saaty, T.L. How to make a decision: The Analytic Hierarchy Process. *Eur. J. Oper. Res.* **1990**, *48*, 9–26. [CrossRef]
58. Saaty, T.L. *Fundamentals of Decision Making and Priority Theory with the Analytic Hierarchy Process*; RWS Publications: Pittsburgh, PA, USA, 1994.
59. Saaty, T.L. *Decision Making with Dependence and Feedback: The Analytic Network Process*; RWS Publications: Pittsburgh, PA, USA, 1996.

sustainability

MDPI

Article

Mutual Support, Role Breadth Self-Efficacy, and Sustainable Job Performance of Workers in Young Firms

Sarah Cheah [1,*]**, Shiyu li** [1] **and Yuen-Ping Ho** [2]

[1] Business School, National University of Singapore, Singapore 119245, Singapore; shiyu.li@nus.edu.sg
[2] Entrepreneurship Centre, National University of Singapore, Singapore 119245, Singapore; yuenping@nus.edu.sg
* Correspondence: sarahcheah@nus.edu.sg; Tel.: +65-65167230

Received: 21 May 2019; Accepted: 12 June 2019; Published: 17 June 2019

Abstract: Coworking space has flourished in the past decade. Unlike traditional shared services organizations, coworking spaces put a much greater emphasis on 'sharing'. Members not only can share the physical office space, but also the virtual social spaces created by the coworking space operators managing the office. As coworking spaces provide a community to foster the culture of sharing, which gives rise to social interactions and thus knowledge and idea exchange, entrepreneurs favor such coworking spaces to achieve a higher level of job performance among their workers. Although it is generally accepted that a worker's job performance varies over time within a job, there have been limited studies on within-person performance sustainability and its comparison with between-person sustainability. We sampled 101 workers of young firms operating in six coworking spaces in Singapore who completed daily surveys twice a day across ten consecutive workdays. By treating participants as the first level and daily observations as the second level, our study develops a dual-path model to explain how daily mutual support influences daily job performance. Our results indicated that daily mutual support is positively related to sustainable job performance after controlling for sleep quality, job requirements and workload stress. Within-person sustainability in mutual support was found to account for part of within-person variance in job performance. We established that mutual support not only predicts job performance, but also varies across workdays. As the collaboration of team members depends on cooperation rather than competition, mutual support is considered essential for team work and thus employees' job performance. Our study also demonstrated the importance of role breadth self-efficacy as a moderator in the link between mutual support and sustainable job performance. Role breadth self-efficacy refers to the extent to which people feel confident that they are able to carry out a broader and more proactive role, beyond traditional prescribed technical requirements. The results revealed an enhancing moderation effect, where increasing the role breath self-efficacy would enhance the effect of the mutual support predictor on sustainable job performance of workers in young firms operating in the coworking space.

Keywords: young firms; job performance; mutual support; role breadth self-efficacy; coworking space

1. Introduction

Individual job performance, referring to things that people actually do and actions they take that contribute to the organization's goals [1], drives the entire sustainable economy [2]. Without the sustainability of individual job performance, there is no sustainable team performance, organizational performance, economic sector performance, nor gross domestic product (GDP). Due to the importance of individual job performance, considerable studies on the subject have been conducted across various fields including service [3,4], education [5], marketing [6], management [7] and psychology [8]. From the extant literature, it is apparent that a worker's job performance depends on a range of factors comprising job type, self-esteem, emotional stability and workload [8,9]. According to Callewaert and Robert [10], the culture of sustainability in job performance is a notion that describes a set of behaviors, degrees of engagement and contributions to sustainable development at individual and organizational levels. By postulating the concept of employee sustainable performance, Jiang, Zhao, and Ni [11] reveal that an individual's sustainable performance is positively influenced by transformational leadership. Based on job demands–resources theory [12,13] that explains how job stress and motivation are affected by job demands and job resources, Bakker and Demerouti [14] used multilevel approach to demonstrate how managers and supervisors can help employees to avoid job stress and enhance well-being and job performance. However, so far, job performance literature has not focused on young firms. Our study aims to address this gap by looking at employees' job performance working in young firms located at coworking spaces.

There are several reasons for young firms to turn to coworking spaces. First, with advances in telecommunication technologies and rise in cross-border trade, knowledge workers are increasingly expected to coordinate their tasks with other workers, suppliers, customers or partners operating from diverse geographical locations in different time zones. Due to the changing nature of work enabled by mobile computing, these knowledge workers are able to work anywhere as long as they are given access to the internet, email and telephone. As the workers become more mobile, the need for a firm to enter into long-term lease of a conventional office with fixed space and furniture for them to utilize during regular work hours decreases. With limited financial resources, young firms will find it more cost-effective to get into short-term leases with coworking space operators that offer tenant firms office space and meeting rooms on-demand.

Second, as young firms expand internationally, their need for office space in their target foreign markets increases. Besides housing local hires, these firms will need office space to host meetings with local partners and prospective customers. As coworking space operators compete to meet the internationalization needs of these young firms, the former have also expanded their overseas network by organic growth, acquisition or collaboration with local layers to provide the latter seamless access to the local community. By having such access, young firms are able to plug into the local market quickly for talent, venture capital, technology, and other essential resources for venture expansion [15].

Finally, unlike traditional shared services organizations, coworking spaces put much greater emphasis on 'sharing'. Members not only can share the physical office space, but also the virtual social spaces created by the coworking space operators managing the office. Coworking spaces are generally designed to engender a community to foster the culture of sharing, which gives rise to social interactions and thus knowledge and idea exchange. Believing that the social climate of coworking spaces can promote a sense of belonging, self-efficacy, work enjoyment and job performance among their workers, young firms tend to favor such spaces. Fueled by the above developments, coworking space has flourished in the past decade and gained increasing interest among academics and policymakers.

Although it is generally accepted that a worker's job performance varies over time within a job, very little is known about how and why it varies in this manner in the literature of young firms. This study aims to investigate how a worker's job performance in a young firm varies within oneself (within-person sustainability), and compare it with that between workers (between-person sustainability). In this research, we sampled 101 workers of young firms operating in six coworking spaces in Singapore who completed daily surveys twice a day across ten consecutive workdays. By treating participants as the first level and daily observations as the second level, our study develops a dual-path model based on self-determination theory and social exchange theory to explain how daily mutual support influences daily job performance. With the further application of the expectancy-value theory, we examine how RBSE can influence the link between daily mutual support and daily job performance.

Our results indicated that daily mutual support is positively related to daily job performance after controlling for sleep quality, job requirements and workload stress. Within-person sustainability in mutual support was found to account for part of within-person variance in job performance. We established that mutual support not only predicts job performance, but also varies across workdays. As the collaboration of team members depends on cooperation rather than competition, mutual support is considered essential for team work and thus employees' job performance.

Our study also demonstrated the importance of role breadth self-efficacy (RBSE) as a moderator in the link between mutual support and sustainable job performance. RBSE refers to the extent to which people feel confident that they are able to carry out a broader and more proactive role, beyond traditional prescribed technical requirements. The results revealed an enhancing moderation effect, where increasing RBSE would enhance the effect of the mutual support predictor on sustainable job performance of workers in young firms operating in the coworking space.

2. Background and Hypotheses

2.1. Daily Mutual Support and Sustainable Job Performance

In the research of entrepreneurship, the concept of social interaction refers to the interaction among members of entrepreneurial teams. Based on a study of more than 150 German entrepreneurial teams, Lechler [16] empirically established that social interaction is a significant factor to business success. Social interaction was posited to comprise six dimensions [16]: communication [17], cohesion [18], work norms [19], mutual support, coordination and the balance of member contributions [20]. In particular, mutual support concerns the cooperation rather than competition among team members. It is considered critical for teamwork [21,22]. In its most basic form, mutual support is defined as "a process in which persons voluntarily come together to help each other address common problems or shared concerns" [23] (p. 168). In a work environment where there is mutual support, workers will attempt to complement each other and strive to engage in constructive and beneficial discussion, with the view to reaching consensus on important issues. In a cooperative atmosphere, workers can feel mutual respect when discussing their proposals and contributions for meaningful development.

As a high level of social support buffers the individual against the negative consequences of stressors at work [24], a supportive environment is important for the individual to develop work enjoyment and productivity. Baruch-Feldman et al. highlighted that the supervisor also plays an important role in rendering support to workers by demonstrating that immediate supervisor support was positively correlated to employees' job satisfaction and productivity [25]. Earlier research has confirmed that an increase in productivity can lead directly to an increase in job performance [26].

An alternative explanation for the positive relationship between mutual support and job performance could be the role of the worker's psychological state. Genero et al. found that low spouse or partner mutuality was predictive of significant depressive symptoms which can negatively impact the cognitive and emotional states of a person [27]. Mutual support has been proven to be associated with affective commitment [28,29] and positive psychological outcomes [30]. According to the self-determination theory [31], the fulfillment of three basic psychological needs—need for autonomy, need for competence and need for relatedness—could result in the state of well-being, social development, and positive behaviors of individuals such as high level of job performance [32]. Ilardi et al. illustrated that psychological needs satisfaction is essential for well-being at work [33].

Numerous studies have examined the relationship between mutual support and job performance, most of which focus on the leader–follower mutuality [29,34]. The social exchange theory is frequently used and defined as the "voluntary actions of individuals that are motivated by the returns they are expected to bring and typically do in fact bring from others" [35] (p. 91). Based on the theory, Clarke and Mahadi found that mutual respect between leaders and followers is positively associated with followers' job performance [29]. In a young firm that is relatively small in staff strength and flat in its hierarchical structure compared to a mature firm, workers in the former are likely to play more multiple roles and interact more closely as a founding team than those in the latter. This means the relationships between superiors and subordinates might be weaker while the mutual support among coworkers stronger in young firms than those in mature firms.

To understand the sustainability of job performance, Jiang, Zhao and Ni's study of 389 project teams analyzed task sustainable performance and relational sustainable performance, which refer to, respectively, the extent to which employees achieve their own sustainable development by meeting their tasks on time, and the extent to which employees contribute to the organizational goal and the sustainability of organizational culture [11]. A recent study by Nguyen found several important determinants for the sustainable performance of small and medium enterprises (SMEs), such as managerial support, environment, motivation, and engagement of all members in the organization [36].

Building on their works [11,36], we hypothesize that workers who receive daily mutual support are likely to achieve sustainable job performance on the same day.

Hypothesis 1 (H1): *Daily mutual support will be positively related to sustainable job performance on the same day.*

2.2. The Moderating Role of Role Breadth Self-efficacy (RBSE)

The concept of self-efficacy was first developed by Bandura [37] as "an individual's conviction (or confidence) about his or her abilities to mobilize the motivation, cognitive resources, and courses of action needed to successfully execute a specific task within a given context" [38] (p. 66). This suggests that workers having the same abilities may perform differently from one another depending on how their self-confidence about their abilities boost or hinder their motivation or efforts. In Anderson, Chen and Carter's health promotion study of US church institutions, self-efficacy was found to contribute to individuals' physical activity levels, although its effect was relatively less significant compared to other social-cognitive variables such as self-regulation [39]. Using a multilevel approach, Yeo and Neal found that task-specific self-efficacy was negatively correlated to task performance at the within-person level. However, the average levels of task-specific self-efficacy were positively correlated to task performance at between-person level [40]. These findings highlight the significance of adopting a multilevel approach in explaining self-efficacy.

Building on the self-efficacy concept, Parker developed a particular type of self-efficacy RBSE, which describes the extent to which people feel confident that they are able to carry out a broader and more proactive role, beyond traditional prescribed technical requirements [41]. Employees with high RBSE are more likely to feel that they can control the situation and be capable of accomplishing more challenging tasks [42]. On the other hand, those with low RBSE tend to be less proactive as they have less confidence in their capabilities [43].

Drawing on the self-determination theory [31] and expectancy-value theory [44], which is a process theory of motivation that defines three components (effort, rewards, valence) relating positively to level of performance, Fuller et al. argued that RBSE reflects the "can do" motivational states [45]. They also found RBSE to be an essential predictor of proactive behavior. Once coworkers decide to behave proactively, they become intrinsically motivated and attempt to meaningfully alter the self to make some contributions to the organization [46]. As Zapata-Phelan et al. demonstrated, intrinsic motivation can lead employees to perform better tasks [47].

Some studies have found that RBSE relates positively to job performance because it influences both the activities that people pursue and how much effort they allocate to these activities. However, others have revealed that high levels of RBSE may impair performance [48]. This might happen when employees are given ambiguous tasks. When employees have a clear overall goal and specific feedback about their work, RBSE was posited to positively predict job performance [49]. Although these mixed findings might be attributed to situational factors such as goal clarity, more studies are required to empirically investigate the relationship between RBSE and job performance.

Extending the works of Tims et al. which established that day-level self-efficacy has a positive relationship with day-level performance [50], we hypothesize that, at day level, the relationship between mutual support and sustainable job performance would be stronger for employees with high RBSE, compared with those with lower RBSE.

Hypothesis 2 (H2): *Daily role breadth self-efficacy (RBSE) will moderate the relationship between daily mutual support and sustainable job performance on the same day.*

Analysis at day level would allow us to make cross-sectional comparison across employees, track an individual employee over time and study the sustainability of job performance within coworkers. The conceptual model is shown in Figure 1.

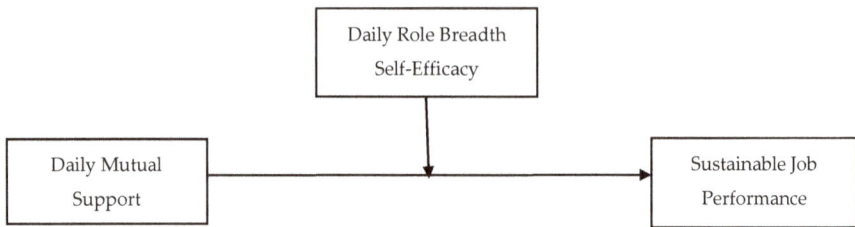

Figure 1. Conceptual model.

3. Methods

3.1. Data Collection and Sample

The sample comprised employees from young firms operating in coworking spaces in Singapore. Coworking spaces refer to a shared working environment where diverse groups of people who do not necessarily work for the same company or on the same project, work alongside each other and share the office space and resources [51]. According to Davidson et al. [23] (p. 168), mutual support can be provided by persons who "voluntarily come together to help each other address common problems or shared concerns". The persons offering mutual support do not necessarily work for the same company or the same project, as in a coworking space. They may simply participate in mutual support to increase their social network, receive social acceptance or seek solutions [52,53]. Of the seven coworking space operators we contacted, six agreed to help us inform their tenant firms about the study. Their tenants were primarily young firms that rented office space from the operators to house their workers. When recruiting their employees working in the coworking space in Singapore, we emphasized voluntary participation, assuring data confidentiality, and identity anonymity.

3.1.1. Daily Noon Time Survey, Daily Evening Survey, and One-Time Peer Survey

Among the 281 members who were working at the six coworking spaces at the time of the study, 204 members agreed to participate. After prospective participants registered online, they were invited to complete a one-time baseline survey, which captured their background information such as gender, age, designation and nationality. In the baseline survey, participants were also requested to nominate one of their coworkers as peers for objective rating of the participants' job performance. These participants were then asked to complete two daily surveys using their mobile phone for ten consecutive workdays. The first daily survey was conducted at noon, before the participants started their afternoon work. The purpose of the noon survey was to assess the level of participants' RBSE and the mutual support they received from their coworkers during the morning. The second daily survey was conducted at the end of workday, when participants were asked to report their job performance. All assessments were time stamped in the online survey system.

After the participants completed the daily surveys for ten working days, we invited their peers (one peer per participant) to respond to a one-time survey on the participant's job performance. In the individual differences literature, some studies suggest self-reported measures of job performance may be biased due to participants' desire for social acceptance [54] and hence advocated the need for peer ratings of job performance [55]. Other studies, on the other hand, found that self-reported measures were affected by individuals' observations or experiences rather than bias and established convergence between self-measures and peer-based measures [56]. Building on these works, this study captured peer ratings to assess the validity of participants' self-reported responses on the latter's job performance.

To compensate them for their time, the participants were paid S$ 100 each upon successful completion of the ten-day diary study, while their nominated peers were given $10 each for their one-time survey completion.

3.1.2. Participant Overview

To ensure the accuracy of data analysis, we required the participants to complete surveys during the specific time slots. Of the 204 participants, we first excluded those participants whose data had incompatible time stamps with the instructions given to them. Second, the measures of all variables were not collected on holidays or weekends. Data with missing values were also excluded. Third, we excluded those days on which participants were on leave, as we aimed to analyze the relationship between mutual support and job performance at the coworking space, so their physical presence at the space was a requirement for valid response.

This procedure led to a total number of 101 participants, showing a response rate of 49.5%. The 101 participants comprised Singaporeans (83%), Chinese (7%), Malaysians (4%), Filipinos (2%), Indians (2%), and Koreans (2%). 60 of the participants were male (59%) while 41 are female (41%). The mean age was 28.77 (SD = 6.28), ranging from 20 to 54 years old and the average job tenure was 29.24 weeks (SD = 32.15). As young firms are more likely than mature firms to rent desks compared to rooms at the coworking spaces, we found that our sample was generally made up of younger and more male individuals with little work experience.

3.2. Measures and Variables

3.2.1. Independent Variable

The independent variable 'mutual support' is operationally defined as support provided by the staff of young firms operating at the coworking space. We measured 'mutual support' with the first survey at noon. Four items were adapted from previous social interaction research at the Stevens Institution of Technology [16]. The items including "the coworking team members/tenants support and complement each other as well as they can", "discussions among the coworking team members/tenants are constructive and beneficial", "proposals and suggestions of coworking team members/tenants are respected", "I work within a cooperative ambience", were answered on five-point Likert scales ranging from 1 = strongly disagree to 5 = strongly agree. Cronbach's Alpha for this scale is 0.98.

3.2.2. Moderating Variable

The moderating variable, 'RBSE' is operationally defined as the RBSE of the staff of young firms operating at the coworking space. It was assessed at noon time survey, using a seven-item measurement based on a cross-sectional study by Parker [41]. Coworkers were asked to report at the noon survey how confident they felt on "analyzing a long-term problem to find a solution", "designing new procedures for their work", "contributing to discussion about the company's strategy", "writing a proposal to request for funding in their work", "helping to set targets/goals in their work area", "contacting people outside company (e.g., suppliers, customers) to discuss problems", "presenting information to a group of colleagues", on a five-point scale ranging from 1 = not at all, 2 = slightly, 3 = somewhat, 4 = moderately, and 5 = extremely. Cronbach's Alpha for this scale is 0.94.

3.2.3. Dependent Variable

The dependent variable 'sustainable job performance' is operationally defined as the daily job performance of the staff of young firms operating at the coworking space. From every individual worker, we captured ten different self-reported job performance ratings in the evening survey during a period of ten consecutive working days. Daily 'sustainable job performance' was measured by a four-item scale from Welbourne, Johnson, and Erez [57]. Individuals responded to items "quantity of work output", "quality of work output", "accuracy of work", and "customer service provided", with a Cronbach's Alpha of 0.81.

As 101 participants completed daily questionnaires over a period of ten days, we successfully collected a total of 1010 observations for each of the three variables: 'mutual support', 'RBSE', and 'sustainable job performance'.

3.2.4. Control Variables

Three variables were controlled when we tested our model. Nebes et al. suggested that poor sleep is associated with decreased concentration, which may lead to poor job performance [58]. Daily sleep quality was measured, in the noon survey, by a single item that "How do you evaluate your sleep quality last night" with a scale from 1 = very poor to 5 = very good. In the evening survey, we included 'job requirements' and 'workload stress' as control variables, which may account for differences in creative behaviors.

We controlled for daily 'job requirements' as organizations require different levels of performance in different jobs. Daily 'job requirements' was measured with five items adopted from Yuan and Woodman [59], "my job duties include searching for new technologies and techniques", "introducing new ideas into the organization is part of my job", "I don't have to be innovative to fulfil my job requirements", "my job requires me to try out new approaches to problems", and "suggesting new ideas is part of my job duties". Cronbach's alpha of 'job requirements' is 0.80.

It is important to control for daily 'workload stress' as excessive or undesirable constraints may interfere with individuals' ability to accomplish their daily tasks. Daily 'workload stress' was measured by five-item scale from Cavanaugh et al. [60]. The items were "today, I worked on many tasks and assignments", "today, I had a lot of work to do", "today, I experienced time pressure", "today, I had a lot of responsibilities", "today, I had to work fast" with Cronbach's alpha of 0.97.

Among the seven study variables, alpha values range from 0.79 to 0.98. The strength of these reliability estimates indicate a high homogeneity among the scale items.

3.3. *Data Analysis*

For robust data analysis, there is a need to address the issue of potential bias in self-reported survey data. As self-reported questionnaires and performance-based evaluations have inherent limitations, such as poor recall, both intentional and unintentional distortions by participants [54,61,62], we gathered peer-ratings on the participants' job performance as more objective evaluations, which were not the dependent variable, but were used only to assess the validity of participants' responses on their own job performance [55,56]. We proceeded to compare the difference between the average of ten measurements provided by each of the participants' and their nominated peers' scores on job performance. One-way analysis of variance (ANOVA) was used to determine whether there were any significant differences between the participants' responses on job performance and their nominated peers' rating on their job performance. Job performance was centered by subtracting its mean value since the average of job performance from participants was 3.67, while that from colleagues, who preferred to rate their coworkers higher, was 4.28. After centralization, one-way ANOVA generated a

F-statistic of 0.244, with a *p*-value of 0.622, showing no significant difference between mean values of job performance from the two groups. Hence, the validity of participants' job performance was confirmed.

Multilevel modelling (MLM) is appropriate for the analysis of longitudinal data, given that ten-wave measurement points (level 1) in our case are nested within 101 individuals (level 2). Ignoring the nested structure of such longitudinal data can result in biased estimates of standard errors and subsequent increase in Type I error, the rejection of true null hypothesis [63]. More importantly, we group-centered the predictors by calculating the difference between a single observation and the mean of ten observations from one individual. As indicated by Wooldridge [64], centering is an effective way to avoid collinearity caused by highly correlated random intercepts and slopes in MLM. Moreover, the group centering approach eliminates all the between-individual variance in the predictors and therefore the estimates represent strictly within-individual relations [64–66]. Using the group mean centered values of predictors in the analysis would therefore mean that we are investigating the relationship between an individual's sustainable job performance over a period of time and their daily mutual support.

The two hypotheses were tested through MLM in R [67]. To examine Hypothesis 1, we used the independent variable 'mutual support' and three control variables to predict 'sustainable job performance'. In Hypothesis 2, 'RBSE' was tested as a moderator in the link between 'mutual support' and 'sustainable job performance'. If Hypothesis 2 is supported, the direction of the moderation effect needs to be discussed as well. The analyses of Hypothesis 1 and Hypothesis 2 were based on a sample of 101 coworkers, and involved a total of 1010 observations each of 'mutual support', 'RBSE', and 'sustainable job performance' over ten days.

4. Results

Table 1 presents the mean, standard deviation, between- and within-individual correlations among the variables used in this study. Since high correlations up to 0.77 have been observed between certain variables, variance inflation factor (VIF) values are calculated, which are found to be less than 2 and well below the threshold of ten, addressing any possible concerns about multi-collinearity issues [68].

Table 1. Descriptive statistics and the within and between correlations

	Variables	Mean	SD	1	2	3	4	5	6	CA	VIF
1	Sustainable job performance (evening, self-rated)	3.67	0.71	-	0.18 **	0.48 **	0.59 **	0.28 **	0.54 **	0.81	
2	Sleep quality (noon)	2.87	0.72	0.29 **	-	0.12 **	0.05	0.15 **	0.19 **		1.05
3	Job requirements (evening)	3.46	0.71	0.61 **	0.23 **	-	0.46 **	0.24 **	0.57 **	0.80	1.63
4	Workload stress (evening)	3.50	0.97	0.71 **	0.11	0.60 **	-	0.07 *	0.46 **	0.97	1.38
5	Mutual support (noon)	3.73	0.76	0.38 **	0.19 **	0.32 **	0.07	-	0.26 **	0.98	1.11
6	Role breadth self-efficacy (noon)	3.68	0.75	0.74 **	0.25 **	0.77 **	0.67 **	0.28 **	-	0.94	1.69
7	Performance (peer-rated; one-time rating)	4.28	0.66	0.06	0.02	−0.05	0.00	0.06	0.05	0.79	

Notes: * $p < 0.05$; ** $p < 0.01$ (two-tailed), N = 1010, VIF: variance inflation factor, CA: Cronbach's Alpha for the within-individual variables, CA was averaged over 10 measurements. The correlation above the diagonal represents within-individual correlations with 1010 observations. The correlation below the diagonal represents between-individual associations by using individuals' average scores during 10 days, N = 101.

At the between-individual level, it is important to note that the peer ratings on the participants' job performance did not correlate consistently with the average daily job performance provided by the participants themselves. A plausible explanation of the low cross-sectional validity may be the augmented effects of rating biases such as 'sleep quality' [58]. To reassure the validity of the self-reported 'sustainable job performance', as demonstrated in the previous section, a F-statistic of

0.244, with p-value of 0.622 generated by one-way ANOVA confirms the validity of 'sustainable job performance' [69]. Furthermore, at the intra-individual level, 'mutual support' and 'RBSE' correlated with 'sustainable job performance' in the expected directions.

4.1. Main Effect Hypothesis

Hypothesis 1 suggests that on days when coworkers experience high 'mutual support', they report a higher level of 'sustainable job performance' for that day, compared to days when they experience low 'mutual support'. We used the following two-level model to test this hypothesis, where SQ, JR, WS, MS represent 'sleep quality', 'job requirements', 'workload stress', and 'mutual support', respectively.

Level 1:

$$Y_{ij} = \beta_{0j} + \beta_{1j}SQ_{1j} + \beta_{2j}JR_{2j} + \beta_{3j}WS_{3j} + \beta_{4j}MS_{4j} + \varepsilon_{ij}$$

Level 2:

$$\beta_{0j} = \gamma_{00} + U_{0j}$$

$$\beta_{1j} = \gamma_{10}$$

$$\beta_{2j} = \gamma_{20}$$

$$\beta_{3j} = \gamma_{30}$$

$$\beta_{4j} = \gamma_{40}$$

In the level 1 model, Y_{ij} represents the 'sustainable job performance' for individual j measured at each day (1, 2, ..., 10). The intercept β_{0j} can be intercepted as individual j's mean job performance over time. While in level 2 model, β_{0j} was entered as an outcome and was divided into two parts: γ_{00}, a fixed effect because it remains constant across all individuals, and U_{0j}, a random effect which varies from individual to individual. γ_{00} can be interpreted as the general mean value for 'sustainable job performance' when all control variables and 'mutual support' equal to zero. γ_{10} through γ_{40} express the relationship between controllers, predictors, and the outcome variable. For instance, holding everything else constant, larger values of γ_{40} (positive or negative) indicate a stronger linear relationship between daily 'mutual support' and 'sustainable job performance'.

At level 2, we assumed that the individuals' intercepts were random but other slopes were fixed across individuals. Our implication of the model above is that coworkers' 'sustainable job performance' is impacted by individuals' daily fluctuation (within-person variation), variations among individuals (between-person variation), an overall mean to all individuals (γ_{00}), and the impact of the control variables and predictor as measured by γ_{10} to γ_{40}, which are common to all individuals as well. β_{4j} is of our primary interest, representing the individual slope effect of the time-varying predictor 'mutual support' on the coworkers' 'sustainable job performance'. Essentially, the goal of this model was to examine the extent to which the control variables and the dynamic predictor 'mutual support' could predict the coworkers' 'sustainable job performance'.

In line with our expectations (see Table 2), coworkers with higher 'mutual support' demonstrated a higher level of 'sustainable job performance'. The coefficient of 0.08 for 'mutual support' in Model 1 indicates that coworkers scoring 1 point higher on the daily mutual support could be expected to report 0.08 more 'sustainable job performance' on the same day. Hypothesis 1 was therefore supported. Model 2 further showed that coworkers with higher 'sleep quality', 'job requirements', 'workload stress', and 'RBSE' were more likely to report higher 'sustainable job performance'. For example, holding all the other variables constant, coworkers with higher 'RBSE' reported 0.18 more 'sustainable job performance', compared with coworkers in lower 'RBSE'.

Table 2. Hierarchical linear modeling with daily mutual support to predict sustainable job performance

Variables	DV: Sustainable Job Performance		
	Model 1	Model 2	Model 3
Fixed effects:			
Intercept	3.65 ** (0.05)	3.64 ** (0.05)	3.64 ** (0.05)
Sleep quality	0.07 ** (0.02)	0.05 * (0.02)	0.05 * (0.02)
Job requirements	0.20 ** (0.03)	0.17 ** (0.03)	0.16 ** (0.03)
Workload stress	0.29 ** (0.02)	0.28 ** (0.02)	0.28 ** (0.02)
Mutual support	0.08 ** (0.03)	0.05 † (0.03)	0.05 † (0.03)
Role breadth self-efficacy		0.18 ** (0.03)	0.18 ** (0.03)
Mutual support * Role breadth self-efficacy			0.05 * (0.03)
Random effects:			
Between-person	0.49	0.44	0.44
Within-person	0.44	0.43	0.43

† $p < 0.10$; * $p < 0.05$; ** $p < 0.01$ (two-tailed), N = 101 with 1010 total observations.

4.2. Moderating Effect Hypothesis

Hypothesis 2 concerns the moderation role of 'RBSE' and demonstrates that among coworkers who are high on 'RBSE', those with higher daily 'mutual support' achieve higher level of 'sustainable job performance'. Conversely, among coworkers low on 'RBSE', those with lower daily 'mutual support' achieve lower level of 'sustainable job performance'. As shown in Model 3, the data supported Hypothesis 2 in that the interactive effect of 'mutual support' and 'RBSE' was positively significant when predicting 'sustainable job performance'. The predictor 'mutual support' and moderator 'RBSE' are both significant with the interaction term added, where partial moderation has occurred. Figure 2 depicts this moderation effect graphically, showing that coworkers with high 'mutual support' experience a strong, positive relationship between daily 'mutual support' and 'sustainable job performance', whereas the relationship was weak for those with low 'RBSE'.

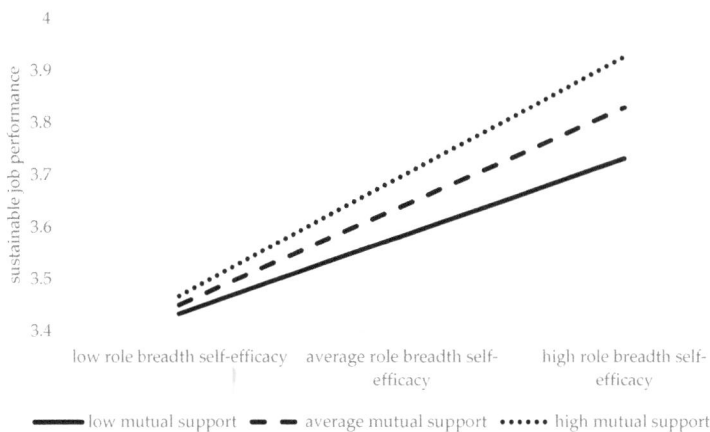

Figure 2. Moderation effect of role breadth self-efficacy.

Notably, the between-person variation reflects the variation in coefficients across individuals, the within-person variation demonstrates the fluctuation of job performance over ten days within individual. A relatively larger value of this between or within-person variation indicates that the relationship between the predictor and 'sustainable job performance' differs on inter- and intra-individual level. As the random effects have shown, the variation from individual differences is slightly larger than the time variation within individual, both of which provide the source of random variation in 'sustainable job performance'.

Low mutual support and low RBSE represent participants scored one standard deviation below the grand mean on the respective measures. High mutual support and high RBSE represent participants scored one standard deviation above the grand mean.

5. Discussion and Concluding Remarks

The purpose of this study is to investigate how a worker's daily job performance in a young firm operating in coworking space varies within oneself (within-person sustainability), and compare it with that between workers (between-person sustainability). In the recent decade, coworking space has flourished as it has been regarded by the governments of innovation-driven economies as an important aspect of the city's startup ecosystem to encourage entrepreneurship. As a result, more new firms are formed and house their knowledge workers in these spaces on a periodic lease or on-demand, rather than the traditional office space on a fixed-term lease [70,71]. Despite the growing interest in the sustainability of young firms among the policymakers and research scholars, the extant literature has still left the dynamic predictors of young firms' sustainability almost unexplored. Few studies have attempted multilevel studies of employees' sustainable job performance in young firms characterized by working alongside other firms in a coworking space.

Our study supported all the hypotheses. Daily mutual support that a worker receives in a young firm operating in a coworking space was found to be positively related to the worker's daily sustainable job performance after controlling for daily sleep quality, daily job requirements and daily workload stress, validating Hypothesis 1. A worker's daily RBSE was empirically established as a significant positive moderator in the link between the daily mutual support the worker receives and the worker's daily sustainable job performance, confirming Hypothesis 2.

5.1. Theoretical Implications

With ten waves of data from 101 members working at young firms in coworking spaces (1010 observations over a period of ten days), our study offers several contributions to the literature that has limited multilevel studies on young firms' sustainability. Specifically, we put forward current thinking about the sustainability of workers' daily job performance by testing the significance of daily mutual support as an essential predictor, as well as the potential moderating role of daily RBSE in the relationship between daily mutual support and workers' daily sustainable job performance. In addition, we made comparison between within-person and between-person differences in daily job performance.

While past research has focused on the direct relationship among social interaction, organizational support and job performance [72,73], we have drawn attention to one crucial dimension of social interaction in the context of young firms, that is, coworkers' mutual support by examining the extent to which daily mutual support influences workers' sustainable job performance. As coworkers' mutual support showed a positive effect on workers' sustainable job performance, this finding suggests a supportive environment can have a beneficial effect on workers' sustainable job performance such that on a day that workers perceive higher coworker support, they would report higher job performance for that day.

Second, based on the established relationship between daily mutual support and daily sustainable job performance, we further tested the moderating role of daily RBSE within this relationship. Vancouver et al. did not find any significant relationship between RBSE and job performance due to the existence of overconfidence [74]. We expand this process theoretically by analyzing daily job performance in the context of young firms. The result that daily RBSE is a significant moderator for the effect of daily mutual support on daily job performance can be explained by the fact that participants' self-reported ratings on their performance were measured every evening over ten days, enabling participants to estimate how they carry out their daily tasks. Their awareness that their performance would also be evaluated by their peers might lead them to reduce overconfidence and avoid underperformance.

Last but not least, a diary design and a novel multilevel longitudinal analysis help us find that the state fluctuations within individual accounts for almost half the variation in job performance, the rest of which are explained by the differences across individuals. Apart from the importance of traits on job performance, significant variability in within-individual level suggests daily mutual support and RBSE may increase the workers' sustainable job performance as well as the sustainability of young firms. The level of invisible external support and RBSE fluctuate on a daily basis [75,76]. Sustainable job performance has also been found to be highly fluctuating, with 44.57 per cent of variation explained at the within-individual level [77]. In line with previous diary studies, we extend the research on job performance into a coworking space context, aiming to provide new perspectives and suggestions on sustainable job performance for young firms.

5.2. Managerial Implications

Our results have several important implications for the managers of both coworking space operators and tenant firms. First, employees are the backbone of any organization. It is their continuous effort and sustainable job performance that contribute to company performance and thus drive business success. Based on a study of digital economy companies, Jabłoński observed that managers can be inspired to consider sustainability-related factors in their projects [78]. Managers in young firms should find ways to enhance workers' sustainable job performance by helping workers realize how their work contributes towards company's sustainability goals and find meaning in their work. Once workers understand the meaning of their contributions, they are likely to work with more passion and excitement, and therefore be more productive. This will in turn enable the young firm to sustain a high level of performance.

Second, as higher daily mutual support is found to be associated positively with a higher level of job performance, managers of coworking spaces should build a friendly and cooperative environment rather than a competitive one. To ensure everyone's ideas are respected and discussions among coworkers are constructive and beneficial, ground rules that promote collaboration and eliminate rude behavior should be emphasized at the workplace. Disrespectful behavior not only hinders coworkers from performing actively, but also can be contagious, causing problems ranging from increased stress to lost productivity. Such behavior should be stamped out by putting in place processes for incident reporting and management. Coworking space managers should be trained and empowered to deal with disrespectful behavior by providing clear and constructive feedback and coaching to the offending coworkers. In more severe situations, disciplinary actions might be required. In such ways, a psychologically safe and collaborative environment can be established.

Third, the positive relationship between mutual support and sustainable job performance will be enhanced with a high level of RBSE. This result suggests that managers can implement practices to foster workers' RBSE, thereby developing their abilities and sustaining their job performance. RBSE can be enhanced via organizational intervention such as increased task control, training and membership of an active improvement group [79]. In young firms, most workers are required to multi-task to optimize limited resources. So, inherently, RBSE is important in young firms, and our findings strengthen this argument. To help expand workers' task control and raise RBSE, managers in young firms can consider granting workers who are high in skills but low in RBSE greater autonomy. Managers can organize training involving horizontal skills such as conflict resolution (to do the job) or vertical skills such as preventative maintenance (to gain technical mastery). Equipped with a range of skills, workers will feel more confident when facing challenging tasks. By encouraging workers to join professional development groups in the form of monetary support (e.g., reimbursement of membership fees) or non-monetary support (e.g., time off), managers in young firms can bolster their workers' RBSE.

5.3. Policy Implications

Our findings have important implications for policy makers. First, in innovation-driven economies, entrepreneurship has gained increasing attention as a key driver for socio-economic growth. To encourage formation of new ventures, local governments can formulate policies to set aside land and buildings for development of infrastructure such as coworking space. To foster the growth of young firms, public policymakers can introduce programs to develop the coworking spaces into key nodes of a larger innovation and startup ecosystem in the city [70]. Joining the membership of coworking space will enable young firms to gain access to government-sponsored venture-friendly support programs. Second, to provide greater level of support for entrepreneurs, coaching programs can be introduced to render the required assistance for problem solving. For example, an online coaching program between established and young entrepreneurs in the north of England was found to furnish the required quality and quantity of support in all functional aspects [80].

5.4. Limitations and Future Research

The current study entails several limitations. First, although the peer responses of participants' job performance converged with self-reports, other factors besides objective performance may have influenced the peer ratings. For example, participants were inclined to nominate peers who got along well with them to rate on their job performance. It is therefore possible that participants shared the highlights or lowlights of their workdays with their peers during break time or lunch time, thereby influencing the peers to make inferences about the participants' overall job performance. Future research on job performance may include a measure assessing the extent to which individuals discuss their workdays with their coworkers.

Second, although there are various dimensions in job performance, our study focuses on task performance such as the quantity and quality of work output. Katz and Kahn first divided job performance into task performance and contextual performance, which is also known as relational performance [81]. The former refers to the effectiveness of activities contributing to business development. The latter reflects the effectiveness of social environment and cultural context that serve as catalysts for task activities and process, which is also an important element of job performance. Future studies could explore how mutual support relates to other dimensions in job performance (e.g., contextual performance) and other outcomes important to young firms, which would help us to better understand their sustainability.

Author Contributions: Conceptualization, S.C. and Y.-P.H.; Methodology, S.C.; Software, S.C.; Validation, S.C. and S.L.; Formal Analysis, S.C., S.L., and Y.P.-H.; Investigation, S.C., S.L., and Y.P.-H.; Resources, S.C.; Data Curation, S.C. and S.L.; Writing—Original Draft Preparation, S.L., and S.C.; Writing—Review & Editing, S.C. and Y.P.H.; Visualization, S.C. and S.L.; Supervision, S.C.; Project Administration, S.C.; Funding Acquisition, S.C.

Funding: This research was funded by Ng Teng Fong Charitable Foundation (NTFCF) Research Funding, grant number R-317-000-133-720. The APC was funded by NTFCF Research Funding, grant number R-317-000-133-720.

Conflicts of Interest: The authors declare no conflict of interest. The funders had no role in the design of the study; in the collection, analyses, or interpretation of data; in the writing of the manuscript, or in the decision to publish the results.

References

1. Campbell, J.P.; Wiernik, B.M. The modeling and assessment of work performance. *Annu. Rev. Organ. Psychol. Organ. Behav.* **2015**, *2*, 47–74. [CrossRef]
2. Kim, Y.; Ployhart, R.E. The effects of staffing and training on firm productivity and profit growth before, during, and after the Great Recession. *J. Appl. Psychol.* **2014**, *99*, 361. [CrossRef] [PubMed]

3. Barrick, M.R.; Stewart, G.L.; Piotrowski, M. Personality and job performance: Test of the mediating effects of motivation among sales representatives. *J. Appl. Psychol.* **2002**, *87*, 43. [CrossRef] [PubMed]

4. He, H.; Wang, W.; Zhu, W.; Harris, L. Service workers' job performance: The roles of personality traits, organizational identification, and customer orientation. *Eur. J. Mark.* **2015**, *49*, 1751–1776. [CrossRef]

5. Masa'deh, R.; Shannak, R.; Maqableh, M.; Tarhini, A. The impact of knowledge management on job performance in higher education: The case of the University of Jordan. *J. Enterp. Inf. Manag.* **2017**, *30*, 244–262. [CrossRef]

6. Cano, C.R.; Carrillat, F.A.; Jaramillo, F. A meta-analysis of the relationship between market orientation and business performance: Evidence from five continents. *Int. J. Res. Market* **2004**, *21*, 179–200. [CrossRef]

7. Barrick, M.R.; Mount, M.K. The big five personality dimensions and job performance: A meta-analysis. *Pers. Psychol.* **1991**, *44*, 1–26. [CrossRef]

8. Judge, T.A.; Thoresen, C.J.; Bono, J.E.; Patton, G.K. The job satisfaction-job performance relationship: A qualitative and quantitative review. *Psychol. Bull.* **2001**, *127*, 376–407. [CrossRef]

9. Judge, T.A.; Bono, J.E. Relationship of Core Self-Evaluations Traits-Self-Esteem, Generalized Self-Efficacy, Locus of Control, and Emotional Stability-With Job Satisfaction and Job Performance: A Meta-Analysis. *J. Appl. Psychol.* **2001**, *86*, 80–92. [CrossRef]

10. Callewaert, J.; Marans, R.W. Measuring progress over time: The sustainability cultural indicators program at the University of Michigan. In *Handbook of Theory and Practice of Sustainable Development in Higher Education*; Springer: Cham, Switzerland, 2017; pp. 173–187.

11. Jiang, W.; Zhao, X.; Ni, J. The Impact of Transformational Leadership on Employee Sustainable Performance: The Mediating Role of Organizational Citizenship Behavior. *Sustainability* **2017**, *9*, 1567. [CrossRef]

12. Bakker, A.B.; Demerouti, E. Job Demands–Resources theory. In *Wellbeing: A Complete Reference Guide*; Cooper, C., Chen, P., Eds.; Wiley-Blackwell: Chichester, UK, 2014.

13. Bakker, A.B.; Demerouti, E. Job Demands–Resources theory: Taking stock and looking forward. *J. Occup. Health Psychol.* **2017**, *22*, 273–285. [CrossRef] [PubMed]

14. Bakker, A.B.; Demerouti, E. Multiple levels in job demands-resources theory: Implications for employee well-being and performance. In *Handbook of Wellbeing*; Diener, E., Oishi, S., Tay, L., Eds.; DEF Publishers: Salt Lake City, UT, USA, 2018.

15. Sedláček, P.; Sterk, V. The growth potential of startups over the business cycle. *Am. Econ. Rev.* **2017**, *107*, 3182–3210. [CrossRef]

16. Lechler, T. Social Interaction: A Determinant of Entrepreneurial Team Venture Success. *Small Bus. Econ.* **2001**, *16*, 263–278. [CrossRef]

17. Pinto, M.B.; Pinto, J.K. Project team communication and cross-functional cooperation in new program development. *J. Prod. Innov. Manag.* **1990**, *7*, 200–212. [CrossRef]

18. Mullen, B.; Copper, C. The relation between group cohesiveness and performance: An integration. *Psychol. Bull.* **1994**, *115*, 210. [CrossRef]

19. Levine, J.M.; Moreland, R.L. Progress in small group research. *Ann. Rev. Psychol.* **1990**, *41*, 585–634. [CrossRef]

20. Gemünden, H.G.; Högl, M. Teamarbeit in innovativen Projekten: Eine kritische Bestandsaufnahme der empirischen Forschung. *Ger. J. Hum. Resour. Manag.* **1998**, *12*, 277–301. [CrossRef]

21. Tjosvold, D.; Tjosvold, M.M. Cooperation theory, constructive controversy, and effectiveness: Learning from crises. In *Team Effectiveness and Decision Making in Organizations*; Jossey-Bass: San Francisco, CA, USA, 1995; pp. 79–112.

22. Sroka, W.; Jabłoński, A.; Jabłoński, M. Cooperative business models in steel enterprises in Poland. *Metalurgija* **2013**, *52*, 565–568.

23. Davidson, L.; Chinman, M.; Kloos, B.; Weingarten, R.; Stayner, D.; Tebes, J.K. Peer support among individuals with severe mental illness: A review of the evidence. *Clin. Psychol. Sci. Pract.* **1999**, *6*, 165–187. [CrossRef]

24. Marcelissen, F.H.G.; Winnubst, J.A.M.; Buunk, B.; de Wolff, C.J. Social support and occupational stress: A causal analysis. *Soc. Sci. Med.* **1988**, *26*, 365–373. [CrossRef]

25. Baruch-Feldman, C.; Brondolo, E.; Ben-Dayan, D.; Schwartz, J. Sources of social support and burnout, job satisfaction, and productivity. *J. Occup. Health Psychol.* **2002**, *7*, 84. [CrossRef] [PubMed]

26. Murphy, K.R. Job performance and productivity. *Psychol. Organ. Integr. Sci. Pract.* **1990**, *157*, 176.

27. Genero, N.P.; Miller, J.B.; Surrey, J.; Baldwin, L.M. Measuring Perceived Mutuality in Close Relationships: Validation of the Mutual Psychological Development Questionnaire. *J. Fam. Psychol.* **1992**, *6*, 36–48. [CrossRef]

28. Murray, S.L.; Holmes, J.G. The Architecture of Interdependent Minds: A Motivation-Management Theory of Mutual Responsiveness. *Psychol. Rev.* **2009**, *116*, 908–928. [CrossRef] [PubMed]

29. Clarke, N.; Mahadi, N. Mutual recognition respect between leaders and followers: Its relationship to follower job performance and well-being. *J. Bus. Eth.* **2017**, *141*, 163–178. [CrossRef]

30. Coyne, J.C.; Bolger, N. Doing without social support as an explanatory concept. *J. Soc. Clin. Psychol.* **1990**, *9*, 148–158. [CrossRef]

31. Deci, E.L.; Ryan, R.M. SpringerLink (Online service). In *Intrinsic Motivation and Self-Determination in Human Behavior*; Plenum: New York, NY, USA, 1985.

32. Andersen, S.M.; Chen, S.; Carter, C. Fundamental Human Needs: Making Social Cognition Relevant. *Psychol. Inq.* **2000**, *11*, 269–275.

33. Ilardi, B.C.; Leone, D.; Kasser, T.; Ryan, R.M. Employee and supervisor ratings of motivation: Main effects and discrepancies associated with job satisfaction and adjustment in a factory setting. *J. Appl. Soc. Psychol.* **1993**, *23*, 1789–1805. [CrossRef]

34. Brickson, S. The impact of identity orientation on individual and organizational outcomes in demographically diverse settings. *Acad. Manag. Rev.* **2000**, *25*, 82–101. [CrossRef]

35. Blau, P. *Exchange and Power in Social Life*; Routledge: Abingdon, UK, 2017.

36. Nguyen, T. STEAM-ME: A Novel Model for Successful Kaizen Implementation and Sustainable Performance of SMEs in Vietnam. *Complexity* **2019**, *2019*, 6048195. [CrossRef]

37. Bandura, A.; Walters, R.H. *Social Learning Theory*; Prentice-Hall: Englewood Cliffs, NJ, USA, March 1977.

38. Stajkovic, A.D.; Luthans, F. Social cognitive theory and self-efficacy: Goin beyond traditional motivational and behavioral approaches. *Organ. Dyn.* **1998**, *26*, 62–74. [CrossRef]

39. Anderson, E.S.; Wojcik, J.R.; Winett, R.A.; Williams, D.M. Social-cognitive determinants of physical activity: The influence of social support, self-efficacy, outcome expectations, and self-regulation among participants in a church-based health promotion study. *Health Psychol.* **2006**, *25*, 510. [CrossRef] [PubMed]

40. Yeo, G.B.; Neal, A. An examination of the dynamic relationship between self-efficacy and performance across levels of analysis and levels of specificity. *J. Appl. Psychol.* **2006**, *91*, 1088. [CrossRef] [PubMed]

41. Parker, S.K. Enhancing Role Breadth Self-Efficacy: The Roles of Job Enrichment and Other Organizational Interventions. *J. Appl. Psychol.* **1998**, *83*, 835–852. [CrossRef] [PubMed]

42. Parker, S.K.; Williams, H.M.; Turner, N. Modeling the antecedents of proactive behavior at work. *J. Appl. Psychol.* **2006**, *91*, 636. [CrossRef]

43. Griffin, M.A.; Parker, S.K.; Mason, C.M. Leader vision and the development of adaptive and proactive performance: A longitudinal study. *J. Appl. Psychol.* **2010**, *95*, 174. [CrossRef] [PubMed]

44. Vroom, V.H. *Work and Motivation*; Wiley: New York, NY, USA, 1964.

45. Fuller, J.B., Jr.; Marler, L.E.; Hester, K. Bridge building within the province of proactivity. *J. Organ. Behav.* **2012**, *33*, 1053–1070. [CrossRef]

46. Grant, A.M.; Ashford, S.J. The dynamics of proactivity at work. *Res. Organ. Behave.* **2008**, *28*, 3–34. [CrossRef]

47. Zapata-Phelan, C.P.; Colquitt, J.A.; Scott, B.A.; Livingston, B. Procedural justice, interactional justice, and task performance: The mediating role of intrinsic motivation. *Organ. Behav. Hum. Decis. Process.* **2009**, *108*, 93–105. [CrossRef]

48. Vancouver, J.B.; Kendall, L.N. When self-efficacy negatively relates to motivation and performance in a learning context. *J. Appl. Psychol.* **2006**, *91*, 1146. [CrossRef]

49. Cervone, D.; Wood, R. Goals, feedback, and the differential influence of self-regulatory processes on cognitively complex performance. *Cogn. Ther. Res.* **1995**, *19*, 519–545. [CrossRef]

50. Tims, M.B.; Bakker, A.; Derks, D. Daily job crafting and the self-efficacy–performance relationship. *J. Manag. Psychol.* **2014**, *29*, 490–507. [CrossRef]

51. DeGuzman, G.V.; Tang, A.I. *Working in the Unoffice: A Guide to Coworking for Indie Workers, Small Businesses, and Nonprofits*; Night Owls Press LLC: San Francisco, CA, USA, 2011.

52. Carpinello, S.E.; Knight, E.L.; Janis, L. A qualitative study of the perceptions of the meaning of self-help, self-help group processes and outcomes by self-help group leaders, members, and significant others. 1991; Unpublished manuscript.

53. McAdam, M.; Marlow, S. Building futures or stealing secrets? Entrepreneurial cooperation and conflict within business incubators. *Int. Small Bus. J.* **2007**, *25*, 361–382. [CrossRef]

54. Podsakoff, P.M. Organ DW. Self-reports in organizational research: Problems and prospects. *J. Manag.* **1986**, *12*, 531–544.

55. Meyer, J.P.; Allen, N.J. *Commitment in the Workplace: Theory, Research, and Application*; Sage: Newcastle upon Tyne, UK, 27 January 1997.

56. Goffin, R.D.; Gellatly, I.R. A multi-rater assessment of organizational commitment: Are self-report measures biased? *J. Organ. Behav. Int. J. Ind. Occup. Organ. Psychol. Behav.* **2001**, *22*, 437–451. [CrossRef]

57. Welbourne, T.M.; Johnson, D.E.; Erez, A. The role-based performance scale: Validity analysis of a theory-based measure. *Acad. Manag. J.* **1998**, *41*, 540–555.

58. Nebes, R.D.; Buysse, D.J.; Halligan, E.M.; Houck, P.R.; Monk, T.H. Self-Reported Sleep Quality Predicts Poor Cognitive Performance in Healthy Older Adults. *J. Gerontol. Ser. B* **2009**, *64B*, 180–187. [CrossRef]

59. Yuan, F.; Woodman, R.W. Innovation behaviour in the workplace: The role of performance and image outcome expectations. *Acad. Manag. J.* **2010**, *53*, 323–342. [CrossRef]

60. Cavanaugh, M.A.; Boswell, W.R.; Roehling, M.V.; Boudreau, J.W. An Empirical Examination of Self-Reported Work Stress Among U.S. Managers. *J. Appl. Psychol.* **2000**, *85*, 65–74. [CrossRef]

61. Azar, B. Poor recall mars research and treatment: Inaccurate self-reports can lead to faulty research conclusions and inappropriate treatment. *APA Monitor* **1997**, *28*.

62. Schwarz, N. Self-reports: How the questions shape the answers. *Am. Psychol.* **1999**, *54*, 93. [CrossRef]

63. Hox, J.J. *Multilevel Analysis: Techniques and Applications*, 2nd ed.; Routledge: New York, NY, USA, 2010.

64. Wooldridge, J.M. Fixed-Effects and Related Estimators for Correlated Random-Coefficient and Treatment-Effect Panel Data Models. *Rev. Econ. Stat.* **2005**, *87*, 385–390. [CrossRef]

65. Ilies, R.; Scott, B.A.; Judge, T.A. The Interactive Effects of Personal Traits and Experienced States on Intraindividual Patterns of Citizenship Behavior. *Acad. Manag. J.* **2006**, *49*, 561–575. [CrossRef]

66. Sonnentag, S. Recovery, Work Engagement, and Proactive Behavior: A New Look at the Interface Between Nonwork and Work. *J. Appl. Psychol.* **2003**, *88*, 518–528. [CrossRef] [PubMed]

67. Finch, W.H. *Multilevel Modeling Using R*; Taylor & Francis Group/CRC Press: Boca Raton, FL, USA, 2014.

68. Chatterjee, S.; Hadi, A.S. *Regression Analysis by Example*; John Wiley & Sons: Hoboken, NJ, USA, 2015.

69. Berman, S.L.; Montgomery, M.J.; Kurtines, W.M. The development and validation of a measure of identity distress. *Id. Int. J. Theory Res.* **2004**, *4*, 1–8. [CrossRef]

70. Cheah, S.; Ho, Y.P. Coworking and Sustainable Business Model Innovation in Young Firms. *Sustainability* **2019**, *11*, 2959. [CrossRef]

71. Cheah, S.; Ho, Y.P.; Lim, P. Role of Public Science in Fostering the Innovation and Startup Ecosystem in Singapore. *Asia Res. Policy* **2016**, *7*, 78–93.

72. Hochwarter, W.A.; Witt, L.A.; Treadway, D.C.; Ferris, G.R. The Interaction of Social Skill and Organizational Support on Job Performance. *J. Appl. Psychol.* **2006**, *91*, 482–489. [CrossRef]

73. Sandoval, L.R.; González, B.L.; Stone, W.S.; Guimond, S.; Rivas, C.T.; Sheynberg, D.; Kuo, S.S.; Eack, S.; Keshavan, M.S. Effects of peer social interaction on performance during computerized cognitive remediation therapy in patients with early course schizophrenia: A pilot study. *Schizophr. Res.* **2019**, *203*, 17–23. [CrossRef]

74. Vancouver, J.B.; Thompson, C.M.; Tischner, E.C.; Putka, D.J. Two studies examining the negative effect of self-efficacy on performance. *J. Appl. Psychol.* **2002**, *87*, 506. [CrossRef]

75. Bolger, N.; Zuckerman, A.; Kessler, R.C. Invisible support and adjustment to stress. *J. Pers. Soc. Psychol.* **2000**, *79*, 953. [CrossRef] [PubMed]

76. Tims, M.; Bakker, A.B.; Derks, D. Development and validation of the job crafting scale. *J. Vocat. Behav.* **2012**, *80*, 173–186. [CrossRef]

77. Xanthopoulou, D.; Baker, A.B.; Heuven, E.; Demerouti, E.; Schaufeli, W.B. Working in the sky: A diary study on work engagement among flight attendants. *J. Occup. Health Psychol.* **2008**, *13*, 345. [CrossRef] [PubMed]

78. Jabłoński, M. Value Migration to the Sustainable Business Models of Digital Economy Companies on the Capital Market. *Sustainability* **2018**, *10*, 3113. [CrossRef]

79. Axtell, C.M.; Parker, S.K. Promoting role breadth self-efficacy through involvement, work redesign and training. *Hum. Relat.* **2003**, *56*, 113–131. [CrossRef]

80. Fielden, S.L.; Hunt, C.M. Online coaching: An alternative source of social support for female entrepreneurs during venture creation. *Int. Small Bus. J.* **2011**, *29*, 345–359. [CrossRef]

81. Katz, D.; Kahn, R.L. The social psychology of organizations. *Adm. Sci. Q.* **1978**, *46*, 118.

sustainability

MDPI

Article

Coworking and Sustainable Business Model Innovation in Young Firms

Sarah Cheah [1,*] and Yuen-Ping Ho [2]

1   Business School, National University of Singapore, Singapore 119245, Singapore
2   Entrepreneurship Centre, National University of Singapore, Singapore 119245, Singapore;
     yuenping@nus.edu.sg
*   Correspondence: sarahcheah@nus.edu.sg; Tel.: +65-65167230

Received: 1 May 2019; Accepted: 22 May 2019; Published: 24 May 2019

Abstract: In larger cities, we see a rising trend of more people working outside their traditional offices, and engaging in a practice called co-working by sharing office space. The public policy makers of innovation-driven economies, on the other hand, have been availing co-working spaces and related support to promote innovation and entrepreneurship. Despite the growing significance of this area, there has been limited research on the link between coworking and innovation among young firms. This research examines the relationship between coworking space and innovation, particularly business model innovation (BMI) for sustainable performance. Based on an empirical study of 258 young tenant firms operating in 13 coworking spaces in Singapore, we establish that the space creativity of coworking spaces is positively related to the BMI outcome of tenant firms. Tenant firms' opportunity recognition and exploitation (ORE) process positively mediates the relationship between the space creativity of coworking spaces and the BMI outcome of tenant firms. While the social climate of the coworking space is found to have no direct effect on the BMI outcome of tenant firms, tenant firms' ORE process positively mediates the relationship between the social climate of coworking spaces and the sustainable BMI outcome of tenant firms.

Keywords: coworking space; creativity; social climate; sustainable business model innovation; opportunity recognition and evaluation

1. Introduction

Since the global financial crisis of 2008, a new economic order has been taking shape and is characterized by low-level growth equilibrium, affecting the business climate that firms operate in. This has brought about not only fundamental changes in the governance and structure of many organizations, but also significant shifts in the policies of many governments in the 21st century. A phenomenon that has emerged, particularly in innovation-driven economies, is the rising popularity of coworking spaces and their increasing association with innovation and inclusive growth. We observe that the new economic conditions contribute to the growing significance of coworking and innovation in several ways.

First, the reduction in foreign direct investment and capital flows between countries after the 2008 crisis has increased the cost of capital for the business community. This has precipitated the expansion of the role of governments in finding alternative engines of economic growth, such as innovation and entrepreneurship [1]. We have seen the introduction of new public policies that encourage coworking as low-cost alternatives to office spaces in support of the formation of new ventures and the sustenance of existing businesses. The deliberate co-location of coworking spaces with key innovation ecosystem stakeholders such as public research institutes and institutes of higher learning underscores the importance the governments have accorded to their roles in fuelling innovation-driven economic development.

Second, the decline in trade in goods and services in the new economic conditions would spell increasing burden of regulation and taxation [2]. The increasing rigidity of labour markets in response to populist opposition in many countries have led to a shortfall in the global supply of engineers and technical professionals [3]. As firms find it more challenging to deploy fund and shift activities across borders in the traditional way, they look towards coworking as alternative channels to acquire resources such as space, professional talent, and value chain partners [1].

Third, in the face of economic volatility pursuant to the worldwide financial crisis, companies have become more wary of making investment in capital assets such as land, buildings and equipment. As these capital assets take a longer time than current assets to recover the cash investment used to acquire the assets, the investing firms are exposed to monetary policy risks (e.g., interest rate and exchange rate changes) that may devalue their assets. To minimize such risks, firms prefer to rent coworking spaces that come with a range of facilities and services to support their operations, an expense that can recorded immediately for computation of their net profits [4].

Fourth, before the crisis, multi-national enterprises (MNEs) were welcome as benefactors that could provide opportunities for the local communities to get employment and upgrade skills. However, after the crisis, the political sentiments have shifted to support local businesses and community. To respond to this change, MNEs take their cue from the local communities for their stakeholder engagement strategy. MNEs begin to tie up with coworking space operators to gain visibility in supporting local innovation and startup ecosystem stakeholders. For example, Procter and Gamble and JP Morgan have collaborated with coworking space operator, Impact Hub Singapore, to introduce innovation and impact laboratory programs to grow the local startup landscape [5]. Other MNEs such as L'Oréal have partnered coworking space operator, Block71 Singapore, to launch startup challenge to invite collaboration with early-stage startups and small enterprises in the Asia Pacific region [6].

All these developments emphasize the increasing significance of coworking space and innovation in new economic conditions, especially for innovation-driven economies that are characterized by intense rivalry among firms in wages as well as the development of new products, production processes and business models [7]. However, there is limited research on the link between coworking and innovation. Is this just about locating firms in the coworking space where they will flourish automatically? Are there specific characteristics about the coworking space that encourage certain types of innovation among tenant firms? Do tenant firms need to have certain processes in place to optimize their innovation outcome for sustainable performance at the coworking space?

The purpose of our study is to examine and explain the relationship between coworking space and innovation, particularly business model innovation (BMI) in innovation-driven economies. We also examine the key process that enables tenant firms to enhance and sustain their BMI outcome at the coworking space.

Empirically, we conducted a survey on 258 tenant firms operating in 13 coworking spaces in 2016. Our analysis of the survey results establish that the space creativity of coworking spaces is positively related to the BMI outcome of tenant firms. Tenant firms' opportunity recognition and exploitation (ORE) process positively mediates the relationship between the space creativity of coworking spaces and the BMI outcome of tenant firms. While the social climate of the coworking space is found to have no direct effect on the BMI outcome of tenant firms, tenant firms' ORE process positively mediates the relationship between the social climate of coworking spaces, and the sustainable BMI outcome of tenant firms.

Our findings contribute to the management literature in several ways. First, our research has shed light on an emerging topic in the study of firm-level innovation, namely BMI by demonstrating that the coworking space creativity can have important effects on the BMI of tenant firms. Prior research tends to examine the activities and outcome of BMI in general, rather than investigating the antecedents of BMI in the context of firms located in coworking spaces. Second, our empirical study of 258 tenant firms across 13 coworking space operators will extend and add generalizability to the extant coworking studies. Extant studies have largely focused on conceptual models and qualitative studies of the coworking spaces, rather than quantitative research of their tenant firms. Third, we complement current research on entrepreneurship by considering the tenant firms' ORE process within the coworking space under the conditions of the new economic conditions that are characterized by volatility, uncertainty, complexity and ambiguity, rather than in a general environment.

2. Background and Hypotheses

The conceptual framework in this paper uses as a starting point Assenza's [8] proposed model for empirical measurement of the interaction between spatial dimensions and economic value creation. Drawing on Assenza's theoretical propositions, we develop and test hypotheses examining whether the innovation outcome of firms is influenced by coworking space characteristics. Innovation is a well-established antecedent for firm's economic performance in the literature [9]. An original contribution of this paper is the focus on an emerging topic in the study of firm-level innovation, namely BMI. The empirical literature, although sparse, shows that business model design and innovation have an impact on firm performance [10,11].

2.1. Business Model Innovation

The concept of the business model (BM) has only recently received growing scholastic attention although business models have been an integral part of economic behavior even in ancient civilizations, as noted by Teece [12]. In their wide-ranging review of the management literature, Zott, Amit, and Massa [13] linked the growth in BM studies to the broad diffusion information and communications technology, especially the Internet. These technological advances transformed how businesses use and share information, leading the way to more experimentation with BMs and the way that business activities are organized and structured [14].

There are multiple conceptualizations of the BM as pointed out by Zott et al. [13] and Massa and Tucci [15]. However, by synthesizing the commonalities across multiple views, a broad definition is derived: a BM is a systemic understanding of how an organization orchestrates its activities for the purpose of value creation. A BM is not just what the firm does, but how it does it. A more in-depth definition provided by Amit and Zott [14] (p. 511) describes the business model as 'the content, structure, and governance of transactions designed so as to create value through the exploitation of business opportunities'. In studies of BMs and firm strategy, the perspective is widened to encompass the firm's exchanges with external parties, in service of delivering customer-focused value [16,17].

There is general consensus in the literature that innovation and the BM are related concepts. One strand of the literature views the BM as a vehicle for firms to commercialize innovative ideas. By designing and implementing appropriate BMs, firms can better translate technology into value creation [17–19]. Technology and innovative ideas in and of themselves have no economic value. The BM is the mediating mechanism that connects technologies and ideas to the market.

A second complementary strand of the literature posits that the BM represents a new dimension of innovation [15]. In this view, firms consider the BM itself as a subject of innovation [20]. The term BMI emerged from this school of thought and is gaining increasing prominence. The BMI concept argues that a firm can compete through its novel business model [21] and that the business model can be part of a firm's intellectual property [22]. In fact, Chesbrough [23] suggested that BMI may be more important strategically than other forms of innovation, as having a better business model than competitors is more advantageous than possessing a better idea or technology.

Researchers have developed different approaches to examining the BMI phenomenon, reflecting the multi-dimensionality of the concept. Massa and Tucci [15] propose that BMI may refer to (1) business model design (BMD), which is the entrepreneurial activity of creating a business model in a new firm, or (2) business model reconfiguration (BMR), which is the process of changing an existing business model. Zott and Amit [24] view the BM as a system of boundary-spanning interdependent activities and suggest that BMI can be achieved by (1) adding new activities, (2) linking activities in novel ways, and (3) changing which party performs the activity. Giesen, Berman, Bell and Blitz [25] adopt a more outcome-driven perspective, classifying BMI into three groups: (1) industry model innovation, which consists of innovating the industry value chain by moving into new industries, redefining industries or creating new industries, (2) revenue model innovation, which innovates the way that revenues are generated, and (3) enterprise model innovation, which changes the role the firm plays in its value chain.

In this paper, we examine the outcome of BMI in firms. We adapt from the three categories of BMI proposed by Giesen et al. [25] to derive three groups of outcome, namely (1) new or expanded markets, (2) new sources of revenues and profit, and (3) improved efficiency and productivity.

Several studies have established that BMI is key to firm performance [25–27]. This justifies the focus on BMI outcome as the dependent variable in our conceptual framework. Research on antecedents of BMI has identified the importance of leadership and management agenda [28] and configuration of resources [29]. Cheah, Ho and Li [30] have demonstrated that the positive mediating role of BMI in the relationship between industry turbulence and firms' sustainable competitive advantage in the retail and hospitality industries. Significantly, no prior studies have examined BMI in the context of firms located in coworking spaces, nor of the role of space design in fostering BMI in firms.

2.2. Coworking Space Characteristics

Coworking spaces are designed to be extremely open and inclusive. The space is shared by people from all walks of life with different backgrounds and fulfilling distinct economic roles: entrepreneurs, freelancers, artists, researchers, students, and so on. Flexibility is inherent to coworking spaces as tenants can rent a table in an open space for any desired period. Many coworking spaces feature movable dividers and desks that allow for reconfiguration of work areas to adapt to developing businesses as well as community activities such as physical or online conferences [31].

The modern coworking space has evolved beyond its beginnings as a "desk share" space providing independent contractors with professional settings to work and meet customers. It draws inspiration from open sources, human interaction and professional training. The principles of co-location, collaboration and shared resources explain the economic rationale for firms to choose coworking spaces [32,33]. However, the physical design of the space itself and the community in the space are often highlighted by coworking space operators as important factors [34]. Open areas, modern furnishings, bright colors, architectural lighting, access to amenities such as coffee and tea, games and videos are all common [8]. Tenants also seek a sense of community from the space [35], to make connections, foster collaboration, and share knowledge.

The characteristics of coworking space are based on important values of openness, interaction, sharing and participation [31]. We will introduce two aspects of space characteristics, which we postulate to impact on the BMI outcome of firms in coworking spaces.

2.2.1. Space Creativity

Previous studies have inferred that the design of a work place, including architecture and layout, can inspire and motivate people to be creative [36]. In the framework of coworking space, we focus on the physical aspect of space creativity, which can affect an enterprise's performance through space structuring [37].

Many organizations are now paying attention to the design of the physical environment to raise their levels of innovation [38]. The work areas in most coworking spaces are designed to stimulate creativity, modelled after the offices in high-tech corporations such as Apple and Google [8]. These design elements are intended to interact with the cognitive and social functioning of tenants to generate novel ideas and foster collaborative connections. The structural configuration of a space in terms of architecture, decoration and layout influences the behavior of occupants [39]. Kristensen [40] and Magadley and Birdi [41] found that the design and configuration of physical space influenced the creativity and idea generating process of individuals. Spaces designed to encourage creative thinking, such as innovation labs and brainstorming rooms, would eliminate elements of the traditional office environment such as rectangular rooms and tables [42]. Coworking spaces have borrowed these ideas and typically feature multiple working rooms, round tables, exhibition spaces, refreshment areas, and creative cues such as pictures or irregular geometric shapes.

A conducive physical design also allows tenants to easily and effectively exchange existing knowledge. The overall "openness" of the coworking space layout creates potential opportunities for interacting in a spatial environment. In addition, the space visibility has been found to promote both team communication and interaction [43]. By facilitating tenants' participation in community activities and personal interaction opportunities, the spatial space design can afford unplanned interaction that allows for creative "collisions" that can increase the transfer of ideas [8,44,45]. Space creativity in coworking space is also important to provide a basis for value creation. The space is designed not only as physical space, but also as a lived social context and as a conceptual space, within which production or individualized personal practice occurs [8]. The physical proximity in the coworking space also provides additional space for informal communication and resource acquisition [37,43].

The physical design of a coworking space is intended to anticipate the needs of the participants, providing a work environment where multiple creative and ultimately productive activities are encouraged. Spatial design should attract entrepreneurs and other participants who feel comfortable enough to interact with the space [8]. Space creativity stimulates the cognitive process of tenants to actively seek new knowledge and materialize new ideas and concepts [40]. Additionally, space creativity encourages informal knowledge exchange in the coworking space. By effectively acquiring internal and external information from noncompetitive, complementary tenants within the community, innovative ideas are more likely to emerge. Therefore, we propose the following hypothesis:

Hypothesis 1 (H1a). *Space creativity of coworking spaces is positively related to sustainable business model innovation outcome of tenant firms.*

2.2.2. Social Climate

Several previous studies have produced results that support the relationship between social climate and innovative outcome. Innovation often occurs in the cyclic and iterative process which is established and maintained in collaborative environment through social interaction [46]. Thus, innovation is considered a social process in which social interaction provides a variety of input and improvement [47].

To some extent, the coworking space arrangement brings socialization back into the workplace. A coworking space can be seen as a work community that can be instrumental to enrich networks [48]. Coworkers are attempting to work in flexible ways, seeking workplaces that are used by other creative self-employed people who understand the value of forming networks and the power that derives from collaboration [48,49]. In the coworking space, entrepreneurs can share their experience in a harmonious social environment of like-minded individuals [31]. The formation of networks and collaborations is enhanced by a favorable social climate.

An essential purpose of coworking is the community that is constructed by physical co-location and as such, relationships within the community are less confounded by external motivations roles, and structures [35]. A community is a mode of relating [50]. According to McMillan and Chavis [51] the sense of community is characterized by four basic properties: membership, influence, integration and emotional support. This view of community underlines our conceptualization of social climate, which emphasizes interpersonal relationships [52] and trust [53]. Coworking can be seen as trust-based community-oriented environments which stimulate encounters and collaborations inside [54]. Trust supports learning and continuous improvement innovation development, and encourages greater information sharing and improved coordination between partners [55].

A favorable social climate fundamentally contributes to the well-being of tenant firms by reducing or eliminating workplace frictions. Psychological security confers a common understanding that coworkers can safely take risks, express opinions, share knowledge and try new ideas [56,57]. When there is overlapping knowledge and opportunities for spillovers, a positive social atmosphere and sense of trust enhance the capabilities of coworkers to adopt others' views and ideas [58].

The coworking space is a convergence of creators and innovators. It is believed that this concentration of creative types will shift the interpretation of a task towards a cognitive frame that desires creativity over routine performance, and may motivate creative actions [59,60]. Previous studies established that creative emulation is linked to an increase in creative potential [61]. Creative emulation among coworkers is facilitated by a positive social climate as there are less relational tension and struggle between proponents of established versus novel approaches.

Thus, we find the theoretical evidence supports a hypothesis that a positive social climate will positively influence the sustainable BMI outcome of firms in coworking spaces. We propose the following hypothesis:

Hypothesis 2 (H2a). *Social climate in coworking spaces is positively related to sustainable business model innovation outcome of tenant firms.*

2.3. Opportunity Recognition and Exploitation

The process of identifying and developing opportunity process is a key part of entrepreneurship [62] and innovation strategy of established firms [63]. Timmons argues that an opportunity "has the qualities of being attractive, durable, and timely and is anchored in a product or service which creates or adds value for its buyer or end user" [64] (p. 87). Opportunity recognition is defined as an individual's efforts in searching and identifying opportunities [65,66], which has been argued as a key contributor to competitive advantage and superior performance [67,68]. Opportunity development is centered on seeking and gaining information. Firms have long tapped different external sources of knowledge to develop new products, processes, systems, and business models. Much knowledge-based research has suggested that firms access external knowledge in order to deploy such knowledge in the context of innovation [69–72], thus linking the opportunity process to innovation.

Tapping into external knowledge sources may help firms not only to recognize new strategic opportunities [62,73] but also to exploit them to gain competitive advantage [63]. As argued by Ardichvilli, Cardozo and Ray [74], opportunities are intended to deliver value and the opportunity process should therefore extend to the implementation of the opportunity. There are three important concepts in the opportunity process: Opportunity recognition, development, and evaluation. We adopt this wider view of opportunity, which we term opportunity recognition and exploitation (ORE).

The fundamental nature of coworking is aligned to the conditions for ORE to take place. Coworking provides a creative physical space which promotes collaboration, networking and incubator-like sharing of ideas. By engaging in peer-to-peer interactions in different configurations, coworkers can network their activities and activity systems within the space [75]. Activities such as organizational design, networking, and knowledge management [63,76,77] aid firms in exploiting opportunities.

We posit that the ORE process positively mediates the relationship between coworking space characteristics and BMI outcome. The reinvention of a business model requires the firm to build a boundary-spanning business network with its external stakeholders to effectively exploit opportunities and capture value [78].

As earlier hypothesized in H1a, space creativity is associated with better BMI outcome. Drawing on conceptual and empirical studies, Ardichvilli et al. [74] concluded that creativity is one of five key factors in the opportunity development process. Specifically, it is proposed that creativity is related to "alertness" which is the propensity to be sensitive to information about unsolved problems, unmet needs and novel combination of resources. Coworking firms that engage in ORE are able to capitalize more on the creative design of the physical space. As such, we hypothesize that:

Hypothesis 1 (H1b). *Opportunity recognition and exploitation positively mediates the relationship between space creativity of coworking spaces and sustainable business model innovation outcome of tenant firms.*

The quality and strength of social ties are important to the opportunity identification process [74,79]. Gravonetter [80] argues that more distant or casual acquaintances are bridges to information that may not be available within a strong-ties network of close friends or family. Extended networks contribute to higher levels of opportunity discovery.

Coworking spaces are carefully designed to foster connections and to increase opportunities for collaboration and conversation among tenants from vastly disparate backgrounds. Coworkers operate in different industries and markets, and have different strategies and business models. Such heterogeneity can lead to the discovery of potential collaborations and innovations on the peripheries [81]. The community aspect of coworking facilitates the formation of informal networks by promoting a friendly and trust-based social environment. In short, a favorable social climate can help a tenant firm to improve its ORE process.

Mu and Di Benedetto [82] hypothesized that opportunity discovery mediates the relationship between networking capability and the firm's performance in new product development. They argue that the network serves as a conduit of information through which important technological news can be brought to the early notice of the firm. In this way, the opportunity discovery process helps firms to validate technology trends and reduce the probability of errors on untried projects. As a corollary, we propose that the social climate in a coworking space provides the setting for a firm to interact with an extensive network of coworkers and to obtain unique information. The diversity of coworkers provides insights on different business models for value creation and value capture. At the same time, a positive social atmosphere and sense of trust enhance the firm's capability to exploit opportunities by adopting new ideas [58] and practicing creative emulation [59,60]. The ORE process therefore increases the likelihood of BMI in the firm. We thus hypothesize that firms that engage in ORE can better leverage on social climate to achieve sustainable BMI outcome.

Hypothesis 2 (H2b). *Opportunity recognition and exploitation positively mediates the relationship between social climate in coworking spaces and sustainable business model innovation outcome of tenant firms.*

The conceptual model and hypotheses developed in this paper are summarized in Figure 1.

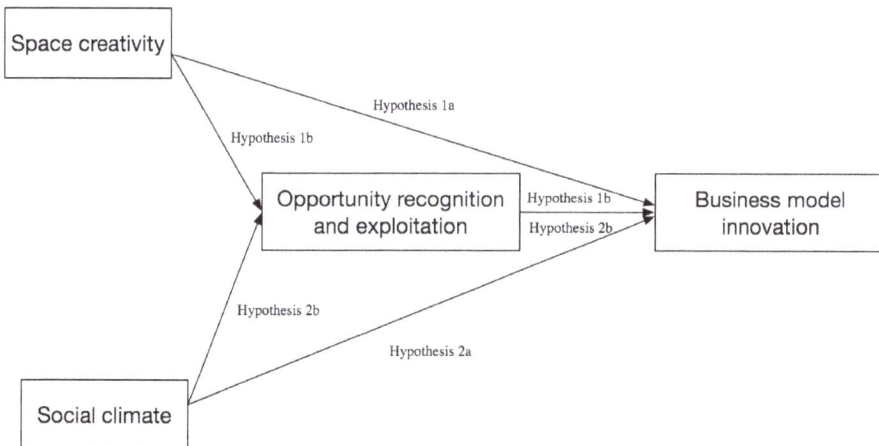

Figure 1. Conceptual model.

3. Methods

3.1. Data Collection and Sample

Singapore is an ideal research context. The Singapore government has long understood the important role of entrepreneurship in maintaining Singapore's leading position as an innovation-driven economy. Due to the lack of natural resources, Singapore has no choice but to rely on its human resources and intellectual capital as a source of competitive advantage. As part of the effort to develop a dynamic entrepreneurship ecosystem, its policy makers have invested in building infrastructure to support the formation and growth of new enterprises, including coworking spaces.

This research adopts the quantitative research method to understand the impact of coworking on the tenant firms and their business model innovation outcome. As of March 2016, we scanned the coworking landscape in Singapore and found a total of 36 operators from a variety of sources such as major media channels that focus on startups and innovators. Of these operators, there were two broad categories. The first category was made up of 13 operators that catered mainly to individuals such as professionals, hobbyists, freelancers and craftsmen, while the second had 23 operators that targeted at setups, startups and small businesses. As our study focuses on companies as units of analysis, we reached out in August 2016 to the second group, of which 13 responded positively to our request for surveys. After we had explained to them the purpose and scope of our study, 13 operators welcomed and supported our survey of their 447 tenant firms. By November 2016, we collected responses from 279 tenant firms, of which 21 were unusable due to errors. The final sample size thus consisted of 258 company responses, which falls within the recommended range of 30 to 500 that is appropriate for most research studies [83]. Table 1 provides a breakdown of the sample size by coworking space operator.

Table 1. Breakdown of Sample Size by coworking space (CS) operator.

Coworking Space (CS)	Population of CS	No. of Responses Collected at CS	Response Rate of CS
CS1	3	2	67%
CS2	33	20	61%
CS3	62	33	53%
CS4	60	30	50%
CS5	10	9	90%
CS6	8	4	50%
CS7	56	43	77%
CS8	60	32	53%
CS9	20	13	65%
CS10	20	10	50%
CS11	15	8	53%
CS12	70	38	54%
CS13	30	16	53%
Total	447	258	60%

3.2. Measures and Variables

We use innovation performance as the dependent variable, specifically focusing on sustainable performance in business model innovation (BMI). The independent variables are two characteristics of coworking space – space creativity and social climate. The process of opportunity recognition and exploitation (ORE) is included as a mediating variable.

The dependent, independent and mediator variables are measured using multi-item constructs scored on a five-point Likert scale (1 = strongly disagree to 5 = strongly agree). In order to ensure the reliability and discriminatory validity of items included our survey questionnaire, we draw on the literature and adapt items that have been successfully used in previous studies. The items and measures of construct validity are shown in Table 2.

Table 2. Measures and validation.

Items	Loading
Space creativity (Alpha = 0.829; CR = 0.840; AVE = 0.642)	
Our coworking space design encourages creative thinking	0.863
Our coworking space design encourages playfulness	0.627
Our coworking space design generates idea of higher quality	0.887
Social climate (Alpha = 0.895; CR =0.895; AVE = 0.518)	
In our coworking space, the coworking community has a full sense of cooperation among members	0.747
In our coworking space, mutual aid, sharing and cooperation is important in the coworking community	0.679
In our coworking space, there is a friendly atmosphere	0.531
In our coworking space, the relationships in the coworking community are close and cosy	0.737
In our coworking space, there is a sincere relationship in the coworking community	0.744
The coworking community members can depend on one another even in difficult situation	0.791
The coworking community members typically look out for one another	0.805
The coworking community members have faith in the integrity of one another	0.687
Opportunity recognition and exploitation (Alpha = 0.916; CR =0.917; AVE = 0.648)	
We can take advantage of product development opportunities with the help of the coworking community	0.789
We are very responsive to the technological opportunities that circle in the coworking community	0.762
We can develop new products to catch market opportunities with the help of coworking community	0.848
We get insights into new ways to approach product development	0.794
We can make several alternative solutions for each problem the project team encountered with the help of coworking community	0.861
We can learn the technical know-how held by the coworking community	0.769
Business model innovation (Alpha = 0.922; CR =0.921; AVE = 0.665)	
The coworking space services enabled us to open new market(s)	0.786
The coworking space services enabled us to increase market share	0.867
The coworking space services enabled us to generate new sources of revenues	0.951
The coworking space services enabled us to generate new sources of profits	0.939
The coworking space services enabled us to improve operational efficiency	0.660
The coworking space services enabled us to raise productivity level/reduce reliance on manpower	0.631

3.2.1. Dependent Variable

The dependent variable is a construct that measures the sustainable outcome of BMI in coworking tenant firms. We developed items by adapting from the three categories of BMI proposed by [25]. We derived six items that encompass three groups of outcome from achieving BMI, namely (1) new or expanded markets, (2) new sources of revenues and profit, and (3) improved efficiency and productivity.

3.2.2. Independent Variables

We developed items that measure space creativity and social climate in coworking spaces. Space creativity items capture the extent to which the physical design and configuration of the space encourage creativity, playfulness and idea generation [41]. Social climate items measure the congeniality of atmosphere of the coworking community and the degree of trust among tenant firms, reflecting the interpersonal relationships in the coworking space. Items are drawn from adapting previous studies by Erdil and Ertosun [52] and Daly and Finnigan [53].

3.2.3. Mediating Variable

ORE is included as the mediating variable in our analysis framework. Six items were used to measure the tenant firms' process for opportunity recognition and exploitation, adapted from Mu and Di Benedetto [82].

3.2.4. Control Variables

Control variables are included in the analysis in order to control for structural differences in the survey sample. As innovation performance can be affected by industry and business characteristics, we use industry, firm size and firm age as control variables. We use 11 dummy variables to control for the industry classification of the focal firms following Mu and Di Benedetto [82]. Firm size is measured as a firm's annual revenue in natural log form. Firm age is measured as the squared term of a firm's number of years since founding.

4. Results

To determine the adequacy of our hypothesized measurement model, we used confirmatory factor analysis (CFA) in MPlus 7.0 [84]. Items for the two components of space characteristics (space creativity and social climate), ORE and BMI were included in the CFA. The results shown in Table 3 suggest that a 4-factor model provides a good fit to the data ($c2$ = 759.069, df = 224, CFI = 0.878, RMSEA = 0.096, SRMR = 0.062). We also tested a series of alternative models, all of which provide a significantly worse fit. The results of our CFAs consistently suggested that the hypothesized measurement model provides the best fit to the data.

Table 3. Confirmatory factor analysis.

Model	X^2	Df	X^2/DF	CFI	TLI	SRMR	RMSEA
1	759.069	224	3.389	0.878	0.862	0.062	0.096
2	949.690	227	4.184	0.835	0.816	0.072	0.111
3	1372.577	229	5.994	0.738	0.711	0.094	0.139
4	1994.564	230	8.672	0.596	0.556	0.110	0.172

Note: CFI = comparative factor index; TLI = Tucker-Lewis index; SRMR = standardized root of approximation; Model 1: Space creativity, social climate, ORE, BMI; Model 2: Space creativity + social climate, ORE, BMI; Model 3: Space creativity + social climate + ORE, BMI; Model 4: Space creativity + social climate + ORE + BMI.

Table 4 presents the means, standard deviations, and correlations among variables. It shows that the independent variables (space characteristics) are positively related to the mediating variable (ORE) and dependent variable (BMI). Moreover, the mediator variable ORE is also positively related to dependent variable BMI.

Table 4. Means, standard deviations, and correlations of the variables.

Variables	(1)	(2)	(3)	(4)	(5)	(6)	(7)	Mean	SD
1. Size (log)	1							5.969	0.629
2 Age (squared)	0.241 **	1						97.28	853.078
3. Industry	−0.052	0.071	1					6.60	2.759
4. Space creativity	0.011	0.079	0.055	1				3.680	0.860
5. Social climate	0.087	0.093	−0.032	0.585 **	1			3.728	0.715
6. Opportunity recognition and exploitation	−0.009	0.005	−0.008	0.475 **	0.595 **	1		3.309	0.875
7. Business model innovation	0.092	0.080	−0.034	0.467 **	0.459 **	0.655 **	1	3.273	0.955

Note: * $p < 0.05$; ** $p < 0.01$; all two-tailed tests.

4.1. Main Effect Hypotheses

To validate the main effect Hypotheses 1a and 2a, we tested our proposed model using path analysis in MPlus 7.0. We included all possible direct paths between the space characteristics constructs and the mediator and dependent variables, controlling for the possible influence of firm age, firm size and industry. The results are summarized in Table 5. The direct path between space creativity and BMI was significant, and the estimated coefficient was positive (β = 0.222, $p < 0.01$), thereby supporting Hypothesis 1a. In contrast, social climate does not have a significant direct effect on BMI (β = −0.009). Thus, Hypothesis 2a is not supported.

Table 5. Results of path analysis.

Dependent Variable	Independent Variable	Effect
Opportunity recognition and exploitation	Space creativity	0.195 **
	Social climate	0.600 ***
Business model innovation	Space creativity	0.222 **
	Social climate	−0.009
	Opportunity recognition and exploitation	0.616 ***

Note: * $p < 0.05$; ** $p < 0.01$; *** $p < 0.001$.

4.2. Mediating Effect Hypotheses

To test the mediating effect Hypothesis 1b and 2b, we estimate the mediating effects, also known as indirect effects, of space creativity and social climate on BMI. The indirect effect of each independent variable is the product of coefficients from regressing (1) the mediator ORE on the independent variable, and (2) the dependent variable BMI on the mediator ORE. We used the bootstrapping approach for mediation analysis to test for the significance of the indirect effect [85–87]. In this non-parametric approach, the indirect effect of independent variables on the dependent variable is estimated multiple times by resampling with replacement from the dataset. A sampling distribution is generated from the multiple estimates and forms the basis for significance testing of the estimated indirect effect. The bootstrapping approach has been used extensively in empirical studies in sociology, psychology, and management research [88–90].

This approach is implemented using bootstrapping procedure in MPlus 7.0 (across 10,000 samples) to estimate indirect effects for each of the space characteristics on the dependent variable BMI, through the mediator variable ORE, as depicted in Table 6. Space creativity is found to have a significant indirect effect on BMI (unstandardized indirect effect 0.120, 95% CI 0.029, 0.228) through ORE, showing support for Hypothesis 1b. Similarly, our results suggested that social climate had a significant indirect effect on BMI (unstandardized indirect effect 0.370, 95% CI 0.262, 0.526) through ORE, in support of Hypothesis 2b.

Table 6. Results of mediating effect.

Relationship	Effect	95% CI
Space creativity → Opportunity recognition and exploitation → Business model innovation	0.120 *	[0.029, 0.228]
Social climate → Opportunity recognition and exploitation → Business model innovation	0.370 ***	[0.262, 0.526]

Note: * $p < 0.05$; ** $p < 0.01$; *** $p < 0.001$.

The path coefficients computed using structured equation modelling for our conceptual model are presented in Figure 2.

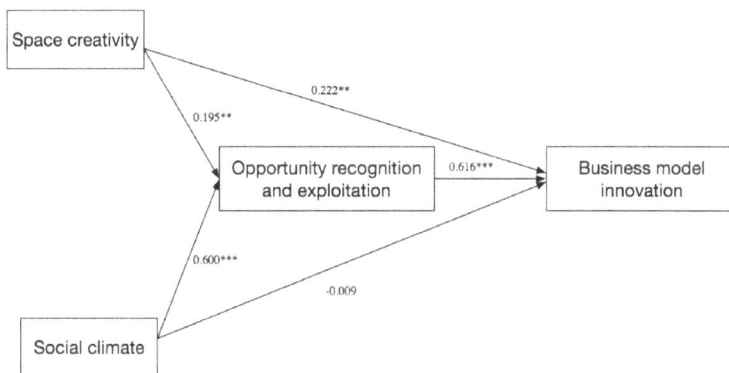

Figure 2. Structural equation modeling results. Note: * $p < 0.05$; ** $p < 0.01$; *** $p < 0.001$.

5. Discussion

Prior studies on BMI have largely focused on the activities and outcome of BMI in general [24,25]. In contrast, our research considers the relatively understudied antecedents of BMI in the context of firms located in coworking spaces in the innovation-driven economy Singapore. We begin to examine the link between coworking space and BMI. Our research illuminates not just the relationship between coworking space characteristics and BMI outcome, but also the key process that enables tenant firms to enhance and sustain their BMI outcome at the coworking space.

In this study, it is evident that the mere provision of coworking space is not enough to foster BMI. The empirical results support our view that a coworking space design that encourages creativity can drive BMI outcome. Our survey results support our hypothesized relationship between the space creativity of coworking spaces and the BMI outcome of tenant firms (H1a). The physical design of the space plays a role in not only encouraging creative thinking and playfulness, but also generating ideas of higher quality, thereby helping tenant firms achieve greater levels of BMI.

We then proceed to address the key mechanisms that firms employ at the coworking space to optimize and sustain their BMI outcome. Our empirical results support our arguments that tenant firms' ORE process positively mediates the relationship between the space creativity of coworking spaces and the sustainable BMI outcome of tenant firms (H1b). As creativity is one of the key factors in opportunity development [74], tenant firms that have internal ORE process in place are in a better position than those that have not, to identify, evaluate and commercialize the higher-quality ideas generated in a coworking space that is well-designed for creativity.

The internal ORE process of tenant firms is also instrumental in enabling them to harness the power of a favorable social climate provided by the coworking space. Our findings lend support to our postulations that tenant firms' ORE process positively mediates the relationship between the social climate of coworking spaces and the sustainable BMI outcome of tenant firms (H2b). A conducive social climate in a coworking space enables tenant firms to interact with extensive network of other tenants to provide useful social ties and knowledge, which are the key factors of opportunity development process [74]. To maximize the benefits of a conducive social climate, tenant firms should have established ORE process to leverage the social ties and market and technology knowledge that are pivotal for enhancing and sustaining their BMI outcome.

We had anticipated that the social climate of the coworking space would be important to allow tenant firms to freely exchange ideas for opportunity identification and evaluation, as well as facilitate discussion for collaboration on idea exploitation, thereby positively impacting their innovation performance [59,60]. Contrary to the expectations we formulated in Hypothesis 2a, the social climate is found to have no direct effect on the sustainable BMI outcome of tenant firms. This finding could reflect the challenges that coworking space operators face in configuring their social climate to meaningfully support the ORE process of their tenant firms. To address this challenge, the operators should develop greater familiarity and empathy with their tenant firms' profiles and processes, before working closely with their event partners to ensure their activities, such as hackathons, idea pitching sessions and investor presentations, seamlessly address the needs, goals and opportunity development processes of their tenant firms [91].

5.1. Policy Implications

This study has important policy implications, particularly for innovation-driven economies. First, to improve the social climate of coworking space in support of ORE and BMI of tenant firms, the public policymakers can play a more active role to enhance the quantity and diversity of tenant firms. Applying the principles of co-location, collaboration and shared resources [32,33], the government may formulate policies or programs to encourage the inshoring of foreign ventures in local coworking space. In Singapore, for example, the government has funded the operation of several coworking spaces (e.g., Block71 Singapore) to attract foreign ventures to use these sites as a launch pad to enter the Southeast Asian market.

Second, in a similar way, the government can support offshoring of domestic ventures into overseas coworking space. By supporting the construction of overseas coworking space facilities (e.g., Block71 San Francisco, US), the public policymakers can enable domestic ventures to use the overseas site to make foray into foreign markets.

Third, the government can provide incentives to encourage coworking service providers to offer a range of complementary services to meet the needs of young tenant firms to foster innovation. Operators granting access to physical resources and office support are found to enhance the survival rate of the tenant firms, while those offering programs to gain access to venture capital and supply chain network are more likely to increase investment in new ventures [1,54,92].

5.2. Managerial Implications

Our research has identified implications for management practice. First, coworking space operators should understand that the physical design and social climate of their space can play a bigger role than merely providing colocation for economic reasons [8]. While the tenant firms value a conducive environment for generating and bouncing off ideas, they also demand some form of idea protection. Further thoughts should therefore be put into the design, policies and practices of coworking spaces, which are expected to balance between the collaboration and privacy needs of the firms. Coworking space operators should also be mindful of increasing cost pressures as they face the need to differentiate themselves from the growing population of coworking spaces fueled in part by the new economic conditions [4].

Second, as MNEs partner local coworking spaces to engage innovators and entrepreneurs, it is inevitable that differences in their culture and approaches to innovation may give rise to tension and conflicts, thereby adversely affecting the quality of new knowledge shared and new ideas generated [57]. To effectively leverage the partnership to achieve their objectives, the MNEs should define and implement appropriate internal processes to guide their interactions with their coworking space partners and the tenant firms.

Finally, even the best coworking space boasting creativity-enhancing design and favorable social climate can be lost on a firm that has under-developed process for opportunity development. It is therefore imperative for tenant firms to establish efficient and effective ORE process internally to optimize the benefits of operating in a coworking space.

5.3. Limitations and Future Research

Although this research offers illuminating insights into the relationships among coworking space characteristics, tenant firms' ORE process and their BMI under the new economic conditions, it has several limitations, which open up opportunities for future research.

First, we used cross-sectional data, where the results represent only a snapshot perspective of dynamic processes. Although this limitation does not invalidate the basic logic of our argument, we recommend future research to employ a longitudinal study design, where the dynamic phenomena may be observed and causal relationships investigated.

Second, survey-based studies traditionally suffer from common method bias. Due to systematic measurement error, the estimates of self-reported data could be biased [93]. To ascertain such bias, this study adopted the guidelines of Radicic and Pugh [94], where Harmon's one-factor test was used to check the validity of our data with exploratory factor analysis on all the independent variables. From our unrotated principle component factor analysis, the first unrotated factor was found to account for only 47.4 per cent of the total variation in the other independent variables of our conceptual model, suggesting that the common method bias is unlikely to take place.

Future studies could use more objective data (e.g., percent of sales from new products also known as innovative sales) to measure the innovation performance of the tenant firms, as a proxy for commercial success of innovation. Third, this study focuses on tenant firms that are already operating in coworking spaces. Further research should find matched sample of companies that are not located in coworking spaces so as to control for possible factors that contribute to variances in their BMI performance.

6. Conclusions

We make at least three significant contributions to the literature on management. First, we investigate the relatively understudied antecedents of BMI in the new economic order prevailing for innovation-driven economies. Prior research tends to examine the activities and outcome of BMI in general, rather than investigating the antecedents of BMI in the context of firms located in coworking spaces. We establish empirically that the coworking space creativity can have important effects on the BMI of tenant firms. The physical design of the space is found to play a role in not only encouraging creative thinking and playfulness, but also generating ideas of higher quality, thereby helping tenant firms achieve greater levels of BMI. Our empirical results support our arguments that tenant firms' ORE process positively mediates the relationship between the space creativity of coworking spaces and the sustainable BMI outcome of tenant firms. This process is also found to positively mediate the relationship between the social climate of coworking spaces and the sustainable BMI outcome of tenant firms. Tenant firms that have internal ORE process in place are in a better position than those that have not, to identify, evaluate and commercialize the higher-quality ideas generated in a coworking space that is designed for creativity. To benefit from a conducive social climate, tenant firms should have well-defined ORE process to leverage the social ties and market and technology knowledge that are pivotal for enhancing their sustainable BMI outcome. Second, our empirical study of 258 tenant firms across 13 coworking space operators will extend and add generalizability to the extant coworking research. Current studies have largely focused on conceptual models and qualitative studies of the coworking spaces, rather than quantitative research of their tenant firms. Third, we complement prior studies on entrepreneurship by considering the tenant firms' ORE process within the coworking space under the conditions of the new economic order, rather than in a general environment.

Author Contributions: Conceptualization, S.C. and Y.-P.H.; Methodology, S.C. and Y.-P.H.; Software, S.C.; Validation, S.C.; Formal Analysis, S.C. and Y.-P.H.; Investigation, S.C. and Y.-P.H.; Resources, S.C.; Data Curation, S.C.; Writing-Original Draft Preparation, S.C.; Writing-Review & Editing, S.C. and Y.-P.H.; Visualization, S.C. and Y.-P.H.; Supervision, S.C.; Project Administration, S.C.; Funding Acquisition, S.C.

Funding: This research was funded by Ng Teng Fong Charitable Foundation (NTFCF) Research Funding, grant number R-317-000-133-720. The APC was funded by NTFCF Research Funding, grant number R-317-000-133-720.

Conflicts of Interest: The authors declare no conflict of interest. The funders had no role in the design of the study; in the collection, analyses, or interpretation of data; in the writing of the manuscript, or in the decision to publish the results.

References

1. Cheah, S.; Ho, Y.P.; Lim, P. Role of public science in fostering the innovation and startup ecosystem in Singapore. *Asia Res. Policy* **2016**, *7*, 78–93.
2. Sharma, R. *The Rise and Fall of Nations: Forces of Change in the Post-Crisis World*; W.W. Norton & Company: New York, NY, USA, 2016.
3. Autor, D.H.; Dorn, D.; Hanson, G.H. *The China Shock: Learning from Labor Market Adjustment to Large Changes in Trade*; National Bureau of Economic Research: Cambridge, MA, USA, 2016.
4. Merkel, J. Coworking in the city. *Ephemera* **2015**, *15*, 121.
5. Impact Hub The Hub Singapore Expands to Support the Growing Number of Startups and Entrepreneurs 2015. Available online: http://singapore.impacthub.net/impact-hub-singapore-press-room/the-hub-singapore-expands-to-support-the-growing-number-ofstartups-a (accessed on 12 December 2017).
6. Block71. L'Oréal Innovation Runway. Available online: http://www.blk71.com/events/l%E2%80%99or%C3%A9al-innovation-runway (accessed on 12 December 2017).
7. Crowley, F.; McCann, P. Firm innovation and productivity in Europe: Evidence from innovation-driven and transition-driven economies. *Appl. Econ.* **2018**, *50*, 1203–1221. [CrossRef]
8. Assenza, P. If you build it will they come? The influence of spatial configuration on social and cognitive functioning and knowledge spillover in entrepreneurial co-working and hacker spaces. *J. Manag. Policy Pract.* **2015**, *16*, 35.
9. Klomp, L.; Van Leeuwen, G. The importance of innovation for company performance. *Neth. Off. Stat.* **1999**, *14*, 26–35.
10. Zott, C.; Amit, R. Business model design and the performance of entrepreneurial firms. *Organ. Sci.* **2007**, *18*, 81–199. [CrossRef]

11. Patzelt, H.; Zu Knyphausen-Aufseß, Z.; Nikol, P. Top management teams, business models, and performance of biotechnology ventures: An upper echelon perspective. *Br. J. Manag.* **2008**, *19*, 205–221. [CrossRef]

12. Teece, D.J. Business models, business strategy and innovation. *Long Range Plan.* **2010**, *43*, 172–194. [CrossRef]

13. Zott, C.; Amit, R.; Massa, L. The business model: Recent developments and future research. *J. Manag.* **2011**, *37*, 1019–1042.

14. Amit, R.; Zott, C. Value creation in e-business. *Strat. Manag. J.* **2001**, *22*, 493–520. [CrossRef]

15. Massa, L.; Tucci, C.L. Business model innovation. *Oxf. Handb. Innov. Manag.* **2013**, *20*, 18.

16. Zott, C.; Amit, R. The fit between product market strategy and business model: Implications for firm performance. *Strat. Manag. J.* **2008**, *29*, 1–26. [CrossRef]

17. Chesbrough, H.; Rosenbloom, R.S. The role of the business model in capturing value from innovation: Evidence from Xerox Corporation's technology spin-off companies. *Ind. Corp. Change* **2002**, *11*, 529–555. [CrossRef]

18. Jabłoński, M. Value migration to the sustainable business models of digital economy companies on the capital market. *Sustainability* **2018**, *10*, 3113. [CrossRef]

19. Cheah, S.; Wang, S. Big data-driven business model innovation by traditional industries in the Chinese economy. *J. Chin. Econ. Foreign Trade Stud.* **2017**, *10*, 229–251. [CrossRef]

20. Mitchell, D.W.; Bruckner Coles, C. Business model innovation breakthrough moves. *J. Bus. Strat.* **2004**, *25*, 16–26. [CrossRef]

21. Casadesus-Masanell, R.; Ricart, J.E. *Competing Through Business Models*; IESE Business School: Madrid, Spain, 2007.

22. Rappa, M. *Managing the Digital Enterprise-Business Models on the Web*; North Carolina State University: Raleigh, NC, USA, 2001.

23. Chesbrough, H. Business model innovation: It's not just about technology anymore. *Strat. Leadersh.* **2007**, *35*, 12–17. [CrossRef]

24. Zott, C.; Amit, R. Business model design: An activity system perspective. *Long Range Plan.* **2010**, *43*, 216–226. [CrossRef]

25. Giesen, E.; Berman, S.J.; Bell, R.; Blitz, A. Three ways to successfully innovate your business model. *Strat. Leadersh.* **2007**, *35*, 27–33. [CrossRef]

26. Demil, B.; Lecocq, X. Business model evolution: In search of dynamic consistency. *Long Range Plan.* **2010**, *43*, 227–246. [CrossRef]

27. IBM Global Business Services. Expanding the Innovation Horizon: The Global CEO Study 2006. Available online: http://www-07.ibm.com/sg/pdf/global_ceo_study.pdf (accessed on 12 December 2017).

28. Svejenova, S.; Planellas, M.; Vives, L. An individual business model in the making: A chef's quest for creative freedom. *Long Range Plan.* **2010**, *43*, 408–430. [CrossRef]

29. Chesbrough, H. Business model innovation: Opportunities and barriers. *Long Range Plan.* **2010**, *43*, 354–363. [CrossRef]

30. Cheah, S.; Ho, Y.P.; Li, S. Business Model Innovation for Sustainable Performance in Retail and Hospitality Industries. *Sustainability* **2018**, *1011*, 3952. [CrossRef]

31. Leforestier, A. *The Co-Working Space Concept: CINE Term Project*; Indian Institute of Management (IIMAHD): Ahmedabad, India, 2009.

32. Capdevila, I. *Different Inter-Organizational Collaboration Approaches in Coworking Spaces in Barcelona*; ESG Management School: Paris, France, 2014.

33. Capdevila, I. Co-working spaces and the localised dynamics of innovation in Barcelona. *Int. J. Innov. Manag.* **2015**, *19*, 1540004. [CrossRef]

34. Koh, C.; Cheah, S. Co-working and the creative space—Designing the future organization. In Proceedings of the DRUID-Asia Conference on Asian Innovation, Singapore, 23–25 February 2016.

35. Garrett, L.E.; Spreitzer, G.M.; Bacevice, P. Co-constructing a sense of community at work: The emergence of community in coworking spaces. In *Academy of Management Proceedings*; Academy of Management: Briarcliff Manor, NU, USA, 2014; Volume 1, p. 14004.

36. Haner, U.-E.; Bakke, J.W. On how work environments influence innovation—A case study from a large ICT company. In Proceedings of the XV Annual Conference of the International Society for Professional Innovation Management (ISPIM), Oslo, Norway, 20–24 June 2004.

37. Haner, U.E. Spaces for creativity and innovation in two established organizations. *Creat. Innov. Manag.* **2005**, *14*, 288–298. [CrossRef]

38. Bauer, W. Innovations in Office Design as a Strategy for Survival. In *Office 21®—Push for the Future: Better Performance in Innovative Working Environment*; Spath, D., Kern, P., Egmont, V., Eds.; Cologne: Stuttgart, Germany, 2004; pp. 6–11.

39. Holahan, C.J. *Environmental Psychology*; Random House Inc.: New York, NY, USA, 1982.

40. Kristensen, T. The physical context of creativity. *Create. Innov. Manag.* **2004**, *13*, 89–96. [CrossRef]

41. Magadley, W.; Birdi, K. Innovation labs: An examination into the use of physical spaces to enhance organizational creativity. *Cret. Innov. Manag.* **2009**, *18*, 315–325. [CrossRef]

42. Lewis, M.; Moultrie, J. The organizational innovation laboratory. *Cret. Innov. Manag.* **2005**, *14*, 73–83. [CrossRef]

43. Stryker, J.; Farris, G. *Designing the Workplace to Promote Face-to-Face Communication in R&D Project Teams: A Field Study*; Rutgers University: New Brunswick, NY, USA, 2004.

44. Sailer, K. Creativity as social and spatial process. *Facilities* **2011**, *29*, 6–18. [CrossRef]

45. Taylor, S.; Spicer, A. Time for Space: A narrative review of research on organizational spaces. *Int. J. Manag. Rev.* **2007**, *9*, 325–346. [CrossRef]

46. Kanter, R.M. *The Change Masters*; Simon & Schuster: New York, NY, USA, 1983.

47. Weiss, M.; Hoegl, M.; Gibbert, M. Making virtue of necessity: The role of team climate for innovation in resource-constrained innovation projects. *J. Prod. Innov. Manag.* **2011**, *28*, 196–207. [CrossRef]

48. Rus, A.; Orel, M. Coworking: A community of work. *Teor. Praksa* **2015**, *52*, 10.

49. Davies, A.; Tollervey, K. *The Style of Coworking—Contemporary Shared Workspaces*; Prestel Verlag: New York, NY, USA, 2013.

50. Calhoun, C. Community without propinquity revisited: Communications technology and the transformation of the urban public sphere. *Soc. Inq.* **1998**, *68*, 373–397. [CrossRef]

51. McMillan, D.W.; Chavis, D.M. Sense of community: A definition and theory. *J. Commun. Psychol.* **1986**, *14*, 6–23. [CrossRef]

52. Erdil, O.; Ertosun, Ö.G. The relationship between social climate and loneliness in the workplace and effects on employee well-being. *Proc. Soc. Behav. Sci.* **2011**, *24*, 505–525. [CrossRef]

53. Daly, A.J.; Finnigan, K.S. Exploring the space between: Social networks, trust, and urban school district leaders. *J. Sch. Leadersh.* **2012**, *22*, 493–530. [CrossRef]

54. Fuzi, A. Co-working spaces for promoting entrepreneurship in sparse regions: The case of South Wales. *Reg. Stud. Reg. Sci.* **2015**, *2*, 462–469. [CrossRef]

55. Bunduchi, R. Trust, partner selection and innovation outcome in collaborative new product development. *Prod. Plan. Control* **2013**, *24*, 145–157. [CrossRef]

56. Schein, E.H. *Organizational Culture and Leadership*; Jossey-Bass: San Francisco, CA, USA, 1992.

57. Abu El-Ella, N.; Bessant, J.; Pinkwart, A. Revisiting the honorable merchant: The reshaped role of trust in open innovation. *Thunderbird Int. Bus. Rev.* **2015**. [CrossRef]

58. Un, C.A. An empirical multi-level analysis for achieving balance between incremental and radical innovations. *J. Eng. Technol. Manag.* **2010**, *27*, 1–19. [CrossRef]

59. Unsworth, K.L.; Clegg, C.W. Why do employees undertake creative action? *J. Occup. Organ. Psychol.* **2010**, *83*, 77–99. [CrossRef]

60. Madjar, N.; Greenberg, E.; Chen, Z. Factors for radical creativity, incremental creativity, and routine, noncreative performance. *J. Appl. Psychol.* **2011**, *96*, 730. [CrossRef] [PubMed]

61. Simonton, D.K. Sociocultural context of individual creativity: A transhistorical time-series analysis. *J. Pers. Soc. Psychol.* **1975**, *32*, 1119–1133. [CrossRef]

62. Venkataraman, S. The distinctive domain of entrepreneurship research. *Adv. Entrep. Firm Emerg. Growth* **1997**, *3*, 119–138.

63. Foss, N.J.; Lyngsie, J.; Zahra, S.A. The role of external knowledge sources and organizational design in the process of opportunity exploitation. *Strat. Manag. J.* **2013**, *34*, 1453–1471. [CrossRef]

64. Timmons, J.A. *New Venture Creation: Entrepreneurship for the 21st Century*, 4th ed.; Irwin: Burr Ridge, IL, USA, 1994.

65. Ozgen, E.; Baron, R.A. Social sources of information in opportunity recognition: Effects of mentors, industry networks, and professional forums. *J. Bus. Vent.* **2007**, *22*, 174–192. [CrossRef]

66. Ucbasaran, D.; Westhead, P.; Wright, M. The extent and nature of opportunity identification by experienced entrepreneurs. *J. Bus. Vent.* **2009**, *24*, 99–115. [CrossRef]
67. Chandler, G.N.; Hanks, S.H. Founder competence, the environment, and venture performance. *Entrep. Theory Pract.* **1994**, *18*, 77–90. [CrossRef]
68. Gielnik, M.M.; Zacher, H.; Frese, M. Focus on opportunities as a mediator of the relationship between business owners' age and venture growth. *J. Bus. Vent.* **2012**, *27*, 127–142. [CrossRef]
69. Cohen, W.M.; Levinthal, D.A. Absorptive capacity: A new perspective on learning and innovation. *Adm. Sci. Quart.* **1990**, *35*, 128–152. [CrossRef]
70. Foss, N.J.; Laursen, K.; Pedersen, T. Linking customer interaction and innovation: The mediating role of new organizational practices. *Organ. Sci.* **2011**, *22*, 980–999. [CrossRef]
71. Laursen, K.; Salter, A. Open for innovation: The role of openness in explaining innovation performance among U.K. manufacturing firms. *Strat. Manag. J.* **2006**, *27*, 131–150. [CrossRef]
72. Zahra, S.A.; George, G. Absorptive capacity: A review, reconceptualization, and extension. *Acad. Manag. Rev.* **2002**, *27*, 185–203. [CrossRef]
73. Shane, S.; Venkataraman, S. The promise of entrepreneurship as a field of research'. *Acad. Manag. Rev.* **2000**, *25*, 217–226. [CrossRef]
74. Ardichvili, A.; Cardozo, R.; Ray, S. A theory of entrepreneurial opportunity identification and development. *J. Bus. Vent.* **2003**, *18*, 105–123. [CrossRef]
75. Spinuzzi, C. Working alone together: Coworking as emergent collaborative activity. *J. Bus. Tech. Commun.* **2012**, *26*, 399–441. [CrossRef]
76. Vasilchenko, E.; Morrish, S. The role of entrepreneurial networks in the exploration and exploitation of internationalization opportunities by information and communication technology firms'. *J. Int. Mark.* **2011**, *19*, 88–105. [CrossRef]
77. Dencker, J.C.; Gruber, M. The effects of opportunities and founder experience on new firm performance. *Strat. Manag. J.* **2015**, *36*, 1035–1052. [CrossRef]
78. Zott, C.; Amit, R. The business model: A theoretically anchored robust construct for strategic analysis. *Strat. Organ.* **2013**, *11*, 403–411. [CrossRef]
79. Hills, G.E.; Lumpkin, G.T.; Singh, R.P. Opportunity recognition: Perceptions and behaviors of entrepreneurs. *Front. Entrep. Res.* **1997**, *17*, 168–182.
80. Granovetter, M.S. The strength of weak ties. *Am. J. Soc.* **1973**, *78*, 1360–1380. [CrossRef]
81. Surman, T. Building social entrepreneurship through the power of coworking. *Innovations* **2013**, *8*, 189–195. [CrossRef]
82. Mu, J.; Di Benedetto, A. Networking capability and new product development. *IEEE Trans. Eng. Manag.* **2012**, *59*, 4–19. [CrossRef]
83. Roscoe, J.T. *Fundamental Research Statistics for the Behavioral Sciences*; Holt, Rinehart and Winston: New York, NY, USA, 1975.
84. Muthén, L.K. *Mplus User's Guide*; Muthén & Muthén: Los Angeles, CA, USA, 2010.
85. Bollen, K.A.; Stine, R. Direct and indirect effects: Classical and bootstrap estimates of variability. *Soc. Method.* **1990**, *20*, 115–140. [CrossRef]
86. Preacher, K.J.; Hayes, A.F. SPSS and SAS procedures for estimating indirect effects in simple mediation models. *Behav. Res. Methods Instrum. Comput.* **2004**, *36*, 717–731. [CrossRef]
87. Bolger, N.; Laurenceau, J.-P. *Intensive Longitudinal Methods: An Introduction to Diary and Experience Sampling Research*; Guilford Press: New York, NY, USA, 2013.
88. Bear, S.; Rahman, N.; Post, C. The impact of board diversity and gender composition on corporate social responsibility and firm reputation. *J. Bus. Ethics* **2010**, *97*, 207–221. [CrossRef]
89. De Jong, B.A.; Elfring, T. How does trust affect the performance of ongoing teams? The mediating role of reflexivity, monitoring, and effort. *Acad. Manag. J.* **2010**, *53*, 535–549. [CrossRef]
90. Peng, J.; Li, D.; Zhang, Z.; Tian, Y.; Miao, D.; Xiao, W.; Zhang, J. How can core self-evaluations influence job burnout? The key roles of organizational commitment and job satisfaction. *J. Health Psychol.* **2016**, *21*, 50–59. [CrossRef]
91. Cheah, S.; Koh, C.; Ho, Y.P. Understanding the models of coworking space in Singapore. In Proceedings of the Asialics Conference on Area-based Innovation in Asia, Bangkok, Thailand, 3–4 October 2016.

92. Schwartz, M.A. Control group study of incubators' impact to promote firm survival. *J. Technol. Transf.* **2013**, *38*, 302–331. [CrossRef]
93. Podsakoff, P.M.; Organ, D.W. Self-reports in organizational research: Problems and prospects. *J. Manag.* **1986**, *12*, 531–544. [CrossRef]
94. Radicic, D.; Pugh, G. R&D programmes, policy mix, and the 'european paradox': Evidence from European SMEs. *Sci. Public Policy* **2016**, *44*, 497–512.

sustainability

MDPI

Article

Surviving through Incubation Based on Entrepreneurship-Specific Human Capital Development: The Moderating Role of Tenants' Network Involvement

Li Zhang [1,2], Ping Gao [3,*], Yongtao Zhou [1,2], Yuchuan Zhang [1,2] and Junhua Wang [1,2]

[1]   Business School, Hubei University, Wuhan 430062, China; zhanglipaul@hubu.edu.cn (L.Z.);
     daviszyt@hubu.edu.cn (Y.Z.); zyc@hubu.edu.cn (Y.Z.); 20070036@hubu.edu.cn (J.W.)
[2]   Hubei Center for Studies of Human Capital Development Strategy and Policy, Hubei University,
     Wuhan 430062, China
[3]   Global Development Institute, The University of Manchester, Manchester M13 9PL, UK
*   Correspondence: ping.gao@manchester.ac.uk

Received: 11 April 2019; Accepted: 16 May 2019; Published: 20 May 2019

Abstract: Drawing upon human capital theory and the co-production view of business support processes, this paper investigates the moderating effects of network involvement on entrepreneurship-specific human capital (ESHC) that determines the tenants' survival in an incubator. Longitudinal data between 2006 and 2009 of 71 ventures located in an incubator in China have been collected and analyzed. The research confirms that network involvement strengthens the influence of entrepreneurial experience on tenants' successful graduation, but does not impact the relationship between entrepreneurial family background and tenants' graduation.

Keywords: China; entrepreneurship-specific human capital; incubator; incubation services; network involvement; tenants' graduation

---

1. Introduction

In recent years, the global business landscape has undergone dramatic change. Some companies in emerging economies like China have developed quickly and caught-up with leading foreign companies in the global value chain. This phenomenon has attracted significant research attentions from various perspectives, for example the government supports [1] (like subsidy [2]), foreign research and development (R&D) spillovers [3], and so on. However, little is known about how companies from a disadvantaged context like China can overcome challenges in the early stage of development and survive so that they may further achieve sustainability. This paper sets out to explore this important research theme. We focus on the entrepreneurship-specific human capital (ESHC) issue in Chinese young companies which are still located in an incubator. Specifically, we consider the impacts of ESHC on tenants' survival in an incubator moderated by tenants' network involvement.

The impact of access to networks on the tenants' survival in an incubator presents an interesting research topic [4]. The extant wisdom is that incubation services can be developed or orchestrated by means of multiple accesses to a network. A network embedded in incubation services is found to be critical to the tenants' survival. The effects of incubation services on tenants are treated as a binary independent variable [5]. Furthermore, in-depth case studies indicate that access to networks is a facilitator of tenants' growth [6,7]. Although all tenants have the same access to the network of incubation services, it has varying effects on different tenants. The heterogeneity of tenants' network involvement can be an anchor to exploit the varying effects.

Human capital theory and prior studies have identified the significance of tight-coupling between entrepreneurs' human-capital profiles and the growth and survival of new-technology based firms (NTBFs) [8–10]. Moreover, according to the co-production view [11], an entrepreneur is both a receiver of incubation services and the party immediately involved in co-production with the incubator. In this interdependent co-production dyad, the assistance that tenants have received from incubation services is embedded in various kinds of networks, including social networks, virtual networks and so on. The heterogeneous impacts of the same access to network in the focal incubator are an interesting phenomenon that should be a research focus.

This paper has three research objectives. First, previous research examines either ESHC or entrepreneurs' network involvement. The interactions between ESHC and tenants' graduation (TG) have yet to be fully elucidated. In this study, we examine the influence of network involvement on the ESHC–TG relationship. We will disclose the mediating effects of network involvement on each component of ESHC, which determines TG. Second, existing research models treat network involvement as a binary independent variable, and prior studies have only considered whether network involvement is active or not in the process of incubation. Our research focuses on the effect of network involvement in quantitative terms. Third, this paper highlights the significance mechanism of co-production business assistance. Existing empirical works focus on tenants or the incubator management from the theoretical perspectives of resource-based view, competence-based view, and real option theory [12]. Our focus is the entrepreneur him/herself, especially in terms of ESHC in the context of network involvement.

The paper proceeds as follows. In Section 2, we develop the research hypotheses through a literature review. We review the theoretical and empirical literature relating to the impact of tenants' ESHC on their survival. We focus on the role of network involvement on the ESHC-TG relationship. Section 3 describes the dataset along with the econometric models and the dependent and explanatory variables. Section 4 presents the results of the econometric estimates. In Section 5 we interpret the results, and discuss the implications and future research.

2. Literature Review and Hypotheses

In this paper we explore the moderating effects of the tenants' network involvement on the relation of ESHC and tenants' survival. In this section we develop our research hypotheses from the literature. The research model is shown in Figure 1.

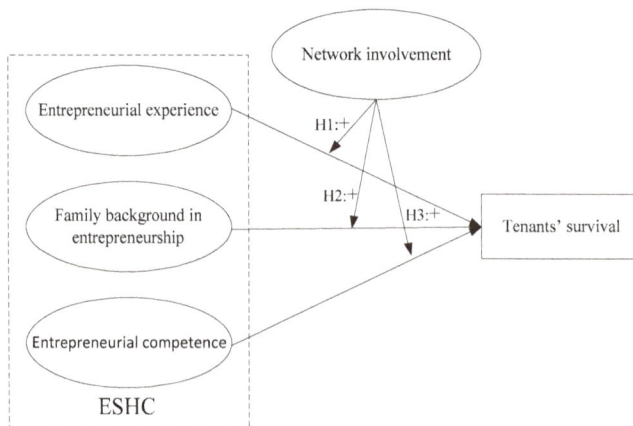

Figure 1. Research model.

2.1. Entrepreneurship-Specific Human Capital–Tenants' Graduation (ESHC–TG) Relationship

Human capital theory defines human capital as the stock of skills, knowledge, experience and capabilities of individuals that are relevant for economic activity and productive uses [13]. Many studies have explored the relationship between human capital "inputs" accumulated by entrepreneurs and the "outputs" that include the survival of the firm. As an example, Monsson and Jørgensen demonstrated that entrepreneurs' human-capital profiles have a significant impact on firm performance; entrepreneurs with more human capital or higher-quality human capital are coupled with superior 'outputs' [14]. This reasoning implies that ESHC is the relevant currency for TG relationships. ESHC is a conception of multi-dimension. It encompasses entrepreneurial experience, family background in entrepreneurship [15], and entrepreneurial competence [16] in entrepreneurship.

Entrepreneurial experience refers to the experience gained by entrepreneurs in previous entrepreneurial practices [15]. Episodically launching a new venture may endow valuable managerial experience, an enhanced reputation and abundant accesses to social and business assistances to entrepreneurs. These experiences help tenants overcome different kinds of bottlenecks embedded in the process of tenants' growth and promote new ventures, and facilitate entrepreneurs to manage complex information and prior knowledge [17]. Entrepreneurial experiences also have a positive effect on the growth of NTBFs. Entrepreneurs with more entrepreneurial experience, particularly portfolio entrepreneurs involved in multiple practice of entrepreneurship, have more diverse knowledge and more resources to promote the tenants' survival than inexperienced entrepreneurs [18,19]. Entrepreneurial experiences have a positive impact on harvest sale [12]. Experienced entrepreneurs have a higher likelihood of receiving venture capital funding and receive higher venture capital valuations. Moreover, entrepreneurial experience enables entrepreneurs to identify and pursue more business opportunities [20]. All these findings underpin the argument that entrepreneurs with prior entrepreneurial experience better facilitate tenants' growth than inexperienced peers [21].

A family background in entrepreneurship means that entrepreneurs have access to stable and trustworthy entrepreneurial assistance from their families which is a Chinese tradition. From the perspective of social capital [22], entrepreneurial family background is associated with relationships within a family, which is a kind of "socially-instituted" relationships. These relationships are particular resources and benefits that can be enjoyed by family members. Entrepreneurial experience from a family provides one source of entrepreneurial assistance that assists an entrepreneur in a range of administrative roles. From the perspective of intergenerational influence theory which focuses on the socialization of children, family has a vital impact on social roles and behaviors of children. The children of entrepreneurs often have access to their parents' workplaces from early childhood, acquiring entrepreneurial qualifications as a byproduct of everyday interactions. Thus, parental self-employment may serve as a mechanism which facilitates an entrepreneur to launch a new venture by means of transmission of information, beliefs, and knowledge within a family [23,24]. A lot of research demonstrates a tight-coupling between family background in entrepreneurship and NTBFs' survival [25,26].

Entrepreneurial competence is the core of entrepreneurship. The classic entrepreneurial logic is that entrepreneurs first scrutinize their own abilities and explore external environments, confirm promising opportunities, and then develop strategies to exploit those opportunities [20,27]. Prior studies, e.g., Obschonka et al. demonstrated the positive relationship between entrepreneurial competence and business opportunity identification and pursuits, which in turn affect the survival of tenants [28].

2.2. Moderating Effects of Entrepreneur's Network Involvement

An incubator offers an entrepreneur an appropriate physical room with discount rent, financial services, entrepreneurial mentoring, technology assistance, and network access [29]. It is the entrepreneur's competence of co-production with different kinds of service providers to make use of these facilitators that lays out the process and output of entrepreneurship [30]. So the emphasis of business incubation should be placed on entrepreneurs' involvement rather than just location. Access to networks has been a primary service that is central to incubation. Although previous studies have identified the tight-coupling between ESHC and NTBFs' survival, the co-production theory of an incubator manifests that the network that entrepreneurs are involved in determines the output of their collaboration [31]. The incubation network is a kind of social network. Its nodes include the incubator management, tenants, financial service providers, entrepreneurial mentors, and partners of technology assistance. Distinct networks can be formed and then expanded when actors involve in specific co-production of financial services, entrepreneurship mentoring, and technology assistance [6]. Moreover, networking infrastructure acts as the intermediary to connect the business assistance to new startups' growth [11]. The heterogeneous network involvement means that the ESHC derived from incubating networks by the focal entrepreneur is heterogeneous. Thus, the entrepreneurs' network involvement can be treated as a moderator when we explore the effect of ESHC on TG which has not yet been fully discussed in the literature.

2.2.1. Moderating Effects of Network Involvement on Entrepreneurial Experience

First, network involvement determines the input of entrepreneurial experience. Considering that the network involvement is an important means by which technology start-ups exchange entrepreneurial experience with other actors embedded in networks, we can argue that the more extensive their network involvement, the more diverse entrepreneurial experience they can receive from other participants. Network involvement helps new startups to access diverse entrepreneurial experience to overcome their vulnerability. Moreover, the experience relating to different industries and business lifecycle enables entrepreneurs to keep abreast of the coming and unpredictable bottle-neck of entrepreneurship, for example, cash flow constraints, inexperienced management, imperfect technology, and so on. In fact entrepreneurial experience can foster successful entrepreneurship only when such experience can synthesize episodic experience embedded in the process of tenants' growth [32]. Network involvement can impact the effect of entrepreneurial experience on tenants' growth in two ways. In one way, network involvement means all kind of communication and cooperation, from which tenants can gain diverse entrepreneurial experience. The intensiveness and commitment of network involvement is a determinant of the stock of entrepreneurial experiences. In another way, network involvement enables tenants to embed in the process of "leaning by doing". Through network involvement they can absorb and internalize tacit knowledge gradually, so they improve their competence in using these entrepreneurial experiences [33].

We can conclude that network involvement determines the stock of inputs of entrepreneurial experience in the process of co-production. It also underpins the improvement of management competence. When providers of incubation services explore partners of network involvement, they have the initiative to co-produce with active tenants because their services are exchanged at equal values at least, or they can even get more profitable enterprise equity as reward if they have made the right choice to pick up potential tenants. Tenants' extensive involvement in multiple social and commercial networks can be a signal of tenants' growth potential, and diverse service providers are more willing to attach to tenants with such a signal [34]. Furthermore, the amount and attribution of relationships determine a tenant's capability to get tangible resource and intangible knowledge [35], thus the tenant's growth and successful graduation. Therefore, network involvement leads to heterogeneous mechanism of attachment, which impacts the positive relationship between entrepreneurial experience and TG.

Moreover, entrepreneurial experience helps tenants gain a good reputation, while a good reputation is relevant to trust and trustworthiness between tenants and service providers [36]. According to social capital theory, tenants' trust and trustworthiness support them to get scarce resource and valuable information. Thus the reputation coupling with network involvement can set heterogeneous scenes when entrepreneurial experience promotes TG [22]. Network involvement facilitates tenants to connect with diverse service providers, and tenants' reputation can be dissimilated through independent paths of multiple networks. Consequently network involvement promotes the amplification of the good reputation of tenants. Entrepreneurial experience facilitates tenants to be involved in multiple social and commercial networks in which valuable resource and knowledge is embedded [4]. We postulate the following:

Hypothesis 1 (H1): *Network involvement moderates the positive relationship between entrepreneurial experience and TG in such a way that the relationship is stronger when entrepreneurs' network involvement is more extensive.*

2.2.2. Moderating Effects of Network Involvement on Family Background

Family background in entrepreneurship usually provides emotional support and financial convenience. The family members develop networks of emotional communication and financial support. The relationships embedded in those networks are characterized by trustworthiness and intimacy [37]. Network involvement means entrepreneurs take active part in different kinds of cooperation resulting from distinct services [38,39]. Tenants can occupy a favorable network location by actively taking part in diverse networks [40]. According to the theory of social network, incremental nodes and attachments embedded in an emotional communication network and financial support networks resulting from network involvement improve tenants' connectivity and hierarchy [41], while a node's connectivity and hierarchy belong to the structural dimension of social capital [22]. This implies that network involvement has a positive impact on the structural dimension of social capital of tenants' emotional communication network and financial support network.

Emotional communication from an entrepreneurial family is a kind of universal emotional support, while network involvement provides multiple points of access to emotional supports for tenants. Emotional support is embedded in specific financial services, entrepreneurial mentoring, and technology assistance [42]. In this case, emotional support becomes a sort of customized service that can express a clear purpose [32]. The more extensive the tenants' network involvement is, the more customized orientation the emotional support is [43]. Highly customized emotional support is more convenient to smooth away entrepreneurs' anxieties and puzzles. It can facilitate entrepreneurs to engage in entrepreneurship in a good mood.

A tenant's network involvement makes an entrepreneurial family focus on only bridging the tenant with the most matched financial service providers, i.e., acting as a "network broker" [35]. As an entrepreneurial family accompanies a tenant in the whole process of entrepreneurship, network involvement of the tenant facilitates an entrepreneurial family to access all kind of financial service providers. When an entrepreneurial family obtains an abundant supply of financial services from multiple providers, the family should scrutinize those providers and pick out competent ones (ibid).

In sum, network involvement of tenants has an impact on the structural dimension of social capital [44], and customization of emotional support from entrepreneurial family [45]. The above suggests that the more extensive network involvement of tenants, the more the stock of structural dimension of social capital and the higher customized emotional support the tenants can obtain. At the same time, entrepreneurial family can play the role of "network broker" better. Therefore, we could postulate the following:

Hypothesis 2 (H2): *Network involvement moderates the positive relationship between family background in entrepreneurship and TG in such a way that the relationship is stronger when entrepreneurs' network involvement is more extensive.*

2.2.3. Moderating Effects of Network Involvement on Entrepreneurial Competence

In general, entrepreneurial competence refers to the ability to kindle potential investor's interest, and the successful access to those investments [29,46]. As tenants are located in an incubator, their entrepreneurial competence mainly refers to the ability to acquire tangible resource and intangible knowledge by means of cooperation with diverse service providers. In the process of acquiring multiple investments, tenants usually will make efforts to convince potential investors of the prospect of technology commercialization by revealing the advantage of their core technology and plausible enterprise operation pattern. The network involvement enables entrepreneurs to receive information about the potential of tenant growth [47], which can attract the proactive engagements of multiple financial service providers [48]. The readiness of service providers has an positive impact on outcomes of co-production [11]. The proactive involvement of financial services providers promotes the tenants' growth as well as their successful graduation.

When tenants are involved in the co-production of entrepreneurial mentoring, their entrepreneurial competence mainly refers to ability to communicate with partners smoothly and to achieve cooperation with partners closely. Network involvement facilitates tenants to "co-produce" with more entrepreneurial tutors, successful entrepreneurs, and professional consulting companies. A real-time response interface of entrepreneurial mentoring is required when there are enough service providers for entrepreneurial mentoring. So network involvement transforms the frequency of entrepreneurial mentoring from episodic to continual mentoring [34,49]. The continual involvement of entrepreneurial mentoring promotes the tenants growth as well as successful graduation [11].

When we focus on technology assistance of incubation services, entrepreneurial competence refers to ability to acquire external knowledge. Network involvement facilitates tenants to acquire more explicit and tactic knowledge by means of cooperation with more partners who sell their technologies or are engaged in joint R&D [50]. Incubation is an important policy tool to facilitate knowledge transfer [51], while tenants with incremental knowledge are inclined to involve in extensive knowledge sharing. Tenants' extensive knowledge sharing and network involvement would evolve into mode of dynamic incubation, which is the most powerful pattern to promote the incumbent firms growth [52].

Therefore we can confirm that network involvement stimulates the readiness of financial providers, build a scenario of continuous entrepreneurial mentoring, and evolve into the mode of dynamic incubation. We postulate the following:

Hypothesis 3 (H3): *Network involvement moderates the positive relationship between entrepreneurial competence and TG in such a way that the relationship is stronger when entrepreneurs' network involvement is more extensive.*

3. Methodology

3.1. Estimation Procedure

Let T represent duration between the start event and the last event. Start event refers to the status of firm's location in the incubator, while the last event refers to the status of a firm's exit, graduation or out of research. We use days to measure the duration between the start event and last event.

T is regarded as a random variable with cumulative distribution function

$$P(t) = pr(T \leq t) = \int_0^t f(x)dx \tag{1}$$

The probability that a tenant has not graduated from incubator in the interval (0, t) is

$$S(t) = pr(T \geq t) = 1 - P(t) = \int_t^\infty f(x)dx \tag{2}$$

then $p(t) = P'(t) = -S'(t)$.

The hazard function h(t) demonstrates the instantaneous probability of graduation at time t, if the ventures have not graduated successfully in the duration interval [0, t]. It also depicts the conditional likelihood that graduation occurs at duration time t, assuming that it has not occurred in the interval [0, t].

Therefore, the hazard function h(t) is defined as

$$h(t) = \lim_{\Delta t \to 0} \frac{pr(t \leq T < t + \Delta t | T \geq t)}{\Delta t} = \frac{\frac{dP(t)}{dt}}{1 - P(t)} = \frac{P'(t)}{S(t)} = \frac{-S'(t)}{S(t)} = -[\ln S(t)]' \tag{3}$$

The survival function is an estimate of probability of staying in the incubator longer than that fixed duration.

The proportional hazards model proposed by Cox [53] was applied in this study, meaning that the firms in the sample present hazard functions that are proportional. Then the hazard function of T given x is specified as (1) in its continuous type version because the ratio $\frac{h(t|x_1)}{h(t|x_2)}$ of two firms x_1 and x_2 will not depend on t:

$$h(t|X) = h_0(t) \exp(\beta X^T)$$
$$\beta = (\beta_1, \beta_2, \ldots \beta_m), X = (X_1, X_2, \ldots X_m) \tag{4}$$

where:

We get baseline hazard function $h_0(t)$ if all covariates are equal to zero, while we get the estimated hazard function $h(t)$ if the covariates $X = (X_1, X_2, \ldots X_m)$ are nonzero;

$X = (X_1, X_2, \ldots X_m)$ is a vector of independent variables which describe various characteristics of incubator or tenants;

$\beta = (\beta_1, \beta_2, \ldots \beta_m)$ represents the vector of unknown parameters.

Based on (3) and (4), we obtain the predicted duration, between a starting point and the time a graduation occurred.

$$S(t|X) = \exp\left[-\int_0^t h(t, X)dt\right] = \exp\left[-\int_0^t h_0(t) \exp(\beta X^T)dt\right] = [S_0(t)]^{\exp(\beta X^T)} \tag{5}$$

Based on (4), we get

$$\ln \frac{h(t|X)}{h_0(t)} = \beta X^T = \beta_1 X_1 + \beta_2 X_2 + \ldots + \beta_m X_m \tag{6}$$

3.2. Research Setting—Wuhan Donghu Innovation Centre

The studied incubator in this paper is the Wuhan Donghu Innovation Centre (WDIC), which was founded in 1987 as the first state-level incubator in China. Similar to other countries, in China the development of an entrepreneurial ecosystem is a major policy tool to promote innovation and entrepreneurship. Incubators, also called "science parks", are an important component of this ecosystem. The Ministry of Science and Technology (MOST) initialized the Torch Program, which aimed to promote the formation of such an ecosystem and provide comprehensive value-added services for the tenants. Since 1988, 1103 ventures have entered into WDIC, and more than 900 hi-tech programs have been launched. By the end of 2010, the graduated ventures amounted to 681 in total, and the survival rate reached approximately 75%, Moreover, in 22 years WDIC has created 66,000 jobs. WIDC provided various incubation services to incubator firms to promote entrepreneurship and stimulate technology transfer from academia to the front lines of industry, which has contributed to the improvement of regional economy in global competition (see http://www.whibi.com/about/intro).

3.3. Sample and Data

According to the Regulation of Identification and Administration of Technology Business Incubator issued by MOST in 2006, a tenant located in a Chinese incubator should graduate within 3 years (1095 days). Accordingly we have selected the sample tenants that were in WDIC for at least three years from 2006 to 2009 so that we can get to know their last three statuses—exit, graduation or the end of the study period. The duration of survey appears to be a bit conservative because tenants tended to fall into one of three categories within 1095 days: (1) failure, i.e., the venture cannot survive and has been eliminated; (2) the firm remains in the incubator for failing to meet the graduation qualifications; and (3) successful graduation, i.e., the firm overcomes its nascent vulnerability and finally is competitive in the market.

The sample consisted of 71 firms admitted to WDIC in 2006. The data were collected through survey. We could obtain longitudinal data which depicted multiple, unequivocal status of tenants' growth by surveying their initial "inputs" and final status i.e., "outcomes". Thus, our sampling was likely to disclose the determinants of new venture creation and successful graduation. At the end of 2009, 31 tenants met the qualifications for graduation, 18 were terminated from the incubation program, and 22 remained in the incubator due to their vulnerability. Because the terminal event of successful graduation was only observed in the first group, the other two groups consisted of right-censored data. In addition, 4 ventures had multiple founders while other 67 firms had just one founder. Among those 4 ventures, only one founder made arbitrary decisions from a position of absolute authority. Thus, the sample allowed us to have the accurate and convenient measurement of predictor variables that can maintain a distance from the unclear effect of multiple founders on the dependent variables.

3.4. Measures

3.4.1. Dependent Variables

The dependent variables include the duration of location and its final status when the last event occurred. Status is coded as 1 if the tenant graduated and 0 if the graduation time is censored or tenant exits because of failure. Duration refers to days between a tenant's admission to an incubator and its graduation or exit.

3.4.2. Explainable Variables: ESHC

As mentioned above and shown in Figure 1, ESHC consists of three components: entrepreneurial experience, family background in entrepreneurship, and entrepreneurial competence. Entrepreneurial experience is measured by the counts that a firm founder had previously launched new ventures. The founder is included in the counts as long as it is in the primary stages of growth, no matter the venture is successful or not.

Family background in entrepreneurship is assessed with three questions adopted from Carr and Sequeira [23]: does your parent currently own a business or have they ever launched a new venture? Does your family member other than parents currently own a business or have they ever launched a new venture? Have you ever worked in those ventures owned by family members? Family background in entrepreneurship could be assessed by summing the time of "Yes" responses.

Entrepreneurial competence is measured using six-item scale obtained from Chandler and Hanks [16]: (1) I am conscious of potential consumer needs accurately; (2) My time and energy focus mainly on exploring and exploiting products or services that will meet my customer needs; (3) One of my greatest strengths is concentrating on developing goods and services to meet customer needs; (4) One of my prominent abilities is to make use of high-quality business opportunities; (5) I am extremely willing to push forward this venture through to full of competition; and (6) One of my prominent abilities is to develop novel goods and services that are technically advanced. Each item is measured using a seven-point Likert scale ranging from 1 to 7 (1 = strongly disagree, 7 = strongly agree). The items measuring entrepreneurial competence focus on entrepreneur's ability to develop products or services that can meet consumer needs. The scale has exhibited eligible internal consistency, with a Cronbach's alpha of 0.92. There is no increment of Cronbach's alpha if we deleted any items. It indicates that six items as whole are appropriate.

3.4.3. Moderator

Network involvement is measured by a four-item scale obtained from Hughes, Ireland and Morgan [52]: (1) We often take part in diverse business network organizations since we are admitted to the incubator; (2) We find it is good to embed in a business network deeply; (3) We often resort to business networks embedded in the incubator for assistance; (4) We often engage in all kinds of networks available by means of the incubator. We assess each item by using a seven-point Likert scale. The response scores of these items range from 1 to 7 (1 = strongly disagree, 7 = strongly agree). We can explore network involvement of entrepreneurs by means of these items. This scale possesses excellent internal consistency because its Cronbach's alpha is 0.96, and there is no any increment of Cronbach's alpha even if the deletion of any items. It indicates that all items should be retained in the scale.

3.4.4. Control Variables

Theoretically, human capital contributes to the success of new firms. Prior research shows that a founder's human capital plays a vital important role for tenants' growth and success [10,27]. According to Firkin [15], human capital consists of general human capital and specific human capital. General human capital refers to status of formal education, prior work experience, and a range of individual characters of entrepreneurs. Specific human capital consists of industry-specific and entrepreneur-specific components. To assess the distinct contribution of ESHC to TG, we have controlled general and industry-specific human capital variables in this study.

The status of formal education refers to years of education for entrepreneurs. Considering an additional one year of formal education may have little marginal effect on start-up success, we convert the years of formal education into three categories according to their degrees: 1 = bachelor's degree or less; 2 = master's degree; 3 = doctor's degree. The time of involving in full-time jobs previously is used to measure work experience. It is a proper proxy to ascertain the amount of and the level of attainment of work experience [20]. We square the number of full-time jobs to eliminate the variance.

In the literature, an entrepreneur's age [54] and gender [55] have been used as proxies of personal attributes of the entrepreneur. A dummy variable is a proxy for the gender of entrepreneurs. Female is marked as a value of "0", while male is marked a value of "1".

Industry-specific human capital captures the founders' prior work experience in a specific industry. Thus, we use how many years the founders have worked in the same industry to assess industry-specific human capital.

3.5. Uni-Dimensionality and Reliability

We use multiple-item scales to assess two independent variables—entrepreneurial competence and entrepreneur's network involvement. It is necessary to conduct a principal components factor analysis (PCFA) to assess their uni-dimensionality. The result indicates that one factor explains 49.91% and 37.45% of the original variance of these two constructs respectively, with an initial eigenvalue of 4.99 and 3.75, respectively. This implies that they are scales of uni-dimensionality.

We assess the statistical reliability of the multiple-item scales by computing Cronbach's alpha. Cronbach's alpha is 0.92 for the six items of entrepreneurial competence, and 0.96 for the four items of network involvement. Hence, the multi-item scales applied in our econometric model are reliable.

3.6. Common Method Bias

All of the items to assess the dependent, independent and control variables are included in a single PCFA to conduct a Harman one factor test in order to make it clear whether one component can account for most of the variance. First, there are six components with eigenvalues greater than 1.0. Second, those six components account for 83.31% of the variance, while the largest component only accounts for 32.31%. These evidences indicate that there is no common method bias that can affect the results.

4. Results

We have performed descriptive statistics on all of the firms in the population. The results are summarized in Table 1. Table 2 presents a correlation matrix. The correlation analysis indicates that several variables are positively correlated to one another. In order to ascertain whether there is a serious multi-collinearity, we have analyzed the VIF (variance inflation factor) and the tolerance of variance, and tested the eigenvalues. Since VIF < 10, Tolerance of Variance > 0.1, Eigenvalues ≠ 0 and the corresponding condition index < 30, there is no multi-collinearity. Table 3 presents the results obtained from the hierarchical Cox regression models associating ESHC, incubation services and control variables with the hazard rate of tenants' graduation.

Table 1. Descriptive statistics.

Variables	Minimum	Maximum	Mean	Std. Deviation
Bachelor's degree or less	0	1	0.52	0.503
Master's degree	0	1	0.34	0.476
Doctorate degree	0	1	0.14	0.355
Work experience	0	3	1.10	0.679
Age	31	49	40.75	4.711
Gender	0	1	0.58	0.497
Industry-specific human capital	1	11	4.65	2.673
Entrepreneurial experience	0	5	1.87	1.362
Family background in entrepreneurship	0	3	1.21	0.791
Entrepreneurial competence	1.00	5.50	3.288	1.315
Network involvement	1.00	6.25	2.370	1.479

Table 2. Correlation analysis.

	1	2	3	4	5	6	7	8	9	10
2.Master's degree	−0.745 **									
3.Doctorate degree	−0.422 **	−0.289 *								
4.Work experience	−0.027	0.160	−0.179							
5.Age	0.087	−0.305 **	0.290 *	−0.099						
6.Gender	0.135	−0.129	−0.018	−0.210	0.040					
7.Industry-specific human capital	0.000	0.061	−0.084	0.263 *	0.160	0.017				
8.Entreneurial experience	−0.027	0.199	−0.231	0.230	0.071	0.080	0.572 **			
9.Entrepreneurial Family background	−0.029	0.225	−0.263 *	0.200	−0.005	0.024	0.454 **	0.741 **		
10.Entrepreneurial competence	−0.144	0.211	−0.079	0.197	−0.017	−0.084	0.365 **	0.474 **	0.592 **	
11.Network involvement	−0.044	0.167	−0.164	0.282 *	0.020	0.022	0.455 **	0.699 **	0.732 **	0.521 **

* $p < 0.05$, ** $p < 0.01$ (two-tailed). 1–Bachelor's degree or a lower degree.

Table 3. Results of survival analysis.

Variables		Model 1 β	Model 1 p	Model 2 B	Model 2 p	Model 3 β	Model 3 p	Model 4 B	Model 4 p	Model 5 β	Model 5 p
Control variables											
Formal education (degree 1 as reference)	Master	0.493	0.234	−0.549	0.282	1.117	0.099	0.945	0.145	1.244	0.064
	Doctor	−0.082	0.901	1.037	0.163	0.387	0.637	0.361	0.661	0.512	0.535
Prior work experience		−0.004	0.990	0.257	0.447	−0.411	0.292	−0.380	0.309	−0.418	0.270
Age		−0.017	0.708	−0.086	0.067	−0.115	0.105	−0.113	0.097	−0.126	0.094
Gender (female as reference)		0.316	0.399	0.009	0.982	0.247	0.590	0.311	0.488	0.387	0.389
Industry-specific human capital		0.373	0.000	0.203	0.030	0.372	0.017	0.362	0.016	0.483	0.003
Explainable variables: ESHC											
Entrepreneurial experience		0.720	0.172	0.658	0.014	−7.627	0.017	0.323	0.473	0.361	0.438
Entrepreneurial family background				1.171	0.000	−0.672	0.366	0.274	0.881	0.070	0.915
Entrepreneurial competence				0.550	0.019	1.440	0.000	1.283	0.001	−1.549	0.183
Moderators											
Network involvement						0.955	0.321	3.706	0.001	−0.923	0.543
Interactive effects											
Entrepreneurial experience × Network involvement						2.835	0.011				
Entrepreneurial family background × Network involvement								−0.092	0.880		
Entrepreneurial competence × Network involvement										1.137	0.012
−2Log likelihood		223.207		179.081		105.661		111.545		106.034	
overall score Chi-square (p-value)		0.000		0.000		0.000		0.000		0.000	

As the base model, Model 1 includes control variables directly related to the probability of tenants' graduation. Model 2 tests the collective impacts of ESHC components with the objective of calculating their total contribution to the tenants' graduation. Model 3, Model 4 and Model 5 test the interactive effects of each components of ESHC and network involvement based on the cross-products between the two.

The overall significance of Model 1 is assessed using overall χ^2. The Chi-square statistics for all models is significant at $p < 0.001$; thus, the hypothesis that all of the parameters in the model equal to 0 is rejected. This base model for the control variables indicates that a founder's status of formal education and duration of prior work are not statistically significant, in line with findings by Montgomery, Johnson and Faisal [56]. A range of entrepreneurs' personal attributes variables, such as an entrepreneur's age and gender, are not statistically significant as well. In addition, our results yield a significant finding regarding the impact of industry-specific human capital on the survival of a new venture, lending support to studies by Ucbasaran, Westhead and Wright [20].

As demonstrated in Model 2 of Table 3, ESHC exhibits significant independent effects on the survival of new ventures while the variables related to ESHC are all included; the regression coefficients for ESHC are statistically significant at $p < 0.05$. Moreover, the -2log likelihood in Model 2 is smaller than that of Model 1. This demonstrates the increased fit of Model 2 when ESHC components are all included.

We have further specified the models including interactive terms. When comparing the differences in −2log likelihood between Model 2 and Models 3, 4 and 5, the reduction in −2log likelihood indicates superior fit for the Models 3, 4 and 5 if the interaction terms are entered. It indicates that the interactive term included in the models contributes to the explanation.

H1 predicts the moderating effect of network involvement when we uncover the impact of entrepreneurial experience on the probability of tenants' graduation. The interaction of entrepreneurial experience and network involvement is significant at the 0.05 level (Table 3, Model 3), and the interaction of entrepreneurial competence and network involvement are significant at 0.05 level (Table 3, Model 5), indicating that network involvement moderates the impact of entrepreneurial experience on TG as well as the entrepreneurial competence on TG. In other words, the more extensive network involvement, the greater the impact of entrepreneurial experience as well as entrepreneurial competence on the probability of tenants' graduation, lending strong support for H1 and H3.

The interaction between entrepreneurial family background and network involvement is not significant (Table 3, Model 4). It means that a high or low level as well as positive or negative variations of entrepreneurs' network involvement does not affect the relationship of entrepreneurial family background and the hazard rate of tenants' graduation, therefore H2 is not supported.

To interpret the effect of network involvement, we have conducted cluster analysis to subdivide the tenants by means of their relative degrees of network involvement. The final cluster solution has created three groups of network involvement, i.e., low, medium, and high ones corresponding to the degree of network involvement. The difference of survival curves among the three groups illustrates the impact of varying network involvement on the survival probability of TG (Figure 2): the group labeled as high reach the average graduation rate 43.7% after 559 days, whereas the medium-level group fail to reach the benchmark in 613 days, and the other group are far from the benchmark till the end of the period of location.

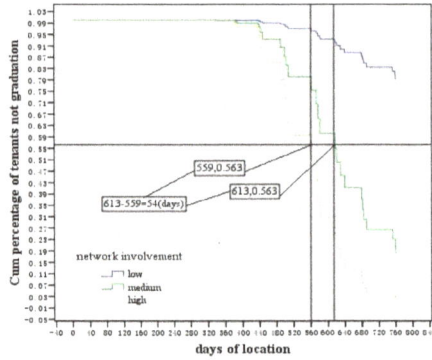

Figure 2. The impact of network involvement on the survival probability of tenants' graduation (TG). (Note: The graduation rate is 0.437, i.e., 31 of 71 tenants graduated; un-graduation rate is 0.563).

To further interpret the interaction effects, which are statistically significant in the models, we have plotted the regression equations for all conditions of network involvement. Figure 3a,b graphically depict the entrepreneurial experience and TG relationship, and entrepreneurial competence and TG relationship as moderated by network involvement, respectively.

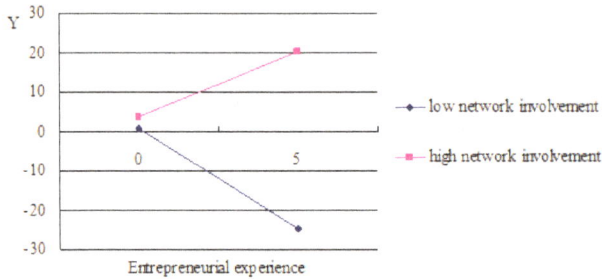

Entrepreneurial experience

Figure 3a

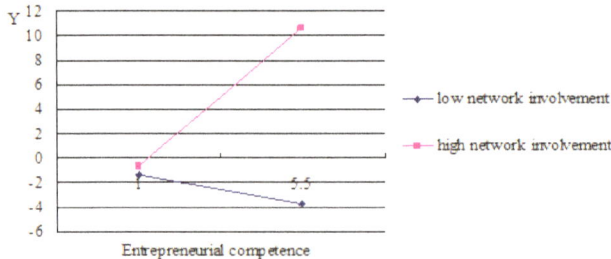

Entrepreneurial competence

Figure 3b

Figure 3. The network involvement as a moderator of entrepreneurship-specific human capital (ESHC)–Y relationship. (Note: The Y axes is $\ln \frac{h(t|X)}{h_0(t)}$, for $(\ln x)' = \frac{1}{x} > 0$ ($x > 0$), the $\ln x$ is monotonically increasing, thus $\ln \frac{h(t|X)}{h_0(t)}$ and $\frac{h(t|X)}{h_0(t)}$ are positively relative in a strict way, and the impact of covariates on $\ln \frac{h(t|X)}{h_0(t)}$ and $\frac{h(t|X)}{h_0(t)}$ should be in the same direction according to (4) and (6)).

5. Discussion and Conclusions

5.1. Theoretical Reflections

Our research contributes to the study on ESHC and network involvement in the context of incubators. It demonstrates that network involvement sets the baseline for the impact of ESHC on client ventures' graduation. Our analytical results expose the factors common in most incubators that lead to the varying effectiveness of the network involvement.

Previous research focuses on either ESHC or network involvement of entrepreneurs but not both, collectively and interactively. This study adds to the literature and demonstrated the impact of network involvement on the relationship between ESHC and TG. Specifically, entrepreneurial experience and entrepreneurial competence significantly impact ventures' survival in the presence of network involvement, while network involvement does not moderate the effect of family background in entrepreneurship on TG. The plausible explanation is that entrepreneurial experience and entrepreneurial competence are in tacit forms and are embodied in entrepreneurs themselves. Face-to-face communication and immediate cooperation facilitate the transfer of tacit knowledge among tenants, as well as between tenants and service providers. When entrepreneurs' network involvement promotes a co-production dyad, which enables entrepreneurs to pursue entrepreneurial experience and entrepreneurial competence by themselves, tacit knowledge can be transferred among different parties embedded in the incubating process. This explains the moderating effects of network involvement on entrepreneurial experience and entrepreneurial competence when those two ESHC factors facilitate tenants' survival in incubators.

H2 on the relation of family background in entrepreneurship and network involvement is not supported. The reason is that a Chinese entrepreneur is not accustomed to share the resource and knowledge within his (or her) own family. As the saying goes, 'every miller draws water to his own mill.' Resource and knowledge obtained from Chinese family are deeply embedded in its own "GUANXI" network, which cannot be substituted by those from incubation network [42]. Moreover, Chinese people like to turn to their family when meeting challenges, rather than outside help. Traditional family ties in China lead to the phenomenon that assistance from family is just close at hand. Due to the excessive reliance on family, a Chinese entrepreneur is often reluctant to resort to incubating network; in turn, network involvement does not strengthen the pooling of knowledge and resource from entrepreneurial family. Moreover, the expertise and knowledge derived from entrepreneurial family is highly customized, which in most cases cannot be used by other entrepreneurs at all. Consequently, as we have observed, network involvement does not amplify the effect of an entrepreneurial family background on the tenants' graduation.

5.2. Managerial and Policy Implications

The study results have useful implications for the incubator management and policy makers that sponsor and initiate incubation services. Incubator management should take effective measures to assist tenants to access to networks and have network involvement so that they can make use of knowledge and resource embedded in incubating networks proactively. Furthermore, an incubator should strive to be 'core node' for the flow of resource and expertise, which may ultimately affect tenants. The government should stimulate the 'nodes' to engage in networking, including entrepreneur, incubator and other resource providers involved in co-production.

Institutionalizing the incubating network should be a priority of the incubator management in enhancing incubation services. Network institutionalization refers to mechanisms and norms that drive actors to take active part in formal and informal networks and contribute to cooperation practices. On the one hand, incubator management can institutionalize formal networking through measures like bringing external experts on site; establishing regular processes for exchanging information and know-how across the incubator; implementing economic incentives for networking initiatives; etc. [6]. On the other hand, incubator management can institutionalize informal networking by means of appropriating layout of incubated firms' physical location [57]; appealing social interaction scenes [38]; and so on.

In particular, the roles of information and communication technology (ICT) in supporting efficient networking should be recognized [58]. In China the government has supported the construction of nationwide ICT infrastructure and ensured the affordability and availability of Internet services and mobile technologies to society. An incubator should leverage different ICT tools such as socialising applications e.g., WeChat and on-line platforms like Alibaba etc. to support web-based collaboration between tenants, and their contacts with external sources. The government can consider building a national ICT-based incubating platform for different incubators to exchange their best practices of offering incubation services, and for tenants in different incubators to explore broader business opportunities.

5.3. Limitations and Future Research

In this paper we investigate the relationship between ESHC, network involvement, and tenants' survival. We focus on the process of incubation co-production of tenants, the incubator management, and external service providers [11] as the theoretical anchor. We have examined three ESHC dimensions—entrepreneurial experience, family background in entrepreneurship, and entrepreneurial competence. Further research can consider other factors, and focus on the impact of network involvement on general human capital rather than ESHC. The conclusions of our study should encourage future exploration on contextual variables which can impact the co-production of all of the "inputs" embedded in the process of incubation.

Our research context is an incubator. We have considered financial services, entrepreneurial mentoring, and technology assistance provided by an incubator to tenants when examining the moderating effects of tenants' network involvement on entrepreneurial competence that determines the tenants' survival. The ability to develop novel goods and services is a facilitator for acquiring additional financial services, entrepreneurial mentoring, and technology assistance, which may help tenants survive eventually. In this condition, it is assumed innovation has no direct link with the tenants' survival. Moreover, the ability to develop novel goods and services is not the focus of this research. As suggested by Chandler and Hanks [16], we have included it in the dimension of entrepreneurial competence. According to Colombelli, Krafft and Vivarelli [59], innovation is a source of a "survival premium". Future research on tenants' survival can include a proxy for innovation, and analyze the impacts of tenants' ability to develop novel goods and services separately.

Our research points directions for future research. Researchers may consider establishing a new scale to examine the new dimensionality of network involvement, and evaluating network involvement derived from questionnaire responses focusing on the cooperation embedded in on-line social networks.

Author Contributions: Formal analysis, L.Z. and J.W.; methodology, L.Z.; supervision, P.G., Y.Z. (Yuchuan Zhang); writing original draft preparation, L.Z. and Y.Z. (Yongtao Zhou); writing review and editing, L.Z. and P.G.; project administration, L.Z.; funding acquisition, L.Z. and Y.Z. (Yongtao Zhou).

Funding: This research was funded by the National Natural Science Foundation of China. Grant No. 15GBL026: Customized Incubation Based on Big Data Embedded in Incubator Network.

Conflicts of Interest: The authors declare no conflict of interest. The funder had no role in the design of the study; in the collection, analyses, or interpretation of data; in the writing of the manuscript, and in the decision to publish the results.

References

1. Gao, P. Government in the catching-up of technology innovation: Case of administrative intervention in China. *Technol. Forecast. Soc. Chang.* **2015**, *96*, 4–14. [CrossRef]
2. Shao, Y.; Deng, X.; Qing, Q.; Wang, Y. Optimal battery recycling strategy for electric vehicle under government subsidy in China. *Sustainability* **2018**, *10*, 4855. [CrossRef]

3. Liu, J.; Lu, K.; Cheng, S. International R&D spillovers and innovation efficiency. *Sustainability* **2018**, *10*, 3974.
4. Rothaermel, F.T.; Thursby, M. Incubator firm failure or graduation? The role of university linkages. *Res. Policy* **2005**, *34*, 1076–1090. [CrossRef]
5. Tumelero, C.; Sbragia, R.; Borini, F.M.; Franco, E.C. The role of networks in technological capability: A technology-based companies perspective. *J. Glob. Entrep. Res.* **2008**, *8*, 1–19. [CrossRef]
6. Hansen, M.T.; Chesbrough, H.W.; Nohria, N.; Sull, D.N. Networked incubators: Hothouses of the new economy. *Harv. Bus. Rev.* **2008**, *78*, 74–84.
7. Rothschild, L.; Darr, A. Technological incubators and the social construction of innovation networks: An Israeli case study. *Technovation* **2005**, *25*, 59–67. [CrossRef]
8. Bosma, N.; Van Praag, M.; Thurik, R.; De Wit, G. The value of human and social capital investments for the business performance of startups. *Small Bus. Econ.* **2004**, *23*, 227–236. [CrossRef]
9. Gimeno, J.; Folta, T.B.; Cooper, A.C.; Woo, C.Y. Survival of the fittest? Entrepreneurial human capital and the persistence of underperforming firms. *Adm. Sci. Q.* **1997**, *42*, 750–783. [CrossRef]
10. Wright, M.; Hmieleski, K.M.; Siegel, D.S.; Ensley, M.D. The role of human capital in technological entrepreneurship. *Entrep. Theory Pract.* **2007**, *31*, 791–806. [CrossRef]
11. Rice, M.P. Co-production of business assistance in business incubators: An exploratory study. *J. Bus. Ventur.* **2002**, *17*, 163–187. [CrossRef]
12. Hackett, S.M.; Dilts, D.M. A systematic review of business incubation research. *J. Technol. Transf.* **2004**, *29*, 55–82. [CrossRef]
13. Becker, G.S. *Human Capital: A Theoretical and Empirical Analysis*; National Bureau of Economic Research: New York, NY, USA, 2009.
14. Monsson, C.K.; Jørgensen, S.B. How do entrepreneurs' characteristics influence the benefits from the various elements of a business incubator? *J. Small Bus. Enterp. Dev.* **2016**, *23*, 224–239. [CrossRef]
15. Firkin, P. *Entrepreneurial Capital: A Resource-based Conceptualization of the Entrepreneurial Process*; Massey University: Albany, New Zealand, 2001.
16. Chandler, G.N.; Hanks, S.H. Founder competence, the environment, and venture performance. *Entrep. Theory Pract.* **1994**, *18*, 77–89. [CrossRef]
17. Shane, S. Prior knowledge and the discovery of entrepreneurial opportunities. *Organ. Sci.* **2000**, *11*, 448–469. [CrossRef]
18. Ardichvili, A.; RCardozo Ray, S. A theory of entrepreneurial opportunity identification and development. *J. Bus. Ventur.* **2003**, *18*, 105–123. [CrossRef]
19. Lamine, W.; Mian, S.; Fayolle, A.; Wright, M.; Klofsten, M.; Etzkowitz, H. Technology business incubation mechanisms and sustainable regional development. *J. Technol. Transf.* **2008**, *43*, 1121–1141. [CrossRef]
20. Ucbasaran, D.; Westhead, P.; Wright, M. Opportunity identification and pursuit: Does an entrepreneur's human capital matter? *Small Bus. Econ.* **2008**, *30*, 153–173. [CrossRef]
21. Shane, S.; Khurana, K. Career experience and firm founding. *Ind. Corp. Chang.* **2003**, *12*, 519–544. [CrossRef]
22. Redondo, M.; Camarero, C. Social capital in university business incubators: Dimensions, antecedents and outcomes. *Int. Entrep. Manag. J.* **2019**, *15*, 599–624. [CrossRef]
23. Carr, J.C.; Sequeira, J.M. Prior family business exposure as intergenerational influence and entrepreneurial intent: A theory of planned behavior approach. *J. Bus. Res.* **2007**, *60*, 1090–1098. [CrossRef]
24. Moore, E.S.; Wilkie, W.L.; Lutz, R.J. Passing the torch: Intergenerational influences as a source of brand equity. *J. Market.* **2002**, *66*, 17–37. [CrossRef]
25. Lussier, R.N. A nonfinancial business success versus failure prediction model for young firms. *J. Small Bus. Manag.* **1995**, *33*, 8–20.
26. Lussier, R.N.; Pfeifer, S. A crossnational prediction model for business success. *J. Small Bus. Manag.* **2001**, *39*, 228–239. [CrossRef]
27. Colombo, M.G.; Grilli, L. Founders' human capital and the growth of new technology-based firms: A competence-based view. *Res. Policy* **2005**, *34*, 795–816. [CrossRef]
28. Obschonka, M.; Silbereisen, R.K.; Schmitt-Rodermund, E.; Stuetzer, M. Nascent entrepreneurship and the developing individual: Early entrepreneurial competence in adolescence and venture creation success during the career. *J. Vocat. Behav.* **2011**, *79*, 121–133. [CrossRef]

29. Xiao, L.; North, D. The graduation performance of technology business incubators in China's three tier cities: The role of incubator funding, technical support, and entrepreneurial mentoring. *J. Technol. Transf.* **2017**, *42*, 615–634. [CrossRef]

30. Eriksson, P.; Vilhunen, J.; Voutilainen, K. Incubation as co-creation: Case study of proactive technology business development. *Int. J. Entrep. Innov. Manag.* **2014**, *18*, 382–396. [CrossRef]

31. Eriksson, P.; Montonen, T.; Vilhunen, J.; Voutilainen, K. Incubation manager roles in the co-innovation context. *Int. J. Entrep. Innov. Manag.* **2016**, *20*, 285–297. [CrossRef]

32. Zane, L.J.; DeCarolis, D.M. Social networks and the acquisition of resources by technology-based new ventures. *J. Small Bus. Entrep.* **2016**, *28*, 203–221. [CrossRef]

33. Cantù, C. Entrepreneurial knowledge spillovers: Discovering opportunities through understanding mediated spatial relationships. *Ind. Market. Manag.* **2017**, *61*, 30–42. [CrossRef]

34. Lecluyse, L.; Knockaert, M.; Spithoven, A. The contribution of science parks: A literature review and future research agenda. *J. Technol. Transf.* **2018**, *44*, 559–595. [CrossRef]

35. Van Rijnsoever, F.J.; van Weele, M.A.; Eveleens, C.P. Network brokers or hit makers? Analyzing the influence of incubation on start-up investments. *Int. Entrep. Manag. J.* **2017**, *13*, 605–629. [CrossRef]

36. Ebbers, J.J. Networking behavior and contracting relationships among entrepreneurs in business incubators. *Entrep. Theory Pract.* **2014**, *38*, 1159–1181. [CrossRef]

37. Pettersen, I.B.; Aarstad, J.; Høvig, Ø.S.; Tobiassen, A.E. Business incubation and the network resources of start-ups. *J. Innov. Entrep.* **2016**, *5*, 7. [CrossRef]

38. Nijssen, E.J.; van der Borgh, M. Beyond the water cooler: Using socialization to understand use and impact of networking services on collaboration in a business incubator. *R&D Manag.* **2017**, *47*, 443–457.

39. Pellinen, K. The interplay of entrepreneurial and network activities in the entrepreneurial process: A relational analysis. *Int. J. Entrep. Innov.* **2014**, *15*, 17–29. [CrossRef]

40. Tello, S.; Yang, Y.; Latham, S. Nascent entrepreneurs access and use of network resources in a technology incubator. *J. Small Bus. Entrep.* **2012**, *25*, 375–397. [CrossRef]

41. Paredes-Frigolett, H.; Pyka, A. A model of innovation network formation. *Innov. Organ. Manag.* **2017**, *19*, 245–269. [CrossRef]

42. Burt, R.S.; Burzynska, K. Chinese entrepreneurs, social networks, and Guanxi. *Manag. Organ. Rev.* **2017**, *13*, 221–260. [CrossRef]

43. Vanderstraeten, J.; van Witteloostuijn, A.; Matthyssens, P.; Andreassi, T. Being flexible through customization—The impact of incubator focus and customization strategies on incubatee survival and growth. *J. Eng. Technol. Manag.* **2016**, *41*, 45–64. [CrossRef]

44. Kapucu, N.; Demiroz, F. A social network analysis approach to strengthening nonprofit collaboration. *J. Appl. Manag. Entrep.* **2015**, *20*, 87–101. [CrossRef]

45. Theodorakopoulos, N.; Kakabadse, N.K.; McGowan, C. What matters in business incubation? A literature review and a suggestion for situated theorizing. *J. Small Bus. Enterp. Dev.* **2014**, *21*, 602–622. [CrossRef]

46. Díez-Vial, I.; Fernández-Olmos, M. The effect of science and technology parks on a firm's performance: A dynamic approach over time. *J. Evol. Econ.* **2017**, *27*, 413–434. [CrossRef]

47. Apa, R.; Grandinetti, R.; Sedita, S.R. The social and business dimensions of a networked business incubator: The case of H-Farm. *J. Small Bus. Enterp. Dev.* **2017**, *24*, 198–221. [CrossRef]

48. Soetanto, D.P.; Jack, S.L. Business incubators and the networks of technology-based firms. *J. Technol. Transf.* **2013**, *38*, 432–453. [CrossRef]

49. Zardini, A.; Ricciardi, F.; Orlandi, L.B.; Rossignoli, C. Business networks as breeding grounds for entrepreneurial options: Organizational implications. *Rev. Manag. Sci.* **2018**, 1–18. [CrossRef]

50. Rothaermel, F.T.; Thursby, M. University-incubator firm knowledge flows: Assessing their impact on incubator firm performance. *Res. Policy* **2005**, *34*, 305–320. [CrossRef]

51. Díez-Vial, I.; Montoro-Sánchez, A. How knowledge links with universities may foster innovation: The case of a science park. *Technovation* **2016**, *50–51*, 41–52. [CrossRef]

52. Hughes, M.; Ireland, R.D.; Morgan, R.E. Stimulating dynamic value: Social capital and business incubation as a pathway to competitive success. *Long Range Plan.* **2007**, *40*, 154–177. [CrossRef]

53. Cox, D.R. Regression models and life-tables. *J. R. Stat. Soc.* **1972**, *34*, 187–220. [CrossRef]

54. Schwartz, E.J.; Harms, R.; Grieshuber, E. New venture performance: Initial and emerging factor—A longitudinal approach. In Proceedings of the Babson-Kauffman Entrepreneurship Research Conference (BKERC), Boston, MA, USA, 8–11 June 2005.

55. Baptista, R.; Karaoz, M.; Mendonça, J. The impact of human capital on the early success of necessity versus opportunity-based entrepreneurs. *Small Bus. Econ.* **2013**, *24*, 63–78. [CrossRef]

56. Montgomery, M.; Johnson, T.; Faisal, J. What kind of capital do you need to start a business: Financial or human? *Q. Rev. Econ. Financ.* **2005**, *45*, 103–122. [CrossRef]

57. Bøllingtoft, A.; Ulhøi, J.P. The networked business incubator—Leveraging entrepreneurial agency? *J. Bus. Vent.* **2005**, *20*, 265–290. [CrossRef]

58. Zhou, Q.; Gao, P.; Chimhowu, A. ICTs in the transformation of rural enterprises in China: A multi-layer perspective. *Technol. Forecast. Soc. Chang.* **2019**, *145*, 12–23. [CrossRef]

59. Colombelli, A.; Krafft, J.; Vivarelli, M. To be born is not enough: The key role of innovative start-ups. *Small Bus. Econ.* **2016**, *47*, 277–291. [CrossRef]

sustainability

MDPI

Article

What Are the Features of Successful Medical Device Start-Ups? Evidence from KOREA

Munjae Lee [1], Sewon Park [1] and Kyu-Sung Lee [1,2,*

[1] Department of Medical Device Management and Research, SAIHST, Sungkyunkwan University, Seoul 06351, Korea; emunjae@skku.edu (M.L.); se10919@g.skku.edu (S.P.)
[2] Department of Urology, Samsung Medical Center, Sungkyunkwan University School of Medicine, Seoul 06351, Korea
* Correspondence: medevice@skku.edu; Tel.: + 82-2-3410-6830

Received: 22 February 2019; Accepted: 26 March 2019; Published: 2 April 2019

Abstract: This study analyzes the factors determining the success of medical device start-ups, focusing on the healthcare sector as the starting point of the Fourth Industrial Revolution. The government is also working to establish a business model to revitalize medical device start-ups as a new driving force for the economy. Accordingly, such start-ups based on innovative technologies have been actively developed, but it seems that there is a limit to growth. We employed an analytical hierarchy process to derive an activation strategy for medical device start-ups. A survey was administered to experts in such start-ups, including medical device companies and venture capital firms, prospective start-up entrepreneurs, medical device developers, and professors. A total of 18 responses were obtained for analysis. The results revealed the following priorities for the success of medical device start-ups: technical skills, marketability, entrepreneurial capacity, and funding. In addition, medical device and venture capital firms were divided into separate groups and compared and analyzed. Technical skills are considered a priority for those in the medical industry. However, entrepreneurial skills are a priority for venture capitalists. Based on these results, we suggest measures for the success of medical device start-ups.

Keywords: medical device industry; medical device start-ups; start-ups; success factor; Korea; analytical hierarchy process

---

1. Introduction

Healthcare is increasingly important in Korea due to the improvement of living standards and an aging population, and the service paradigm in the health and medical sectors is changing from treatment to prevention. Accordingly, the focus is shifting to personal day-to-day care and customized services. Moreover, with the advent of the Fourth Industrial Revolution, there is a surge in the number of medical device start-ups that use the Internet of Things, cloud computing, big data, artificial intelligence, mobiles, and wearable robots [1].

The medical device industry is rapidly transforming into a convergence of state-of-the-art information and communication technologies (ICT) and healthcare. In addition, countries facing excessive medical expenses due to an aging population are attempting to reduce the burden of medical expenses through policy support for the medical device industry centered on healthcare. Medical devices are made of various products, and they are becoming more complex and diversified with the advance in technology. In addition, start-ups based on innovative technologies are being actively advanced by the development of new-technology medical devices using IT/BT (information technology/biotechnology) fusion technology. Global medical device companies have established incubation centers or venture capital to foster start-ups and to promote innovation. However, Korean medical device companies are mostly small, and the market for such devices has not yet become international; thus, growth is limited. Since existing companies are very small, start-ups have not been activated because of limited investment. It is difficult for new medical devices to enter the market due to the regulatory system. Medical devices can have a direct impact on people's lives, and the licensing system is complex. To launch new medical devices, the device must be approved by the Ministry of Food and Drug Safety (MRDS). New medical technology is evaluated by the National Evidence-based Healthcare Collaborating Agency (NECA). Benefits are evaluated by the Health Insurance Review & Assessment Service. This process takes up to 390 days, and the government has stated that it would shorten this to 80 days, but no full-scale implementation has yet taken place. Therefore, medical start-ups must be invested in the licensing system for a long time, but it is difficult to prepare the regulatory system due to the lack of professional labor. In addition, it is difficult to compete with existing companies because it is a challenge to acquire distribution networks even if they enter the market with permission to produce medical devices. Other difficulties such as clinical or R&D costs, patent application, and registration also exist.

Start-ups are companies that start businesses based on cutting-edge technology. Since the mid-2000s, start-ups have become more important in the global economy and the business environment is changing accordingly. To survive in a rapidly changing business environment, start-ups need the capacity for sustainable growth as well as competence in the market [2,3]. Interest in start-ups has increased due to the global economic recession and rising unemployment. Start-ups with the right diversity and flexibility can create a base industry and promote economic growth through competition and innovation [4]. The number of successful start-ups is on the rise due to the start-up wave, but the reality is that most companies fail. Changes in the domestic and overseas business environment caused by the global financial crisis have led to fierce competition among global companies to take the initiative, thereby causing serious damage to start-ups. The journey from idea and commercialization is complicated and 90 percent of start-up companies struggle to enter the market. Unless they establish core strategies tailored to the rapidly changing market conditions and respond accordingly, it can be difficult for start-ups to enter the market upon their initial attempt.

With the recent growth of the healthcare sector influenced by the advent of the Fourth Industrial Revolution, medical device start-ups are seeing growth in wearable devices as their main product. Medical devices in the healthcare field enable early diagnosis of disease and can be used extensively, from simple healthcare to treatment of serious diseases. Thus, innovative medical devices developed by medical device start-ups will enable personalized healthcare, which will help bolster the public's continued health. Accordingly, the government is also extending its support to provide a basis for start-up growth, but there seems to be a limit to the success of medical device start-ups. Medical expenses continue to increase with age and the use of advanced medical devices helps reduce these expenses by improving patient health. In particular, the medical device industry has been selected by the government as a major industry to secure innovative growth engines and aims to expand its future growth engine through the development of medical device start-ups. That is, the medical device industry's development will bring about economic benefits, resulting in the continued improvement of people's health and the securing of medical expenses [5,6]. Start-ups must build a sustainable business model that can prosper over time. The medical device industry is intertwined with complex stakeholders and needs to interact with understanding stakeholders. Therefore, deriving the key factors of each stakeholder for the initial growth of medical device start-ups will lead to their sustainable growth, which will aid Korea's economic development [7,8]. In this study, we will seek to derive an activation strategy for medical device start-ups based on a priority analysis using the analytical hierarchy process (AHP), with experts as targets, to determine the success factors for medical device start-ups [4]. The success of such start-ups through these measures will result in the promotion of medical device start-ups based on innovative technologies, which will lead to the development of the domestic medical device industry.

2. Literature Review

2.1. The Start-Up Business in the New Market

Start-ups are companies that develop new products and services to create new markets in uncertain environments. They are also defined as new businesses started by entrepreneurs that combine ideas and resources. If these conditions are met, the company is considered a start-up regardless of its size or shape. Thus, a company is defined as a start-up if it combines new ideas and advanced technologies to create new markets and business opportunities. In Korea, start-ups and venture capital firms are close to each other in concept, but there are differences between the two. First, in terms of business activities, venture firms are new companies of whom high growth is expected because they have a systematic organizational structure and a major focus on research and development. By contrast, start-ups operate in smaller sizes around a common project aiming at high risk and high returns, based on innovative ideas or advanced technology, while focusing on commercialization. From a legal standpoint, venture capital firms are those that are provided with policy support as they meet the conditions set out in the Special Measures for the Growth of Venture Businesses Act. Start-ups, however, receive investment and support from venture capitalists or angel investors, and there are no legal requirements [2].

Start-ups create new businesses in highly competitive environments and galvanize the national economy. However, to commercialize their ideas, start-ups must allocate funds to their products based on their growth potential. Without market analysis and experience, it is difficult to operate reliably because the market is uncertain, and start-ups are a new form of business. Hence, for start-ups, it is important to identify marketability, users, competitors, and suppliers based on innovative products [9]. In Silicon Valley, US, there are over 298,800 angel investors available to make the necessary investments in the development and success of start-up products. Korea is expanding its investment in ICT services and biotechnology, but there are only 3984 angel investors in the country. In the US, investment by venture companies is strengthening regarding start-ups, but this is not the case in Korea, which is focused on growth. Therefore, in most countries other than the US, start-ups fail in the initial phase of market entry. Hence, long-term strategy and support are needed. Korea began supporting start-ups in 2013 with a government policy called Creating Jobs by Revitalizing Investment in Start-ups. The government is also encouraging start-ups with a 2018 policy for financial support and deregulation. By doing so, the government aims to ease the financial burden of start-ups and create an environment for growth by establishing a cooperative ecosystem among start-ups [3,10].

2.2. Start-Up Businesses in the Medical Device Industry

One characteristic of medical devices is that they use interdisciplinary technologies such as clinical medicine, electrics, electronics, mechanics, material, and optics. Recently, the medical device market has been expanding into the new convergence sector in connection with the Fourth Industrial Revolution, and it is seeing greater growth with the development of digital healthcare, u-health, wearable medical devices, and so on. As medical devices directly and indirectly affect people's promotion of health and their securing of health rights, regulation and government approval are needed. Hence, the government is regulating the manufacture of medical devices, the safety rules for clinical tests, as well as the distribution and sale of such devices. In addition, as the main demand for medical devices comes from hospitals that are conservative regarding the use of existing devices because of safety and reliability issues, the industry has a high barrier to entry [11–13].

The medical device industry is a promising sector that will create new jobs and secure new growth engines as the medical paradigm shifts to one that is focused on healthcare [14]. In particular, as consumer demands for medical services are increasing rapidly, a new market is being created through convergence of and integration with new technologies such as BT, ICT, and Nano Technology (NT). Medical device start-ups are actively developing wearable devices that collect and manage personal biometric information, medical mobile consultation services, information services for medical institutions and pharmacies, and personalized healthcare services. Such start-ups have been on the rise in recent years, but more than half fail in the first one to three years of business [15].

The medical device industry requires much time and a large amount of investment before research results are commercialized. Uncertainties regarding success are also very high. In Korea, researchers that want to found a start-up have to look for support programs or investors. There is almost no systematic support system or policy in Korea that can connect the demand for start-up companies in the medical device industry with actual start-ups and make them successful. The medical device industry requires the development and assessment of clinical ideas, connecting with hospitals in the process of technological commercialization, and supporting government licensing regulations. Thus, we need a start-up support service that includes all of these aspects [16].

2.3. Success Factors of Start-Up Businesses

For a start-up to succeed, technology-based infrastructure must be in place for the entrepreneur to utilize. It must also secure key resources such as manpower, technology, and finance [17]. If we analyze previous studies on the success factors of start-ups, Stuart [18] claims that the following are very likely to be successful: companies in markets with low entry barriers and high expected growth, products with innovative technologies, entrepreneurs with strategic marketing skills, experience, and a wide network, and organizations where free communication is possible. Chorev [19] also claims that the following are core success factors for high-tech start-ups: entrepreneurs skilled at market analysis and management, strategies to achieve a competitive advantage, marketing capabilities to identify customer needs, products wanted by the market, organizations that have expertise, financing through venture capital, and external environment for maintaining competence. Nam [20] argues that entrepreneurial competences such as entrepreneurs' level of education, experience in start-ups, and preparedness for start-ups; economic features such as financial resources and start-up investment; and circumstantial features such as government policy and market environment lead to success. Start-up ecosystems are created with start-up growth, recovery, and reinvestment. However, most start-ups do not achieve results in the early stages. Entrepreneurial competence plays a key role in the start-up phase and requires entrepreneurial commercialization, such as finding ideas and opportunities for the business, and building a complete business model. In the early stage of the start-up, network competence is crucial, and cooperation with external companies and corporate resources such as knowledge and technology should be utilized. That is, the start-up preparation phase should have a foundation to support entrepreneurship and commercialization capabilities, and in the early stage, it should be supported by the relevant agency to reduce the likelihood of failure.

Since start-ups are based on new technology and face challenges in the journey from idea to commercialization, they find it difficult to enter the market successfully. According to government statistics for 2016 on the success and failure of companies, the 3-year survival rate of start-ups is 39.1%; it seems difficult for them to stay afloat [2]. Sandberg and Hoffer [21] developed an ERI model, believing that the performance of start-ups is related to the structure of resources and industries as well as the characteristics of entrepreneurs. Thus, in the ERI model, the founders, resources, and the industrial environment influence the performance of a start-up. In particular, the performance of start-ups is influenced by the characteristics of entrepreneurs as well as the company's structure and strategy [21]. Han [22] developed the ERIS model by adding a strategic factor to the ERI model. The ERIS model indicates that the performance of start-ups consists of the interaction between entrepreneurs, resources, industrial environments, and strategic factors. Entrepreneurs need to use their capabilities to manage risks and build management systems in the process of commercializing start-ups. Resources are an important factor in start-up success. The source of competitive advantage for a product or service depends on the level of resources held by the company. In the case of start-ups, they should be able to mobilize resources that contribute to creating capabilities that are difficult to imitate. The industrial environment can be viewed in terms of industrial growth rate, market size, and competition intensity since the industrial structure determines the intensity of competition and the profitability of the industry. In establishing strategies, the entrepreneur can identify whether the product will create a competitive advantage and whether such an advantage will be sustainable [22]. The ERIS model is shown in Figure 1.

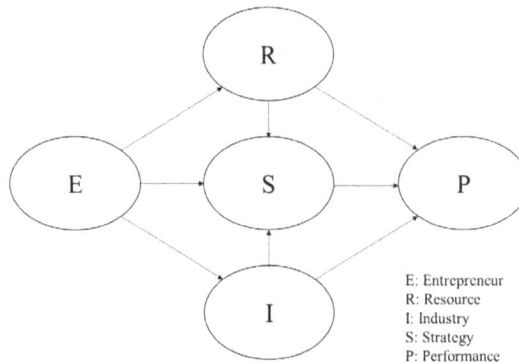

E: Entrepreneur
R: Resource
I: Industry
S: Strategy
P: Performance

Figure 1. ERIS Model [18].

2.4. Research Purpose

The research purpose of this study is twofold.

First, we wish to derive the priority of medical device start-up success factors. This will help medical device start-ups that lack experience and resources to enter the market smoothly, and create new businesses in a highly competitive environment to galvanize the national economy.

Second, based on these priorities, we will present strategies for activating medical device start-ups that contribute to continuous health promotion. The sustainable operation of medical device start-ups will realize the public value possessed by the medical device, enhance the safety of the public, and reduce the medical burden of the patient.

3. Method

3.1. Analytic Hierarchy Process

An AHP analysis was conducted to derive the success factors of medical device start-ups. The AHP method, developed by Saaty [23], is a method for ranking various factors and distinguishing the important ones. It views the problem to be addressed as a structure consisting of several hierarchies, analyzes them, and decides their relative priority. The AHP is useful for solving complex problems and is primarily used to solve unstructured problems in areas such as politics, economics, society, and management [24]. The AHP method derives the factors that make up the decision-making hierarchy by conducting pairwise comparison on a 9-point scale. If the evaluator's consistency ratio (CR) is less than 0.1, it is considered logical and reliable [16,25].

If the consistency ratio is less than 10%, the pairwise comparison matrix is consistent. If the CR value is less than 0.1, the pairwise comparison is considered to have a reasonable consistency [26–30].

An AHP analysis enables decision-making through the integration of qualitative and quantitative factors, and it is possible to measure or prioritize relative importance even with the participation of only very few experts. It is useful because it can be used both publicly and privately. On the other hand, it is not easy to recruit experts who can participate, and if the logic consistency is not secured, the research results become meaningless. In addition, there is a limitation in that the number of layers that can be measured is limited, and logical consistency decreases when the number of measurement elements increases [31,32].

Park and Kim (2011) conducted AHP analysis of 10 medical industry experts in the Wonju Medical Device Cluster to present a credit evaluation model for medical industry venture firms [33]. Lee (2018) conducted AHP analysis of 18 medical device industry experts to elucidate the key strategies and direction of the medical device industry [12]. Dhochak and Sharma (2016) used the AHP method to prioritize the factors that influence the investment decisions of venture capitalists. AHP analysis was conducted on 20 venture capital experts. The major factors influencing investment decisions were entrepreneurial characteristics, profitability, and market size [34]. Vanhala and Kasurinen (2014) used AHP analysis to rank the key elements of the business model of computer game start-ups. To this end, a survey of nine experts on computer games were interviewed and the key factors were human capital, marketing, and partners [35]. AHP analysis is applied not only to the medical device industry but also to the research for establishing the start-ups business model and is used to derive the relative importance of evaluation items in various fields. When we examine previous studies using AHP analysis, we can obtain valid results even when at least 10 experts participate. In particular, the higher the consistency among experts, the smaller the magnitude that is not related to the internal validity and reliability. Therefore, the sample number of this study is similar to that of the previous study, meaning that at least the minimum value is secured, and the consistency ratio of each factor is within 0.1, which is considered to be logical consistency [36–38].

3.2. Research Framework and Variables

Kim's [3] Critical Success Factors of a Design Start-up Business was used as the main criteria for the success of medical device start-ups. The AHP analysis was conducted based on entrepreneurship, innovation, technology, and capital environment as success factors for design venture capital firms; the results indicated that continuous investment and commercialization of ideas are important for the success of design start-ups. In addition, entrepreneurial capacity is also important to maintain the technological and capital environment. Frank [39] argued that ICT start-ups require critical growth factors of capital size and marketable technology to succeed. Based on these, the following were derived as success factors for medical device start-ups: entrepreneurial skills, technical skills, marketability, and funds. The definition of each factor is as follows. Entrepreneurial skills are defined as the entrepreneurial experience, education, skills, and knowledge needed to successfully lead medical device start-ups, and ability to communicate with the outside world. Technical skills are defined as technology and products that can make a medical device start-up successful. Marketability is defined as the market orientation of medical device start-ups with high professionalism. Finally, funds are defined as the ability of medical device start-ups to generate profits in the medical device market.

First, according to Tutar [40], a company's strategic market orientation and aggressive innovation orientation, as subcategories of entrepreneurs' capabilities, play an important role in business performance, and corporate culture has an impact on organizational performance. Based on these, corporate culture, as a comprehensive concept of innovation and market orientation, was derived. In addition, network utilization was derived based on Tur-Porcar's [41] argument that building relationships between people and the environment is important for the sustainable development of businesses. Diamonto [42] argues that the founder's career, expertise, and experience enhance ability to cope with new technologies or the environment when doing business. Since the medical device industry is heavily influenced by regulations, competitive advantage can be achieved through the manager's experience in starting businesses and market analysis skills. Founders who have experience in medical device start-ups can have a positive impact on start-up success due to the interaction of product innovation and the ability to utilize market information. Gelderen [43] found that, in terms of success and risk factors, entrepreneurial competence, organizational culture, and corporate surroundings influence the success of venture companies in the pre-start-up phase. Accordingly, start-up experience, market analysis skills, organizational culture, and network utilization were derived as subcategories of entrepreneurial competences. Second, with regard to the subcategory of technological capacities, Lee [2] identified research and development, innovative technology, and patent holding as factors that determine early market advance of medical devices in a study of the success factors in the initial success of a start-up. Sohn [44] states that in the case of latecomers like Korea, an increase in R&D investment influences the financial performance of a company. He also argues that improving employees' expertise is a way to strengthen corporate capabilities. In particular, the medical device industry is dependent on capital and technology and it takes three to five years for a product to be developed and manufactured, resulting in a long payback period. In addition, as individual products have small markets and a short product cycle, continuous investment in R&D is necessary. Based on these arguments, the following were factors derived: technology innovativeness, R&D facilities and infrastructure, patent retention, and securement of a professional workforce. Third, as a subcategory of marketability, Chesbrough [45] identified the business model as more important than original ideas or R&D for new technology. He noted that if significant financial resources are invested to develop a product that is found to be unmarketable or is delivered to customers through the wrong channel, then the company's profit will be poor. Hyytinen [46] asks does innovativeness reduce start-up survival rates? For the entrepreneurial enterprise to survive, market performance products should have profitability. Furthermore, product competitiveness may help maintain start-up companies lacking capital. Korea's medical device market has a very weak competitive structure compared to the US, Europe, and Japan, where global companies are located. Therefore, for a medical device start-up to be successful, profitability should be created based on product competitiveness. In addition, it is necessary to increase the market size of products by using marketing skills to create a new distribution channel of the medical device market. Based on this, the following factors were derived: the product's market size, product competitiveness, product profitability, and marketing and sales skills. Fourth, as a subcategory of finance, Kohler [47] argues that investment of capital, improved reliability through strategic partnerships, and distribution network support for increasing market accessibility are being implemented to revitalize start-up companies. Park [33] developed an evaluation model for medical venture businesses using the AHP, that author presents a credit rating model for medical venture firms. The top indicators of financial factors are profitability, fundraising ability, and safety. The top indicators of nonfinancial factors are technical, business, and reliability. In addition, securing the capital of venture companies is crucial for securing initial capital, since it can help achieve stable management. Medical device start-ups that are based on innovative technologies require a lot of capital because they need to demonstrate the safety and effectiveness of technology through clinical trials. In addition, due to the nature of the medical device industry, it takes about three to five years from the development to the production of products, and hence, the long payback period, which requires funding capacity. Based on these, the following factors were derived: initial capital, funding capacity, available funds, and potential profit growth. The main factors for the AHP analysis are shown in Figure 2, and the selection criteria of each factor are shown in Table 1.

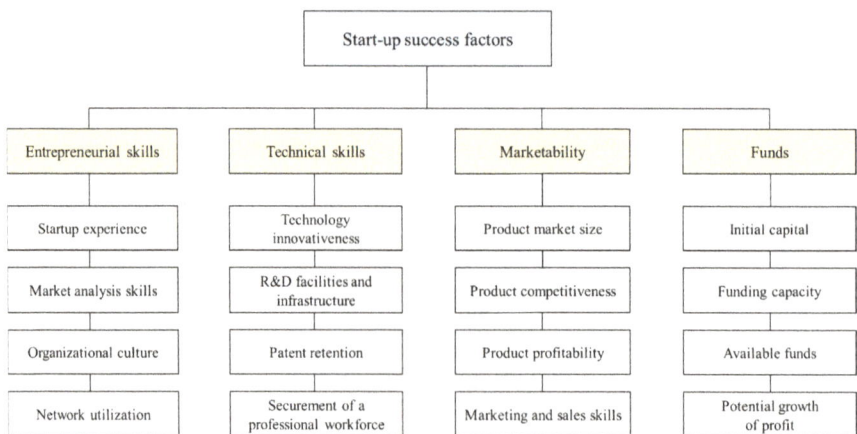

Figure 2. Research framework.

Table 1. Evaluation items and criteria for medical device start-up success.

Area	Item	Selection Criteria	Related References
Entrepreneurial skills	Start-up experience Market analysis skills Organizational culture Network utilization	Founder's career, academic background, expertise Market-based business model Flexible corporate culture and innovation orientation Cooperation with industry stakeholders	[3,40–43]
Technical skills	Technology innovativeness R&D facilities and infrastructure Patent retention Securement of a professional workforce	Originality of new technology Facilities and infrastructure for R & D Efforts for intellectual property and technology patents Secure workforce for R & D	[2,3,44]
Marketability	Product's market size Product competitiveness Product profitability Marketing and sales skills	Market formation status of products Competitiveness of products Market competition situation and profit prospect Market expansion through marketing	[3,45,46]
Funds	Initial capital Funding capacity Available funds Potential growth of profit	Financial stability using venture capital Financing for business expansion Availability of corporate funds Profit-making ability through product selling	[3,33,47]

3.3. Research Process

A previous study that analyzed start-ups' success factors was reviewed to conduct the AHP analysis. Major issues were derived based on opinions of experts from medical device and venture capital firms. First, we selected the main factors and defined each factor through the analysis of previous research that derived start-up success factors. Next, we selected three medical and entrepreneurial venture capital experts and examined whether the extracted factors influenced the success of medical device start-ups. This was done from 24 September 2018 to 3 October 2018, and a consensus was reached on the criteria for success in medical device start-ups. Finally, a questionnaire survey was prepared using literature reviews and brainstorming each of the factors identified by the experts. The survey focused on experts in medical device start-ups, including medical device companies and venture capital firms, prospective start-up founders, medical device developers, and professors. In the case of medical device companies, surveys were conducted mainly on entrepreneurs working in these companies or start-ups. In the case of medical device start-ups, there is often no distinction between management and employees in small-sized companies. Venture capital was targeted at companies with experience in investing in start-up medical devices. For start-up candidates and medical device developers, medical devices were developed to target those who were developing medical devices or who were developing medical devices with the goal of starting their own businesses. Professors and experts selected people working on promoting the medical device industry as research subjects. A total of 30 questionnaires were distributed through the selected research targets (Table A1). A total of 18 valid responses were obtained from an online and offline survey. The survey period was from 29 October 2018 to 19 November 2018.

3.4. Data Collection

The AHP analysis in this study was conducted using DRESS 1.7.00, which is a solution designed for the AHP. A total of 18 valid responses were obtained from medical device start-up experts. The AHP result was judged to be reliable as the CR was less than 0.1. First, demographic characteristics indicate that men account for the majority. In terms of job category, more than half worked in medical device companies and held a diverse range of responsibilities. Professors were divided into other categories because they do not work for a medical device company and do not have any responsibilities (Table 2).

Table 2. Demographic information.

Characteristics		Frequency	Ratio (%)
Gender	Male	14	77.8
	Female	4	22.2
Age (years)	30s	1	5.6
	40s	9	50.0
	50s	7	38.9
	Over 60s	1	5.6
Work experience in the related field	Under 5 years	4	22.2
	5–10 years	2	11.1
	10–20 years	7	38.9
	Over 20 years	5	27.8
Occupation	Medical device company	10	55.6
	Venture capital	2	11.1
	Professor	2	11.1
	Others	4	22.2
Assigned task	Management	6	33.3
	licensing	6	33.3
	Marketing/Sales	1	5.6
	R&D	1	5.6
	Funding and investment	2	11.1
	etc.	2	11.1

4. Results

4.1. Comparing Success Factors

To derive the importance through the AHP analysis, we conducted a pairwise comparison of the top and sub-items and selected their importance and priority. Next, the importance and the priority of the sub-item were obtained through the conducting pairwise comparison of the items, and the importance and priority of the items were selected. Priority was derived based on entrepreneurial skills, technical skills, marketability, and funds, which are the main criteria for success factors in medical device start-ups. The following results were obtained: technical skills (0.38), marketability (0.29), entrepreneurial skills (0.22), and funds (0.11). Based on this, it can be said that to be successful, it is necessary for start-ups to commercialize a marketable medical device based on innovative technology.

Next, priorities were derived based on subcategories of success factors. The priorities for the subcategory of entrepreneurial skills were market analysis skills (0.33), network utilization (0.30), entrepreneurship experience (0.26), and organizational culture (0.11). Priorities in the subcategory of technical skills were securement of a professional workforce (0.44), technological innovativeness (0.27), patent retention (0.15), and R&D facilities and infrastructure (0.13). Priorities in the subcategory of marketability were marketing and sales skills (0.39), product competitiveness (0.32), product profitability (0.18), and product market size (0.11). Finally, priorities in the subcategory of funds were revenue growth potential (0.34), available capital (0.30), funding capacity (0.25), and initial capital (0.11). The results are shown below (Table 3).

Table 3. Analysis of medical device start-up success factors.

Top Item	Factor Weights		Subitem	Factor Weights		
	Importance	Priority		Importance	Priority	CR
Entrepreneurial skills	0.22	3	Start-up experience	0.26	3	0.03
			Market analysis skills	0.33	1	
			Organizational culture	0.11	4	
			Network utilization	0.30	2	
Technical skills	0.38	1	Technology innovativeness	0.27	2	0.02
			R&D facilities and infrastructure	0.13	4	
			Patent retention	0.15	3	
			Securement of a professional workforce	0.44	1	
Marketability	0.29	2	Product's market size	0.11	4	0.03
			Product competitiveness	0.32	2	
			Product profitability	0.18	3	
			Marketing and sales skills	0.39	1	
Funds	0.11	4	Initial capital	0.11	4	0.05
			Funding capacity	0.25	3	
			Available funds	0.30	2	
			Potential growth of profit	0.34	1	
Total	1.0			4.0		

4.2. Comparative Analysis of Major Factors by Job

The major criteria for success factors were determined separately for employees in medical device companies and those in venture capital firms, which were then compared and analyzed. Therefore, we excluded professors from the analysis because they are not directly engaged or do not invest in medical device companies. In the case of those working in the medical device industry, the success factors of start-up companies were technical skills (0.45), marketability (0.30), entrepreneurial skills (0.15), and funds (0.09). For venture capital firms, however, it was entrepreneurial skills (0.34), technical skills (0.29), marketability (0.24), and funds (0.13). Medical device start-ups are increasingly focusing on healthcare. Healthcare is a convergence industry to which ICT-based technologies are mainly applied. Since, in the case of medical device start-ups, competitive advantage must be gained through ICT convergence by securing technology, technical skill was seen as a key success factor. On the other hand, experience and expertise play a leading role in commercialization based on innovation. Since experience with start-ups predicts a company's financial performance and improves its business performance, venture capital firms that raise funds view entrepreneurial skills as the key factor in the success of medical device start-ups [48] (Table 4).

Table 4. Analysis of key factors.

Top Item	Weights of Factors					
	Medical Device Company			Venture Capital Firm		
	Importance	Priority	CR	Importance	Priority	CR
Entrepreneurial skills	0.15	3		0.34	1	
Technical skills	0.45	1	0.03	0.29	2	0.08
Marketability	0.30	2		0.24	3	
Funds	0.09	4		0.13	4	
Total	1.0			1.0		

4.3. Comparative Analysis of Start-Up Success Factors by Job

Subcategories of success factors for medical device start-ups were divided into those for medical device companies and those for venture capital firms. For the former group, the priorities in the subcategories for entrepreneurial skills were network utilization (0.37), market analysis skills (0.35), entrepreneurship experience (0.21), and organizational culture (0.07). In the case of technical skills, the following were identified: securing experts (0.48), technology innovativeness (0.27), patent retention (0.13), and R&D facilities and infrastructure (0.12). The priorities for marketability were arranged as follows: marketing and sales skills (0.37), product competitiveness (0.36), product profitability (0.17), and product market size (0.10). Finally, in the case of funds, profit growth potential (0.35), funding capacity (0.30), available capital (0.24), and initial capital (0.10) were identified as priorities. Next, for venture capital firms, entrepreneurship experience (0.31), market analysis skills (0.28), network utilization (0.22), and organizational culture (0.19) were identified as priorities in the subcategory of entrepreneurial skills. In the case of technical skills, the following priorities were identified: securing experts (0.41), technology innovativeness (0.28), patent retention (0.18), and R&D facilities and infrastructure (0.14). The priorities for marketability were marketing and sales skills (0.40), product competitiveness (0.27), product profitability (0.18), and product market size (0.14). Finally, in the case of funds, profit growth potential (0.31), funding capacity (0.31), available capital (0.26), and initial capital (0.12) were identified as priorities.

Both groups (medical device companies and venture capital firms) showed agreement on the following subcategories: technical skills, marketability, and funds; however, their view of entrepreneurial skills as a priority for the success of medical device start-ups differed. Medical device companies considered network utilization a priority among the subcategories of entrepreneurial skills. This appears to be because the ecosystem of medical devices consists of a variety of stakeholders, and experts in each field must work together to meet the needs of stakeholders for new products to enter the market quickly. Venture capital firms, in contrast, considered entrepreneurship experience a priority among the subcategories of entrepreneurial capacities. This seems to be because venture capital firms consider the future potential of the company they are investing in, and the expertise and experience of the entrepreneur play a key role in their decision to invest funds [49] (Table 5).

Table 5. Analysis of medical device start-up success factors.

| Top Item | Subitem | Weights of Factor | | | |
| | | Medical Device Company | | Venture Capital Firm | |
		Importance	Priority	Importance	Priority
Entrepreneurial skills	Start-up experience	0.21	3	0.31	1
	Market analysis skills	0.35	2	0.28	2
	Organizational culture	0.07	4	0.19	4
	Network utilization	0.37	1	0.22	3
Technical skills	Technology innovativeness	0.27	2	0.28	2
	R&D facilities and infrastructure	0.12	4	0.14	4
	Patent retention	0.13	3	0.18	3
	Securement of a professional workforce	0.48	1	0.41	1
Marketability	Product's market size	0.10	4	0.14	4
	Product competitiveness	0.36	2	0.27	2
	Product Profitability	0.17	3	0.18	3
	Marketing and sales skills	0.37	1	0.40	1
Funds	Initial capital	0.10	4	0.12	4
	Funding capacity	0.24	3	0.26	3
	Available funds	0.30	2	0.31	1
	Potential growth of profit	0.35	1	0.31	1
Total		4.0		4.0	

5. Discussion

As of 2017, Korea's medical device market was worth 6.2 trillion won, accounting for 1.7 percent of the world market and ranking ninth globally. However, since imports account for 63.8 percent, the market competitiveness of Korean products is considered low [50]. As the medical device industry has a high value-added rate and a job creation effect, the activation of medical device start-ups based on innovative technologies is expected to lead to job creation. In this study, an AHP analysis was conducted to derive the success factors of medical device start-ups. The results indicated that the main criteria for the success factors were technical skills, marketability, entrepreneurial skills, and funds. Priorities in the subcategories of the major criteria were market analysis skills, network utilization, entrepreneurship experience, and organizational culture. In the case of marketability, marketing and sales skills, product competitiveness, product profitability, and product market size were identified as priorities. Market analysis skills, network utilization, entrepreneurship experience, and organizational culture were identified as priorities for entrepreneurial skills. For funds, profit growth potential, available capital, funding capacity, and initial capital were identified. Based on these results, we propose the following measures for the success of medical device start-ups:

First, there must be a professional workforce for developing innovative technology. A start-up is a company based on new ideas and technologies. Securing innovative technologies therefore creates a constant competitive advantage. Since medical devices converge with other fields, and because this leads to increased competition in the industry, they need to be better equipped than competitors in other fields. To do so, they need to maintain a competitive edge through technical development by securing an expert workforce. The increasing demand for improved quality of medical devices is increasing the number of medical device start-ups that combine ideas and IT technologies. However, the steady growth of such start-ups is proving to be a challenge due to the lack of experts in medical device R&D, licensing, quality management, and clinical testing. Medical device start-ups need to have products that are more refined than those in other industries. They can succeed in commercialization only when funding and licensing are available and when they understand the needs of medical staff, who are their major customers. It is essential to plan for marketability assessments, clinical tests, licenses, and salaries. In this process, securing skilled professionals with expertise in each field is essential. To this end, field-oriented workforce development should be carried out in the medical device industry by introducing graduate schools geared toward the medical device industry. Currently, a graduate school that specializes in the medical device industry is operating in Korea to impart interdisciplinary knowledge of convergence and work experience to mid-level managers. However, a degree program is needed to train high-quality human resources by balancing learning, industry, and employment. Accordingly, training core leaders in the medical device industry through a specialized graduate school is expected to revitalize medical device start-ups.

Second, we need to expand the marketability of products with marketing that identifies customer needs. Byun (2017) conducted a weighted analysis of the key elements of strategies for each phase of medical device commercialization and found that users, hospitals and buyers, pricing factors, and product differentiation strategies during the commercialization phase were highly weighted. He also states that when selecting products, they should be chosen not based on entrepreneurs' preferences but on the needs of the market and stakeholders [51]. Since medical devices take a long time from technology development to clinical testing, licensing, insurance registration, and distribution, they require a sustained strategy to enter the market. Furthermore, since ideas alone are insufficient for start-up success, it is necessary to accurately identify major customers and needs during the R&D process. The primary consumer of medical devices is the hospital or doctor. Therefore, it is important to know who the product users are, whether the product is helping to treat patients, and if there is a demand. Whether the product has better technical capacities than existing products should also be considered [52]. Safety and reliability are considered first because medical devices directly affect people's health and well-being, which is why market consumers tend to continue to use popular products. There is a high preference for global corporate products that remain competitive, and this leads to high barriers to entry. In addition, price elasticity is low, and awareness of the product and brand power are very important. Thus, when entering the market, medical device start-ups should develop strategies that consider the purchase history, price, and willingness to purchase existing products existing products for their target customers.

Third, the company should enhance its entrepreneurial skills to commercialize the product through market analysis. Unlike the ecosystem of general start-ups, there are a large number of stakeholders in the ecosystem of medical device start-ups, such as regulators, the government, businesses, patients, hospitals, and venture capital firms. Thus, medical device start-ups require a streamlined process for managing stakeholders during the initial market entry phase. For medical devices to enter the market, they need to undergo procedures such as approval screening by the Ministry of Food and Drug Safety and registering for insurance at the Health Insurance Review and Assessment Service. Therefore, it is essential for medical device start-ups to perform market analyses such as analysis of similar products, status of use, and life cycle. They also need to go obtain approval from the Ministry of Food and Drug Safety, and determine, when registering for insurance, whether they are subject to assessment for new medical technology. To enter the market, medical device start-ups should include strategies for market analysis, licensing, and salary. Accordingly, if medical device start-ups are to enter the market quickly, entrepreneurs must have expertise in the entire life cycle of medical devices. Currently, the medical device comprehensive support center supports early start-up companies. However, it is composed of a one-time consultation focusing on regulation and is not particularly effective. Therefore, we need to ascertain consultation outcomes and provide practical support that is linked to the relevant department's approval process for market entry.

In addition, to enhance entrepreneurial skills, educational courses on the medical device industry are needed. Currently, the National Institute of Medical Device Safety provides practical skill-reinforcement courses. However, as these courses are offered only twice a year, it is necessary to extend the training period. By extending these courses, we will be able to reinforce entrepreneurial skills and increase the success rate of medical device start-ups. Advances in medical device start-ups based on innovative technologies will play a positive role in creating jobs and corporate structures in Korea. In particular, since medical device start-ups need connections with hospitals and support related to government licensing regulations when conceiving and assessing clinical ideas and commercializing, we need a comprehensive start-up support service. To this end, we need to build a medical device start-up platform linking start-up companies with government and regulatory agencies. The active market entry of medical device start-ups based on innovative technologies will lead to the advancement of medical technology and will ultimately improve people's health.

6. Conclusions

This study derived the success factors of medical device start-ups through an AHP analysis. These findings are likely to help medical device start-ups that have difficulty entering the market. Medical devices are heavily regulated given their potential impacts on human health/life. It is also difficult to launch start-ups if policy support is not provided. Therefore, based on the aforementioned discussion, the following policy efforts are necessary. First, a graduate school for the medical device industry should be introduced to secure skilled professionals. The global health market is growing 5.2 percent annually, from 10 trillion dollars in 2017 to an estimated 12.3 trillion dollars in 2021. In addition, the number of jobs in the health industry is expected to increase 3.5 percent to 860,000, including an increase of 2800 in the medical device sector. However, Korean medical device start-ups, which are small in size compared to those in other developed countries, lack the capacity to invest in private R&D, and the institutional basis for promoting new industry fusion is weak. As a result, it is difficult to secure skilled professionals. Therefore, with the introduction of a graduate school for the medical device industry, it is expected that the professionalization of the Korean medical device start-up business and demand for labor will be achieved by fostering pre-emptive and customized medical device specialists. The introduction of the graduate school will contribute to rapid market growth by strengthening the site-centered human resource development function by providing advanced and diversified programs.

Second, support for the development of hospital-enterprise-linked medical devices technology should be expanded to increase marketability. If hospitals, which are a major consumer of medical devices, establish a cooperative system in which clinicians and consultants participate in the development of medical devices, the reliability of medical device start-up products will be enhanced.

Since such products are newly developed medical equipment, the scientific and clinical grounds are insufficient and the use rate in Korean medical institutions is low. Therefore, if the ideas and clinical experience of a hospital are linked to the research and development of a company, a medical device that meets customer needs will be developed. This will ensure marketability and reliability of medical device start-up products. Third, it is necessary to conduct intensive consulting for companies to commercialize medical device products. To this end, it should strengthen initial medical device start-up support in cooperation with the Bio-health Innovation Start-up Center. It is necessary to conduct basic training for the medical device industry by holding a briefing session for start-ups, and to concentrate consultation on practical details after deriving the difficulties faced by start-ups.

The limitations of this study are as follows: In the case of medical device companies, no distinction has been made between the employees of existing companies and start-ups. Medical device companies comprise various types, including those that began as start-ups and succeeded, and foreign medical device companies distributing global medical device products. Therefore, the success factors of medical device start-ups will be different according to the characteristics of medical device companies. In future research, it is necessary to classify and analyze the employees of medical device companies. In addition, the size of the sample as a whole is small, and job distribution of respondents is focused on the employees of medical device companies. Thus, it will be possible to make more objective conclusions in future research if we enlarge the sample size and job distribution is appropriately distributed and analyzed.

Author Contributions: Conceptualization, M.L.; Methodology, M.L. and S.P.; Software, S.P.; Writing—original draft, S.P.; Writing—review & editing, M.L.; Supervision, K.S.L.; Project administration, M.L.; Funding acquisition, K.S.L.

Funding: This research was supported by a grant of the Korea Health Technology R&D Project through the Korea Health Industry Development Institute (KHIDI), funded by the Ministry of Health & Welfare, Republic of Korea (grant number: HI14C3229).

Conflicts of Interest: The authors declare no conflict of interest.

Appendix A

Table A1. Questionnaire Sample. Here are five areas on the key factors for medical device start-up success. Please mark ($\sqrt{}$) to indicate their degree of importance.

Item (A)	A Is Important								1	B Is Important								Item (B)
	9	8	7	6	5	4	3	2		2	3	4	5	6	7	8	9	
Entrepreneurial skills																		Technical skills
Entrepreneurial skills																		Marketability
Entrepreneurial skills																		Funds
Technical skills																		Marketability
Technical skills																		Funds
Marketability																		Funds

Note: 1: equal, 3: low importance, 5: important, 7: very important, 9: extremely important.

References

1. Dang, A.; Sharma, J.K. Economics of Medical Devices in India. *Value Health Reg. Issues* **2019**, *18*, 14–17. [CrossRef]
2. Lee, H.H.; Hwangbo, Y.; Gong, C.H. A Study on the Factors that Determine the Initial Success of Start-Up. *Asia-Pac. J. Bus. Ventur. Entrep.* **2017**, *12*, 1–13.
3. Kim, B.; Kim, H.; Jeon, Y. Critical Success Factors of a Design Startup Business. *Sustainability* **2018**, *10*, 2981. [CrossRef]
4. Watson, K.; Hogarth-Scott, S.; Wilson, N. Small business start-ups: Success factors and support implications. *Int. J. Entrep. Behav. Res.* **1998**, *4*, 217–238. [CrossRef]

5. Pammolli, F.; Riccaboni, M.; Magazzini, L. The sustainability of European health care systems: Beyond income and aging. *Eur. J. Health Econ.* **2012**, *13*, 623–634. [CrossRef]

6. Yang, A.; Farmer, P.E.; McGahan, A.M. 'Sustainability' in global health. *Glob. Public Health* **2010**, *5*, 129–135. [CrossRef]

7. Heirman, A.; Clarysse, B. The imprinting effect of initial resources and market strategy on the early growth path of start-ups. *Acad. Manag. Proc.* **2005**, *2005*, A1–A6. [CrossRef]

8. Clinton, L.; Whisnant, R. Business Model Innovations for Sustainability. In *Managing Sustainable Business*; Springer: Berlin, Germany, 2019; pp. 467–507.

9. Tripathi, N.; Seppänen, P.; Boominathan, G.; Oivo, M.; Liukkunen, K. Insights into startup ecosystems through exploration of multi-vocal literature. *Inf. Softw. Technol.* **2019**, *105*, 56–77. [CrossRef]

10. Moroni, I.; Arruda, A.; Araujo, K. The design and technological innovation: How to understand the growth of startups companies in competitive business environment. *Procedia Manuf.* **2015**, *3*, 2199–2204. [CrossRef]

11. Ahn, J.-G.; Seo, G.-S.; Jung, E.-S.; Lee, S.-M.; Lee, D.-H. Medical Device Industry Trends and Investment Promotion Plan. 2017. Available online: http://news.kotra.or.kr/user/reports/kotranews/20/usrReportsView.do?reportsIdx=7614 (accessed on 28 March 2019).

12. Lee, M. Strategies for Promoting the Medical Device Industry in Korea: An Analytical Hierarchy Process Analysis. *Int. J. Environ. Res. Public Health* **2018**, *15*, 2659. [CrossRef] [PubMed]

13. Lee, M.; Yoon, Y.; Ryu, G.H.; Bok, H.S.; Yoon, K.; Park, S.; Lee, K.-S. Innovative distribution priorities for the medical devices industry in the fourth industrial revolution. *Int. Neurourol. J.* **2018**, *22*, S83. [CrossRef] [PubMed]

14. Lee, M.; Yoon, K. Ecosystem of the medical device industry in South Korea: A Network Analysis Approach. *Health Policy Technol.* **2018**, *7*, 397–408. [CrossRef]

15. Manbachi, A.; Kreamer-Tonin, K.; Walch, P.; Gamo, N.J.; Khoshakhlagh, P.; Zhang, Y.S.; Montague, C.; Acharya, S.; Logsdon, E.A.; Allen, R.H. Starting a medical technology venture as a young academic innovator or student entrepreneur. *Ann. Biomed. Eng.* **2018**, *46*, 1–13. [CrossRef] [PubMed]

16. Lee, M.; Yoon, K.; Lee, K.-S. Social network analysis in the legislative process in the Korean medical device industry. *Inq. J. Health Care Organ. Provis. Financ.* **2018**, *55*. [CrossRef]

17. Lee, Y.H.; Park, S.H. A Study on the Success Factors of Venture Entrepreneurs and Entrepreneurship Education. *Asia-Pac. J. Bus. Ventur. Entrep.* **2014**, *9*, 231–244.

18. Stuart, R.; Abetti, P.A. Start-up ventures: Towards the prediction of initial success. *J. Bus. Ventur.* **1987**, *2*, 215–230. [CrossRef]

19. Chorev, S.; Anderson, A.R. Success in Israeli high-tech start-ups; Critical factors and process. *Technovation* **2006**, *26*, 162–174. [CrossRef]

20. Nam, J.M. A Study on the Factors Affecting Success of Start-up in Korea. *Asia-Pac. J. Bus. Ventur. Entrep.* **2014**, *9*, 13–20.

21. Sandberg, W.R.; Hofer, C.W. Improving new venture performance: The role of strategy, industry structure, and the entrepreneur. *J. Bus. Ventur.* **1987**, *2*, 5–28. [CrossRef]

22. Han, J.-H.; Shin, J.K. Analysis of failure factors: Dynamic ERIS. *J. Strateg. Manage. Conf. Proc.* **2004**, *1*, 75–97.

23. Saaty, T.L. The analytic hierarchy process in conflict management. *Int. J. Confl. Manag.* **1990**, *1*, 47–68. [CrossRef]

24. Álvarez Pérez, C.; Rodríguez Montequín, V.; Ortega Fernández, F.; Villanueva Balsera, J. Integrating Analytic Hierarchy Process (AHP) and Balanced Scorecard (BSC) Framework for Sustainable Business in a Software Factory in the Financial Sector. *Sustainability* **2017**, *9*, 486. [CrossRef]

25. Bai, L.; Wang, H.; Shi, C.; Du, Q.; Li, Y. Assessment of SIP buildings for sustainable development in rural China using AHP-grey correlation analysis. *Int. J. Environ. Res. Public Health* **2017**, *14*, 1292. [CrossRef] [PubMed]

26. Nikou, S.; Mezei, J. Evaluation of mobile services and substantial adoption factors with Analytic Hierarchy Process (AHP). *Telecommun. Policy* **2013**, *37*, 915–929. [CrossRef]

27. Kil, S.-H.; Lee, K.D.; Kim, J.-H.; Li, M.-H.; Newman, G. Utilizing the Analytic Hierarchy Process to Establish Weighted Values for Evaluating the Stability of Slope Revegetation based on Hydroseeding Applications in South Korea. *Sustainability* **2016**, *8*, 58. [CrossRef]

28. Chen, M.K.; Wang, S.-C. The critical factors of success for information service industry in developing international market: Using analytic hierarchy process (AHP) approach. *Expert Syst. Appl.* **2010**, *37*, 694–704. [CrossRef]

29. Saaty, T.L. Relative measurement and its generalization in decision making why pairwise comparisons are central in mathematics for the measurement of intangible factors the analytic hierarchy/network process. RACSAM-Revista de la Real Academia de Ciencias Exactas, Fisicas y Naturales. Serie A. *Matematicas* **2008**, *102*, 251–318.

30. Cho, Y.-C. A Study on the Determinants of Decision Making for Officetel Development Project. Ph.D. Thesis, Graduate School of Jeonju University, Jeonju, Korea, 2015.

31. Forman, E.H. AHP is intended for more than expected value calculations. *Decis. Sci.* **1990**, *21*, 670–672. [CrossRef]

32. Thanki, S.; Govindan, K.; Thakkar, J. An investigation on lean-green implementation practices in Indian SMEs using analytical hierarchy process (AHP) approach. *J. Clean. Prod.* **2016**, *135*, 284–298. [CrossRef]

33. Park, C.S.; Kim, M.S. Credit Evaluation Model for Medical Venture Business by the Analytic Hierarchy Process. *Asia-Pac. J. Bus. Ventur. Entrep.* **2011**, *6*, 133–147.

34. Dhochak, M.; Sharma, A.K. Identification and prioritization of factors affecting venture capitalists' investment decision-making process: An analytical hierarchal process (AHP) approach. *J. Small Bus. Enterp. Dev.* **2016**, *23*, 964–983. [CrossRef]

35. Vanhala, E.; Kasurinen, J. The role of business model and its elements in computer game start-ups. In Proceedings of the International Conference of Software Business, Paphos, Cyprus, 14–17 June 2014; pp. 72–87.

36. Beom Soo, H.; Seung Jun, C. Research Articles: Assessment of "Visit Gyeonggi 2005": The Analytic Hierarchy Process. *J. Tour. Sci.* **2006**, *30*, 183–202.

37. Kino Sita, E.; Ooya, T.; Kwon, J.H. *Strategic Decision Making Method AHP*; Cheongram: Seoul, Korea, 2012.

38. Darko, A.; Chan, A.P.C.; Ameyaw, E.E.; Owusu, E.K.; Pärn, E.; Edwards, D.J. Review of application of analytic hierarchy process (AHP) in construction. *Int. J. Constr. Manag.* **2018**, 1–17. [CrossRef]

39. Lasch, F.; Le Roy, F.; Yami, S. Critical growth factors of ICT start-ups. *Manag. Decis.* **2007**, *45*, 62–75. [CrossRef]

40. Tutar, H.; Nart, S.; Bingöl, D. The effects of strategic orientations on innovation capabilities and market performance: The case of ASEM. *Procedia Soc. Behav. Sci.* **2015**, *207*, 709–719. [CrossRef]

41. Tur-Porcar, A.; Roig-Tierno, N.; Llorca Mestre, A. Factors Affecting Entrepreneurship and Business Sustainability. *Sustainability* **2018**, *10*, 452. [CrossRef]

42. Politis, D. Does prior start-up experience matter for entrepreneurs' learning? A comparison between novice and habitual entrepreneurs. *J. Small Bus. Enterp. Dev.* **2008**, *15*, 472–489. [CrossRef]

43. Van Gelderen, M.; Thurik, R.; Bosma, N. Success and risk factors in the pre-startup phase. *Small Bus. Econ.* **2005**, *24*, 365–380. [CrossRef]

44. Sohn, D.W.; Hur, W.; Kim, H.J. Effects of R&D and patents on the financial performance of Korean venture firms. *Asian J. Technol. Innov.* **2010**, *18*, 169–185.

45. Chesbrough, H. Business model innovation: it's not just about technology anymore. *Strateg. Leadersh.* **2007**, *35*, 12–17. [CrossRef]

46. Hyytinen, A.; Pajarinen, M.; Rouvinen, P. Does innovativeness reduce startup survival rates? *J. Bus. Ventur.* **2015**, *30*, 564–581. [CrossRef]

47. Kohler, T. Corporate accelerators: Building bridges between corporations and startups. *Bus. Horiz.* **2016**, *59*, 347–357. [CrossRef]

48. Seo Han, L.; Seung Hoon, N. A study on the success factors of ICT Convergence type-specific start-up enterprise—Mainly the case study. *J. Digit. Converg.* **2014**, *12*, 203–215.

49. Schwienbacher, A. The entrepreneur's investor choice: The impact on later-stage firm development. *J. Bus. Ventur.* **2013**, *28*, 528–545. [CrossRef]

50. Kim, D.S.; Lee, J.S.; Cho, S.H.; Kim, M.S.; Kim, N.H. An Analysis of the Patent Trend of Korean Medical Equipment Manufacturers: 98 companies holding domestic registered patents through R&D. *J. Bus. Econ.* **2018**, *34*, 165–187.

51. Byun, J.Y.; Sung Min, K. Road Map in Increased Efficiency from Medical Device Product Planning to Technology Commercialization. *Regul. Res. Food Drug Cosmet.* **2017**, *12*, 59–74.
52. Mas, J.-P.; Hsueh, B. An investor perspective on forming and funding your medical device start-up. *Tech. Vasc. Interv. Radiol.* **2017**, *20*, 101–108. [CrossRef]

sustainability

MDPI

Article

Socially Responsible Human Resource Management as a Concept of Fostering Sustainable Organization-Building: Experiences of Young Polish Companies

Edyta Bombiak * and Anna Marciniuk-Kluska *

Faculty of Economic and Legal Science, Siedlce University of Natural Sciences and Humanities, Konarskiego 2, 08-110 Siedlce, Poland
* Correspondence: edyta.bombiak@uph.edu.pl (E.B.); anna.marciniuk-kluska@uph.edu.pl (A.M.-K.);
  Tel.: +025-643-17-09 (E.B.); +025-643-17-09 (A.M.-K.)

Received: 16 December 2018; Accepted: 13 February 2019; Published: 17 February 2019

Abstract: There has been increased interest over recent years in socially responsible human resource management (SRHRM) oriented at developing good relations with employees as a function fostering sustainable organization-building. This is a consequence of our awareness of the fact that employees and personnel processes play a vital role in translating the policy of sustainable development into practice. The objective of this research has been to diagnose the activity of young Polish enterprises in the area of SRHRM as an important corporate social responsibility (CSR) component and to assess relations between SRHRM practices and the sustainable development of organizations. The studies conducted on a representative sample of 150 entities demonstrate both the scope of SRHRM practical implementation and the fields which have disparity in this respect. It has been determined that SRHRM practices are quite frequently adopted by young Polish enterprises. Research has shown that there is a correlation between the assessment of the relationship of SRHRM practices with the sustainable development of organizations and their practical implementation. It has been established that the higher the assessment of the strength of the relations of a given practice, the more often it is implemented in the enterprises studied. Simultaneously, the research has demonstrated a low level of maturity with respect to SRHRM implementation, as evidenced by the adoption of basic practices.

Keywords: sustainability development; corporate social responsibility; sustainable enterprises; young companies; socially responsible human resource management

---

1. Introduction

In contemporary knowledge economies, one of the crucial elements determining an organization's ability to create added value, and hence its long-term competitiveness, is skillful interaction with one's surroundings [1]. What is expected from today's businesses, however, is not only for them to generate profits but also to limit and reduce their negative impact on the environment and to address threats to our civilization [2]. In response to higher global social awareness as well as the sensitivity of interested parties, the number of organizations which have based their strategies on sustainable development principles is growing [3].

Sustainable development is a present-day idea of civilizational development, born out of the necessity to mitigate and counteract the adverse impacts of economic growth. It is the kind of development that aims to satisfy the needs of present generations while preserving the ability of future generations to meet their own aspirations [4]. Its mechanism is built around the pursuit of three primary goals [5–8]:

(1) Ecological—which involves a reduction of environmental degradation;

(2) Economic—expressed by satisfying basic material human needs with the application of technology and techniques which do not destroy the environment;

(3) Social—which assumes the maintenance of a social minimum (eradication of hunger and poverty), health protection, development of human spiritual sphere (culture), safety and education.

A consideration of the above mentioned three categories of objectives is referred to as the "triple-bottom line" [9]. The concept highlights that social, economic and environmental goals are interrelated and mutually reinforcing [10].

Therefore, the idea of sustainable development has three characteristic features: sustainability, durability and self-sustainability. Sustainability involves the need to maintain a balance between developmental needs and the need to protect the environment. Durability requires the provision of access to environmental resources. Self-sustainability draws attention to the interdependence of economic, environmental and social factors in the stimulation of a long-term economic growth [11].

The application of the principles of sustainable development entails profound consequences at the microeconomic level. For the idea to be implemented and to assess its effectiveness, business entities need to account not only for economic aspects but also for social and environmental criteria [12]. Consequently, this means support should be provided to organizations which are socially responsible, environmentally friendly and which promote economically valuable solutions as part of their business activities [13]. A tool that fosters sustainable organization-building is the concept of CSR.

CSR refers to a firm fulfilling its legal, economic, ethical, and philanthropic responsibilities to society [14]. The ISO 26000 standard (International Organization for Standardization) defining social responsibility as the responsibility of an organisation for the impact of its decisions and activities on society and the environment, through transparent and ethical behaviour which contributes to sustainable development, including the health and well-being of society [10]. Hart defines CSR as "the company's considerations of and response to issues above the narrow economic, technical and legal requirements of the company to accomplish social and environmental benefits alongside with the traditional economic benefits which the company seeks to achieve" [15].

CSR is a set of activities which serves the implementation of the sustainable development strategy at the microeconomic level [1]. It is a business model based on the development of long-term relations with all participants of the socio-economic system, having regard for their diversity and developmental needs. Thus, CSR stands for a rejection of the strategy oriented purely towards the interests of the owner of the capital [1]. According to this concept, the objective of an enterprise is to create value for all stakeholders, which allows sustainable development and encourages the ongoing involvement of social partners [16]. It is reflected by the voluntary adoption of these expectations into company strategy, which leads not only to economic benefits but also social effects.

CSR concentrates on the organization, yet it is strictly connected to sustainable development [10]. The connection between CSR and sustainable development is emphasized by the definition formulated by the World Bank, stating CSR is the commitment of the business in contributing to the sustainable development through the cooperation of human employees, their families, local communities and society, aimed at improving the quality of life and thus both business and social development [17]. The CSR concept has been defined by the World Business Council for Sustainable Development as "the commitment of business to contribute to sustainable economic development, working with employees, their families, the local community, and society at large to improve their quality of life" [18]. The stated purpose of CSR is "minimizing compromise and maximizing synergies" resulting from company interactions with the economic, community and natural environment where it operates [19]. According to ISO 26000, caring for the compliance with law is especially important when implementing CSR [10]. Also, Cohen at al. [20] underline that respecting the labor law is the starting point for SRHRM. Therefore, it can be concluded that complying with legal regulations is a necessary but not sufficient condition for CSR.

In recent years one can see a kind of integration of CSR and corporate governance (CG) [21]. According to ISO 26000 corporate governance is a system enabling an organization to take and implement decisions serving the realization of its goals. The corporate governance framework is there to encourage the efficient use of resources and equally to require accountability for the stewardship of those resources [22]. The governance mechanism is multidimensional and should ensure that stakeholders interests are protected in all respects. There should be complete transparency about the activities of the company. The conduct of the company should be in line with the legal and ethical framework. That is why some authors believe that CSR is a part of corporate governance [21,22]. Firms use governance mechanisms, along with CSR engagement, to reduce conflicts of interest between managers and non-investing stakeholders. When managers use CSR activities to resolve conflicts between managers and various stakeholders, CSR engagement enhances firm value and performance [23]. CSR and CG have some common ground. Both concepts relate to the general relationships of an enterprise with its internal and external environment, accept the company's responsibility, and aim at ensuring a stable performance and good communication with stakeholders [24]. That is why they can complement each other in heading towards sustainable development of the organization. Giroud and Mueller [25], Coles et al. [26], Core and Guay [27], Li [28] write more about corporate governance and its impact on sustainable development and its connected practices.

Even though the ideas of sustainable development and CSR have been evolving over recent decades [29], in published works concerning the matter focus is mainly placed on aspects related to the environmental and economic dimensions, whereas far less attention is paid to the social dimensions of sustainable development [30,31]. It seems so far that the full potential of human resource management (HRM) within the process of sustainable organization-building and the attainment of sustainable development goals is yet to be revealed [32]. Therefore, in recent years there has been an increase in interest from both theoreticians and practitioners in the concept of sustainable human resource management (SHRM). As highlighted by authors dealing with SHRM, personnel processes and HR leaders play vital roles in translating the policy of sustainable development into practice [33–40]. Thanks to SHRM support, companies may attain their sustainable development goals more effectively [31,41].

It should be noted that the SHRM concept is a result of connecting HRM with the idea of sustainable development [20,42,43]. The idea emphasizes the need to develop the objectives of the personnel function in a broader manner—not only in categories of economic interest, but also in the social and environmental categories [44,45]. A direct consequence of the implementation of SHRM is the development of sustainable human resources, i.e., highly qualified employee who understand and follow the principles of sustainable development throughout the course of their work [46–48].

SHRM is a new approach to the realization of personnel function, which aims at the integration of potentially contradictory economic, ecological and social goals. The SHRM model consists of three components: economic HRM, green HRM and SRHRM [45]. SRHRM is one of the key components of SHRM. Its essence is a socially-sensitive approach to human resources implemented by personnel practices within both HRM and CSR. De facto SRHRM pertains to CSR's internal dimension and fosters corporate social responsibility with a view to attaining environmental and social values by developing ethical attitudes based on honesty and trust in employees. Thus, the concept of SRHRM provides conditions promoting sustainable development.

Despite a marked increase in the studies and practices regarding both sustainable development and HRM and CSR, analyses of the correlations between the fields conducted to date have been sparse [37]. Above all, there is a small number of publications on SRHRM implementation in the context of sustainable organization-building in Poland. A review of the Polish source literature revealed a gap with respect to empirical studies in the field of the relationships between SRHRM and sustainable development. What is more, there has been no attempt to assess the relationship between SRHRM practices and the sustainable development of Polish organizations, which provided the author with an impulse to undertake research in the field.

The objective of the study is to diagnose the activity of young enterprises operating across Poland in the field of SRHRM oriented at developing good relations with the primary group of stakeholders, which includes employees, and to carry out an evaluation of the effect of SRHRM practices on sustainable development of organizations. The analysis includes an identification of SRHRM practices embraced by organizations and their prioritization in accordance with their effect on the sustainable development of organizations. The main research problem was to establish correlation between the assessment of the relation of SRHRM practices with the sustainable development of organizations and their practical implementation.

In the course of analyses, the following research questions were addressed:

—Which SRHRM practices are most often implemented in young Polish enterprises?
—Which SRHRM practices are key to the sustainable development of organizations in the Polish reality?
—Is there a correlation between the assessment of the relation of SRHRM practices with the sustainable development of organizations and its practical implementation in the young Polish enterprises analyzed?

In order to solve the above presented problems, the study was based on a review of literature, a diagnostic survey method, and statistical and comparative analyses.

The interest of the authors in Polish enterprises grows from the fact that usually modern methods in the field of management are implemented in Polish organizations with delay. That is why some practices, which in Western countries have been realized for years, are new in Poland. The authors intended to survey to what extend Polish enterprises have advanced in implementing SRHRM practices, which are the element of a new model of the personnel function evolution, that is SHRM. Finding the gap in the area of desired practice of HRM may, according to the authors, give impetus to improving this field of management in the future.

The first years of functioning of a young enterprise on the market are a test of its survival. That is why in this period of time managers very often concentrate on the realization of economic goals. Social aspects of performance, especially voluntary ones, are usually relegated to secondary status. The authors tried to inquire, whether, and if yes, how deeply, young Polish enterprises are familiar with the concept of SRHRM, and to what extent they are willing to realize this practice in the time of start-up. The authors believe that the scope of implementation of SRHRM is a kind of barometer of the level of CSR importance in the successful organization building.

The principal restriction encountered in the course of research was the shortage of studies conducted in the young enterprise population, which made it difficult to carry out a comparative analysis of the results of research. The reason behind this is that the results of published analyses are typically presented in the form of a profile of the number of entities expressed by the number of employed workers, and less often accounting for the time period of their operation on the market.

The article is composed of five sections. The introductory part presents the essence of the concept of sustainable development and its relation to CSR, which is the background of the study considerations. In addition, it presents the reasons for the growth of interest in SHRM and SRHRM. Further on, there is an outline of the research gap identified in source literature which prompted the author's motivation to carry out personal research. It includes a definition of the research objective, a brief overview of research problems, applied methods, study limitations, the composition of the article and its contribution to science.

In Section 2, the theoretical background of the considerations in question is presented in the context of the world's literature review. Here, the focus is on the determination of the role of human resources and human resource management in sustainable development and sustainable organization-building. Next, the nature of SRHRM and the benefits of its implementation are presented and the relationship between SRHRM and CSR is examined. Furthermore, there is a review of the SRHRM practices.

Section 3 outlines the subject matter of the research and the population studied, formulates research hypotheses and describes the methods employed. Thereafter, there is a discussion involving the research findings. It includes an assessment of the impact of SRHRM on the sustainable development of young organizations and a diagnosis of the scope of their implementation in the enterprises studied. Analysis of the research outcome was performed in the context of studies conducted by other authors. The final section demonstrates key conclusions, references to the extent of verification of research hypotheses and recommendations for future research directions.

This study shall contribute to source literature by diagnosing a gap associated with SRHRM use as a vehicle for increasing the sustainable development of organizations in the Polish reality. In the opinion of the study authors, research findings may stimulate interest in the implementation of the SRHRM concept in Polish organizations and in extending the scope of its application as an instrument for sustainable organization-building. This is particularly important in relation to young organizations' development since the implementation of socially responsible HRM practices during the early stage of development of an organization provides it with an opportunity to improve its sustainability performance.

2. Literature Review

2.1. The Role of HRM in the Creation of Sustainable Organizations Development

Continuing along the path of sustainable development is becoming a necessity given our rapidly deteriorating natural environment and the increase in social challenges. It is mostly expected from enterprises, as they grossly contribute to environmental degradation [46]. Enterprises choosing to base their operations on the triple-bottom line principle [49] are referred to as sustainable enterprises.

According to Grudzewski et al., sustainable enterprises are enterprises capable of ongoing development, adaptation, learning, revitalization and reorientation [50]. The purpose of sustainable enterprise activities is to achieve an economic, social and environmental balance [49]. Economic sustainability requires enterprise profitability to be increased by efficient resource use, effective undertakings, good management, planning and control. Environmental sustainability necessitates the prevention of adverse and irreversible consequences for the environment through efficient use of natural resources, soil and water protection, and skillful waste management. Social sustainability involves the obligation to respond to the needs of all company stakeholders [3,51]. As a result, the prospects of succeeding in the case of sustainable enterprises go far beyond the financial dimension. These are companies which not only yield economic profits, but also take care of the environment and contribute to the social balance. Enterprises following the sustainable development principle apply systems and processes which adhere to the principles of efficient use of natural energy and resources, low pollutant emissions, safety assurance, and satisfaction of employees, consumers and communities [52].

Such business entities would not exist without appropriate staff. The environmental and social conscience of workers, fostered by their activity and competencies, constitutes the foundation of effectiveness and efficiency of actions in the area of sustainable development [46]. Thus, more and more frequently attention is paid to the key role of human resources and HR management in the implementation of the idea of sustainable development. Many authors agree with the thesis that the HR function is a potent instrument of sustainable organization-building [34,53,54]. The group of researchers which explore the issue of the HRM role in the implementation of the strategy of sustainable development is constantly expanding. Source literature emphasizes that the objective of the human resource department is to support the organization on the road to sustainable development [37], whereas HRM practices are essential for attracting and retaining personnel who will strive to attain the goals of sustainable development [37,38,55].

Human resources play a crucial role in the creation of sustainable development culture [38,56]. This is because responsibility culture development starts with the HR function. HRM policies and strategies create a framework for sustainable development culture by raising employee awareness in the field. Most of all, it is underpinned that the HR function may facilitate CSR strategy development and implementation [57–62]. Appropriate personnel policy favors intensification of desirable socially- and environmentally-oriented behaviours [56]. Therefore, it is emphasized that the HR function has a strategic role to play in CSR initiatives of organizations [63]. The role of the HR function in the development of sustainable enterprises is further expressed by the development of sustainable personnel. This term refers to highly qualified employees who understand and follow the principles of sustainable development at work [46].

For HRM to fulfill such a leading role, the HR function should be treated as a strategic partner participating in the policy of sustainable development. Needless to say, one of the main challenges for modern HRM is its fusion with the idea of sustainable development and its orientation at supporting aims related to economic, social and environmental equilibrium [64]. This is reflected in the SHRM concept.

According to Ehnert, SHRM means taking up such practices that allow organizations to attain goals in a long-term perspective and that at the same time reflect their great concern for their employees [65]. Kramar would broaden the definition to include the minimization of the negative effect of enterprise operations on the natural environment, employees and communities [42]. Cohen et al. [20] adds that sustainable human resources management promotes the strategy of sustainable development in organizations by:

- just treatment, commitment to employee development and welfare;
- building employee trust and increasing their motivation to work for the benefit of sustainable development;
- taking care of internal stakeholders' (employees) and external stakeholders' health;
- fostering environment-friendly practices.

Given the above, SHRM contributes not only to the attainment of economic goals but also to the achievement of a far-reaching balance between inter-generational needs, thus preventing serious future environmental or social problems [46,49]. The implementation of this concept involves the need to modify the HRM philosophy so as to include socioenvironmental objectives in all subareas of HRM, from employment planning, to recruitment, selection, employee motivation and development, to employee assessment and impact on the conditions of work. This implies recruiting sustainable employees, broadening employee knowledge about sustainability, encouraging employees to undertake socially and environmentally oriented actions [44] and reward them for the effects produced. Rather than performed occasionally, these practices should become a permanent element of the personnel strategy.

One crucial component of SHRM is SRHRM. It is a manifestation of a responsible and honest approach to employees, which preconditions the use of their knowledge and stimulation of their participation in pursuing the objectives of sustainable development.

2.2. The Essence and Benefits of SRHRM Implementation

A sustainable enterprise is the one which is concerned with satisfying the needs and interests of equal groups of stakeholders. This is because positive relations with the stakeholders reduce operation costs, minimize risks, increase knowledge capital and promote goodwill. In relation to an organization's success creation, employees are particularly vital stakeholders. Commitment to good relations with workers is of the utmost importance in these times of the knowledge economy, where the foundation for the creation of added value is the intellectual capital. Relations with employees are unique in nature given their sensitivity to ill-treatment. To develop effective relations, organizations need to show respect for the rights and personal dignity of the employed. However, despite the fact that human resources and their management are seen as critical in terms of an organizations' success [66], in practice the prevailing approach is that of HR exploitation [67]. The introduction of SRHRM favors counteracting this negative tendency.

SRHRM is a concept which derives from and is strongly correlated with CSR. Authors tackling the issue indicate that there is a feedback loop between the two fields [68–78]. While CSR has an impact on HR, HRM has a key role to play in CSR implementation [56,73]. Relations between CSR and HRM in available literature usually fall under two broad categories [68,79,80]:

—CSR supported by HRM (HRM practices used to involve employees in CSR implementation);
—HRM supported by CSR (CSR practices used to attract, keep and motivate employees).

SRHRM is a concept founded upon the integration of both domains and accounting for the two-way CSR-HRM relation [72,81]. SRHRM comprises a socially-conscious approach to human resources implemented by personnel practices within both HRM and CSR [82]. They are a means by which HRM effectiveness is increased by incorporating employees' needs into the needs of organizations, which leads to greater involvement and satisfaction. On the other hand, given that SRHRM pertains to CSR's internal dimension, it can foster corporate social responsibility with a view to attaining environmental and social values by developing ethical attitudes based on honesty and trust in employees. SRHRM as a social dimension of SHRM is consistent with broadly understood corporate social responsibility oriented at the optimum use of employee potential with simultaneous respect for their rights and needs. The said dimension of HRM is manifested by an employee-centred approach according to which employees are treated as crucial stakeholders [45]. SRHRM can be seen in, amongst other things, voluntary non-business actions aimed at meeting long-term employee needs, ensuring job satisfaction and development opportunities [83]. The principle of SRHRM is to engage in an active dialogue with employees. This fosters trust capital development. Trust is a crucial element of cooperation. It promotes and maintains it, encourages information exchange, enriches relations, prompts growth in candor and mutual acceptance, and aids conflict resolution [84].

Practical implementation of the trust-based SRHRM is manifested by an observation of ethical principles in relations with employees throughout all stages of the personnel process (from recruitment and selection to motivation, assessment and development, to employment restructuring). Table 1 shows a selection of SRHRM practices.

Table 1. Selected SRHRM practices.

Area	Examples of Practices
Employee selection (recruitment, selection, adaptation)	—honest, non-discriminating job offers —ethical job interview —implementation of the "candidate experience" concept —friendly employee adaptation
Employee motivation	—generous remuneration —transparent and objective criteria of gratification —timely payment of remunerations —comprehensive social package (extra insurance, healthcare, pension plans) —employee participation in management
Employee assessment	—transparency of the system of period performance appraisals —objectivity of evaluation criteria —elimination of errors in the process of periodic appraisals —conduct of constructive assessment interviews
Employee development	—investment in employee development —assurance of equal access to training —employee development support (mentoring, coaching) —counseling and support with respect to professional career management

Table 1. *Cont.*

Area	Examples of Practices
Health prophylaxis and work safety	—workshops on coping with stress —training and workshops on healthy eating —vaccinations —health-oriented modifications of working places —sport activities —relax rooms at the workplace —additional health leaves —compliance with periodic health examinations of employees —compliance with the industrial health and safety law —commitment to ergonomic work space design
Diversity Management	—integration programmes —equal opportunities programmes —improvements for persons with disabilities —multicultural teams —work-life balance programmes (nonstandard forms of employment, improvements for parents, additional parental leaves)
Developing relations and attitudes	—transparent rules of communication —corporate volunteering (voluntary participation in social campaigns) —prevention of mobbing and discrimination —development and implementation of ethical codes
Employment restructuring	—dismissal having regard to the values of respect for human dignity and employee rights —just and clear disciplinary procedures —outplacement

Socially responsible practices in the field of HRM generate a number of direct benefits. Most of all, they have a positive effect on internal and external employer branding. The reason behind this is that the most important factor affecting an organization's reputation as a workplace is the way in which it treats employees [80,85]. The research carried out among 100 most reputable firms in Spain showed that socially responsible practice implemented for employees, directly and positively influenced the reputation of the employer [86]. Subject literature emphasizes that a corporate social strategy may be employed in order to attract, maintain and motivate employees [68,73]. An increase in employee motivation and morale, on the other hand, has a positive impact on their involvement [87], productivity [88] and company loyalty, which in turn may improve financial results [63,73]. The application of socially responsible practices in the area of development, the development of working conditions and relations between humans may also contribute directly to a decrease in absences and personnel rotation [37]. More and more SRHRM practices seem to be indispensable to meeting economic and demographic challenges concerning personnel policy, such as the aging of society, the workforce shortage, or the talent war [65,73]. The implementation of the SRHRM concept may also become a panacea for increasing personnel fluctuation, a decrease in employee loyalty to their companies, an increase in levels of work stress, and falling employee satisfaction [31]. Even though this mode of applying the CSR perspective to HRM does not amend the HRM goals, it does contribute to their improved realization [63,73] for it becomes a mechanism for unlocking the human capital, which is fundamental to the development of sustainable organizations and to their ability to gain a long-term competitive advantage [56,89].

3. Materials and Methods

The subject matter of the research comprised SRHRM practices followed by young Polish enterprises. The list of activities included in the research is presented in Table 2. The diagnosis was conducted with reference to 35 activities implemented at various stages of the personnel process. The list of practices was identified pursuant to the analysis of source literature.

Table 2. The list of SRHRM practices included in the research.

Activity Number	Activities
1	Commitment to fairness of one's employment offer
2	Commitment to non-discrimination of vacancy advertising, i.e., eliminating elements which could discriminate because of sex, age, appearance, disability, etc.
3	Employing persons with disabilities
4	Employing people from the age group of 50 and above
5	Commitment to good relations with candidates who have not been employed (candidate experience)
6	Facilitating new employee adaptation
7	Transparent system of periodic performance appraisals
8	Investing in employee development
9	Commitment to equal access to employee training
10	Supporting employees who are made redundant (helping to find accommodation, psychological support)
11	Compliance with the industrial health and safety law
12	Providing generous remuneration
11	Transparent rules of remuneration
14	Comprehensive social benefits
15	Applying solutions facilitating the attainment of a work-life balance (such as flexible working hours)
16	Ability of employees to co-decide on matters relating to company operation (participation)
17	Just and clear dismissal procedures
18	Development and implementation of an ethical code
19	Conduct of environmental audits
20	Award of ethical certificates
21	Cooperating only with those business partners who are certified to be in compliance with ethical requirements
22	Implementing procedures for combating discrimination, mobbing and harassment at work
23	Ethical Code training organization
24	Organization of training sessions on combating discrimination, mobbing and harassment
25	Promoting a healthy lifestyle and civilization disease prevention among employees
26	Conducting health-oriented training and workshops (such as coping with stress, etc.)
27	Financial support for employees with respect to healthy lifestyles (such as money to buy sportswear, sports equipment, gym or swimming-pool memberships, etc.)
28	Investment in infrastructure promoting a healthy lifestyle (such as bicycle parking stations, healthy food canteens)
29	Employee involvement in social projects (aiding shelters, renovating preschools) as part of corporate volunteering
30	Adjustment of working conditions to meet the needs of various employee groups (such as people from the age group of 50 and above, the disabled)
31	Inclusion of social goals of HRM in company strategy
32	Measurement of effectiveness of environmental actions in HRM
33	Provision for socially responsible HRM activities-related expenditure in the budget
34	HRM socially responsible action progress monitoring
35	Drafting reports on social responsibility in HRM

With a view to analyzing the effect of the above-listed socially responsible practices on the policy of sustainable development, a (partial) survey was conducted among a random, representative population of 150 young enterprises with their headquarters in Poland. Young enterprises were defined as those operating on the market for less than three years. The study was conducted in January 2018 with the application of the CATI technique [90]. The study sample was selected on a layer basis.

First, 25 entities from each of the six Polish regions were drawn: Central, South, East, North-West, South-West and North. The survey targeted individuals in charge of HRM policy development in the analyzed enterprises. The characteristic features of the study population are shown in Table 3.

Table 3. Details of young enterprises included in the study.

Criterion	Number of Enterprises	Percentage
Time on the market:		
up to 1 year	14	9.3
1–3 years	136	90.7
Employment number:		
50–249 employees	100	66.7
250–499 employees	42	28.0
More than 500 employees	8	5.3
Main type of activity:		
production	43	28.7
services	99	66.0
trade	8	5.3
Scope of operations		
local	37	24.7
regional	20	13.3
national	44	29.3
international	49	32.7
Respondent's position:		
HR Director	8	5.3
Head of HR Department	126	84.0
CEO	12	8.0
other	4	2.7

The enterprises which prevailed in the population studied were those operating on the market for more than one year. They accounted for as much as 90.7% of the study population. The size of the companies which dominated the population studied was medium, i.e., employing between 50 and 249 employees. Their percentage was established at 66.7%. The prevailing type of business activity of the study entities was provision of services (66%). In terms of the type of ownership, the largest group was that of limited liability companies, which constituted 57.3% of the study group. Next, with respect to the scope of operations, the dominant enterprises were domestic enterprises (29.3%). Respondents were mainly heads of human resource departments (84%).

One of the most important criterion of the surveyed enterprises choice was their size measured with the number of employees. In our research we concentrated on medium and large companies, which—as it has been proven in other research—are more interested in CSR initiatives implementation than small firms [91] and also have better qualified managers [92]. It is worth noticing that this criterion is not very often used in analysis, which is confirmed by the results of the Dang and Li's research [93]. These authors analyzed 100 empirical papers from top finance, accounting, and economics journals and ascertained that the most popular firm size proxies in empirical corporate finance research are total assets, sales, and market value of equity. However, they believe that size is a firm fundamental variable, any small difference may have critical impact on the dependant variable and other independent variables in empirical study. Besides, great caution must be exercised when some variables are collinear with the different firm size measures. They also underline that the choice of company size depends on the concrete goal of research [93].

Other important criterion in our research was the period of time when a company was functioning on the market, which allowed us to determine a group of young enterprises. The justification of this criterion choice was the possibility of obtaining data concerning the scale of SRHRM implementation in the first phase of the life cycle of the surveyed organizations. The results may, on the one hand, fill in the diagnosed in the literature gap, and, on the other hand, create the ground for further analysis giving the possibility to compare in the future the scope of the SRHRM implementation in young and mature companies.

Research allows the following:

- Acknowledgement of the Polish managers' opinions concerning the meaning of particular socially responsible human resource practices in shaping sustainable development of young enterprises
- Identification of practices which are key to sustainable enterprise-building in the opinion of Polish managers;
- Diagnosis of practices which in the opinions of respondents have a marginal role to play in sustainable enterprise-building;
- Determination of the frequency of implementation of individual socially responsible activities in the field of human resource management within the studied enterprises;
- Identification of practices most popular under Polish conditions;
- Diagnosis of practices which are rarely implemented by young enterprises under Polish conditions;
- Analysis of the correlation between the assessment of the relation of SRHRM practices with the sustainable development of organizations and their practical implementation in young Polish enterprises;
- Description of the above-mentioned correlation with the application of a mathematical model and a calculation of standard errors of the estimates.

Over the course of research, attempts were made to verify the following research hypotheses:

Hypothesis 1. *Socially responsible activities declared by Polish managers in the area of HRM have an irregular relation with the sustainable development of young organizations.*

Hypothesis 2. *There is correlation between the assessment of the relation of SRHRM practices with the sustainable development of organizations and their implementation in young enterprises.*

To verify Hypothesis 1, measures of central tendency, both classic and location (in the case of impact asymmetry), measures of dispersion, i.e., the extent to which a distribution is scattered, and measures of dispersion, demonstrating the mean deviation of individual activities from the average and the force of activity variability, were applied. The measures of asymmetry allowed determination of the force and the direction of asymmetry of assessment of individual SRHRM activities; whereas the measures of concentration let us analyze the spread of activity assessment round their mean value.

In the process of verification of Hypothesis 2, Spearman's rank correlation coefficient was used, which allowed the authors to determine the strength and direction of correlations between the impact of SRHRM activities on the sustainable development of young companies, and their practical implementation. Furthermore, the parameters of the linear regression model were estimated, which allowed the modelling of the relationship between the studied variables.

All of the above permitted an assessment of the extent of SRHRM concept implementation under Polish conditions in the context of supporting the sustainable development policy within young organizations.

4. Results and Discussion

4.1. Assessment of the Relationship between SRHRM Practices and the Sustainable Development of Young Organizations

The assessment of the relationship between SRHRM practices and the sustainable development of young organizations was conducted with the application of a five-level Likert scale, where 1 signified a very low relation and 5 a very strong relation of a given practice. To analyze the relation, the structure of the group was described by the calculation of measures of central tendency, both classic and location (in the case of impact asymmetry), measures of dispersion, specifying the extent to which a distribution is scattered, and measures of asymmetry and concentration (Table 4).

Table 4. Evaluation of the relationship between SRHRM practices and the sustainable development of organizations *.

Activity No.	Total (Points)	The Average Strength of the Relation (Points)	Mode (Points)	Median (Points)	Standard Deviation (Points)	Coefficient of Variation (Points)	Strength of Asymmetry (Points)	Kurtosis (Points)
11	725	4.83	5	5	0.424	8.78	−0.39	6.24
2	690	4.6	5	5	0.835	18.16	−0.48	6.12
6	672	4.48	5	5	0.739	16.50	−0.70	5.13
13	667	4.45	5	5	0.710	15.96	−0.78	2.66
1	654	4.36	5	5	0.813	18.65	−0.79	2.99
9	649	4.33	5	5	0.901	20.83	−0.75	2.92
8	646	4.31	5	4	0.835	19.39	−0.83	2.47
12	643	4.29	5	4	0.814	18.98	−0.88	0.63
17	617	4.11	5	4	1.053	25.59	−0.84	1.47
14	604	4.03	5	4	1.080	26.83	−0.90	0.83
22	593	3.95	5	4	1.200	30.36	−0.87	0.50
7	583	3.89	5	4	1.207	31.06	−0.92	0.23
4	568	3.79	5	4	1.097	28.96	−1.11	−0.11
18	561	3.74	5	4	1.353	36.18	−0.93	−0.50
3	553	3.69	5	4	1.221	33.13	−1.08	−0.37
5	546	3.64	4	4	1.166	32.03	−0.309	−0.17
30	535	3.57	3	4	1.228	34.44	0.46	−0.53
31	531	3.54	3	4	1.145	32.34	0.47	0.03
16	518	3.45	3	3	1.267	36.69	0.36	−0.70
15	500	3.33	3	3	1.278	38.34	0.26	−0.62
25	495	3.30	3	3	1.309	39.68	0.23	−0.72
24	460	3.07	3	3	1.299	42.35	0.05	−0.86
27	459	3.06	3	3	1.352	44.19	0.04	−0.96
28	451	3.01	3	3	1.363	45.35	0.00	−1.04
26	443	2.95	3	3	1.372	46.47	−0.03	−1.06
19	439	2.93	3	3	1.296	44.28	−0.06	−0.84
33	438	2.92	3	3	1.282	43.92	−0.06	−0.84
23	432	2.88	3	3	1.295	44.96	−0.09	−0.97
34	425	2.83	3	3	1.255	44.31	−0.13	−0.82
29	423	2.82	3	3	1.336	47.39	−0.13	−1.03
32	417	2.78	3	3	1.268	45.63	−0.17	−0.85
10	416	2.77	3	3	1.275	45.98	−0.18	−0.86
35	405	2.70	3	3	1.225	45.36	−0.24	−0.87
20	362	2.41	3	3	1.275	52.85	−0.46	−0.92
21	360	2.40	3	3	1.221	50.86	−0.49	−0.93

* respondents made assessments whether or not a given activity was implemented within a given enterprise.

To identify socially responsible HRM practices which, according to respondents, had a strong relation with the sustainable development of organizations, the study sample was divided into quartiles. The first quartile was composed of SRHRM activities of primordial importance for the sustainable development of organizations in the opinion of Polish managers. The third quartile, on the other hand, consisted of activities which did not contribute significantly to sustainable development-building.

The analyses demonstrated that it was compliant with the industrial health and safety law (activity no. 11), which had the greatest relation with the sustainable development of young enterprises. The point here is a special care of health and safety at work and not only minimal compliance with the regulations defined in the labor law. This approach is named as sustainable HRM practice also by other authors [94]. Most frequently, respondents evaluated its relation as being very high (mode and median 5) and the average strength of the relation of this activity was 4.83. Another practice deemed crucial within SRHRM was company commitment to nondiscrimination of vacancy advertising, i.e., eliminating elements which could discriminate because of sex, age, appearance, disability, etc. (activity no. 2). The relation of the above activity was most often assessed as very high, with an average rating of 4.6. Other activities the respondents identified as crucial were: facilitating new employee adaptation (activity no. 6) and transparent rules of remuneration (activity no. 13). The average strength of the relation of these activities was 4.48 and 4.45, correspondingly, while the strength of variation of the relation extended from 16.5% to 15.9%. Furthermore, the following activities were considered important for the sustainable development of organizations:

—commitment to fairness of one's employment offer (activity no. 1), with an impact average of 4.36;
—equal access to training (activity no. 9), with an impact average of 4.33;
—investment in employee development (activity no. 8), with an impact average of 4.31;
—provision of generous remuneration (activity no. 12), with an impact average of 4.29;
—just and clear dismissal procedures (activity no. 17), with an impact average of 4.11.

With respect to the above-listed activities, the mode observed was at the level of 5, whereas the (relation diversity)—between 18.65 and 25.59.

Most managers opined that the SRHRM activity considered as having the weakest relation with the sustainable development of enterprises was cooperating only with those business partners who were certified to be in compliance with ethical requirements (activity no. 21). The mean impact of this activity was assessed at 2.41. An equally insignificant activity was the impact of an award of ethical certificates (activity no. 20). In the opinion of the respondents, the average relation of this practice with sustainable development was 2.40. There were also other activities that were seen as having a low relation.

—drafting reports on social responsibility in HRM (activity no. 35);
—support for dismissed employees (activity no. 10);
—measurement of effectiveness of environmental actions in HRM (activity no. 32);
—employee involvement in social projects as part of corporate volunteering (activity no. 29);
—HRM socially responsible action progress monitoring (activity no. 34);
—provision for socially responsible HRM activities-related expenditure in the budget (activity no. 23);
—ethical code training organization (activity no. 33).

The effect of the above activities was deemed to be average, oscillating around 2.70 and 2.92. The coefficient of variation of the strength of relationship of the activities in the last quartile, regarded as less vital for company development, was much higher than the coefficient of variation in the first quartile. It oscillated around 43% to 53%, which signifies strong dispersion.

Given the average assessment of the relation of all SRHRM practices, which was 3.5 in the 5-level scale, we can affirm the following conclusion: the importance of SRHRM practices as instruments of support of sustainable development of organizations is appreciated by the studied entities. Nonetheless, some depreciation of the importance of activities associated with the implementation of procedural activities is evident. The managers covered by the research clearly chose to belittle the importance of practices such as:

—HRM socially responsible action progress monitoring;
—drafting reports on social responsibility in HRM;
—measurement of effectiveness of environmental actions in HRM; and
—provision for socially responsible HRM activities-related expenditure in the budget.

In the light of the fact that contractual partners' commitment to ethical principles was considered—according to our findings—an activity that was the least important of all, it may be assumed that the relevant entities have not yet fully developed a culture of responsibility, which guarantees an authentic social involvement of enterprises. Needless to say, the implementation of SRHRM practices should be a direct result of the canon of values, rules, and norms of conduct respected and followed by a given company. It would be difficult to discuss the effective and comprehensive implementation of the SRHRM concept in the absence of an appreciation of the above practices. Some interesting conclusions in this respect may be drawn from the analysis of the scope of SRHRM concept implementation under Polish conditions conducted in the subsequent part of the study.

4.2. Evaluation of the Scope of SRHRM Concept Implementation in Polish Enterprises

On the basis of data regarding the number of enterprises pursuing individual SRHRM practices, characteristics of their structures were developed. The data analysis covered the following statistical parameters: measures of location, dispersion, asymmetry and concentration. The mean number of enterprises pursuing a SRHRM activity was 97; the standard deviation of the number of enterprises implementing social activities from their mean value was by 39 companies. Half of the activities were accomplished by 105 enterprises at most, whereas another half—in no less than 105 entities. The range of the number of enterprises pursuing an activity was 126 (activity no. 11 was implemented by as many as 149 enterprises, whereas activity no. 21 by 23 companies only). The coefficient of variation of 39.97% indicates a moderate strength of differentiation in the number of enterprises implementing social activities. Approximately 67% of social activities were accomplished by 58 to 136 young enterprises. The left side asymmetry is indicative of the fact that the mean number of enterprises pursuing SRHRM activities (97) was understated in relation to the median value (central value). The structure index (the frequency of activities) oscillated between 15.3% and 99.3% (Table 5). We ought to emphasize that 63% of SRHRM practices were pursued in over 50% of young enterprises. This means that a few activities were conducted more rarely than others.

Table 5. Implementation of SRHRM practices in young Polish enterprises.

Activity No.	Number of Young Enterprises Performing the Activity	Percentage of Young Enterprises Performing the Activity (%)
1	147	98.00
2	143	95.33
3	113	75.33
4	129	86.00
5	119	79.33
6	146	97.33
7	120	80.00
8	142	94.67
9	142	94.67
10	47	31.33
11	149	99.33
12	141	94.00
13	147	98.00
14	130	86.67
15	96	64.00
16	112	74.67
17	130	86.67
18	105	70.00

Table 5. *Cont.*

Activity No.	Number of Young Enterprises Performing the Activity	Percentage of Young Enterprises Performing the Activity (%)
19	50	33.33
20	25	16.67
21	23	15.33
22	119	79.33
23	62	41.33
24	77	51.33
25	86	57.33
26	68	45.33
27	71	47.33
28	64	42.67
29	56	37.33
30	97	64.67
31	106	70.67
32	56	37.33
33	66	44.00
34	62	41.33
35	49	32.67

Among the SRHRM practices most frequently implemented by the studied entities, the following should be listed:

- Activity no. 11, i.e., Compliance with industrial health and safety, was implemented by the greatest number of entities: 149 (99.33% of the total)
- Activity no. 1, i.e., Commitment to fairness of one's employment offer and activity no. 13, i.e., Transparent rules of remuneration, accomplished by 147 enterprises (98% of the total);
- Activity no. 6, i.e., Facilitating new employee adaptation, implemented by 146 companies (97.33% of the total);
- Activity no. 2, i.e., Commitment to nondiscrimination in vacancy advertising, i.e., Eliminating elements which could discriminate because of sex, age, appearance, disability, etc., declared by 143 companies (95.33% of the total);
- Activity no. 8, i.e., Investment in employee development, and activity no. 9, i.e., Equal access to training, pursued by 142 enterprises (94.67% total);
- Activity no. 12, i.e., Providing generous remuneration, implemented by 141 of the studied entities (94% of the total).

Analysis of the above data demonstrates that the analyzed entities quite frequently implement SRHRM practices. The findings show the widespread popularity of selected practices. This is further confirmed by other authors' research studies.

The study conducted by A. Pocztowski in the year 2013, which covered 50 Polish enterprises operating internationally, manifested that the studied entities were greatly involved with diversity management. The initiatives most often found in their company policies were: bullying prevention (64% indications), anti-discriminatory activities (52%), sexual harassment prevention (32%), flexible working hours (32%), accommodation for people with disabilities (30%), age management (24%) and ensuring work-life balance (18%) [45]. Employers in Poland have adopted more and more serious approaches to the policy of diversity, as manifested by corporate practices, such as the organization of workshops on tolerance and the prevention of discrimination and participation in external projects, e.g. company presence at marches promoting equality [95].

On the other hand, in a survey conducted in December 2014 across the whole territory of Poland on a population of 850 entities, an activity which was implemented most often, and which fit within the framework of SRHRM practices, was investment in employee development, as declared by 30% of respondents [96]. Against the backdrop of original research presented herein, we can observe considerable progress in the field, for in the year 2018, investment in staff development was cited by as many as 96.7% of the 150 studied entities. This speaks of Polish entrepreneurs' growing awareness of the need to invest in human capital and to view this kind of expenditure not only in terms of cost but, above all, as a long-term investment.

Other research, conducted among 200 companies included in two rating lists: "Business Gazelles" and "Deloitte Technology Fast 50 in Central Europe" revealed that Polish employers pay considerable attention to the improvement of work conditions. The research demonstrated that 96% of enterprises have invested in industrial health and safety improvements, a reduction of the occupational disease risk, and/or an improvement of social conditions in the workplace over the course of the last three years. Eighty-three percent of the entities incorporated solutions aimed at improving the welfare of employees through the provision of healthcare packages, subsidized sports/recreational memberships and/or holidays. Seventy-seven percent introduced the work-life balance concept, and 60% declared involvement in improving employees' qualifications through the implementation of various training methods (e-learning, coaching, and others) or by subsidizing external forms of education (such as post-graduate university courses) [97].

Our analysis of the presented study findings shows that the widespread presence of socially responsible practices within HRM is a growing trend in the Polish reality. It is a consequence of the fact that the CSR topic is gaining popularity in Poland, as evidenced by the rising number of social initiatives undertaken by employers [98]. According to annual reports concerning CSR published in Poland, Polish entrepreneurs' involvement in the implementation of socially responsible practices is growing [95,99] and so is the use of social media in CSR. An analysis of the latest report on CSR issued in 2017 indicated that out of the 117 cited in the report, as many as 100 followed socially responsible work practices. The number of work-post-related practices nearly doubled compared to the preceding year. This trend may be justified by, most notably, employee market development in Poland. At the same time, the cited reports seem to confirm the hypothesis that the SRHRM concept is not implemented in a comprehensive manner in Poland. The majority of the studied entities pursue individual practices or several basic activities. The leader of the researched companies, Volkswagen Motor Poland, implemented 16 socially responsible work practices [95]. The lack of a comprehensive approach to SRHRM implementation is further demonstrated by the findings of research conducted by the authors of this study on a population of young enterprises.

Despite the positive growth trend with respect to SRHRM, original studies show that there are other, disturbing phenomena. First of all, it should be highlighted that practices listed as those most frequently implemented are of an obligatory nature, for entrepreneurs are obliged to follow them by law. These are activities, such as observance of the industrial health and safety law; commitment to non-discrimination in vacancy advertising and equal access to training. The Constitution of the Republic of Poland and the Labour Code prohibit any type of discrimination in employment, whether direct or indirect, in particular, due to sex, age, disability, race, religion, nationality, political belief, trade union membership, ethnic origin, denomination, and sexual orientation. Frequent implementation of obligatory practices may not necessarily be an indication of the implementation of the SRHRM concept in a given company as the essence of SRHRM is the voluntary adoption of socially responsible practices. Hence, it may be assumed that rather than SRHRM concept implementation, we may be dealing with PR-oriented CSR in some organizations. Obrad and Gherhes also highlight the likeliness of this risk [37]. According to them, it continues to be quite a frequent occurrence in the Romanian corporate environment. In Poland as well as in Romania, CSR is at times used solely as a marketing instrument [100]. Here, attention should be drawn to the risk incurred by adopting such an approach. A consequence of PR-oriented CSR is ignorance regarding employees' real needs and the employment of human resource practices only as a PR instrument used to manipulate society with a view to generating profit. Such actions are not reliable in the eyes of company stakeholders, whereas the benefits of their adoption may be apparent and short-term. Therefore, we need to emphasize that SRHRM concept's implementation may be considered comprehensive and authentic only when companies are truly committed to their employees, their safety and broadly understood physical and mental health, and when they provide optimum conditions for work and development.

Another negative symptom revealed during the research is the limited scope of the implementation of numerous human resource practices which are vital to SRHRM. Studies demonstrate that the least popular activity was exclusive cooperation with business partners who are certified in terms of compliance with ethical requirements (activity no. 21). This activity is practiced the least frequently—by only 23 of the studied enterprises (15.33% of the group). Among other equally infrequent activities were:

- Activity no. 20, i.e., The award of ethical certificates, implemented by a mere 25 entities (16.67% of the population);
- Activity no. 10, i.e., Supporting employees who are made redundant (help with finding a new job, psychological support), declared by 47 enterprises (31.33% of the group).
- Activity no. 35, i.e., Drafting reports on social responsibility in HRM, pursued by 49 companies (32.67% of the population);
- Activity no. 19, i.e., The conduct of ethical audits, implemented by 50 entities (33.33% of the population);
- Activity no. 32, i.e., Measurement of effectiveness of environmental actions in hrm; and activity no. 29, i.e. Employee involvement in social projects as part of corporate volunteering, implemented by 56 enterprises (37.33& of the group);
- Activity no. 34, i.e., Hrm socially responsible action progress monitoring and activity no. 29, i.e., Ethical code workshop organization, implemented by 62 enterprises (41.33% of the group).

The above-presented results point to the low popularity of activities associated with the implementation of SRHRM procedures by organizations, i.e., HRM socially responsible action progress monitoring, drafting reports on social responsibility in HRM, measurement of the effectiveness of socially responsible activities in HRM, and provision for socially responsible HRM activities-related expenditure in the budget. The comprehensive implementation of the SRHRM concept is impossible in the absence of the above-mentioned practices. It should be underlined that the lack of CSR practice implementation can be caused by a short period of the surveyed organizations functioning on the market. Especially that realizing some practices may take more time that three years.

We opine that a particularly important, scarce activity is the reporting of SRHRM practices which plays a vital role in the popularization of the SRHRM concept and, consequently, the scope of its practical application. For the reporting companies, in turn, this presents yet another opportunity to arrange, systematize and develop SRHRM practices. By bringing together all information regarding socially responsible HRM practices, it allows a broad view of the manner in which human resource policy is pursued from the point of view of its inclusion of the principles of sustainable development. Data included in such reports show not only where a given organization is, but also what it intends to achieve in the nearest future. Additionally, social reports facilitate an analysis of the effectiveness of conducted activities and their adoption to the needs of their stakeholders. Despite the above-specified benefits of reporting, the practice was pursued by a mere 32.67% of the entities in the studied group of young enterprises.

The minor scale of CSR reporting has been confirmed by other research studies. In 2013, a study was carried out covering the top 100 companies listed in the "Rzeczpospolita" newspaper's ranking of Poland's 500 largest companies. The results of the analysis demonstrated that only 12 of those companies had drafted social reports [100]. In the interest of comparison, according to the British FTSE 100, as many as 76% of all registered companies reported non-financial matters [101]. What is more, a study carried out in 2014 on a population of 300 Polish companies revealed that only one out of five enterprises had a CSR report prepared [102].

An analysis of the annual CSR reports in Poland shows that there is growing interest in social reporting. However, reporting non-financial data in Poland is still considered to be of marginal importance. One of the reasons behind Polish companies not going public about their social involvement is that such practices may be viewed as a source of risk in terms of competitive information publication [103].

The authors of the study opine that in the Polish reality it is still necessary not only to make the companies aware of the need for social reporting, including SRHRM reporting but also to extend such reporting by introducing a broader range of factors related to SRHRM practices. Under Polish conditions, the key elements of social reports made public by enterprises are environmental indicators (such as energy and water consumption, sewage and waste), data referring to responsibility owed towards the community (such as corruption, competitive behavior) and responsibility for products (such as consumers' health and safety, product marking, compliance with requirements). Data pertaining to SRHRM practices are significantly less prevalent. If they happen to be reported, they are usually limited to information concerning the conditions of work, training, and compliance with human rights (such as anti-discriminatory practices and work safety).

Given the foregoing, we may conclude that enterprises in Poland are characterized by a low level of maturity with respect to the implementation of the SRHRM concept. Original studies conducted on a group of young enterprises as well as studies carried out by other authors tend to confirm this.

In a study conducted in the year 2014 on 300 companies (consisting of 100 large and 200 small and medium enterprises), employee-oriented activities were declared by over 85% of entities. However, only half of the large companies (54%) and every fifth enterprise from the SME sector (19%) have implemented the CSR strategy. This indicated that the remaining entities conducted socially responsible activities on an ad hoc basis, if at all. What is more, only a small percentage of companies (31% large and 16% SME) had the effects of their CSR activities assessed [102]. In comparison with the findings of our original research, it is fair to say that there have been no significant changes in this respect. Measuring the effectiveness of environmental actions in HRM continues to be a rare practice, declared a mere 37.33% of young entities. The reason behind this could be the fact that sustainable HRM is a relatively new concept which requires further analyses, above all with respect to defining indicators for measuring and reporting [103].

Jastrzębska, in turn, draws our attention to the conditions that are characteristic of Poland and which have a slower impact than in other states' evolution of the CSR concept and, consequently, the rate of SRHRM implementation. She claims that in Poland there is an absence of strong social movements that stimulate the social participation of citizens, control the commercial sector or motivate social responsibility. Furthermore, a typical feature of Polish CSR is the lack of institutionalism, which can also be observed in the political sphere. This is evidenced, above all, by the absence of a superior governmental strategy referring to CSR development, the shortage of budgetary resources allocated to CSR development-related activities, and the assignment of participants to local governments pursuing various, dispersed EU-funded projects with respect to CSR [2]. Under such conditions, it is difficult to follow the worldwide CSR trends, and the SRHRM concept is, without a doubt, one of them.

Needless to say, the first signs of Polish public administration's involvement in CSR-related matters should be seen in positive terms. This is demonstrated by, among other things, the project named "Partnership for the Attainment of Sustainable Development Goals" initiated in 2017 by the

Ministry for Enterprise and the Ministry for Technology to integrate representatives of different environments for the purpose of effective realization of objectives on sustainable development. The above initiative is bound to raise awareness across a broader audience in terms of sustainable development's objectives as adopted by the international community, their importance for individual social groups, and the need of cooperation in their effective application [104], which may contribute to an increase in the interest in a comprehensive SRHRM implementation. A vital role in the popularization of practices of the broadly understood CSR, binding since the year 2017, is also played by Directive 2014/95/EU of the European Parliament and of the Council. This is because the Directive obliges large undertakings to disclose statements containing information relating to environmental matters, social and employee-related matters, respect for human rights, anti-corruption and bribery matters, but also to relate these practices with company strategies, the risk entailed and key outcome indicators [105]. In the opinion of the authors of this study, the reporting obligation may become a catalyst for positive change in the field of SRHRM and a precursor to a strategic approach to social responsibility in HRM. Hopefully, this will also contribute to an increase in the number of initiatives in the field.

4.3. The Correlation Between the Assessment of the Relation of SRHRM Practices with the Sustainable Development of Organizations and Their Realization in Young Enterprises

Over the course of the original research, an attempt was made to examine the correlation between the assessment of the relation of SRHRM practices with the sustainable development of organizations and their practical implementation. With a view to establishing the strength and direction of the interdependence of the variables, the Spearman's rank correlation coefficient was calculated (Table 6).

Table 6. The correlation between the assessment of the relation of SRHRM practices with the sustainable development of organizations and their realization in young enterprises.

Activity No.	The Assessment of the Strength of the Relation [1] (Variable X)	Activities Pursued in Enterprises [2] (Variable Y)	Rank X [3]	Rank Y [4]	Di Distance	Square of Distance di [2]
1	654	147	5	2	3	9
2	690	143	2	5	−3	9
3	553	113	15	15	0	0
4	568	129	13	11	2	4
5	546	119	16	13	3	9
6	672	146	3	4	−1	1
7	583	120	12	12	0	0
8	646	142	7	6	1	1
9	649	142	6	7	−1	1
10	416	47	32	33	−1	1
11	725	149	1	1	0	0
12	643	141	8	8	0	0
13	667	147	4	3	1	1
14	604	130	10	9	1	1
15	500	96	20	20	0	0
16	518	112	19	16	3	9
17	617	130	9	10	−1	1
18	561	105	14	18	−4	16
19	439	50	26	31	−5	25
20	362	25	34	34	0	0
21	360	23	35	35	0	0
22	593	119	11	14	−3	9
23	432	62	28	27	1	1
24	460	77	22	22	0	0

Table 6. Cont.

Activity No.	The Assessment of the Strength of the Relation [1] (Variable X)	Activities Pursued in Enterprises [2] (Variable Y)	Rank X [3]	Rank Y [4]	Di Distance	Square of Distance di [2]
25	495	86	21	21	0	0
26	443	68	25	24	1	1
27	459	71	23	23	0	0
28	451	64	24	26	−2	4
29	423	56	30	29	1	1
30	535	97	17	19	−2	4
31	531	106	18	17	1	1
32	417	56	31	30	1	1
33	438	66	27	25	2	4
34	425	62	29	28	1	1
35	405	49	33	32	1	1
Sum	-	-	-	-	-	116

[1] the sum of rating given to a particular practice by all the surveyed managers, with the adopted rating scale 1–5.; [2] the number of enterprises in which, according to the manager, a particular practice has been realized; [3] the position of a given practice in the ranking due to the sum of ratings awarded by managers; [4] the position of a given practice in the ranking due to the number of enterprises where it is realized.

$$r_d = 1 - (6 \times 116/35 \times (35^2 - 1)) = 0.984 \tag{1}$$

The 0.984 rank correlation coefficient demonstrates a very strong correlation between the assessment of the relation between socially responsible practices and the sustainable development of organizations and their practical implementation in the studied enterprises. This indicated that the practices which are pursued are those which—in the opinion of the management—are vital to the policy of sustainable development, as expressed by the high rating of their relation.

To describe the correlations between the impact of the above-mentioned variables, we used regression analysis. Figure 1 represents a linear regression function type II, which specified the development of correlations between the realization of SRHRM practices under the influence of changes in the rating of their assessment of the relation of SRHRM practices with the sustainable development of organizations in the study sample.

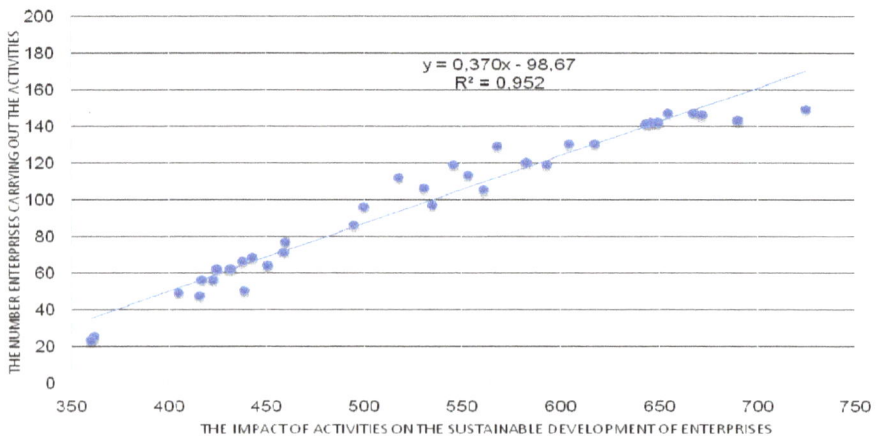

Figure 1. Correlation between the assessment of the relation of SRHRM practices with the sustainable development of organizations and their implementation in young Polish enterprises.

The resultant regression coefficient a_y = 0.3706 tells us that, in the study population, a 1-point impact growth in the assessment of the relation of SRHRM practices with the sustainable development of organizations results in an average increase of its realization by 0.3706. The coefficient of determination R^2 = 0.9529 determines that in 95.29% the changeability of the number of enterprises pursuing socially responsible HRM practices was explained by the estimated regression function (through the variability of the effect of activities on the sustainable development of young companies). Next, the coefficient of linear indetermination (1 − 0.9529 = 0.0471 = 4.71%) yields information that in the studied sample of enterprises, the mere 4.7% changeability in the number of companies realizing social activity was not explained by the variability of the impact of activities on the sustainable development of enterprises.

The above-described regression function type II is a proxy variable of the function describing the studied relationship in all young enterprises in Poland. In the case of concluding with respect to unknown parameters of equations on the basis of data from the sample, a standard error of estimate of the regression coefficient S_a, a standard error of estimate of the polynomial S_b, and residual standard deviation S_z were calculated. The linear regression model is represented by the following equation:

$$y_i = 0.3706 \times x_i - 98.678 + z_{yi} \tag{2}$$

$$[S_{ay} = 0.014] \quad [S_{by} = 7.708] \quad [S_{zy} = 8.54]$$

The standard error of estimate of the regression coefficient S_a informs us that when estimating the regression coefficient in a population of generally young companies on the basis of the regression equation we may err by 0.014. The standard error of estimate of the polynomial S_b informs us that when estimating the polynomial, we may go wrong by 7.708, whereas the residual standard deviation S_z informs us that the real value of the dependent variable differs by 8.54 from its theoretical value computed on the basis of the equation. The following hypotheses were made when drawing conclusions about the regression to the whole body of young enterprises:

$$H_0 : \alpha_y = 0 \quad H_0 : \beta_y = 0$$

$$H_1 : \alpha_y \neq 0 \quad H_1 : \beta_y \neq 0$$

The zero hypotheses presumed that the regression coefficient α_y and the polynomial β_y in the population were statistically insignificant; while the alternative hypotheses assumed that the specified parameters were statistically significant. To verify the validity of assumptions stated in H_0 the t-Student statistics was employed.

$$t = a_y / S_{ay}; \quad t = 0.3706/0.014 = 26.471; t = b_y / S_{by}; \quad t = -98.678/7.708 = -12.802; \tag{3}$$

The critical area is marked by the relation $P(|t| \geq t_{\alpha;s}) = \alpha$ assuming the level of confidence to be α = 0.05 and the degrees of freedom s = n − 2, the result obtained was t = 2.037. When comparing the computed test values with the critical value, it was demonstrated that the parameters α_y, $P(26.471 > 2.037) = 0.05$, and β_y, $P(12.802 > 2.037) = 0.05$ are statistically significant. This shows that the regression function describing the rating of the assessment of the relation of SRHRM practices with the sustainable development of organizations and their implementation in young Polish enterprises computed on the basis of the sample constitutes the basis for concluding on the presence of the said correlation in the whole body, i.e., in all young Polish enterprises.

5. Conclusions

Socially responsible activities of enterprises in our modern world have become one of the fundamental elements of assessment of the position of an undertaking on the global market and a unique measure of its competitiveness. Therefore, the CSR concept—and SRHRM as its vital

Sustainability **2019**, *11*, 1044

component—are becoming increasingly popular. The analysis of source literature demonstrates that SRHRM not only aids the development of sustainable organizations but is also an effective instrument for gaining a competitive advantage, favouring improvement of relations with company employees, increasing their satisfaction, loyalty, and motivation, while boosting both the internal and external company image. Those undertakings that consider SRHRM practices to be a permanent element of the business model they pursue and one of the key competencies are predestined to top the list of global companies and continue to increase their capacity to constantly generate added value. The implementation of the SRHRM concept is, without a doubt, evidence of the HRM system maturity. Maturity in the field of SRHRM may, in turn, be indicative of the general maturity of a given entity in the CSR area. Therefore, analysis of the social aspects of social HRM responsibility should become a more frequent component of assessments of one's developmental potential and enterprise valuations.

To evaluate the scope of implementation of the SRHRM concept in the Polish reality, empirical studies have been conducted on a representative sample of young Polish enterprises. The said studies allowed the positive verification of the following hypotheses:

Hypothesis 1. *Socially responsible activities declared by Polish managers in the area of HRM have an irregular relation with the sustainable development of young organizations.*

Hypothesis 2. *There is correlation between the assessment of the relation of SRHRM practices with the sustainable development of organizations and their implementation in young enterprises.*

The analysis of correlations demonstrated a very strong positive correlation between the evaluation of the relation of SRHRM practices with the sustainable development of organizations and their practical implementation. Research demonstrated that the higher the rating of the relation of a given activity in the opinion of Polish managers, the more often it was implemented in the studied companies. This allowed the formulation of the following conclusion: in order to increase the scope of implementation of the SRHRM concept in the Polish reality, it is necessary to raise awareness of the importance of SRHRM practices at managerial level for the sustainable development of organizations.

Furthermore, the empirical studies show that SRHRM practices are adopted relatively frequently by young Polish enterprises. Nonetheless, there seems to be a low level of maturity with respect to the implementation of the SRHRM concept under Polish conditions. The following symptoms are evidence of the above conclusion:

—the focus of a significant rate of the studied entities on obligatory practices, i.e., Those required by law;
—a low rate of entities which hold ethical certificates;
—low interest in the issue of compliance with ethical requirements by contractual partners;
—a widespread lack of developed measurement and reporting procedures regarding SRHRM.

The analysis of regression defining the assessment of the impact of actions concerning CSR in the area of HRM on their realization in young enterprises is the basis for the conclusion that this correlation is present in the whole collection, that is in all Polish enterprises. However, the results cannot be extrapolated directly to any other country, because the work environment in different countries has its own specific conditions. One of the drawbacks of the results gained with the usage of this research method is the fact that the obtained data express only the managers' opinions. However, it should be underlined that the respondents were managers responsible for the realization of the surveyed HR functions in their organizations, that is people having the required knowledge and experience to properly assess the impact of HRM practices on the sustainable development of the enterprises. Sustainable development of enterprises is difficult to be surveyed because it is shaped by many various factors. In this paper the authors concentrated on one of them, that is SRHRM practices. This creates a limitation in the interpretation of the obtained results.

Sustainability **2019**, *11*, 1044

It appears that in the Polish reality, there are still many entrepreneurs who do not see SRHRM as an effective instrument of HR function improvement. This suggests that the need to disseminate knowledge concerning the usefulness of the society-oriented attitude in the field of human resource management and the emphasis on the relationships between the realization of the said assumptions and the attainment of personnel goals and sustainable development objectives. CSR should feature permanently on the personnel agenda of organizations, for this is the only way in which it can bring long-term positive outcomes as expressed through an accurate perception of an enterprise by its internal and external stakeholders. In the long term, SRHRM activities should be seen as a type of investment which pays off in terms of the increased involvement of employees, improved employee performance, broadened perspectives of development, and strengthened investor confidence, which favors the effective allocation of capital, facilitates the achievement of investment goals, and stimulated sustainable organization-building.

Given the dynamic situation on the labor market, affected by tendencies such as the natural growth rate, the aging of societies, falling unemployment rates, and migration, we should expect SRHRM to be more and more frequently used as an inseparable and permanent element of the personnel strategy. For it must be emphasized that the implementation of the concept may not be limited to an ad hoc participation and may not focus on selected activities only. These must not be pseudo-social initiatives treated as a marketing tool, directed purely at the attainment of image benefits as part of employer branding. Durability (strategic persistence) must be an immanent feature of personnel initiatives taken up as part of SRHRM. Only a long-distance SRHRM strategy, with the potential to become firmly rooted in the organizational culture, may become a foundation for the development of sustainable employees who support the idea of sustainable development of organizations.

Given the advantages of SRHRM implementation and its proven importance for sustainable development of organizations on the one hand and the determined low level of maturity in the field of its practical implementation in the studied entities on the other hand, the authors opine that a significant area for further research is the identification and analysis of factors that precondition the realization of this concept in Polish enterprises. The authors' intention is to continue research directed at the diagnosis of stimuluses and barriers to the implementation of the SRHRM concept.

Author Contributions: E.B. proposed the research concept, reviewed source literature, and wrote the article. A.M.-K. designed the methodology of quantitative research, carried out the statistical analysis of the study findings, and wrote the article.

Acknowledgments: The results of the research carried out under the research theme No. 430/15/S were financed from the science grant granted by the Ministry of Science and Higher Education.

Conflicts of Interest: The authors declare no conflicts of interest.

References

1. Rosińska-Bukowska, M. Społeczna odpowiedzialność biznesu w procesie kreacji wartości dodanej przedsiębiorstwa. In *Kreacja Wartości Przedsiębiorstw. Nowe Trendy i Kierunki Rozwoju*; Jabłoński, M., Zamasz, K., Eds.; WSB: Dąbrowa Górnicza, Poland, 2012; pp. 331–357, ISBN 978-83-62897-34-6.
2. Jastrzębska, E. Ewolucja społecznej odpowiedzialności biznesu w Polsce. *Kwartalnik Kolegium Ekonomiczno-Społecznego Studia i Prace SGH* **2016**, *4*, 85–101.
3. Jabłoński, A. *Zrównoważony Rozwój a Zrównoważony Biznes w Budowie Wartości Przedsiębiorstw Społecznie Odpowiedzialnych*; Zeszyty Naukowe Wyższej Szkoły Humanitas; Oficyna Wydawnicza Humanitas: Zarządzanie, Poland, 2010; Volume 2, pp. 15–30.
4. Report of the World Commission on Environment and Development: Our Common Future. Available online: http://www.un-documents.net/our-common-future.pdf (accessed on 27 August 2018).
5. Mazur-Wierzbicka, E. Koncepcja zrównoważonego rozwoju jako podstawa gospodarowania środowiskiem przyrodniczym. In *Funkcjonowanie gospodarki polskiej w warunkach integracji i globalizacji*; Kopycińska, D., Ed.; Katedra Mikroekonomii Uniwersytetu Szczecińskiego: Szczecin, Poland, 2005; pp. 33–44, ISBN 9788391748763.

6.   Colbert, B.A.; Kurucz, E.C. Three conceptions of triple bottom line business sustainability and the role of HRM. *Hum. Resour. Plan.* **2007**, *30*, 21–29.

7.   Rimanoczy, I.; Pearson, T. Role of HR in the new world of sustainability. *Ind. Commer. Train.* **2010**, *42*, 11–17. [CrossRef]

8.   Skowroński, A. Zrównoważony rozwój perspektywą dalszego postępu cywilizacji. *Probl. Ekorozw.* **2006**, *2*, 47–57.

9.   Elkington, J. *Cannibals with Forks: The Triple Bottom Line of Twenty-First Century Business*; Capstone: Mankato, MN, USA, 1997.

10. ISO 26000:2010 Guidance on Social Responsibility. Available online: https://www.iso.org/standard/42546 .html (accessed on 17 May 2018).

11. Adamczyk, J.; Nitkiewicz, T. *Programowanie Zrównoważonego Rozwoju Przedsiębiorstw*; PWE: Warszawa, Poland, 2007; ISBN 83-208-1705-8. (In Polish)

12. Porter, M.E.; Kramer, M.R. Tworzenie wartości dla biznesu i społeczeństwa. *Harv. Bus. Rev. Polska* **2011**, *5*, 80–87. (In Polish)

13. Rok, B. *Odpowiedzialny Biznes w Nieodpowiedzialnym Świecie*; Akademia Rozwoju Filantropii w Polsce, Forum Odpowiedzialnego Biznesu: Warszawa, Poland, 2001. (In Polish)

14. Carroll, A.B. Carroll's Pyramid of CSR: Taking Another Look. 2016. Available online: https://doi.org/10.1 186/s40991-016-0004-6 (accessed on 15 February 2019).

15. Hart, S. *Capitalism at the Crossroads: Aligning Commerce, Earth, and Humanity*, 2nd ed.; FT Press: Upper Saddle River, NJ, USA, 2007.

16. Pichola, I.; Nocoń, A. *Jak Angażować Interesariuszy Firmy do Budowania jej Wartości, Odpowiedzialny Biznes*; Harvard Business Review: Warszawa, Poland, 2008. (In Polish)

17. Szumiak-Samolej, J. *Odpowiedzialny Biznes w Gospodarce Sieciowej*; Poltext: Warszawa, Poland, 2013; ISBN 978-83-7561-360-5. (In Polish)

18. Hys, K.; Hawrysz, L. Corporate Social Responsibility Reporting. *China-USA Bus. Rev.* **2012**, *11*, 1515–1524.

19. Hediger, W. Welfare and capital-theoretic foundations of corporate social responsibility and corporate sustainability. *J. Socio-Econ.* **2010**, *39*, 518–526. [CrossRef]

20. Cohen, E.; Taylor, S.; Muller-Camen, M. *HRM's Role in Corporate Social and Environmental Sustainability*; SHRM Report: Alexandria, VA, USA, 2012.

21. Jamali, D.; Safieddine, A.M.; Rabbath, M. Corporate Governance and Corporate Social Responsibility Synergies and Interrelationships. *Corp. Gov. Int. Rev.* **2008**, *16*, 443–459. [CrossRef]

22. Buchholz, A.K.; Brown, J.; Shabana, K. *Corporate governance and corporate social responsibility. The Oxford Handbook of Corporate Social Responsibility*; Crane, A., McWilliams, A., Matten, D., Moon, J., Siegel, D.S., Eds.; Oxford University Press: New York, NY, USA, 2008; pp. 327–345, ISBN 9780199211593.

23. Harjoto, M.A.; Jo, H. Corporate Governance and CSR Nexus. *J. Bus. Ethics* **2011**, *100*, 45–67. [CrossRef]

24. Wilewska, M. Corporate governance i corporate social responsibility—Powiązania i wzajemne relacje. *Zarządzanie Finans.* **2013**, *2*, 67–75.

25. Giroud, X.; Mueller, H. Corporate governance, product market competition, and equity prices. *J. Financ.* **2011**, *66*, 563–600. [CrossRef]

26. Coles, J.L.; Li, Z.; Wang, A.Y. Industry Tournament Incentives. *Rev. Financial Stud.* **2018**, *31*, 1418–1459. [CrossRef]

27. Core, J.; Guay, W. The use of equity grants to manage optimal equity incentive levels. *J. Account. Econ.* **1999**, *28*, 151–184. [CrossRef]

28. Li, Z. Mutual monitoring and corporate governance. *J. Bank. Financ.* **2014**, *45*, 255–269.

29. Dyllick, T.; Hockerts, K. Beyond the Business Case for Corporate Sustainability. *Bus. Strategy Environ.* **2002**, *11*, 130–141. [CrossRef]

30. Spreitzer, G.; Porath, C.L.; Gibson, C.B. Toward Human Sustainability: How to Enable More Thriving at Work. *Organ. Dyn.* **2012**, *41*, 155–162. [CrossRef]

31. Wilkinson, A.; Hill, M.; Gollan, P. The sustainability debate. *Int. J. Oper. Prod. Manag.* **2001**, *12*, 1492–1502. [CrossRef]

32. Ehnert, I. Sustainability and Human Resource Management: Reasoning and Applications on Corporate Websites. *Eur. J. Int. Manag.* **2009**, *4*, 419–438. [CrossRef]

33. Renwick, D.; Redman, T.; Maguire, D. Green HRM: A Review, Process Model, and Research Agenda. Discussion Paper No 2008.01. The University of Sheffield, April 2008. Available online: https://www.sheffield.ac.uk/polopoly_fs/1.120337!/file/Green-HRM.pdf (accessed on 27 August 2018).

34. Jabbour, J.; Santos, F. The Central Role of Human Resource Management in the Search for Sustainable Organizations. *Int. J. Hum. Resour. Manag.* **2008**, *12*, 2133–2154. [CrossRef]

35. Wirtenberg, J.; Harmon, J.; Fairfield, K.D. HR's Role in Building a Sustainable Enterprise: Insights from Some of the World's Best. *Hum. Resour. Plan.* **2007**, *30*, 10–20.

36. Spooner, K.; Kaine, S. Defining Sustainability and Human Resource Management. *Int. Employ. Relat. Rev.* **2010**, *2*, 70–81.

37. Obrad, C.; Gherhes, V. A Human Resources Perspective on Responsible Corporate Behavior. Case Study: The Multinational Companies in Western Romania. *Sustainability* **2018**, *10*, 726. [CrossRef]

38. Harmon, J.; Fairfield, K.D.; Wirtenberg, J. Missing an Opportunity: HR Leadership and Sustainability. *People Strategy* **2010**, *33*, 16–21.

39. Glade, B. Human Resources: CSR and Business Sustainability-HR's Leadership Role. *N. Z. Manag.* **2008**, *9*, 51–52.

40. Jabbour, C.J.C.; Santos, F.C.A.; Nagano, M.C. Environmental Management System and Human Resource Practices: Is there a link between them in four Brazilian Companies? *J. Clean. Prod.* **2008**, *17*, 1922–1925. [CrossRef]

41. Liebowitz, J. The role of HR in achieving a sustainability culture. *J. Sustain. Dev.* **2010**, *3*, 50–57. [CrossRef]

42. Kramar, R. Beyond strategic human resource management: Is sustainable human resource management the next approach? *Int. J. Hum. Resour. Manag.* **2014**, *25*, 1069–1089. [CrossRef]

43. Ehnert, I.; Harry, W.; Zink, K.J. Sustainability and HRM: An introduction to the field. In *Sustainability and Human Resource Management: Developing Sustainable Business Organizations*; Ehnert, I., Harry, W., Zink, K.J., Eds.; Springer: Heidelberg, Germany, 2014; pp. 3–32, ISBN 978-3-642-37524-8.

44. Pabian, A. Zrównoważone zarządzanie zasobami ludzkimi. Zarys problematyki. *Zesz. Nauk. Politech. Częstochowskiej Zarządzanie* **2015**, *17*, 7–16. (In Polish)

45. Pocztowski, A. Zrównoważone zarządzanie zasobami ludzkimi w teorii i praktyce. *Zarządzanie Finans.* **2016**, *2*, 303–314. (In Polish)

46. Pabian, A. Sustainable personnel—Pracownicy przedsiębiorstwa przyszłości. *Zarządzanie Zasobami Ludzkimi* **2011**, *5*, 9–18. (In Polish)

47. Cohen, S. *Sustainability Management*; Columbia University Press: New York, NY, USA, 2011; ISBN 9780231152587.

48. Majewski, D. Zrównoważeni pracownicy i ich satysfakcja z pracy. *Edukacja Ekonomistów i Menedżerów* **2012**, *2*, 155–167. (In Polish) [CrossRef]

49. Hart, S.L.; Milstein, M.B. Creating sustainable value. *Acad. Manag. Executive* **2003**, *2*, 56–67. [CrossRef]

50. Grudzewski, W.M.; Hejduk, I.K.; Sankowska, A.; Wańtuchowicz, M. *Sustainability w Biznesie, Czyli Przedsiębiorstwo Przyszłości: Zmiany Paradygmatów i Koncepcji Zarządzania*; Warszawa: Poltext, Poland, 2010; ISBN 978-83-7561-257-8. (In Polish)

51. Abidin, N.Z.; Pasquire, Ch.L. Revolutionize value management: A mode towards sustainability. *Int. J. Proj. Manag.* **2007**, *25*, 275–282. [CrossRef]

52. Burchard-Dziubińska, M. Zrównoważony biznes-dlaczego tak trudno o sukces? In *Przedsiębiorstwo w Warunkach Zrównoważonej Gospodarki*; Powichrowska, B., Ed.; Wyższa Szkoła Ekonomiczna: Białystok, Poland, 2011; ISBN 978-83-61247-38-8. (In Polish)

53. Vickers, M.R. Business Ethics and the HR Role: Past, Present, and Future. *Hum. Resour. Plan.* **2005**, *28*, 26–32.

54. Taylor, S.; Osland, J.; Egri, C.P. Guest Editors' Introduction: Introduction to HRM's Role in Sustainability: Systems, Strategies, and Practices. *Hum. Resour. Manag.* **2012**, *5*, 789–798. [CrossRef]

55. Haugh, H.M.; Talwar, A. How Do Corporations Embed Sustainability Across the Organization? *Acad. Manag. Learn. Educ.* **2010**, *9*, 384–396. [CrossRef]

56. Sharma, S.; Sharma, J.; Devi, A. Corporate social responsibility: The key role of human resource management. *Bus. Intell. J.* **2009**, *2*, 205–213.

57. Jang, S.; Ardichvili, A. The Role of HRD in Embedding Corporate Social Responsibility (CSR) in Organizations Working Paper submitted to the 17th International Research Conference on HRD across Europe 2016, Stream: Scholarly Practitioner Research. Available online: https://www.ufhrd.co.uk/wordpress/wp-content/uploads/2016/10/paper_125.pdf (accessed on 30 August 2018).

58. Fenwick, T. Corporate Social Responsibility and HRD. In *Handbook of Human Resource Development*; Chalofsky, N.E., Rocco, T.S., Morris, M.L., Eds.; John Wiley: Hoboken, NJ, USA, 2014; pp. 164–179, ISBN 978-1-118-45402-2.

59. Pfeffer, J. Building sustainable organizations: The human factor. *Acad. Manag. Perspect.* **2010**, *24*, 34–45.

60. Ardichvili, A. The Role of HRD in CSR, Sustainability, and Ethics a Relational Model. *Hum. Resour. Dev. Rev.* **2013**, *4*, 456–473. [CrossRef]

61. Garavan, T.; McGuire, D. Human resource development and society: Human resource development's role in embedding corporate social responsibility, sustainability, and ethics in organizations. *Adv. Dev. Hum. Resour.* **2010**, *5*, 487–507. [CrossRef]

62. Wilcox, T. Human Resource Development as an Element of Corporate Social Responsibility. *Asia Pac. J. Hum. Resour.* **2006**, *44*, 184–196. [CrossRef]

63. Inyang, B.J.; Awa, H.O.; Enuoh, R.O. CSR-HRM Nexus: Defining the Role Engagement of the Human Resources Professionals. *Int. J. Bus. Soc. Sci.* **2011**, *5*, 118–126.

64. Boudreau, J.W.; Ramstad, P.M. Talentship. Talent Segmentation and Sustainability: A New HR Decision Science Paradigm for a New Strategy Definition. *Hum. Resour. Manag.* **2005**, *2*, 129–136. [CrossRef]

65. Ehnert, I. *Sustainable Human Resource Management: A Conceptual and Exploratory Analysis from a Paradox Perspective*; Physica-Verlag: Heidelberg, Germany, 2009; ISBN 978-3-7908-2187-1.

66. Guest, D.E. Human Resource Management and Performance: Still Searching for Some Answers. *Hum. Resour. Manag. J.* **2011**, *21*, 3–13. [CrossRef]

67. Thom, N.; Zaugg, R. Nachhaltiges und innovatives Personalmanagement: Spitzengruppenbefragung in europäischen Unternehmungen und Institutionen. In *Nachhaltiges Innovationsmanagement*; Schwarz, E.J., Ed.; Gabler: Wiesbaden, Germany, 2004; pp. 217–245.

68. Voegtlin, Ch.; Greenwood, M. Corporate social responsibility and human resource management: A systematic review and conceptual analysis. *Hum. Resour. Manag. Rev.* **2016**, *3*, 181–197. [CrossRef]

69. Ardichvili, A. Sustainability of nations, communities, organizations and individuals: The role of HRD. *Hum. Resour. Dev. Int.* **2011**, *4*, 371–374. [CrossRef]

70. Shen, J. Developing the concept of socially responsible international human resource management. *Int. J. Hum. Resour. Manag.* **2011**, *6*, 1351–1363. [CrossRef]

71. Greenwood, M. Ethics and HRM: A review and conceptual analysis. *J. Bus. Ethics* **2002**, *3*, 261–278. [CrossRef]

72. Cooke, F.L.; He, Q.L. Corporate social responsibility and HRM in China: A study of textile and apparel enterprises. *Asia Pac. Bus. Rev.* **2010**, *3*, 355–376. [CrossRef]

73. Dupont, C.; Ferauge, P.; Giuliano, R. The Impact of Corporate Social Responsibility on Human Resource Management: GDF SUEZ's Case. *Int. Bus. Res.* **2013**, *12*, 145–155. [CrossRef]

74. De Stefano, F.; Bagdadli, S.; Camuffo, A. The HR role in corporate social responsibility and sustainability: A boundary-shifting literature review. *Hum. Resour. Manag.* **2018**, *2*, 549–566. [CrossRef]

75. Jamali, D.R.; Dirani, A.E.; Harwood, I.A. Exploring Human Resource Management Roles in Corporate Social Responsibility: The CSR-HRM Co-creation Model. *Bus. Ethics A Eur. Rev.* **2015**, *2*, 125–143. [CrossRef]

76. Becker, W.S.; Carbo, J.A.; Langella, I.M. Beyond self-interest: Integrating social responsibility and supply chain management with human resource development. *Hum. Resour. Dev. Rev.* **2010**, *2*, 144–168. [CrossRef]

77. Becker, W.S. Are you leading a socially responsible and sustainable human resource function? *People Strategy* **2011**, *34*, 18–23.

78. Preuss, L.; Haunschild, A.; Matten, D. The rise of CSR: Implications for HRM and employee representation. *Int. J. Hum. Resour. Manag.* **2009**, *4*, 953–973. [CrossRef]

79. Garavan, T.N.; Heraty, N.; Rock, A.; Dalton, E. Conceptualizing the behavioral barriers to CSR and CS in organizations: A typology of HRD interventions. *Adv. Dev. Hum. Resour.* **2010**, *5*, 587–613. [CrossRef]

80. Bhattacharya, C.B.; Sen, S.; Korschun, D. Using corporate social responsibility to win the war for talent. *Sloan Manag. Rev.* **2008**, *2*, 37–44.

81. Davies, I.A.; Crane, A. Corporate social responsibility in small-and medium-size enterprises: Investigating employee engagement in fair trade companies. *Bus. Ethics A Eur. Rev.* **2010**, *2*, 126–139. [CrossRef]

82. Gond, J.P.; Igalens, J.; Swaen, V.; El Akremi, A. The human resources contribution to responsible leadership: An exploration of the CSR–HR interface. *J. Bus. Ethics* **2011**, *98*, 115–132. [CrossRef]

83. Wachowiak, P. *Wrażliwość Społeczna Przedsiębiorstwa. Analiza i Pomiar*; Oficyna Wydawnicza SGH: Warszawa, Poland, 2013; ISBN 978-83-7378-851-0. (In Polish)

84. Paliszkiewicz, J. *Zaufanie w Zarządzaniu*; PWN: Warszawa, Poland, 2013; ISBN 978-83-01-19371-3. (In Polish)

85. Greening, D.W.; Turban, D.B. Corporate social Performance as a competitive advantage in attracting a quality workforce. *Bus. Soc.* **2000**, *39*, 254–280. [CrossRef]

86. Odriozola, M.D.; Martín, A.; Luna, L. The relationship between labour social responsibility practices and reputation. *Int. J. Manpow.* **2015**, *36*, 236–251. [CrossRef]

87. Valentine, S.; Fleischman, G. Ethics programs, perceived corporate social responsibility and job satisfaction. *J. Bus. Ethics* **2008**, *77*, 159–172. [CrossRef]

88. Lindgreen, A.; Swaen, V. Corporate social responsibility. *Int. J. Manag. Rev.* **2010**, *12*, 1–7. [CrossRef]

89. Fapohunda, T.M. The Human Resource Management Dimensions of Corporate Social Responsibility. *Eur. J. Res. Reflect. Manag. Sci.* **2015**, *2*, 1–14.

90. Bombiak, E.; Marciniuk-Kluska, A. Green Human Resource Management as a Tool for the Sustainable Development of Enterprises: Polish Young Company Experience. *Sustainability* **2018**, *10*, 1739. [CrossRef]

91. Rogowski, R. Praktyka wdrażania CSR w polskich przedsiębiorstwach w opinii doradców. *Ann. Ethics Econ. Life* **2016**, *19*, 37–54. (In Polish) [CrossRef]

92. Himmelberg, C.; Hubbard, R. Incentive Pay and the Market for CEOS: An Analysis of Pay-for-Performance Sensitivity (June 2000). Presented at Tuck-JFE Contemporary Corporate Governance Conference; 2000. Available online: https://ssrn.com/abstract=2360891 (accessed on 2 January 2019).

93. Dang, C.; Li, F. Measuring Firm Size in Empirical Corporate Finance. *J. Bank. Financ.* **2018**, *86*, 159–176. [CrossRef]

94. Stankevičiūtė, Ž.; Savanevičienė, A. Designing Sustainable HRM: The Core Characteristics of Emerging Field. *Sustainability* **2018**, *10*, 4798. [CrossRef]

95. Raport Odpowiedzialny Biznes w Polsce 2017. Dobre Praktyki. Available online: http://odpowiedzialnybiznes.pl/publikacje/raport-2017/ (accessed on 7 September 2018). (In Polish)

96. Wolska, G. Zaangażowanie przedsiębiorstw w realizację koncepcji społecznej odpowiedzialności biznesu. Studia Ekonomiczne. *Zeszyty Naukowe Uniwersytetu Ekonomicznego w Katowicach* **2015**, *236*, 85–95. (In Polish)

97. Furmańska-Maruszak, A.; Sudolska, A. Relacje z pracownikami jako obszar wdrażania CSR. *Organ. Kier.* **2017**, *2*, 253–267. (In Polish)

98. Raport Odpowiedzialny Biznes w Polsce 2016. Dobre Praktyki. Available online: http://odpowiedzialnybiznes.pl/publikacje/raport-2016/ (accessed on 7 September 2018). (In Polish)

99. Raport Odpowiedzialny Biznes w Polsce 2011. Dobre Praktyki. Available online: http://odpowiedzialnybiznes.pl/wp-content/uploads/2014/01/Raport2011.pdf (accessed on 7 September 2018). (In Polish)

100. Głuszek, E. Wykorzystywanie inicjatyw społecznych w budowaniu atrybutów dobrej reputacji przedsiębiorstwa. *Prace Naukowe Uniwersytetu Ekonomicznego we Wrocławiu* **2013**, *288*, 22–36. (In Polish)

101. Raport Odpowiedzialny Biznes w Polsce 2010. Dobre Praktyki. Available online: http://odpowiedzialnybiznes.pl/wp-content/uploads/2014/02/Raport_odpowiedzialny_biznes_w_Polsce_2010-1301645271.pdf (accessed on 7 September 2018). (In Polish)

102. Wojtysiak-Sowa, E. Obowiązkowy Raport CSR? Polskie Firmy nie są na Niego Gotowe! Available online: http://jbcomm.pl/aktualnosci/obowiazkowy-raport-csr-polskie-firmy-nie-sa-na-niego-gotowe/ (accessed on 28 August 2018).

103. Ehnert, I.; Parsa, S.; Roper, I.; Wagner, M.; Muller-Camen, M. Reporting on sustainability and HRM: A comparative study of sustainability reporting practices by the world's largest companies. *Int. J. Hum. Resour. Manag.* **2016**, *27*, 88–108. [CrossRef]

104. Partnerstwo na rzecz realizacji celów zrównoważonego rozwoju w Polsce. Ministerstwo Przedsiębiorczości i Technologii. Available online: https://www.mpit.gov.pl/strony/zadania/zrownowazony-rozwoj/agenda-2030/partnerstwo-na-rzecz-realizacji-celow-zrownowazonego-rozwoju-w-polsce/ (accessed on 24 August 2018).
105. Wróbel, M. Raportowanie społecznej odpowiedzialności w Polsce w świetle unormowań Dyrektywy Parlamenty Europejskiego i Rady 2014/95/UE. *Zesz. Nauk. Wyższej Szkoły Humanit. Zarządzanie* **2016**, *2*, 83–94. (In Polish) [CrossRef]

sustainability

MDPI

Article

Value Migration to the Sustainable Business Models of Digital Economy Companies on the Capital Market

Marek Jabłoński

Scientific Institute of Entrepreneurship and Innovation, Faculty in Chorzów, WSB University in Poznań, Sportowa 29, 41-506 Chorzów, Poland; marek.jablonski@ottima-plus.com.pl

Received: 29 June 2018; Accepted: 23 August 2018; Published: 31 August 2018

Abstract: The topic of a sustainable business model is currently the subject of much scientific research that covers a wide range of topics, from terminological aspects to aspects related to the impact of sustainability factors on company development. So far, however, the topic of sustainability in business models operating in electronic markets has only been studied to some extent. This article covers broad research into the value migration to sustainable business models of companies operating in the digital economy on the capital market. The aim of the article is to present key results of research into value migration to sustainable business models of companies operating in the digital economy on the capital market. The relevant literature on the trends in the application of the sustainability concept in the digital economy, the attributes of business models, and the interpretation of value within the concept of business models is also reviewed. The results obtained are ambiguous.

Keywords: value migration; value capture; sustainable business model; digital economy

1. Introduction

The digital economy is shaping many new business models. The development of business models based on the Internet initiates many solutions [1]. The Internet is constantly opening new spaces for creating added value [2]. The dynamic development of networking is driving by the fast-paced evolution of digital technologies that foster the shaping of innovative business models. A key topic for modern approaches to business model design is achieving sustainability.

Digital economy business models based on the assumptions of contemporary trends, such as the sharing economy, the network economy, the Big Data and the circular economy, in addition to being based on IT applications in many cases, are also based on rules that are different from the traditional approaches to the neoclassical economy. The applicability of these solutions means that they are increasingly adopted by business practice, which results in undermining existing business models. Sometimes doubts arise about the integrity and even in some cases, the legality, of the proposed solutions. Their important attribute is that they are based on community development. It ensures better availability of goods, rationality of their use and improvement of people's quality of life. Trends in the digital economy influence changes in the perception and understanding of the essence of the modern world and the approach to social, ecological and economic aspects.

The concept of sustainability, widely explored in science in recent years, can play an important role in shaping and adjusting these innovative business models. As regards the concept of sustainability, the key role is played by a longer perspective of studying business, which, in the context of the dynamic development of new technologies creates new challenges, such as positive or negative perceptions of digital platforms by society.

Generally, Sustainable Development ensures the preservation of natural resources, which ensures the natural function of local ecosystems and of nature in general. Sustainable Development influence on solidarization and cooperation with other communities. Economic Sustainable Development ensures quality of life through economic self-determination and self-development of both individuals and societies [3]. Based on the assumptions of this concept, which ideologically refers to the macroeconomic approach, its narrower trend focused on building the theory and application solutions called sustainability has emerged. It is a model to keep managers predisposing their specific attitude to business management.

Generally, in theory and practice, several approaches to sustainability can be distinguished:

The classic approach broadly described in the literature and well-recognized as the Triple Bottom Line [4]. This approach is often used by mature companies which create the strategy based on stakeholder analysis and corporate social responsibility [5]. Their business model incorporates a balance of ecological, social and economic factors. In their strategy of competitive advantage these companies apply the triple bottom line rules for example by including ecologically friendly products into their offer, undertaking activities for positive impact on environmental protection, and striking a balance between all stakeholders interests. There are different aspects, which are described in the range of classical approaches to sustainability, for example: typology [6], aspect of life cycle of enterprises [7], rules for corporate social responsibility [8], and green supply chain [9].

The second approach is based on assumptions, for example of S. Schaltegger et al., who say that: 'The value proposition must provide both ecological or social and economic value through offering products and services–business models for sustainability describe, analyze, manage, and communicate (i) a company's sustainable value proposition to its customers, and all other stakeholders; (ii) how it creates and delivers this value; (iii) and how it captures economic value while maintaining or regenerating natural, social, and economic capital beyond its organizational boundaries [10]. In this holistic approach 'no sustainable value can be created for customers without creating value to a broader range of stakeholders'. This also includes a management approach which aims at achieving success in a fair manner for employees. This topic is widely developed in the literature [11–13]. Schaltegger approach to sustainability is focused on the assumption that the condition for companies' success is to design business models for sustainability, not as in the approach of Triple Bottom Line to meet conditions adequate to social, economic and ecological behavior. The essence of the newly designed business model is the use of sustainability attributes to build a competitive advantage.

The third approach addresses the specific aspect of economic sustainability in combination with the emerging shared economy business models that are enabled by the networked economy. It is very important for the sustained continuity of these business models to consider topics such as social, ecological and labor rules, which may be captured in legal requirements but also in social norms and values. The concept of the sharing economy is now widely discussed in literature [14–17]. This approach differs significantly from the previous ones because it focuses on the ethics of business behavior in the context of legal conditions. Especially, that new solutions undermine existing business models which raises a lot of controversy. In addition, new concepts using social communication platforms provide opportunities for better access to goods for those social groups that could not afford it. In this way, a new social order is shaped, which requires extensive theoretical research and verification of application solutions.

The fourth approach to the understanding of the concept of sustainability is sustainability's role in creating the New Theory of Property Rights, which will be important in the context of designing business models [18]. Property rights emphasize the importance of individual and transferable property rights for an effective allocation of resources in the economy. The theory of property rights assumes that property rights allow for limiting the scope of non-changeable relations in the economy [19].

This concept refers to the difficult relationship and even contradictions between ownership and the fulfillment of sustainability requirements. These dilemmas are crucial for the success of the implementation of balanced solutions in the social, economic and environmental spheres. To some, sustainability primarily refers to energy efficiency or to the slightly broader principles of efficient resource conservation. To others, sustainability requires radical changes in our social and political institutions. Indeed, some proponents of sustainable development argue for "socially just development world-wide" that "should attempt to address important social and political issues related to the inequitable allocation of the world's resources." Still others envision sustainability as a fundamental human right [18]. In this context the right to property and the freedom to dispose of it can be limited by the demands placed on enterprises in the aspect of social pressure of various groups of stakeholders sensitive to the balance in many aspects of life.

The fifth approach to the sustainability concept that can be distinguished is the approach related to the concept of Corporate Social Responsibility. The assumptions of this concept are presented in the Carrol Pyramid. The key issue is the approach to corporate responsibility towards business. There is a philanthropic, economic, legal and ethical responsibility in this context [20]. The context of creating values through applying the Corporate Social Responsibility (CSR) assumptions is also important [21].

CSR assumptions support the conceptualization and operationalization of sustainability assumptions and may include many approaches depending on many factors. The most important thing, however, is that, instead of emphasizing profits, the most important concern for a company should be value [6].

An important approach to the development of the sustainability concept are the assumptions of the stakeholder theory. Honest relations with stakeholders create a business ecosystem based on respect [22,23].

Modern sustainability approaches are complex and based on a holistic approach [24].

The third approach to the understanding of the sustainability concept can be directly applied to a research problem defined. The social aspect of designing digital business models that provides opportunities for building a community and the creation of environmentally friendly technologies may influence value migration to attractive business models.

Sustainability should thus be seen in the context of building competitive advantage with an ethical approach to market play, supporting innovative solutions that have a positive impact on society, creating social value and social profit. The standard approach based on classic economy is designing innovative business models in the Internet environment that will provide the company a monopoly or dominance position. Often the related business models are based on a comprehensive data platform. Such central position allows these companies to reap the benefits of high margins. Recently this approach is strongly criticized.

In modern business models, classic economics provides only a partial answer as argued above and is furthermore challenged by the emergence of the sharing economy. The latter case requires to investigate sustainability in business models again. A firm's business model is relevant to its ability to capture value because it is through its business model that the firm exercises its bargaining ability [25].

Several key challenges that are developed in the context of creating sustainable business models can be distinguished:

1. Triple bottom line—The co-creation of profits, social and environmental benefits and the balance among them are challenging for moving towards Sustainable Business Models.
2. Mind-set—The business rules, guidelines, behavioral norms and performance metrics prevail in the mind-set of firms and inhibit the introduction of new business models.
3. Resources—Reluctance to allocate resources to business model innovation and reconfigure resources and processes for new business models.
4. Technology innovation—Integrating technology innovation, e.g., clean technology, with business model innovation is multidimensional and complex.
5. External relationships—Engaging in extensive interaction with external stakeholders and business environment requires extra efforts.
6. Business modelling methods and tools—Existing business modelling methods and tools [26].

Companies operating in modern conceptual trends that use the potential of the digital economy are often not focused on maximizing shareholder value, but rather, on creating social value. Although the original intentions may not be of an economic nature, the economic aspect is, however, a priority in the long-run. The technologies underpinning the new digital economy, most importantly and in rough order of maturity, include: (1) advanced robotics and factory automation (sometimes referred to as advanced manufacturing); (2) new sources of data from mobile and ubiquitous Internet connectivity (sometimes referred to as the Internet of things); (3) cloud computing; (4) big data analytics and (5) artificial intelligence (AI). The transformative potential of the New Digital Economy can only be realized if and when these elements mature, become better integrated, more interoperable, and broadly used. This is unlikely to be a simple, even, uncontested, or rapid process. Social and technical factors, such as data security risks or a backlash across various digital divides, could slow or even derail the development of the New Digital Economy [27].

Thus, the concept of strategic value plays a crucial role. Strategic value examined in this way and combining economic and social values determines the design of contemporary sustainable business models in the digital economy.

Digital platforms that ensure the creation of social relationships in the global world influence the emergence of sustainable business models that emerge directly from the assumptions of individual concepts and trends in the digital economy. They include the Circular Economy, Big Data, and the sharing economy. The traditional approach to designing business models following Circular Economy assumptions is based on the stages of the value chain delivery process, such as design, production, remanufacturing, distribution, consumption, use, reuse, repair, collection, recycling and recovery. The use of virgin materials and the development of solutions from the sphere of obtaining residual waste should close the circular economy circulation process. Many different approaches have been proposed for designing either circular or sustainable business models, however there is no consensus of an integrated vision of both concepts [28]. The assumptions of the Circular Economy are based on the application of the following principles, which in whole or in part constitute a configuration of business models focused on their implementation. ReSOLVE is a checklist of Circular Economy (CE) requirements proposed by the Ellen MacArthur Foundation that consists of six actions: regenerate, share, optimize, loop, virtualize, and exchange, each presenting an opportunity for CE implementation [29]. The scope and interpretation of these six activities covers the following areas:

1. Regenerate—shift to renewable energy and materials, reclaim, retain and regenerate health of ecosystems, return recovered biological resources to the biosphere.
2. Share—keep product loop speed low, maximize utilization of products by sharing them among users, reuse products throughout their technical lifetime, prolong life through maintenance, repair and design for durability.
3. Optimize—increase performance/efficiency of a product, remove waste in production and the supply chain, leverage big data, automation, remote sensing and steering.
4. Loop—keep components and materials in closed, loops and prioritize inner loops.
5. Virtualize—deliver utility virtually.
6. Exchange—replace old materials with advanced non-renewable materials, apply new technologies [30].

The literature recognizes digital business models and digital technologies as factors that facilitate the transition to the Circular Economy. They can be used to overcome the challenges of the Circular Economy [31].

Companies' fundamental challenge in implementing circular economy principles is to rethink their supply chains, and as a consequence the way they create and deliver value through their business models [32]. Circular economy business models have powerful innovation potential, which must be released by the creators of modern business.

The assumptions of the Triple Bottom Line concept, in turn, shape the understanding of a pro-ecological, ethical and economic approach to managing limited resources in a traditional way.

Big Data and the sharing economy focus on a completely different approach to the aspects of sustainable business. Their approach creates conditions for the creation of value from fast data processing and using the effect of community activity. While there is no universal definition of big data, there appears to be an emerging consensus about its uniqueness that distinguishes big data from what we recognize a large database to be like in a traditional sense. Three Vs of big data, namely volume, variety and velocity, have been introduced at an early stage of the development of this notion which reflect the continuous expansion of data in terms of multiplicity [33–37]. The use of large data sets for a broad approach to sustainability is developmental and, together with other concepts, is revolutionizing the world's economy. The sharing economy holds the promise for a more sustainable world by giving access to underutilized resources, at a fraction of the cost, to some who cannot or do not want to buy new products, and the chance of making an extra income for those who already own such underutilized resources. The sharing economy is seen as instrumental in facing wicked problems such as overconsumption and income inequality [38]. The sharing economy as: a socioeconomic system enabling an intermediated set of exchanges of goods and services between individuals and organizations which aim to increase efficiency and optimization of under-utilized resources in society [39]. From this perspective, the original assumptions of the sharing economy concept are part of the general assumptions of sustainable management, creating opportunities to implement sustainability assumptions by using innovative technological solutions on a previously impossible scale.

An important and noteworthy problem is value migration from less to more attractive business models. Adrian Slywotzky defines value migration as a flow of economic and shareholder value away from obsolete business models to new, more effective designs that are better able to satisfy customers' most important priorities. It reflects changing customer needs that will be satisfied by new competitive offerings. Value migration occurs when there is a disconnect between customer priorities and existing business designs [40]. The reason why value flows from business models may be the lack of mechanisms built into the way companies operate that ensure meeting environmental protection requirements and social and legal standards, which may generate a risk of lowering the market value of companies. This is especially important for companies at the early stage of development and listed on the stock exchange, including start-up companies, where investors assess potential chances and threats to an increase or decrease in company's market value very carefully. Because this type of market concerns a large number of companies that operate in the digital economy, the problem of value migration is also worth considering in terms of meeting sustainability requirements. Sustainability can generate a positive impact on value migration when sustainability features are a distinctive component of the business model. Then the value may flow from companies that do not apply sustainability assumptions to companies that use business models based on these assumptions. Sustainability can be an attribute that determines value migration. Therefore, a decision was made to conduct scientific research into the migration of the value of the business model of digital economy companies.

The theoretical framework presented was used to identify the theoretical and practical gaps in terms of the impact of sustainability factors built into the business models of digital economy companies on achieving their success. Undoubtedly, sustainability factors in the DNA of business models should have an impact on value migration on capital markets.

The aim of the article is, therefore, to present the key results of research into value migration to sustainable business models of companies operating in the digital economy on the capital market.

2. Trends in the Use of the Concept of Sustainability in the Digital Economy

The development of electronic markets is dominated by modern business. The number of areas implemented through digital technologies increases each year. This evolution has lasted for many years. R. Alt and H.-D. Zimmermann distinguish six stages in the development of the subject of electronic markets Table 1:

Table 1. Development of Digital Economy.

Period	Description
Proprietary era (1970–1990)	• Communication of documents (EDI) via proprietary communication networks (videotex, X.25-based value added networks), • Definition of electronic standards for transactions (e.g., American National Standards Institute (ANSI), Electronic Data Interchange for Administration (EDIFACT), Tradacoms) and directories (e.g., X.500), • Focused electronic markets and interorganizational information systems (e.g., airline reservation systems, financial exchanges, electronic shopping).
Early E-Commerce (1990–1995)	• Basic Internet technologies (e.g., TCP/IP, HTML, XML) are used for static HTML pages and web-based EDI, • Emerging standard application for interorganizational processes (ERP) and business process orientation, • Internet-based electronic malls pave the way for multi-vendor platforms which offer joint functionalities (e.g., directories, payment).
Early E-Business (1995–2000)	• Complex dynamic database-based web presences with more integration with business processes and application systems for online sales etc., • Evolution of XML-based standards for electronic business (e.g., cXML and eClass for electronic catalogs), • Evolution of standard application systems for E-Business (e.g., electronic catalogs, supply chain and customer relationship management).
Early digital value chains (2000–2005)	• Emphasis of E-Commerce shifted from B2C to B2B as well as to B2E (Business-to-Employee), • Integration of electronic business technologies with enterprise applications and emergence of integration solutions (e.g., portals, EAI), • Mobile channel becoming available based on GSM and RFID technologies.
Early digital ecosystems (2005–2010)	• Ecosystems with multi-channel clients linked with centralized electronic (market) platforms (e.g., App stores, open source communities), • Social media as enhancement and/or platforms for E-Business (e.g., Social CRM, Social Shopping), • On-premise solutions are becoming available as shared SaaS and cloud-based solutions.
Early convergence (2010–)	• Omni-channel environments where information is shared among all user locations (e.g., mobile, web, office/shop, car, public transport), • Consumerization shifts control to end user and user-centered life solutions (e.g., for health, mobility, finance) are becoming available, • Leverage technologies for storing and analyzing large volumes of data (big data) for business scenarios.

Source: [41].

The digital economy has provided much stronger change than changes in the previous decades, due to the following unique features (Watanabe et al., 2018b):

• Expanding Information and Communication Technology (ICT) and the digital economy at a tremendous pace;

- Value can be provided free of charge;
- ICT prices decrease and productivity declines;
- Digital goods are mobile and intangible, thus leading to substantially different business models;
- The boundary between consumer and producer is thinning, and consumers are becoming "prosumers;"
- Barriers of entry are low, making companies to innovate seamlessly;
- Companies can enjoy fully network externalities and the subsequent self-propagation phenomenon embedded in ICT products and services6;
- Companies are polarized between those enjoying network externality and those not;
- Digital companies have a tendency toward a gigantic monopoly;
- Contrary to a traditional monopoly, this new monopoly can enhance convenience [42].

It can be expected that in the near future, all the areas of human activity will be implemented with the participation of electronic media. They also contribute to changes in the behavior of consumers, which is important for the development of the sustainability concept [43].

The areas of human activity create new solutions by means of social media and it is important to define how they are used, whether this way is honest and does not harm other people, and whether it is in accordance with generally accepted social norms. This subject certainly requires a lot of research and analysis.

The traditional definitions of business models are based on an economic approach. According to D. Teece, a business model describes the design or architecture of the value creation, delivery, and capture mechanisms [a firm] employs. The essence of a business model is in defining the manner by which the enterprise delivers value to customers, entices customers to pay for value, and converts those payments to profit [44].

Extensive literature research into the issue of business model sustainability conducted by R. Biloslavo, C. Bagnola and D. Edgar indicates that the traditional approach refers to the pro-environmental, ethical and effective conduct of business regardless of whether it is run in the standard or digital form [45].

The sustainability is part of the trend of the verification of the social acceptance and legal and moral compliance of electronic media use. Sustainability is addressed in many areas related to electronic media [46]. As F. Lüdeke-Freund and K. Dembek indicate, foundational beliefs and concepts, a base of practical tools and resources, authorities and a community of actors emerge around the research and practice of sustainable business models that operate in both digital and physical spaces [47].

This approach is part of the European approach to the sustainable business model [48]. Digitalization opens new pathways for sustainability that will also affect the characteristics of sustainable entrepreneurial ecosystems [49,50]. The first attempts at identifying the concept of sustainability have already been made. F. Welle Donker and B. van Loenen referred the concept of sustainability to the concept of Big Data. In resolving the tension between the problem of lost revenue due to open data and the need to maintain adequate data service quality, a solution could be to develop a sustainable business model for open government data providers that ensures the availability of quality open data in the long-run. They focused on the service component as it forms the starting point of any business model, and on the financial component as this component determines the sustainability of all other components, i.e., the finances determine the level of service, the technical and organizational aspects. Their approach provides several hands-on proposals for self-funding agencies having to implement an open data policy whilst ensuring their long-term sustainability [51].

The concept of sustainability is examined in the context of the sharing economy, which is characterized by many features that are part of sustainable business model philosophy. Business models based on the sharing economy share resources, making natural resources less exploited (fuel consumption when sharing space in the car, energy consumption to heat the house in the case of sharing a flat or other resources). In addition, sharing creates a positive attitude and reduces the level of consumption, which, in global terms, affects the social and environmental factors of the quality of life. This approach creates sustainable consumption and makes the users of goods and services seek to use limited resources intelligently. In this case, ownership is not a priority but sharing is preferred, which from an economic point of view, generates less consumption and optimal use of limited resources [38].

The perspectives of the sustainable development of the sharing economy suggest the use of perspectives to measure the performance of sharing economy business models in economic, environmental, social and technological areas.

- The economic area is defined as an organizational domain that emphasizes practices, discourses, and material expressions associated with the production, use, and management of resources.
- The ecological area is defined as an organizational domain that emphasizes the practices, discourses, and material expressions that occur across the intersection between the organizational and the natural realms.
- The social area is defined as an organizational domain that emphasizes the practices, discourses, and material expressions associated with the formal and informal processes; systems; structures; and relationships actively support the capacity of current and future generations to create healthy and liveable communities.
- The technological area is defined as an organizational domain that supports and enhances a "good life" for all of its employees, customers and society as well without compromising the Earth's ecosystem or the prospects of later generations [52].

The discussion on the application of sustainable business model assumptions is also developing in reference to Peer-to-Peer (P2P) sharing platforms.

P2P sharing platforms such as Airbnb, Uber, TaskRabbit and Peerby are 'multisided platforms': intermediaries that bring together two (or more) distinct groups of users (e.g., hosts and guests, drivers and riders) and enable their direct interaction.

The triadic business model, involving a platform operator and two customer groups, the suppliers and consumers of the service of these two-sided markets has been variously referred to 'sharing-based', 'accessibility based' as guests, drivers, riders and enable their direct interaction. Arguably, the criteria to assess the success of sharing-based business models (especially if adopted by social enterprises) should go beyond traditional financial metrics (e.g., revenues) and take into account the platform's market penetration, the level and type of user engagement, and the social and environmental impact [53]. In this aspect psychological drivers shapes customer's willingness to participate in co-creation activities. Being a participant in a larger community conducing similar views builds social identity and sensitivity to social and ecological factors. Co-creation then has significance, not only in the context of business and consumption aspects, but also in the improvement of the world.

The concept of the circular economy, important for sustainability, deals with environmental aspects. The circular economy (CE) can be a driver of sustainability and it can be promoted and supported by the creation of new and innovative business models, which embed CE principles into their value propositions throughout the value chains [30]. The modern concepts of the digital economy require assessment in terms of sustainability, not only in the context of social, economic and environmental assumptions, but also in terms of the concept of value, which can be created. Using a sustainable business model, value can be captured from the market. Company market value and social profit can be created by means of a sustainable business model. Value migration plays a key role in this respect. While value migrates to business models of the digital economy, it disrupts other traditional industries that are becoming unstable and labile.

3. Value Migration to the Sustainable Business Models of Digital Economy Companies

The digital economy is now a turning point and the driving force of global business. This results in the emergence of new business models, whose existence depends on the development of this trend. A crop of concepts as well as related business formulas are emerging. The key trends that create opportunities for the emergence of new and innovative business models include concepts such as the sharing economy, the network economy, the circular economy and Big Data. These solutions are based on technological assumptions and a wide impact on social phenomena. The value captured from an enabling technology is thus likely to be highly limited relative to the social returns to the innovation. Because the private returns do not reflect their value to society, inventors will underinvest compared to the level that would be socially optimal [54].

In the context of these trends, the book value of the company is of less importance, whereas intangible assets play an increasing role. They determine the attractiveness of the business model resulting from its functionality. Data is increasingly the basic component of the assets of digital economy companies. It is evidenced by the dynamic development of the Big Data concept, which changes the approach to the valuation of companies. In many cases, having access to a large number of data sets determines the high market valuation of companies [55]. The trend focused on the creation of strategic value is the concept of the sharing economy. In the relevant literature, this approach has been dynamically developed in recent years. The sharing economy was first used by Prof. Lawrence Lessig from Harvard University, where he described it as consumption resulting from sharing, exchanging and hiring resources without the need for goods. This activity began to spread by sharing unused resources between people [14]. Authors such as R. Botsman and R. Rogers [56], A. Stephany [15], R. Belk [17] and others contributed to the recognition of this approach. In the relevant literature, the concept of sharing resources and relationships between cooperation actors may refer to at least several varieties. The collaborative economy, the peer to peer economy, the sharing economy, the collaborative consumption and the mesh economy can be defined. In practice, the concept of the sharing economy refers mainly to the forms of cooperation in terms of Business to Consumer (B2C) and Consumer to Consumer (C2C) transactions. This is of fundamental importance in the area of the construction of business models and the interfaces that take place between these entities, both in the sphere of relationships and the construction of business models that interact with companies. Contemporary business continuously being disrupted by startups and established firms utilizing sharing economy approaches [38]. The same applies to the concept of the circular economy. It also changes the approach to business, especially in the sphere of environmental protection. In the relevant literature, a significant and dynamic increase in the number of publications devoted to this subject can be observed [30]. The circular economy, indeed, is based on the establishment of closed production systems, where resources are reused and kept in a loop of production and usage, allowing for generating more value and for a longer period. Despite the interest in the circular economy by politicians and practitioners, scholars, particularly in the strategic management field, are still struggling with a lack of a framework explaining how companies willing to become circular adapt their existing business model or create a new one [57]. The development of the digital economy mainly involves the processing of large data sets (Big Data), which has become a leading scientific area with reference to the name of data science. An increased number of companies from the private sector as well as government agencies and public institutions benefit from the results obtained in the analysis of large data sets. This has a significant impact on the creation of innovative business models based on a large amount of data. In recent years, a very dynamic new trend initiating innovative business models has been developing, namely Open Data. Open Data portals collect various data that may be helpful in the design of new and innovative business models, which could not exist without the potential of these databases.

The aforementioned concepts function within the framework of the network paradigm, where a distinctive factor is cooperation and coopetition, disrupting existing business models, creating opportunities to develop new and innovative solutions in the field of business. The dynamics and the impact of new business models generate changes in individual industries and sectors of the economy. Business models may survive by striving to achieve sustainability, which can be considered a decisive feature that determines the investment attractiveness of business models. It can be assumed that a sustainability attribute is the key value of modern business models, which affects business and social ecosystems [30]. According to G. Mahajan, value is balance between the effort and the result, and if the value is positive (that is, the perceived effort is less than the perceived result), value is created. If the reverse happens, value is destroyed. Value is also the benefit one gets versus the cost, and is generally is seen in competitive situations, since actors have alternatives. The difficulty with value is that it is intangible because value depends on the value ecosystem and their perception of value. Value is fundamental, it is what we are seeking (it exist whether we notice it and not see it); value is what is good (or meritorious), useful, important or worthwhile [58]. It is visible on the capital markets, which is manifested in value migration from less attractive to more attractive models. Value migration will depend on the qualitative attributes, which include the features of sustainability, which can be considered as a key platform for the business model formula, which may translate into value migration described by means of quantitative variables. The quantitative variables of value migration include:

- The relationship between market value and sales revenue [40],
- The growth rate of sales revenues,
- The growth rate of company market value,
- The growth rate of the Price-to-Equity (P/E) ratio,
- The growth rate of the Price-to-Book Value (P/BV) ratio,
- The scalability of the business model measured by the quantitative state, in which an increase does not force expenses out of proportion to the scale of growth. A perfectly scalable state is when companies, by gaining increased returns, create ever higher profitability.

Essentially, value migration has three stages which were presented in Figure 1: (A) Value inflow: In this phase, a company or an industry captures value from other industries or companies due to superior value proposition. The market share and profit margins of the company or industry expand. (B) Stability: In this phase, competitive equilibrium is established. Growth rates moderate. (C) Value outflow: Value starts to move away towards companies or industries meeting evolving customer needs. In this phase, market share declines, margins contract, and growth stops [59].

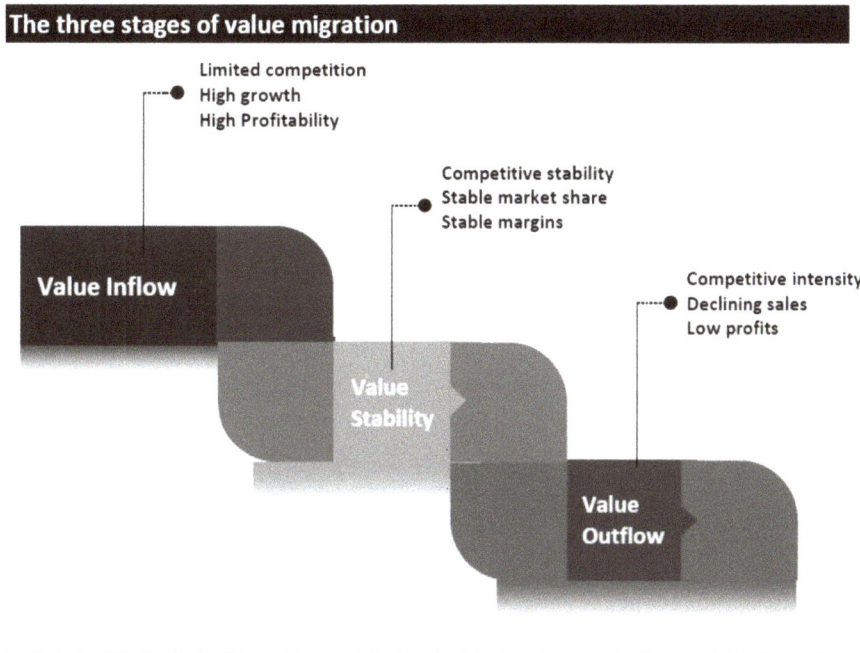

Figure 1. The three stages of value migration. Source: [59].

The causes of value migration are: Customer priorities, an essential catalyst for value migration, change due to a multitude of factors. Hence, there could be several drivers of value migration. Some time-tested drivers are (1) technology; (2) cost; (3) convenience; (4) lowering of entry barriers; (5) lower switching costs; (6) easier access to capital and (7) innovation [60].

Generally, in services, the value is considered from the point of view of two approaches. Value in use and Value in exchange. Value in use refers to the tangible features of a commodity (a tradeable object) which can satisfy some human requirement, want or need, or which serves a useful purpose. Value in exchange it is the ability to trade an asset, such as money, for goods and services. Money has no "value in use." In itself, it does not satisfy wants or needs. To satisfy wants and needs, it must be traded. Although money has no value in use, it has value in exchange [60]. In this article value in exchange has leading character.

In addition to the financial approach to value, other categories of values should be defined, resulting directly from the nature and specificity of the ontological nature of the business model. An aspect leading to value migration is the innovation attribute of the business model. Figure 2 presents the selected types of innovative business models in the context of value migration [61]. Research conducted by F. Hacklin, J. Bjorkdahl and Martin W. Wallin indicates that when value rapidly migrates across industries and between firms, proactively substituting key elements of the primary business model provides a better fit with the new value landscape than launching secondary business models in parallel [61]. Therefore, it is advisable to quickly reconfigure business models in terms of their components to ensure their ability to capture value from the market with the help of the created value proposition for customers, which means that the company, by retaining value, contributes to the growth of value for shareholders/investors.

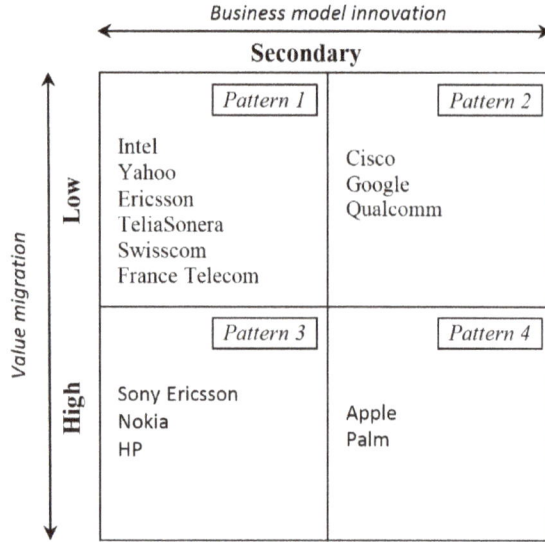

Figure 2. Case firms' selected type of business model innovation versus value migration. Source: [61].

Value migration in the examples of business models presented depends on the primary and secondary innovation of the business model. Primary innovations are based on the initial idea of the component structure of business models, while secondary innovations are created during the life cycle of a company, when the initial principles of the business model operation may change due to new market expectations.

Pattern 1. Secondary business model innovation under lower value migration. A variety of firms who found themselves in an environment of lower value migration—Yahoo, Intel, Ericsson, TeliaSonera, Swisscom and France Télécom—pursued. Pattern 2. Primary business model innovation under lower value migration.

At the same time, a second group of firms in equally stable environments adopted a different response resulting in both better and worse performance than the first group of firms. This group of firms—Cisco, Google, and Qualcomm—chose to probe, pivot and implement substantial changes to their primary business models. Pattern 3. Secondary business model innovation under higher value migration Nokia, Sony-Ericsson, and HP are cases in point. In the case of Hewlett-Packard Company (HP), value started to migrate from their traditional PC business towards online offers. HP complemented their primary business model of selling computing and printing hardware with an ecosystem for online digital photo printing, free online photo albums, and free photo-sharing services. Pattern 4. Primary business model innovation under higher value migration Apple, on the other hand, successfully adapted their primary business model to be at par with a rapidly changing business environment. Apple realized that as computing and mobile technologies converged, value would start to migrate toward smarter devices and services. As they were at that time strongly in a device business related to personal computers (the Mac and later the iMac), in response the company started to pivot their primary business model. Initiating a number of such pivots, Apple launched the iPod in an effort to bring music experience through a new form of MP3 players to a wider consumer market on the basis of a simpler and slicker user interface [61].

The model should therefore be subject to dynamic changes to ensure the ability to retain value and ensure the inflow of value due to the attributes of the business model. When an industry is characterized by rapid value migration, companies are most successful because they adopt a proactive attitude, replacing the key elements of their basic business model by adjusting their business model to current business conditions.

Sustainability as a parameter that describes business models in a positive way for different groups of stakeholders should increase their investment attractiveness. A sustainable business model should inspire increased investor confidence. Therefore, value should migrate from unsustainable to sustainable business models. The relationship between the degree of business model sustainability and value migration is a new research area in the field of value-based management.

4. The Investment Attractiveness of the Sustainable Business Models of Digital Economy Companies on the NewConnect Market

The investment attractiveness of business models is a decisive factor in capturing value in capital markets [62]. Investors are looking for different methods to assess the investment attractiveness of business models. A particular difficulty is the assessment of the attractiveness of business models of companies operating in the digital economy. Therefore, the attribute of sustainability can greatly increase the investment attractiveness of digital economy business models. It may allow, to a greater extent than other criteria of the investment attractiveness of business models, for capturing value from the market where a given company operates, in addition to value from investors.

A business environment was defined for the purposes of scientific research. It is a place where it is possible to find a large number of companies that operate in the digital economy and meet the sustainability criteria. The area of interest was NewConnect, the Alternative Investment Market of the Polish Stock Exchange in Warsaw. This market is dedicated to innovative companies with great development potential. While observing the dynamics of the NewConnect market at the turn of the decade of 2007–2017, their business models were volatile, which resulted in the inability of companies to achieve the expected growth and even in their bankruptcy, loss of competitive advantage, ability to create value, reduced investor interest, and, in particular, loss of market value. This means that very often these models failed, and the original features of the business models designed became unstable. Therefore, this problem needs to be investigated thoroughly from a cognitive perspective. Sustainability may be a factor in making business models less volatile and as a result, capable of capturing more value. The NewConnect market is an interesting environment for testing business models. On 30 August 2007, the Stock Exchange launched an alternative market called NewConnect for small companies with high growth potential. The alternative stock trading system created new links especially between companies in innovative or non-traditional sectors with high growth potential and investors seeking opportunities to participate in these dynamically evolving segments of the economy. The NewConnect market also facilitated access to funding sources for new projects and the tremendous opportunities for information exchange, promotion and customer acquisition. As a result, smaller companies and entrepreneurs in the most innovative sectors are able to implement projects that will change their industry and increase the efficiency of the various sectors of the economy. The market is intended, first of all, for innovative, dynamic companies with high growth potential from different industries, with preferences for the broadly defined IT sector, electronic media, telecommunications, biotechnology, environmental protection, alternative energy supply, various types of modern services and others. NewConnect is an excellent offer for young companies with a short history of activity, aiming to raise funds for development up to a dozen or so million zlotys. The capital raised should enable the company to develop in an accelerated way. It is also assumed that the listed companies will treat NewConnect as an intermediate step on the way to the main WSE floor, which is the target market. It also promotes the best issuers on the NewConnect Lead market, grouping companies with high potential for moving to a regulated market. The development of the capital market in Poland, by creating an alternative trading system, is an undoubted success. The NewConnect market encourages potential newcomers, first and foremost by the possibility of quickly raising the necessary capital, reduced requirements and relatively low debut costs (3.5–5.5% of the topic value). The presence on the NewConnect market also promotes the company and its prestige. The risks associated with NewConnect are primarily the risk of significant fluctuations due to speculation, low liquidity, and in addition, the introduction of new external shareholders to the company may cause difficulties in making decisions or disputes within the company. It should be noted that companies listed on NewConnect are usually young companies at the early stages of development, characterized by the potential high PBV (price to book value) and low dividend yield (DY). This situation is mainly due to the current conditions: the lack of capital at the initial stage of development and the allocation of any profit for further investment. Research into the business models of companies listed on the NewConnect market of the Warsaw Stock Exchange will help identify the strength inherent in sustainability through the measures of value migrations. Based on research, recommendations for the reconfiguration of business models will be indicated by including a sustainability factor in these business models to retain value. The conceptualization of the processes of value migration to digital sustainable business models is presented in Figure 3.

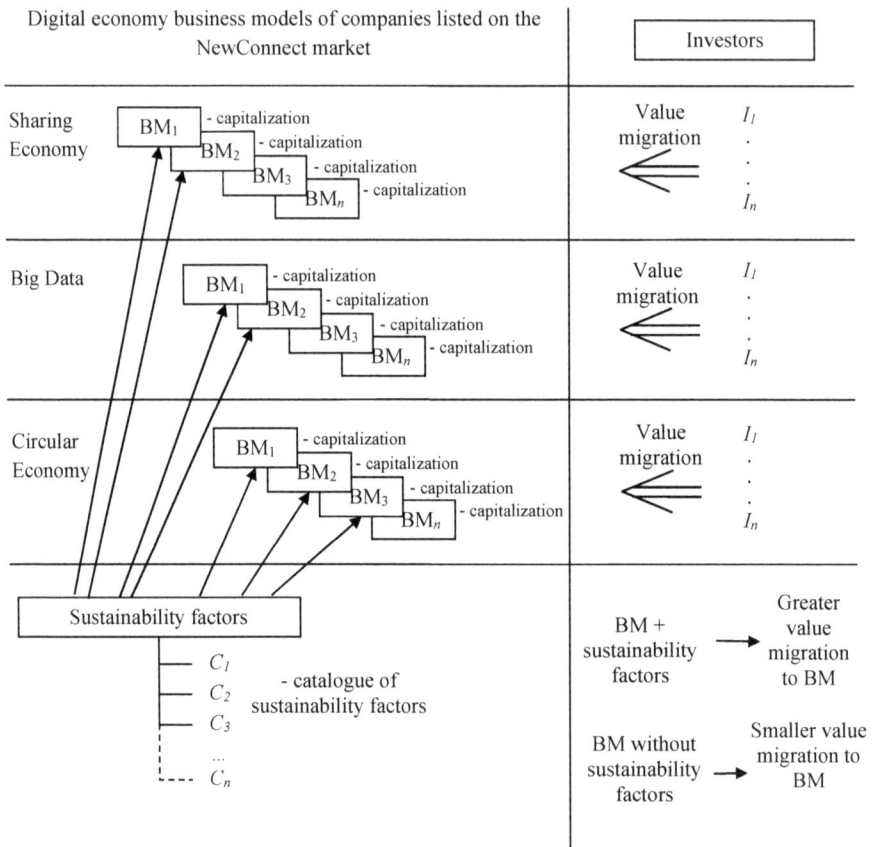

Figure 3. Conceptualization of the processes of value migration to sustainable business models. Source: Own study.

In the presented conceptualization, some business models operating in the digital economy within the framework of the concepts of the sharing economy, Big Data and the circular economy include sustainability factors, which is conducive to capturing value from investors, which subsequently translates into creating a better value proposition for customers and increasing company value in general. This conceptual model presented was verified during the research process adopted.

Variables that describe value migration from the NewConnect market business models operating in the digital economy is presented in Appendix A Table A3.

5. Research Methodology

Qualitative and quantitative research was used to assess value migration to the Sustainable Business Models of digital economy companies. Research triangulation was applied, that is, a combination of different approaches used as one method to strengthen the rigor of the research methodlgy. A method means a procedure covering different methodological approaches. A starting point was the assumption that qualitative and quantitative methods should be perceived as complementary and not competitive [63]. As quantitative research, the analysis of companies' financial performance in terms of market value ratios was adopted, while as regards qualitative research, the analysis of the description of business model features was conducted, which was based on the publicly available information documents of the companies examined. As part of quantitative research, key ratios determining value migration on the capital market, namely the P/BV and P/E ratios were calculated. According to A. Slywotzki, a company is included in the stage of value stabilization if the quotient of the market value to sales revenues is within (1.0 ÷ 2.0). Extreme values are the stage of the outflow of value (the value of the indicator below 1.0), i.e., within the range (0 ÷ 1.0). At the stage of value inflow, the value of this indicator is above 2.0, within the range (2.0 ÷ ∞). A sustainable business model is characterized by stability in the sphere of quantitative and qualitative variables [40]. The calculations were made in 2016 and 2017 based on data from the financial reports of companies listed on the NewConnect market of the Warsaw Stock Exchange.

In order to assess quality criteria that describe the level of saturation of sustainability features in the digital business models of companies listed on the NewConnect market, qualitative research was used and publicly available information documents were analyzed. Appendix A Table A1 presents selected digital economy companies listed on the NewConnect Alternative Investment. As regards the identification of sustainability features, three criteria related to environmental aspects, twelve for ethical ones and one financial criterion were defined. In total, thirteen criteria were used in the assessment of value migration and description of the sustainability features of business models.

The research procedure covered:

1. Collecting the relevant literature on the subject of sustainable business models.
2. Analyzing the evolution of the concept of a sustainable business model and its key trends.
3. Defining the key attributes of digital business models and their development trends, taking into account strategic reflection.
4. Selecting a research sample of value migration to the sustainable business models of companies operating in the digital economy and listed on the NewConnect market.
5. Defining the features of the sustainable business models of companies operating on the NewConnect market based on the analysis of data contained in information documents.
6. Defining and using indicators defining value migration to sustainable business models.
7. Developing the results of research into value migration to sustainable business models.
8. Developing the methodology of value retention through sustainability factors in digital economy business models.
9. Formulating conclusions.

5.1. A Research Sample

From among all the companies surveyed listed on the NewConnect market of the Warsaw Stock Exchange such companies were selected that operate in the digital economy. The total number of these companies is 70, which is 17% percent of all companies. During research, information referring to business models contained in the publicly available information documents of the companies in question was used. Information documents are a simplified version of the prospectus. They are issued in both printed and electronic versions and they can be found on the NewConnect market website and the websites of individual companies and this is mandatory. Information documents contain a lot of reliable data about the company and its industry. The data is verified by an authorized adviser, who bears liability for them. Each information document contains floatation data, data on the company and its activities, risk factors for share buyers, information on company managers and supervisors, data on main shareholders and the financial statements of the company. Information about the company's activity includes basic data on products, goods and services and markets that the company operates in. It is important to discuss the industry and its development prospects. Data on the attributes of business models can be found in the part devoted to the business model, development strategy implemented, and risk factors.

5.2. Research Hypotheses

With reference to the research problem, two research hypotheses were formulated:

Hypothesis 1. *The digital economy is a new space in which it is important to guarantee an ethical approach to designing business models to ensure the long-term success of the company.*

Hypothesis 2. *Sustainability is a factor conducive to the capture of value by the business models of companies operating in the digital economy on the capital markets.*

In order to identify the attributes of sustainable business models, the criteria for qualifying business models in this category were defined. Criteria were defined in terms of the classical approach to the concept of sustainability, defining them in the areas of ecology, ethics and economics.

The following criteria for assessing the application level of sustainability principles in business models were defined. The data proposed, that characterize sustainability features, were developed based on the review of the relevant literature and the selection of such attributes that refer to the specificity of digital economy business models. While selecting the criteria, the proposal of sustainable business model archetypes was used, which were significantly modified [64]. The following criteria for the assessment and classification of business models were adopted.

Within the area of ecology:

1. The business model of the company is oriented towards activities for sustainable development (e.g., for environmental protection with the use of the circular economy, for energy efficiency, renewable energy sources, etc.),
2. A business model exposes the sustainable consumption of goods and services,
3. A company engages in pro-environmental undertakings.

Within the area of ethics:

4. A condition for the existence of a business model is embedding it in the idea of supporting social integration-social values,
5. A business model does not violate the law or the generally accepted principles of business ethics,
6. A business model does not violate the principles of market competitiveness—it does not violate antitrust rules—it does offer excessive prices, which would be an abuse of its position in relation to customers,
7. A business model is not based on using unrealistically low prices, which could be used to eliminate competitors from the market,
8. A business model is not based on discriminating customers,
9. A business model is not based on forcing contractors into certain commercial terms,
10. A business model is not based on the assumption of setting minimum or fixed prices for the sale of products to the distributor/broker,

11. A business model is based on the sales process with the use of transparent regulations, sales conditions and standard contracts, which are easy to understand by the average consumer,

12. A business model is based on activities that provide consumers with an easy and cost-free way of contact, and in particular, it gives the opportunity to contact by phone, informing consumers about the hours of their availability, and in the case of contact via e-mail, it informs consumers about the maximum wait time for a response.

Within the area of economics:

13. The company is focused on creating value for shareholders.

The P/BV ratio was used in the assessment of the economic aspects of business models of the companies surveyed.

Selected NewConnect companies that fulfill qualification criteria for studying sustainability factors Information Technology companies using of the concepts of the sharing economy, the circular economy, and Big Data are presented in Appendix A Table A2.

6. The Results of Research into Value Migration to the Sustainable Business Models of Digital Economy Companies Listed on the NewConnect Alternative Investment Market

The information documents of digital economy companies listed on the NewConnect market were used during research. Information documents and websites of all 70 companies surveyed were analyzed. They indicated that four of them operate in the area of the sharing economy, 1—the circular economy, 15—Big Data, 31—E-commerce and 32—others IT see Figure 4.

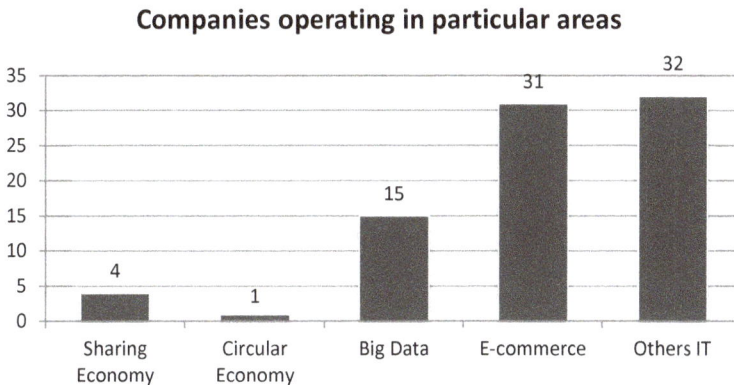

Figure 4. Companies operating in particular areas of the digital economy. Source: Own study based on information documents.

Most companies listed on the NewConnect market of the Warsaw Stock Exchange operate in the field of e-commers and IT systems. Fourteen of them use the Big Data assumptions. The Sharing Economy and Circular Economy concepts are particularly poorly represented. In this respect, there are not many companies in this market yet. Therefore, the research in question is worth replicating in the future.

In order to assess the investment attractiveness of companies in terms of the economic criterion, the P/BV ratio was used. Figure 5.

P/BV (logarithmic scale)

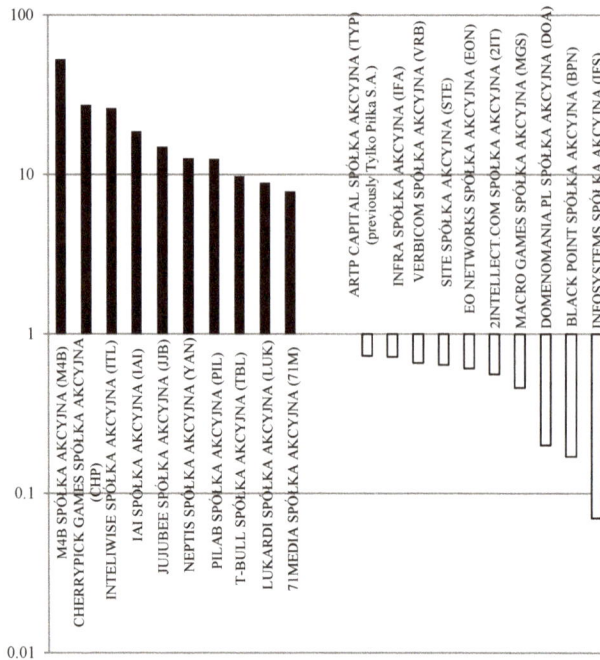

Figure 5. The 10 companies with a maximum Price-to-Book Value (P/BV) value and 10 companies with a minimum P/BV value. Source: Own study.

Figure 5 shows companies with a minimum P/BV value and 10 companies with a minimum P/BV value. For improved readability, a logarithmic scale was used. The best results of the P/BV ratio for the surveyed companies are in the range of 52 to 7, while those characterized by its low value are close to 0.

A total of 10 companies with a maximum P/BV value (outer circle) and 10 companies with a minimum P/BV value (inner circle) by sector are presented in Figure 6. The most companies that have achieved the highest values belong to the group of companies operating in the field of e-commerce and in the field of software development and IT systems.

Eleven companies that meet sustainability criteria were isolated from the digital economy companies that were analyzed. This accounts for 15.71% of the total population surveyed. The list of companies that meet sustainability criteria is presented in Table 2. The research was conducted by identifying individual sustainability features for the area of ecology, ethics and economics, seeking information on the subject and other secondary data in company information documents and on websites. An answer to the question whether sustainability is a new source of company value was sought.

In order to analyze the economization of the business models of companies operating in the digital economy, the analysis of P/BV and P/E ratios achieved by these companies was conducted. Table 3.

Table 2. List of companies that meet sustainability criterion.

No.	Company	Sustainability Criterion	Scope of Activities
1.	4MOBILITY SPÓŁKA AKCYJNA (4MB)	Activity on the Internet marketing and IT services markets	Software
2.	71MEDIA SPÓŁKA AKCYJNA (71M)	Sale of e-readers	E-commerce
3.	BLACK POINT SPÓŁKA AKCYJNA (BPN)	High quality printing materials and the highest quality training and maintenance services, as well as ensuring the receipt and qualified disposal of waste in the form of used printer cartridges.	Information technology-other
4.	DIGITAL AVENUE SPÓŁKA AKCYJNA (DGL)	publisher, among others the largest Polish website for sharing photos-Fotosik.pl, Styl.fm-one of the leaders in the segment of women's fashion and beauty services, and FashionStyle–online games	Web portals
5.	DOOK SPÓŁKA AKCYJNA (DOK)	Design and implementation of innovative solutions using network technologies and native mobile technologies	Software
6.	EDISON SPÓŁKA AKCYJNA (EDN)	Offering solutions for the exchange of electronic documents (including e-invoices) with partners around the world and a system for archiving documents in the electronic form	Software
7.	E-KIOSK SPÓŁKA AKCYJNA (EKS)	creating electronic platforms for the sale of textual content	E-commerce
8.	LOGINTRADE SPÓŁKA AKCYJNA (LGT)	A technology company operating in the e-procurement market, specializing in providing solutions that support purchasing processes in the B2B segment	Software
9.	MAKOLAB SPÓŁKA AKCYJNA (MLB)	Implementation of projects aimed at the digital transformation of global corporations and the largest Polish institutions	Software
10.	NEPTIS SPÓŁKA AKCYJNA (YAN)	Manufacturer, supplier and operator of innovative solutions in the area of vehicle monitoring, car navigation, the reporting systems of mobile workers' work and the creator of the communicator for Yanosik drivers	Software
11.	PILAB SPÓŁKA AKCYJNA (PIL)	Technologically advanced solutions for data analysis by means of its own patented analytical platform	Software

Source: Own study.

10 companies with a maximum P/BV value (outer circle) and 10 companies with a minimum P/BV value (inner circle) by sector

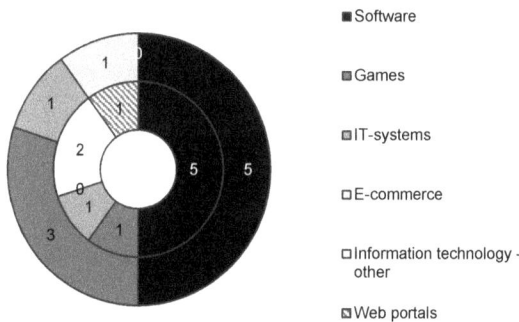

Figure 6. The 10 companies with a maximum P/BV value (outer circle) and 10 companies with a minimum P/BV value (inner circle) by sector. Source: Own study.

Table 3. Values of P/BV and Price-to-Equity (P/E) ratios for companies classified as Digital Sustainability.

No.	Company	P/BV		P/E	
		2016	2017	2016	2017
1.	4MOBILITY SPÓŁKA AKCYJNA (4MB)	75.85	6.53	no data [1]	no data
2.	71MEDIA SPÓŁKA AKCYJNA (71M)	4.16	7.83	10.30	no data
3.	BLACK POINT SPÓŁKA AKCYJNA (BPN)	0.26	0.17	no data	no data
4.	DIGITAL AVENUE SPÓŁKA AKCYJNA (DGL)	3.10	2.26	no data	no data
5.	DOOK SPÓŁKA AKCYJNA (DOK)	no data	5.89	no data	468.70
6.	EDISON SPÓŁKA AKCYJNA (EDN)	1.36	1.09	no data	2.50
7.	E-KIOSK SPÓŁKA AKCYJNA (EKS)	9.02	5.38	26.20	50.90
8.	LOGINTRADE SPÓŁKA AKCYJNA (LGT)	1.50	2.10	no data	16.60
9.	MAKOLAB SPÓŁKA AKCYJNA (MLB)	2.00	2.22	20.10	12.80
10.	NEPTIS SPÓŁKA AKCYJNA (YAN)	9.94	12.62	50.30	72.10
11.	PILAB SPÓŁKA AKCYJNA (PIL)	5.39	12.55	no data	no data
	mean for Digital Sustainability	11.26	5.33	26.73	103.93
	max for Digital Sustainability	75.85	12.62	50.30	468.70
	min for Digital Sustainability	0.26	0.17	10.30	2.50
	mean for 70 Digital Economy companies	53.82	5.29	19.96	46.02
	max for 70 Digital Economy companies	2776.59	52.99	76.10	468.70
	min for 70 Digital Economy companies	0.22	0.07	2.00	2.50

[1] no data—data is not found in the NewConnect Statistic Bulletin. Source: Own study.

Table 3 presents the values of P/BV and P/E ratios achieved by companies that meet the Digital Sustainability criteria in the last two years, i.e., 2016 and 2017. The values of these indices vary.

The Table 3 also presents the results of analyzes of the average value of obtained P/BV and P/E.

The mean value for P/BV for sustainability companies in 2016 (11.26) was lower than the mean value for 70 digital economy companies, which was 53.82. However, in 2017 the situation reversed because the mean value for digital sustainability was 5.33 and the mean for the digital economy was 5.29. Nevertheless, in both cases the maximum value for P/BV was lower for digital sustainability (75.85—2016, 12.62—2017). At the same time, minimum values for P/BV were higher for digital sustainability (0.26—2016, 0.17—2017) than for the digital economy (0.22—2016, 0.07—2017).

P/BV: mean DS < mean DE (2016), mean DS > mean DE (2017)

max DS < max DE (2016), max DS < max DE (2017)

min DS > min DE (2016), min DS > min DE (2017)

The obtained results indicate that companies with sustainability features do not achieve the higher values of market P/BV ratios than other companies operating in the digital economy. This means that these features are not yet perceptible to investors and are not a key factor determining their decisions to buy shares. Better results were achieved in the assessment of the P/E ratio. Taking into account P/E values, the mean value in 2016–2017 for digital sustainability was much higher than for all digital economy companies. The value of a P/E ratio for digital sustainability was then 26.73 in 2016 and 103.93 in 2017, while for the digital economy 19.96 in 2016 and 46.02 in 2017. Interestingly, in 2017, the maximum and minimum values for eleven digital sustainability companies were the same as for all digital economy companies analyzed. This means that companies with both the highest and the lowest P/E value in 2017 were included in the digital sustainability list. In this situation, Hypothesis 2. Sustainability is a factor conducive to the capture of value by the business models of companies operating in the digital economy on the capital markets, was not verified positively.

P/E: mean DS > mean DE (2016), mean DS > mean DE (2017)

max DS < max DE (2016), max DS = max DE (2017)
min DS > min DE (2016), min DS = min DE (2017)

Digital sustainability companies generated about 13% of the total capitalization in the years 2016–2017 in the area of the digital economy Table 4. The mean value of the capitalization of sustainable companies amounted to EUR 92.90 million in 2016 (compared to the mean value for other companies amounting to EUR 121.81 million) and EUR 90.37 million in 2017 (it was EUR 124.17 million for other companies). Thus, the mean value of capitalization for digital sustainability was lower. The median capitalization of sustainability in 2016 (EUR 47.47 million) was higher than the median capitalization for other companies (EUR 43.59 million). However, in 2017 the situation reversed and the median for digital sustainability was EUR 24.21 million, and for the digital economy—EUR 31.26 million.

Table 4. Key results of researched companies.

Key Parameters	2016 [Million Euro]	2017 [Million Euro]	% in 2016	% in 2017
Capitalization of all companies operating in the digital economy	7044.40	7730.22	100	100
Capitalization of sustainable companies	928.97	994.05	13.19	12.86
Capitalization of other companies	6115.43	6736.17		
Mean value of the capitalization of sustainable companies	92.90	90.37		
Mean value of the capitalization of other companies	121.81	124.17		
Median capitalization of sustainable companies	47.47	24.21		
Median capitalization of other companies	43.59	31.26		

Source: Own study.

7. Discussion

The hypotheses presented have been verified.

Extensive research into NewConnect market companies indicates that the subject of sustainability requires further analysis and research in different perspectives, particularly in the context of the dynamic development of the market of the digital business models of technology companies. The research goals set and hypotheses formulated were verified and falsified.

Hypothesis 1: The digital economy is a new space in which it is important to guarantee an ethical approach to designing business models to ensure the long-term success of the company. The analysis of the information documents of 70 companies included in the digital economy sector and a review of the relevant literature and the analysis of information documents and statements about business ethics in periodic reports of listed companies indicates that listed companies operating in the digital economy are trying to take these aspects into account. It is important to them to meet legal requirements and other requirements of the electronic market. In this way, the first hypothesis was verified positively. The sustainability criteria used in research are applied by the companies surveyed and relate to the areas of ecology, ethics and economics.

Hypothesis 2. Sustainability is a factor conducive to the capture of value by the business models of companies operating in the digital economy on the capital markets.

The second hypothesis that sustainability is a factor conducive to the capture of value by the business models of companies operating in the digital economy on the capital markets was not proven. Companies included in digital sustainability do not achieve better results in the area of market value than other digital economy companies. This means that the issue of sustainability, especially as regards electronic markets, is not well recognized in both the theoretical and the application sphere. Investors do not yet appreciate the aspects related to the ethics of business models, as well as factors related to environmental and social aspects. The hypothesis should be rejected. In the future, when ethical, social and ecological aspects will play a greater role in generating risk for investors who purchase high-risk companies' shares, companies at the early stages of development, sustainability factors will definitely play a much greater role and the hypotheses formulated may be falsified in subsequent research. This should result in the best results of market value P/BV and P/E ratios as indicated above, digital sustainability companies generated about 13% of the total capitalization in the years 2016–2017 in the area of the digital economy. The mean value of the capitalization of sustainable companies amounted to EUR 92.90 million in 2016 (compared to the mean value for other companies amounting to EUR 121.81 million) and EUR 90.37 million in 2017 (it was EUR 124.17 million for other companies). Thus, the mean value of capitalization for digital sustainability was lower. The median capitalization of sustainability in 2016 (EUR 47.47 million) was higher than the median capitalization for other companies (EUR 43.59 million). However, in 2017 the situation reversed and the median for digital sustainability was EUR 24.21 million, and for the digital economy—EUR 31.26 million.

8. Conclusions

The topic of sustainability is quite widely recognized in the relevant literature in terms of new approach to business models. However, the concept is only somewhat recognized in the field of electronic markets. Literature research and research into the NewConnect alternative market companies indicate that companies classified as digital sustainability do not differ in terms of market value from the value of companies from the entire market of digital economy companies on this market. It should also be noted that there is no value migration in this case. Research findings do not confirm that value migrates from less attractive companies (in this case, non-digital sustainability companies) to more attractive ones (in this case it was assumed that they should be companies classified into the digital sustainability category). Considering that 70 NewConnect market companies operate in the field of electronic markets, which accounts for 17% of all companies listed on this market, the number of companies included in the digital sustainability category is even lower-only 16% of companies operating in this narrowed area of the digital economy. However, the subject of sustainability seems to be rapidly evolving. Despite the fact that this is not confirmed unequivocally by the research results obtained, business models that fulfill requirements in the area of ethics, ecology and economics, adequately interpreted for electronic markets, should be the key information underlying investment decisions taken by investors. The social aspect of new business models is also a key topic many of them base their ideas on concepts such as the sharing economy, the circular economy and Big Data. These concepts treat an approach to the market differently than the neoclassical method. Economic aspects are not always the drivers; in many cases, a social aspect is a driver for the creation of economic value and it is a priority in this respect. Social profit also counts in addition to economic profit. The impact of the research conducted on the development of the theory and practice of sustainable business models seems worth discussing. Until now, there has been little focus on the search for answers to questions about value migration in terms of sustainable business model criteria. The features of sustainable business models in the context of the digital economy have been poorly researched. Value migration as an important theory of economics and management should be more widely recognized in terms of factors relevant to the sustainability concept. This article shows new trends in the challenges of the digital economy in relation to sustainability requirements in the context of value migration on the capital market. Research results should inspire managers and the creators of business models to take sustainability-related factors into account in their projects.

9. Limitations

Limitations that can be identified result directly from the low effectiveness of the NewConnect market, which may, to some extent, affect the obtained values of P/BV and P/E ratios. This is a problem of many stock exchanges. Although research covers all companies in the Digital Economy sector, there are only 70 companies listed on the NewConnect market that operate in the Circular Economy, the sharing economy, and Big Data. It means that in the future it is worth repeating the research to ensure the replication of scientific research. Another limitation is also the selection of the qualification criteria for companies as those that can be classified as the users of sustainable business models. Replication of scientific research is justified when more companies from the Digital Economy sector will be listed on the Exchange Market, in particular business models based on the assumptions of Sharing Economy, Circular economy and Big Data. In addition, as the securities market efficiency will increase, the credibility of data based on market value indicators will increase.

Funding: This research received no external funding.

Conflicts of Interest: The author declares no conflict of interest.

Appendix

Table A1. Selected digital economy companies listed on the NewConnect Alternative Investment.

No.	Name of the IT Company	Sector	Website	Sharing Economy Company	Circular Economy Company	Big Data Company	E-Commerce	Others IT
1.	BIZTECH KONSULTING SPÓŁKA AKCYJNA (BTK)	IT systems	http://biztech.pl/	X		X		
2.	LUKARDI SPÓŁKA AKCYJNA (LUK)	IT systems	http://lukardi.com/					X
3.	MEGA SONIC SPÓŁKA AKCYJNA (MGA)	IT systems	http://www.megasonic.pl/					X
4.	PROVECTA IT SPÓŁKA AKCYJNA (PRV)	IT systems	http://provectasa.pl/					X
5.	S4E SPÓŁKA AKCYJNA (S4E)	IT systems	https://www.s4e.pl/					X
6.	SEVENET SPÓŁKA AKCYJNA (SEV)	IT systems	https://www.sevenet.pl/					X
7.	SUNTECH SPÓŁKA AKCYJNA (SUN)	IT systems	http://www.suntech.pl/.pl/					X
8.	SURFLAND SYSTEMY KOMPUTEROWE SPÓŁKA AKCYJNA (SSK)	IT systems	http://ssk.com.pl/					X
9.	VERBICOM SPÓŁKA AKCYJNA (VRB)	IT systems	http://verbicom.pl/					X
10.	IMAGIS SPÓŁKA AKCYJNA (IMG)	IT equipment	http://imagis.pl/					X
11.	7IMEDIA SPÓŁKA AKCYJNA (7IM)	E-commerce	http://www.7imedia.pl/				X	
12.	ALEJASAMOCHODOWA.PL SPÓŁKA AKCYJNA (ALS)	E-commerce	http://www.alejasamochodowa.pl/		X		X	
13.	ARENA.PL SPÓŁKA AKCYJNA (ARE) (previously Carbon Invest SA)	E-commerce	https://arena.pl/				X	
14.	E-KIOSK SPÓŁKA AKCYJNA (EKS)	E-commerce	http://www.e-kiosk.pl/			X	X	
15.	INBOOK SPÓŁKA AKCYJNA (INB)	E-commerce	https://www.inbook.pl/				X	
16.	INWESTYCJE ALTERNATYWNE PROFIT SPÓŁKA AKCYJNA (IAP)	E-commerce	http://iaprofit.pl/				X	
17.	MERLIN GROUP SPÓŁKA AKCYJNA (MRG) (previously AdMassive S.A.)	E-commerce	http://www.merlingroup.pl/				X	
18.	MODERN COMMERCE SPÓŁKA AKCYJNA (MCE) (previously Air Market S.A.)	E-commerce	http://moderncommercesa.com/				X	
19.	OUTDOORZY SPÓŁKA AKCYJNA (OUT)	E-commerce	http://www.outdoorzy.pl/				X	
20.	PRESENT24 SPÓŁKA AKCYJNA (P24)	E-commerce	http://www.present24sa.pl/				X	
21.	ARTP CAPITAL SPÓŁKA AKCYJNA (TYP) (previously TYLKO PIŁKA S.A.)	Web portals	http://artpcapital.pl/			X	X	
22.	DIGITAL AVENUE SPÓŁKA AKCYJNA (DGL)	Web portals	http://digitalavenue.pl/			X		
23.	FACHOWCY.PL VENTURES SPÓŁKA AKCYJNA (FAV)	Web portals	https://www.fachowcy.pl/	X		X		

Table A1. *Cont.*

No.	Name of the IT Company	Sector	Website	Sharing Economy Company	Circular Economy Company	Big Data Company	E-Commerce	Others IT
24.	INWESTYCJE.PL SPÓŁKA AKCYJNA (INW)	Web portals	http://spolka.inwestycje.pl/			X		
25.	LANGLOO.COM SPÓŁKA AKCYJNA (LAN)	Web portals	http://langloo.com/			X	X	
26.	2INTELLECT.COM SPÓŁKA AKCYJNA (2IT)	Software	http://2intellect.com/					X
27.	4MOBILITY SPÓŁKA AKCYJNA (4MB)	Software	http://4mobility.pl/	X				
28.	A.P.N. PROMISE SPÓŁKA AKCYJNA (PRO)	Software	http://www.promise.pl/					X
29.	ACREBIT SPÓŁKA AKCYJNA (ACR)	Software	http://www.acrebit.pl/					X
30.	DOOK SPÓŁKA AKCYJNA (DOK)	Software	http://www.dook.pro/					X
31.	EC2 SPÓŁKA AKCYJNA (EC2)	Software	http://ec2.pl/ec2/					X
32.	EDISON SPÓŁKA AKCYJNA (EDN)	Software	https://www.edison.pl/					X
33.	EO NETWORKS SPÓŁKA AKCYJNA (EON)	Software	http://www.eo.pl/					X
34.	EXAMOBILE SPÓŁKA AKCYJNA (EXA)	Software	http://www.examobile.com/				X	
35.	FINHOUSE SPÓŁKA AKCYJNA (FIN)	Software	http://www.finhouse.pl/					X
36.	GRUPA EXORIGO-UPOS SPÓŁKA AKCYJNA (GEU)	Software	https://www.exorigo-upos.pl/en/					X
37.	I3D SPÓŁKA AKCYJNA (I3D)	Software	http://i3d.pl/					X
38.	IAI SPÓŁKA AKCYJNA (IAI)	Software	https://www.idosell.com/pl/				X	
39.	INFOSYSTEMS SPÓŁKA AKCYJNA (IFS)	Software	http://www.infosystems.pl/					
40.	INFRA SPÓŁKA AKCYJNA (IFA)	Software	http://www.infra.pl/				X	
41.	INNOVATIVE COMMERCE A.S. (ICM) (previously iCom Vision Holding, a.s.)	Software	http://www.innocomm.pl/				X	
42.	INTELIWISE SPÓŁKA AKCYJNA (ITL)	Software	https://www.intelliwise.com/				X	
43.	JWA SPÓŁKA AKCYJNA (JWA)	Software	http://jwa.com.pl/					X
44.	KBJ SPÓŁKA AKCYJNA (KBJ)	Software	http://www.kbj.com.pl/					X
45.	LOGINTRADE SPÓŁKA AKCYJNA (LGT)	Software	http://www.logintrade.pl/					X
46.	M4B SPÓŁKA AKCYJNA (M4B)	Software	http://m4b.pl/			X	X	
47.	MADKOM SPÓŁKA AKCYJNA (MAD)	Software	https://madkom.pl/					X
48.	MAKOLAB SPÓŁKA AKCYJNA (MLB)	Software	https://makolab.com.pl-pl					X
49.	MINERAL MIDRANGE SPÓŁKA AKCYJNA (MND)	Software	http://www.mineralmidrange.com/					X
50.	NEPTIS SPÓŁKA AKCYJNA (YAN)	Software	http://www.neptis.pl/	X			X	
51.	NETWISE SPÓŁKA AKCYJNA (NTW)	Software	http://netwise.pl.pl/					X
52.	PILAB SPÓŁKA AKCYJNA (PIL)	Software	https://pilab.pl/					X

Table A1. *Cont.*

No.	Name of the IT Company	Sector	Website	Sharing Economy Company	Circular Economy Company	Big Data Company	E-Commerce	Others IT
53.	SITE SPÓŁKA AKCYJNA (STE)	Software	http://fatdoggames.com/.pl/strona-glowna/			X	X	
54.	STANUSCH TECHNOLOGIES SPÓŁKA AKCYJNA (STT)	Software	https://www.stanusch.com/?q=			X		
55.	UNIFIED FACTORY SPÓŁKA AKCYJNA (UFC)	Software	https://unifiedfactory.com/pl/			X	X	
56.	BLOOBER TEAM SPÓŁKA AKCYJNA (BLO)	Games	http://br.blooberteam.com/pl/					X
57.	CHERRYPICK GAMES SPÓŁKA AKCYJNA (CHP)	Games	http://cherrypickgames.com/				X	
58.	FOREVER ENTERTAINMENT SPÓŁKA AKCYJNA (FOR)	Games	http://www.forever-entertainment.com/pl				X	
59.	HUCKLEBERRY GAMES SPÓŁKA AKCYJNA (HBG)	Games	http://hgames.eu/				X	
60.	IFUN4ALL SPÓŁKA AKCYJNA (IF4)	Games	http://ifun4all.com/				X	
61.	JUJUBEE SPÓŁKA AKCYJNA (JJB)	Games	http://www.jujubee.pl/pl				X	
62.	MACRO GAMES SPÓŁKA AKCYJNA (MGS)	Games	http://macrogames.tv/			X	X	
63.	QUBICGAMES SPÓŁKA AKCYJNA (QUB)	Games	http://qubicgames.com/			X	X	
64.	T-BULL SPÓŁKA AKCYJNA (TBL)	Games	http://t-bull.com/				X	
65.	THE FARM 51 GROUP SPÓŁKA AKCYJNA (F51)	Games	http://www.thefarm51.com/					X
66.	BIT EVIL SPÓŁKA AKCYJNA (BIT)	Information technology-other	http://bitevil.com/			X	X	
67.	BLACK POINT SPÓŁKA AKCYJNA (BPN)	Information technology-other	http://blackpoint.pl/					X
68.	DOMENOMANIA.PL SPÓŁKA AKCYJNA (DOA)	Information technology-other	https://domenomania.pl/			X	X	
69.	EUROSYSTEM SPÓŁKA AKCYJNA (ERS)	Information technology-other	http://www.eurosystem.com.pl/					X
70.	XPLUS SPÓŁKA AKCYJNA (XPL)	Information technology-other	http://www.xplus.pl/					X

X—Assignment to the concept of management or scope of activities. Source: own study based on information documents.

Table A2. Selected NewConnect companies that fulfill qualification criteria for studying sustainability factors (IT companies using of the concepts of the sharing economy, the circular economy, and Big Data.

No.	IT Companies	Criteria for Assessing the Sustainability of the Business Models of IT Companies on the NewConnect Market (Indication of the Occurrence of a Given Criterion)														Range of Activity
		Ecology				Ethics								Economics		
		1. The business model of the company is oriented towards activities for sustainable development (e.g., for environmental protection with the use of the circular economy concept, for energy efficiency, renewable energy sources, etc.).	2. A business model exposes the sustainable consumption of goods and services.	3. A company engages in pro-environmental undertakings.	4. A condition for the existence of a business model is embedding it in the idea of supporting social integration-social values.	5. A business model does not violate the law or the generally accepted principles of business ethics.	6. A business model does not violate the principles of market competitiveness—it does not violate antitrust rules—it does offer excessive prices, which would be an abuse of its position in relation to customers.	7. A business model is not based on the use of unrealistically low prices, which could be used to eliminate competitors from the market.	8. A business model is not based on discriminating customers.	9. A business model is not based on forcing contractors into certain commercial terms	10. A business model is not based on the assumption of setting minimum or fixed prices for the sale of products to the distributor/broker.	11. A business model is based on the sales process with the use of transparent regulations, sales conditions and standard contracts, which are easy to understand by the average consumer.	12. A business model is based on assumptions that provide consumers with an easy and cost-free way of contact, and in particular: it gives the opportunity to contact by phone, informing consumers about the hours of their availability, and in the case of contact via e-mail, it informs consumers about the maximum wait time for a response.	13. The company is focused on creating value for shareholders.	Sustainability	
1.	M4B SPÓŁKA AKCYJNA (M4B)	-[1]	-	-	-	X[2]	X	X	X	X	-	X	X	52.99	-	a technology company specializing in designing and building mobile solutions for business
2.	CHERRYPICK GAMES SPÓŁKA AKCYJNA (CHP)	-	-	-	-	X	X	X	X	X	-	X	-	27.45	-	creating, publishing and distributing computer games to all leading platforms. i.e., iOS, Android, MacOs, Sony PlayStation 4 and Xbox One

Table A2. Cont.

Indication of the Occurrence of a Given Criterion

Criteria for Assessing the Sustainability of the Business Models of IT Companies on the NewConnect Market

No.	Company															Value		Description
3.	INTELIWISE SPÓŁKA AKCYJNA (ITL)	-	-	-	X	X	X	X	X	X	X	X	-	26.19	-			specialized IT solutions that optimize customer service. e-commerce and internet marketing
		-				X							X	X					
4.	IAI SPÓŁKA AKCYJNA (IAI)	-	-	-	X	X	X	X	-	X	X	X	X	18.74	-			Systems for Internet sales
		-				X							X					
5.	JUJUBEE SPÓŁKA AKCYJNA (JJB)	-	-	-	X	X	X	X	-	X	X	X	X	14.95	-			development studio involved in the creation of video games
		-				X							X					
6.	NEPTIS SPÓŁKA AKCYJNA (YAN)	X	X	-	X	X	X	X	-	X	X	X	-	12.62	X			manufacturer, supplier and operator of innovative solutions in the area of vehicle monitoring, car navigation. mobile work reporting systems and the creator of the communicator for Yanosik drivers
		X		X		X							X					
7.	PILAB SPÓŁKA AKCYJNA (PIL)	X	X	-	X	-	X	X	-	X	X	X	-	12.55	X			technologically advanced solutions for data analysis by their own patented analytical platform
		X		X		X							X					
8.	T-BULL SPÓŁKA AKCYJNA (TBL)	-	-	-	X	X	X	X	X	X	X	X	-	9.75	-			design, production and distribution of games for mobile devices
		-				X							X					
9.	LUKARDI SPÓŁKA AKCYJNA (LUK) (previously SAPpeers.com S.A.)	-	-	-	X	X	X	X	X	X	X	X	-	8.87	-			SAP business software
		-		X		X							X					
10.	71MEDIA SPÓŁKA AKCYJNA (71M)	X	X	-	X	X	X	X	X	X	X	X	X	7.83	X			e-reader device sale
		X				X							X					
11.	BIT EVIL SPÓŁKA AKCYJNA (BIT)	-	-	-	X	X	X	-	-	X	X	X	-	7.30	-			web and mobile solutions based on proprietary engines (including mobile games for Android and iOS. mobile applications and e-commerce websites)
		-				X							X					
12.	ARENA.PL SPÓŁKA AKCYJNA (ARE) (previously Carbon Invest S.A.)	-	-	-	X	X	X	X	-	X	X	X	X	7.26	-			online shopping platform
		-		X		X							X					

Table A2. *Cont.*

No.	Company		Indication of the Occurrence of a Given Criterion										Score		Description
			Criteria for Assessing the Sustainability of the Business Models of IT Companies on the NewConnect Market												
13.	4MOBILITY SPÓŁKA AKCYJNA (4MB)	X	X	–	X	–	X	X	X	X	–	6.53	X	activity on the Internet marketing and IT services market
		X				X						X		
14.	IFUN4ALL SPÓŁKA AKCYJNA (IF4)	–	–	–	X	X	X	X	X	X	–	6.4	–	development studio from the Bloober Team group, producing independent computer games (including real-world data type)
		–				X						X		
15.	NETWISE SPÓŁKA AKCYJNA (NTW)	–	–	–	X	–	X	–	X	X	–	5.93	–	integrator of CRM systems (Customer Relationship Management) and CEM (Customer Experience Management) based on Microsoft technologies (Microsoft Dynamics CRM) in Europe
		–				X						X		
16.	DOOK SPÓŁKA AKCYJNA (DOK)	X	–	–	X	–	X	–	X	X	X	5.89	X	design and implementation of innovative solutions using network technologies and native mobile technologies
		X				X						X		
17.	E-KIOSK SPÓŁKA AKCYJNA (EKS)	X	–	X	X	X	X	X	X	X	X	5.38	X	creation of electronic platforms used to sell textual content
		X				X						X		
18.	SUNTECH SPÓŁKA AKCYJNA (SUN)	–	–	–	X	X	X	X	X	X	–	4.56	–	software development and implementation services
		–				X						X		
19.	THE FARM 51 GROUP SPÓŁKA AKCYJNA (F51)	–	–	–	X	–	X	X	X	X	–	4.53	–	computer games for PCs, desktop consoles (Xbox 360 and PlayStation 3) and portable consoles, VR applications
		–				X						X		
20.	MODERN COMMERCE SPÓŁKA AKCYJNA (MCE) (previously Air Market S.A.)	–	–	–	X	X	X	–	–	–	X	3.82	X	sale of IT services
		–				X						X		
21.	KBJ SPÓŁKA AKCYJNA (KBJ)	–	–	–	X	–	X	X	X	X	–	3.63	–	consulting services and creation of dedicated software on the SAP platform for large and medium-sized companies

Table A2. *Cont.*

No.	Company	Criteria for Assessing the Sustainability of the Business Models of IT Companies on the NewConnect Market (Indication of the Occurrence of a Given Criterion)								Value			Description
22.	MINERAL MIDRANGE SPÓŁKA AKCYJNA (MND)	–	–	X	X	X	–	X	X	3.49	X	–	Business Intelligence. Enterprise Planning. Finance Consolidation. a provider of Corporate Performance Management solutions
23.	INWESTYCJE.PL SPÓŁKA AKCYJNA (INW)	–	–	X	X	X	–	X	X	3.46	–	–	the owner and publisher of portals occupies a leading position in Poland in the business/finance/law segment (including Inwestycje.pl. KantorOnline.pl. Waluty.com. Kantory.pl. Fundusze24.pl. Twojefinanse.pl)
24.	INBOOK SPÓŁKA AKCYJNA (INB)	–	–	X	X	X	X	X	X	3.35	X	–	retail sale of consumer goods
25.	FOREVER ENTERTAINMENT SPÓŁKA AKCYJNA (FOR)	–	–	X	X	X	–	X	–	3.28	–	–	production of computer games and broadly defined multimedia entertainment for all currently available platforms (iPad. iPod. Nintendo. PS VITA. Android system. etc.)
26.	ACREBIT SPÓŁKA AKCYJNA (ACR)	–	–	X	X	X	–	X	X	2.91	X	–	ERP systems as well as specialized modules. for example: logistics and sales. Business Intelligence. CRM. human resources management. finance and accounting
27.	OUTDOORZY SPÓŁKA AKCYJNA (OUT)	X	X	X	X	X	X	X	X	2.87	X	–	sale of goods via the online sales platform
28.	BLOOBER TEAM SPÓŁKA AKCYJNA (BLO)	–	–	X	X	X	–	X	X	2.84	–	–	an independent developer of computer games and video games intended for digital distribution to the global market (psychological horrors)
29.	GRUPA EXORIGO-UPOS SPÓŁKA AKCYJNA (GEU)	–	–	X	X	X	X	X	X	2.76	–	–	advanced IT solutions for the retail. banking. insurance. production and public administration sectors
30.	UNIFIED FACTORY SPÓŁKA AKCYJNA (UFC)	–	–	X	X	X	X	X	X	2.62	X	–	manufacturer and global supplier of solutions that make sales and customer service automatic

Table A2. *Cont.*

	Company	Criteria for Assessing the Sustainability of the Business Models of IT Companies on the NewConnect Market										Score	Indication of the Occurrence of a Given Criterion	Description
31.	SEVENET SPÓŁKA AKCYJNA (SEV)	–	–		X	X	X	X	X	X	X	2.4	X	advanced ICT solutions
32.	QUBICGAMES SPÓŁKA AKCYJNA (QUB)	–	–		X	X	X	X	–	X	–	2.38	–	creating multi-platform computer games for iOS, Android, PC (including Steam version and HTML5 Web version), Nintendo 3DS, Sony PS4 and PS Vita and Xbox One, distribution of own games for selected platforms
33.	DIGITAL AVENUE SPÓŁKA AKCYJNA (DGL)	X	X	X	X	X	X	X	–	X	–	2.26	X	publisher, among others, of the largest Polish website for sharing photos–Fotosik.pl. Styl.fm–one of the leaders in the segment of women's fashion and beauty and FashionStyle–an Internet game
34.	MAKOLAB SPÓŁKA AKCYJNA (MLB)	X	X		X	X	X	X	X	X	–	2.22	X	Implementation of projects aimed at the digital transformation of global corporations and the largest Polish institutions
35.	EXAMOBILE SPÓŁKA AKCYJNA (EXA)	X	–		X	X	–	X	X	X	–	2.21	–	functional applications and games for individual users and dedicated applications for business customers
36.	LOGINTRADE SPÓŁKA AKCYJNA (LGT)	X	X		X	X	X	X	–	X	–	2.1	X	a technology company operating on the e-procurement market specializing in providing solutions supporting purchasing processes in the B2B segment
37.	EC2 SPÓŁKA AKCYJNA (EC2)	–	–		X	X	X	X	–	X	–	1.8	–	creating IT solutions, advising on IT projects, auditing and improving existing solutions as well as specifying requirements for systems
38.	MADKOM SPÓŁKA AKCYJNA (MAD)	–	–		X	X	X	X	–	X	–	1.75	–	Supplier and integrator of proprietary software for managing documents, information and processes in public administration.
39.	PRESENT24 SPÓŁKA AKCYJNA (P24)	–	–		X	X	X	X	–	X	X	1.51	X	supplier and integrator of proprietary software for managing documents, information and processes in public administration

Table A2. *Cont.*

Indication of the Occurrence of a Given Criterion

Criteria for Assessing the Sustainability of the Business Models of IT Companies on the NewConnect Market

#	Company	Description	Value
40.	PROVECTA IT SPÓŁKA AKCYJNA (PRV) (previously FINANCIAL INTERMEDIARIES POLSKA S.A.)	communication and IT solutions for enterprises combining competences in the field of telecommunications and IT	1.49
		sale of IT services	1.48
41.	BIZTECH KONSULTING SPÓŁKA AKCYJNA (BTK)		
42.	XPLUS SPÓŁKA AKCYJNA (XPL)	diagnosis and pre-implementation analysis, business consulting, highly-specialized implementations and support of IT systems, solution design and software development	1.42
43.	A.P.N. PROMISE SPÓŁKA AKCYJNA (PRO)	provider of IT solutions for large and medium-sized enterprises, public administration, educational institutions and health care	1.37
44.	S4E SPÓŁKA AKCYJNA (S4E)	services in the scope of implementing data archiving and copying systems	1.32
45.	EUROSYSTEM SPÓŁKA AKCYJNA (ERS)	geodetic and design services for government agencies, state and private sector companies and local governments (services in the field of 3D laser scanning (LIDAR services), digital photogrammetry with the development of digital orthophoto maps and 3D terrain models, measurements and GPS development)	1.23
46.	JWA SPÓŁKA AKCYJNA (JWA)	advanced IT solutions, IT projects consultancy, auditing and improving existing solutions, and specifying IT system requirements	1.15
47.	EDISON SPÓŁKA AKCYJNA (EDN)	offering solutions for the exchange of electronic documents (including e-invoices) with partners all over the world and a system enabling the archiving of documents in electronic form	1.09

Table A2. *Cont.*

Indication of the Occurrence of a Given Criterion

Criteria for Assessing the Sustainability of the Business Models of IT Companies on the NewConnect Market

No.	Company	Criteria (occurrence: X / –)	Value	Description
48.	LANGLOO.COM SPÓŁKA AKCYJNA (LAN)	– – – X X X X – X X	0.99	online educational website and e-learning platform for anyone interested in learning and improving English
49.	ALEJASAMOCHODOWA.PL SPÓŁKA AKCYJNA (ALS)	– – – X – X X – X X	0.81	online sale of spare parts for cars
50.	MEGA SONIC SPÓŁKA AKCYJNA (MGA)	– – – X X X X X X X	0.78	IT systems integrator
51.	ARTP CAPITAL SPÓŁKA AKCYJNA (TYP) (previously Tylko Piłka S.A.)	– – – X X X X X X X	0.73	"Start-up factory", invests mainly in innovative ventures in the digital sector (software, mobile applications, digital media, and e-commerce platforms)
52.	INFRA SPÓŁKA AKCYJNA (IPA)	– – – X X X X X X X	0.72	activity in the sector of IT systems supporting management and work organization in the enterprise and offices
53.	VERBICOM SPÓŁKA AKCYJNA (VRB)	– – – X X X X X X –	0.66	a group of ICT companies
54.				
55.	SITE SPÓŁKA AKCYJNA (STE)	– – – X X X X X – –	0.64	construction, development and management of specialized web portals and the creation of dedicated systems, applications and websites for customers
56.	EO NETWORKS SPÓŁKA AKCYJNA (EON)	– – – X X X X X X X	0.61	an international IT company specializing in systems integration in the search solutions and e-sales solutions sector
57.	2INTELLECT.COM SPÓŁKA AKCYJNA (2IT)	– – – X X X X X X X	0.56	producer and provider of information technology supporting decision-making processes at every level of company management

Table A2. *Cont.*

No.	Company	Criteria for Assessing the Sustainability of the Business Models of IT Companies on the NewConnect Market	Description
58.	MACRO GAMES SPÓŁKA AKCYJNA (MGS)	- - - × × × × × × × - - 0.46 -	web portals related to broadly defined electronic games, a partner of Microsoft Poland in the development, integration and activation of the Minecraft community in Poland
		- ×	×
59.	DOMENOMANIA.PL SPÓŁKA AKCYJNA (DOA)	- - × × × × × × × × × - 0.20 -	one of the largest providers of hosting services and domain registrars in Poland, servicing mainly medium-sized and small companies and individuals
		- ×	×
60.	BLACK POINT SPÓŁKA AKCYJNA (BPN)	× × - × × × × × - × - 0.17 ×	high-quality printing materials and top-quality training and service services, as well as ensuring the collection and qualified disposal of waste in the form of used cartridges for printers
		× ×	×
61.	INFOSYSTEMS SPÓŁKA AKCYJNA (IFS)	- - × × × × - × - × - 0.07 -	solutions improving company management-mainly for the printing industry and consultancy in the field of IT solutions
		- ×	×
62.	SURFLAND SYSTEMY KOMPUTEROWE SPÓŁKA AKCYJNA (SSK)	- - × × - × × × × × × no data[3] -	integration of ICT systems
		- ×	×
63.	IMAGIS SPÓŁKA AKCYJNA (IMG)	- - × × × × × - × × × no data -	geographic information systems (GIS)
		- ×	×
64.	FACHOWCY.PL VENTURES SPÓŁKA AKCYJNA (FAV)	× - × × × × × - × × × no data -	technology development in the scope of winning orders effectively from the Internet for small and medium-sized service and production companies
		- ×	×
65.	FINHOUSE SPÓŁKA AKCYJNA (FIN)	- - × × - × × - × × × no data -	innovative tools facilitating the work of financial advisors; they introduced a search engine for cash loans and mortgages
		- ×	×
66.	I3D SPÓŁKA AKCYJNA (I3D)	- - × × × × × × × × - no data -	new technologies in interactive 3D graphics
		- ×	×

Table A2. *Cont.*

No.	Company	\multicolumn{11}{l}{Indication of the Occurrence of a Given Criterion — Criteria for Assessing the Sustainability of the Business Models of IT Companies on the NewConnect Market}											Value	Description
58.	MACRO GAMES SPÓŁKA AKCYJNA (MGS)	-	-	-	X	X	X	X	-	X	-	X	0.46	web portals related to broadly defined electronic games, a partner of Microsoft Poland in the development, integration and activation of the Minecraft community in Poland
67.	INWESTYCJE ALTERNATYWNE PROFIT SPÓŁKA AKCYJNA (IAP)	-	-	-	-	X	-	X	X	X	X	-	no data	retail trade in bullion, numismatics and precious stones
68.	MERLIN GROUP SPÓŁKA AKCYJNA (MRG) (previously AdMassive S.A.)	-	X	-	X	X	-	X	-	X	-	X	no data	sales activation in digital channels
69.	INNOVATIVE COMMERCE A.S. (ICM) (previously iCom Vision Holding S.A.)	-	-	-	X	X	X	X	X	X	-	X	no data	Internet services and online communication solutions via mobile technologies and online media (the activity market is the Czech Republic)
70.	STANUSCH TECHNOLOGIES SPÓŁKA AKCYJNA (STT)	-	-	-	X	X	X	X	-	X	-	X	no data	research and development into the use of artificial intelligence in company management
71.	HUCKLEBERRY GAMES SPÓŁKA AKCYJNA (HBG)	-	-	-	X	X	X	X	-	X	X	X	no data	production of innovative MMORPG games

Note: [1] "-"—does not include; [2] X—this criterion is met; [3] no data—data is not found in the NewConnect Statistic Bulletin. Source: own study based on information documents and websites.

163

Table A3. Variables that describe value migration from the NewConnect market business models operating in the digital economy.

No.	Company Name	Market Value (Capitalization at the End of the Period) [Million Euro][1]		Sales Revenues [Euro][2]		Market Value/Sales Revenues		Growth Rate of Company Market Value	Growth Rate of Sales Revenues	P/E Ratio[3]		Growth Rate of the P/E Ratio	P/BV Ratio[4]		Growth Rate of the P/BV Ratio
		2016	2017	2016	2017	2016	2017			2016	2017		2016	2017	
							IT systems								
1.	BIZTECH KONSULTING SPÓŁKA AKCYJNA (BTK)	no data[5]	15.34	32,265,085.92	36,385,111.03	-[6]	0.4215	-	1.1277	no data	14.1	-	no data	1.48	-
2.	LUKARDI SPÓŁKA AKCYJNA (LUK)	no data	19.42	7,346,050.01	11,875,768.01	-	1.6352	-	1.6166	no data	no data	-	no data	8.87	-
3.	MEGA SONIC SPÓŁKA AKCYJNA (MGA)	34.80	28.88	253,301,570.53	134,418,335.19	0.1374	0.2148	0.8299	0.5307	10.3	9	0.87	1.03	0.78	0.7573
4.	PROVECTA IT SPÓŁKA AKCYJNA (PRV)	163.82	375.68	7,280,390.62	no data	22.5011	-	2.2933	-	24.8	no data	-	8.04	1.49	0.1853
5.	S4E SPÓŁKA AKCYJNA (S4E)	76.72	74.43	458,898,908.70	625,024,155.90	0.1672	0.1191	0.9701	1.3620	6.1	no data	-	1.25	1.32	1.0560
6.	SEVENET SPÓŁKA AKCYJNA (SEV)	47.88	29.96	no data	no data	-	-	0.6258	-	no data	no data	-	1.03	2.40	2.3301
7.	SUNTECH SPÓŁKA AKCYJNA (SUN)	23.92	16.63	28,512,655.56	28,706,028.65	0.8389	0.5792	0.6951	1.0068	21.2	32.6	1.54	7.63	4.56	0.5976
8.	SURFLAND SYSTEMY KOMPUTEROWE SPÓŁKA AKCYJNA (SSK)	5.63	9.63	16,354,362.78	9,831,524.00	0.3440	0.9791	1.7111	0.6012	no data	no data	-	2.08	no data	-
9.	VERBICOM SPÓŁKA AKCYJNA (VRB)	52.51	28.75	25,769,333.01	49,706,304.21	2.0376	0.5785	0.5476	1.9289	6	13	2.17	1.35	0.66	0.4889
							IT equipment								
10.	IMAGIS SPÓŁKA AKCYJNA (IMG)	no data	43.55	19,543,136.77	19,472,751.08	-	2.2364	-	0.9964	no data	no data	-	no data	no data	-
							E-commerce								
11.	71MEDIA SPÓŁKA AKCYJNA (71M)	33.88	24.21	28,717,642.58	18,297,622.32	1.1798	1.3232	0.7146	0.6372	10.3	no data	-	4.16	7.83	1.8822
12.	ALEJASAMOCHODOWA.PL SPÓŁKA AKCYJNA (ALS)	16.29	33.26	13,712,024.74	118,810,265.25	1.1883	0.2799	2.0409	8.6647	3.8	3.7	0.97	0.58	0.81	1.3966
13.	ARENA.PL SPÓŁKA AKCYJNA (ARE) (Carbon Invest S.A.)	207.61	257.29	0.00	0.00	-	-	1.2393	-	no data	no data	-	5.23	7.26	1.3881
14.	E-KIOSK SPÓŁKA AKCYJNA (EKS)	61.05	40.71	76,534,464.80	95,646,823.61	0.7977	0.4257	0.6669	1.2497	26.2	50.9	1.94	9.02	5.38	0.5965
15.	INBOOK SPÓŁKA AKCYJNA (INB)	17.84	11.92	11,875,355.65	12,838,674.27	1.5019	0.9283	0.6682	1.0811	no data	45.1	-	5.42	3.35	0.6181
16.	INWESTYCJE ALTERNATYWNE PROFIT SPÓŁKA AKCYJNA (IAP)	48.05	no data	725,626.95	no data	66.2172	-	-	-	no data	no data	-	0.60	no data	-

Table A3. *Cont.*

No.	Company Name	Market Value (Capitalization at the End of the Period) [Million Euro] [1]		Sales Revenues [Euro] [2]		Market Value/Sales Revenues		Growth Rate of Company Market Value	Growth Rate of Sales Revenues	P/E Ratio [3]		Growth Rate of the P/E Ratio	P/BV Ratio [4]		Growth Rate of the P/BV Ratio
		2016	2017	2016	2017	2016	2017			2016	2017		2016	2017	
						E-commerce									
17.	MERLIN GROUP SPÓŁKA AKCYJNA (MRG) (previously AdMassive S.A.)	no data	no data	0.00	780,952.02	-	-	-	-	no data	no data	-	no data	no data	-
18.	MODERN COMMERCE SPÓŁKA AKCYJNA (MCE) (previously Air Market S.A.)	302.88	298.25	5000.76	0.00	60,566.67	-	0.9847	-	no data	no data	-	4.97	3.82	0.7686
19.	OUTDOORZY SPÓŁKA AKCYJNA (OUT)	16.63	18.38	15,912,076.73	20,423,466.94	1.0450	0.8998	1.1053	1.2835	76.1	32.1	0.42	2.84	2.87	1.0106
20.	PRESENT24 SPÓŁKA AKCYJNA (P24)	7.33	29.30	2,647,626.75	1,949,021.83	2.7702	15.0312	3.9943	0.7361	no data	22.2	-	0.70	1.51	2.1571
						Web portals									
21.	ARTP CAPITAL SPÓŁKA AKCYJNA (TYP) (previously Tylko Piłka S.A.)	18.17	13.63	5,917,107.60	2,187,660.68	3.0707	6.2291	0.7500	0.3697	no data	no data	-	0.71	0.73	1.0282
22.	DIGITAL AVENUE SPÓŁKA AKCYJNA (DGL)	14.84	10.04	5,131,506.08	4,944,255.91	2.8911	2.0313	0.6770	0.9635	no data	no data	-	3.10	2.26	0.7290
23.	FACHOWCY.PL VENTURES SPÓŁKA AKCYJNA (FAV)	493.66	17.63	11,504,319.93	21,285,142.14	42.9107	0.8282	0.0357	1.8502	no data	no data	-	75.56	no data	-
24.	INWESTYCJE.PL SPÓŁKA AKCYJNA (INW)	53.92	175.32	18,344.45	37,105.64	2939.5729	4724.8428	3.2512	2.0227	no data	no data	-	0.94	3.46	3.6809
25.	LANGLOO.COM SPÓŁKA AKCYJNA (LAN)	7.21	12.59	10,041,545.83	9,692,260.67	0.7180	1.2985	1.7457	0.9652	2	20.2	10.10	0.59	0.99	1.6780
						Software									
26.	2INTELLECT.COM SPÓŁKA AKCYJNA (2IT)	no data	2.00	4,562,429.80	2,736,824.27	-	0.7309	-	0.5999	no data	no data	-	no data	0.56	-
27.	4MOBILITY SPÓŁKA AKCYJNA (4MB)	209.45	146.65	4,922,958.43	4,581,638.26	42.5453	32.0076	1.1053	0.9307	no data	no data	-	75.85	6.53	0.0861
28.	A.P.N. PROMISE SPÓŁKA AKCYJNA (PRO)	244.79	160.11	1,164,534,330.57	1,185,289,341.43	0.2102	0.1351	0.6541	1.0178	8.4	5.4	0.64	2.67	1.37	0.5131
29.	ACREBIT SPÓŁKA AKCYJNA (ACR)	52.63	40.92	7,775,112.68	7,775,112.68	6.7694	5.2633	0.7775	1.0000	48.9	no data	-	3.28	2.91	0.8872
30.	DOOK SPÓŁKA AKCYJNA (DOK)	no data	15.50	no data	no data	-	-	-	-	no data	468.7	-	no data	5.89	-
31.	EC2 SPÓŁKA AKCYJNA (EC2)	6.46	5.04	8,627,914.66	3,901,784.11	0.7487	1.2923	0.7806	0.4522	2.4	no data	-	1.29	1.80	1.3953
32.	EDISON SPÓŁKA AKCYJNA (EDN)	15.63	22.25	10,705,043.21	11,995,773.54	1.4598	1.8551	1.4240	1.1206	no data	2.5	-	1.36	1.09	0.8015
33.	EO NETWORKS SPÓŁKA AKCYJNA (EON)	52.17	49.51	120,180,764.70	160,945,293.30	0.4341	0.3076	0.9489	1.3392	3.6	4.3	-	0.74	0.61	0.8243

Table A3. *Cont.*

No.	Company Name	Market Value (Capitalization at the End of the Period) [Million Euro] [1]		Sales Revenues [Euro] [2]		Market Value/Sales Revenues		Growth Rate of Company Market Value	Growth Rate of Sales Revenues	P/E Ratio [3]		Growth Rate of the P/E Ratio	P/BV Ratio [4]		Growth Rate of the P/BV Ratio
		2016	2017	2016	2017	2016	2017			2016	2017		2016	2017	
						Software									
34.	EXAMOBILE SPÓŁKA AKCYJNA (EXA)	14.67	9.08	1,844,666.05	1,242,922.73	7.9521	7.3092	0.6193	0.6738	18.5	82.8	4.48	3.68	2.21	0.6005
35.	FINHOUSE SPÓŁKA AKCYJNA (FIN)	4.63	1.38	5,058,449.52	4,631,254.34	0.9145	0.2969	0.2973	0.9155	no data	no data	-	7.01	no data	-
36.	GRUPA EXORIGO-UPOS SPÓŁKA AKCYJNA (GEU)	1000.15	430.90	0.00	7,084,410.00	-	60.8235	0.4308	-	29.8	11.6	0.39	7.11	2.76	0.3882
37.	I3D SPÓŁKA AKCYJNA (I3D)	22.09	3.50	13,926,115.86	5,577,398.59	1.5860	0.6276	0.1585	0.4005	no data	no data	-	20.85	no data	-
38.	IAI SPÓŁKA AKCYJNA (IAI)	232.16	628.80	54,643,545.93	80,859,454.60	4.2486	7.7765	2.7085	1.4798	27	39.8	1.47	10.64	18.74	1.7613
39.	INFOSYSTEMS SPÓŁKA AKCYJNA (IRS)	15.75	4.96	8,297,094.30	7,980,379.50	1.8985	0.6214	0.3148	0.9618	no data	no data	-	0.22	0.07	0.3182
40.	INFRA SPÓŁKA AKCYJNA (IFA)	8.13	2.83	2,946,263.31	2,598,983.03	2.7581	1.0903	0.3487	0.8821	59.4	19.1	0.32	2.15	0.72	0.3349
41.	INNOVATIVE COMMERCE A.S. (ICM) (previously iCom Vision Holding S.A.)	no data	no data	no data	no data	-	-	-	-	no data	no data	-	no data	no data	-
42.	INTELIWISE SPÓŁKA AKCYJNA (ITL)	40.17	58.68	5,022,055.78	7,369,318.09	7.9993	7.9621	1.4606	1.4674	no data	71.5	-	22.69	26.19	1.1543
43.	JWA SPÓŁKA AKCYJNA (JWA)	12.84	8.67	12,217,690.14	8,995,157.39	1.0505	0.9636	0.6753	0.7362	3.2	4.9	1.53	2.23	1.15	0.5157
44.	KBJ SPÓŁKA AKCYJNA (KBJ)	37.26	84.64	40,933,141.60	69,126,070.98	0.9102	1.2244	2.2718	1.6888	8.9	10	1.12	2.11	3.63	1.7204
45.	LOGINTRADE SPÓŁKA AKCYJNA (LGT)	9.79	15.67	10,559,322.40	13,157,714.54	0.9274	1.1909	1.6000	1.2461	no data	16.6	-	1.50	2.10	1.4000
46.	M4B SPÓŁKA AKCYJNA (M4B)	47.01	1162.43	44,223,509.41	32,784,088.88	1.0629	35.4570	24.7297	0.7413	4.5	136	30.22	13.85	52.99	3.8260
47.	MADKOM SPÓŁKA AKCYJNA (MAD)	36.76	30.84	12,681,693.66	30,888,190.79	2.8983	0.9984	0.8390	2.4357	no data	5.8	-	2.95	1.75	0.5932
48.	MAKOLAB SPÓŁKA AKCYJNA (MLB)	65.76	81.51	60,302.29	74,471.53	1090.5058	1094.5443	1.2395	1.2350	20.1	12.8	0.64	2.00	2.22	1.1100
49.	MINERAL MIDRANGE SPÓŁKA AKCYJNA (MND)	8.46	8.08	30,892,376.55	25,723,241.80	0.2738	0.3143	0.9557	0.8327	7.3	no data	-	1.56	3.49	2.2372
50.	NEPTIS SPÓŁKA AKCYJNA (YAN)	81.26	125.02	38,715,271.45	43,770,718.60	2.0990	2.8562	1.5385	1.1306	50.3	72.1	1.43	9.94	12.62	1.2696
51.	NETWISE SPÓŁKA AKCYJNA (NTW)	21.21	53.05	27,410,732.46	28,657,412.68	0.7738	1.8512	2.5010	1.0455	no data	16.8	-	3.67	5.93	1.6158
52.	PILAB SPÓŁKA AKCYJNA (PIL)	413.31	498.49	3,094,838.72	4,756,890.77	133.5491	104.7938	1.2061	1.5370	no data	no data	-	5.39	12.55	2.3284

Table A3. *Cont.*

No.	Company Name	Market Value (Capitalization at the End of the Period [Million Euro])[1]		Sales Revenues [Euro][2]		Market Value/Sales Revenues		Growth Rate of Company Market Value	Growth Rate of Sales Revenues	P/E Ratio[3]		Growth Rate of the P/E Ratio	P/BV Ratio[4]		Growth Rate of the P/BV Ratio
		2016	2017	2016	2017	2016	2017			2016	2017		2016	2017	
						Software									
53.	SITE SPÓŁKA AKCYJNA (STE)	4.08	31.67	no data	no data	-	-	7.7551	-	no data	no data	-	1.46	0.64	0.4384
54.	STANUSCH TECHNOLOGIES SPÓŁKA AKCYJNA (STT)	49.51	no data	1,819,638.08	no data	27.2073	-	-	-	no data	no data	-	2776.59	no data	-
55.	UNIFIED FACTORY SPÓŁKA AKCYJNA (UFC)	265.46	419.36	70,379,775.85	95,880,640.68	3.7718	4.3737	1.5797	1.3623	18.4	12.8	0.70	3.65	2.62	0.7178
						Games									
56.	BLOOBER TEAM SPÓŁKA AKCYJNA (BLO)	584.76	309.34	45,209,422.29	46,900,982.28	12.9344	6.5956	0.5290	1.0374	17.9	17.5	0.98	6.43	2.84	0.4417
57.	CHERRYPICK GAMES SPÓŁKA AKCYJNA (CHP)	no data	611.18	no data	no data	-	-	-	-	no data	55.1	-	no data	27.45	-
58.	FOREVER ENTERTAINMENT SPÓŁKA AKCYJNA (FOR)	84.72	103.14	3,446,160.32	8,855,701.49	24.5842	11.6468	1.2174	2.5697	no data	no data	-	4.25	3.28	0.7718
59.	HUCKLEBERRY GAMES SPÓŁKA AKCYJNA (HBG)	no data	no data	no data	no data	-	-	-	-	no data	no data	-	no data	no data	-
60.	IFUN4ALL SPÓŁKA AKCYJNA (IF4)	71.05	66.68	3,543,511.78	4,149,781.88	20.0514	16.0675	0.9384	1.1711	no data	no data	-	5.83	6.4	1.0978
61.	JUJUBEE SPÓŁKA AKCYJNA (JJB)	248.41	127.35	1,540,522.33	4,927,524.99	161.2523	25.8452	0.5127	3.1986	no data	276.3	-	43.08	14.95	0.3470
62.	MACRO GAMES SPÓŁKA AKCYJNA (MGS)	125.44	22.13	15,647,059.57	22,154,600.03	8.0166	0.9988	0.1764	1.4159	23.4	24.4	1.04	2.97	0.46	0.1549
63.	QUBICGAMES SPÓŁKA AKCYJNA (QUB)	76.93	38.88	2,351,957,443.20	2,661,191,939.70	0.0327	0.0146	0.5054	1.1315	no data	40	-	3.99	2.38	0.5965
64.	T-BULL SPÓŁKA AKCYJNA (TBL)	782.54	468.45	40,876,544.87	44,188,057.44	19.1439	10.6012	0.5986	1.0810	43.8	21.9	0.50	29.41	9.75	0.3315
65.	THE FARM 51 GROUP SPÓŁKA AKCYJNA (F51)	294.38	172.23	19,685,719.19	20,952,156.08	14.9539	8.2204	0.5851	1.0643	no data	no data	-	6.93	4.53	0.6537
						Information technology-others									
66.	BIT EVIL SPÓŁKA AKCYJNA (BIT)	no data	23.63	951,340.54	2,577,236.22	-	9.1682	-	2.7091	no data	15.9	-	no data	7.30	-
67.	BLACK POINT SPÓŁKA AKCYJNA (BPN)	24.00	14.00	167,867,743.73	162,009,149.61	0.1430	0.0864	0.5833	0.9651	no data	no data	-	0.26	0.17	0.6538
68.	DOMENOMANIA.PL SPÓŁKA AKCYJNA (DOA)	10.21	3.00	14,788,969.33	12,173,996.62	0.6904	0.2465	0.2939	0.8232	11.4	6.0	0.5263	0.71	0.20	0.2817
69.	EUROSYSTEM SPÓŁKA AKCYJNA (ERS)	4.33	5.21	1,774,200.89	6,840,596.36	2.4428	0.7615	1.2019	3.8556	no data	no data	-	0.70	1.23	1.7571
70.	XPLUS SPÓŁKA AKCYJNA (XPL)	36.51	47.72	60,159,445.01	62,305,325.64	0.6068	0.7658	1.3071	1.0357	4.8	9.3	1.9375	1.17	1.42	1.2137

[1] NewConnect Statistic Bulletin for 2016 and 2017; [2] A unitary quarterly report for 2016 and 2017. Value includes sales revenues for three quarters of a given financial year; [3] NewConnect Statistic Bulletin for 2016 and 2017; [4] NewConnect Statistic Bulletin for 2016 and 2017; [5] no data—data is not found in the NewConnect Statistic Bulletin; [6] "-"—it is not possible to calculate a given ratio; Source: own study based on information documents.

References

1. Timmers, P. Business Models for Electronic Markets. *Electron. Markets* **1998**, *8*, 3–8. [CrossRef]
2. Lumpkin, G.T.; Dess, G.G. E-Business Strategies and Internet Business Models: How the Internet Adds Value. *Organ. Dyn.* **2004**, *33*, 161–173. [CrossRef]
3. Sinakou, E.; Boeve-de Pauw, J.; Goossens, M.; Van Petegem, P. Academics in the field of Education for Sustainable Development: Their conceptions of sustainable development. *J. Clean. Prod.* **2018**, *184*, 321–332. [CrossRef]
4. Elkington, J. *Cannibals with Forks: The Triple Bottom Line of 21st Century Business*; Capstone: Oxford, UK, 1999.
5. Wang, Z.; Sarkis, J. Corporate social responsibility governance, outcomes, and financial performance. *J. Clean. Prod.* **2017**, *162*, 1607–1616. [CrossRef]
6. Bergman, M.M.; Bergman, Z.; Berger, L. An Empirical Exploration, Typology, and Definition of Corporate Sustainability. *Sustainability* **2017**, *9*, 753. [CrossRef]
7. Jabłoński, A.; Jabłoński, M. Research on Business Models in their Life Cycle. *Sustainability* **2016**, *8*, 430. [CrossRef]
8. Mourougan, S. Corporate Social Responsibility for sustainable business. *IOSR J. Bus. Manag.* **2015**, *17*, 94–106.
9. Fahimnia, B.; Sarkis, J.; Davarzani, H. Green supply chain management: A review and bibliometric analysis. *Int. J. Profuction Econ.* **2015**, *162*, 101–114. [CrossRef]
10. Schaltegger, S.; Hansen, E.; Lüdeke-Freund, F. Business Models for Sustainability: Origins, Present Research, and Future Avenues. *Organ. Environ.* **2016**. [CrossRef]
11. Lüdeke-Freund, F. Towards a Conceptual Framework of 'Business Models for Sustainability'. In Proceedings of the Knowledge Collaboration & Learning for Sustainable Innovation: 14th European Roundtable on Sustainable Consumption and Production (ERSCP) Conference and the 6th Environmental Management for Sustainable Universities (EMSU) Conference, Delft, The Netherlands, 25–29 October 2010.
12. Schaltegger, S.; Lüdeke-Freund, F.; Hansen, E.G. Business Models for Sustainability—A Co-Evolutionary Analysis of Sustainable Entrepreneurship, Innovation, and Transformation. *Organ. Environ.* **2016**, *29*, 264–289. [CrossRef]
13. Boons, F.; Montalvo, C.; Quist, J.; Wagner, M. Sustainable innovation, business models and economic performance: An overview. *J. Clean. Prod.* **2013**, *45*, 1–8. [CrossRef]
14. Choi, H.R.; Cho, M.J.; Lee, K.B.; Hong, S.G.; Woo, C.R. The Business Model for the Sharing economy between SMEs. *WSEAS Trans. Bus. Econ.* **2014**, *11*, 625–634.
15. Stephany, A. *The Business of Sharing: Making It in the New Sharing Economy*; Palgrave Macmillan: London, UK, 2015.
16. Cohen, B.; Munoz, P. Sharing Business Model Compass. 2017. Available online: https://ladiaria.com.uy/articulo/2017/4/un-modelo-para-entender-la-economiacolaborativa/# (accessed on 7 June 2017).
17. Belk, R. You are what you can access: Sharing and collaborative consumption online. *J. Bus. Res.* **2014**, *67*, 1595–1600. [CrossRef]
18. Circo, C.J. Does Sustainability Require a New Theory of Property Rights? *Kansas Law Rev.* **2009**, *58*, 91. [CrossRef]
19. Alchian, A.A. *The New Palgrave Dictionary of Economics*; Palgrave Macmillan: London, UK, 2008.
20. Caroll, A.B. *Business & Society, Ethics and Stakeholders Management*, 2nd ed.; South-Western Publishing Co: Cikncinnati, OH, USA, 1995.
21. Husted, B.W.; Allen, D.B. Strategic corporate social responsibility and value creation among large firms. *Longe Range Plan.* **2007**, *40*, 594–610. [CrossRef]
22. Freeman, R.E. *Strategic Management: A Stakeholder Approach*; Pitman: Boston, MA, USA, 1984.
23. Harrison, J.S.; Wicks, A.C. Stakeholder Theory, Value, and Firm Performance. *Bus. Ethics Q.* **2013**, *23*, 97–124. [CrossRef]
24. Lüdeke-Freund, F.; Carroux, S.; Joyce, A.; Massa, L.; Breuer, H. The sustainable business model pattern taxonomy—45 patterns to support sustainability-oriented business model innovation. *Sustain. Prod. Consum.* **2018**, *15*, 145–162. [CrossRef]
25. Casadesus-Masanell, R.; Heilbron, J. *The Business Model: Nature and Benefits*; Working Paper 15-089; Harvard Business School: Boston, MA, USA, 2015.

26. Evans, S.; Vladimirova, D.; Holgado, M.; Van Fossen, K.; Yang, M.; Silva, E.A.; Barlow, C.Y. Business model innovation for sustainability: Towards a unified perspective for creation of sustainable business models. *Bus. Strategy Environ.* **2017**, *26*, 597–608. [CrossRef]

27. *The New Digital Economy and Development*; Technical Note No. 8, UNEDITED TN/UNCTAD/ICT4D/08 October; UNCTAD, Division on Technology and Logistics Science, Technology and ICT Branch ICT Policy Section: Geneva, Switzerland, 2017.

28. De Pádua Pieronia, M.; Pigossoa, D.C.A.; McAloonea, T.C. Sustainable qualifying criteria for designing circular business models. *Procedia CIRP* **2018**, *69*, 799–804. [CrossRef]

29. Ellen MacArthur Foundation (EMF). *Towards a Circular Economy—Business Rationale for an Accelerated Transition*; Ellen MacArthur Foundation (EMF): Cowes, UK, 2015.

30. Manninen, K.; Koskela, S.; Antikainen, R.; Bocken, N.; Dahlbo, H.; Aminoff, A. Do circular economy business models capture intended environmental value propositions? *J. Clean. Prod.* **2018**, *171*, 413–422. [CrossRef]

31. Bressanelli, G.; Adrodegari, F.; Perona, M.; Saccani, N. The role of digital technologies to overcome Circular Economy challenges in PSS Business Models—And exploratory case study. *Procedia CIRP* **2018**, *73*, 216–221. [CrossRef]

32. Lüdeke-Freund, F.; Gold, S.; Bocken, N. A Review and Basic Typology of Circular Economy Business Model Patterns. *J. Ind. Ecol.* **2018**, in press.

33. Laney, D. 3-D Data Management: Controlling Data Volume, Velocity and Variety. META Group Research Note. 2001. Available online: http://blogs.gartner.com/doug-laney/files/2012/01/ad949-3D-Data-Management-Controlling-Data-Volume-Velocity-and-Variety.pdf (accessed on 15 July 2018).

34. Kwon, O.; Lee, N.; Shin, B. Data quality management, data usage experience and acquisition intention of big data analytics. *Int. J. Inf. Manag.* **2014**, *34*, 387–394. [CrossRef]

35. Russom, P. *Big Data Analytics*; TDWI Best Practices Report; Fourth Quarter: Renton, WA, USA, 2011.

36. Sheng, J.; Amankwah-Amoah, J.; Wang, X. A multidisciplinary perspective of big data in management Research. *Int. J. Prod. Econ.* **2017**, *191*, 97–112. [CrossRef]

37. Sivarajah, U.; Kamal, M.M.; Irani, Z.; Weerakkody, V. Critical analysis of Big Data challenges and analytical methods. *J. Bus. Res.* **2017**, *70*, 263–286. [CrossRef]

38. Muñoz, P.; Cohen, B. Mapping out the sharing economy: A configurational approach to sharing business modeling. *Technol. Forecast. Soc. Chang.* **2017**, *125*, 21–37. [CrossRef]

39. McLaren, D.; Agyeman, J. *Sharing Cities: A Case for Truly Smart and Sustainable Cities*; MIT Press: Cambridge, MA, USA, 2015.

40. Slywotzky, A.J. *Value Migration: How to Think Several Moves Ahead of the Competition*; Harvard Business School Press: Boston, MA, USA, 1996.

41. Alt, R.; Zimmermann, H.-D. Editorial 24/3: Electronic Markets and general research. *Electron. Markets* **2014**, *24*, 161–164. [CrossRef]

42. Watanabe, C. Measuring GDP in the digital economy: Increasing dependence on uncaptured GDP. *Technol. Forecast. Soc. Chang.* **2018**. [CrossRef]

43. Directorate General for Internal Policies; Policy Department A: Economic and Scientific Policy; Internal Market and Consumer Protection. *Consumer Behaviour in a Digital Environment*; European Parlament: Brussels, Belgium, 2011.

44. Teece, D.J. Business models, business strategy and innovation. *Long. Range Plan.* **2010**, *43*, 172–194. [CrossRef]

45. Biloslavo, R.; Bagnoli, C.; Edgar, D. An eco-critical perspective on business models: The value triangle as an approach to closing the sustainability gap. *J. Clean. Prod.* **2018**, *174*, 746–762. [CrossRef]

46. Fortunati, L.; O'Sullivan, J. Situating the social sustainability of print media in a world of digital alternatives. *Telemat. Inform.* **2018**. [CrossRef]

47. Lüdeke-Freund, F.; Dembek, K. Research and Practice on Sustainable Business Models: Emerging Field or Passing Fancy? *J. Clean. Prod.* **2017**. [CrossRef]

48. D'Humières, P. *Towards a Sustainable European Business Model?* European Issues n°460; Fondation Robert Schuman: Paris, France, 2018.

49. Neumeyer, X.; Santos, S.C. Sustainable Business Models, Venture Typologies, and Entrepreneurial Ecosystems: A Social Network Perspective. *J. Clean. Prod.* **2018**, *172*, 4565–4579. [CrossRef]

50. Seele, P.; Lock, I. The Game-Changing Potential of Digitalization for Sustainability: Possibilities, Perils, and Pathways. *Sustain. Sci.* **2017**, *12*, 183–185. [CrossRef]

51. Donker, F.W.; van Loenen, B. Sustainable Business Models for Public Sector Open Data Providers. *JeDEM* **2016**, *8*, 28–61. [CrossRef]

52. Daunoriene, A.; Draksaite, A.; Snieska, V.; Valodkiene, G. Evaluating Sustainability of Sharing economy Business Models. *Procedia Soc. Behav. Sci.* **2015**, *213*, 836–841. [CrossRef]

53. Piscicelli, L.; Ludden, G.D.S.; Cooper, T. What makes a sustainable business model successful? An empirical comparison of two peer-to-peer goods-sharing platforms. *J. Clean. Prod.* **2018**, *172*, 4582–4589. [CrossRef]

54. Teece, D.J. Business models and dynamic capabilities. *Longe Range Plan.* **2018**, *51*, 40–49. [CrossRef]

55. Mayer-Schonberger, V.; Cukier, K. *Big Data: A Revolution that Will Transform How We Live, Work, and Think*; Houghton Mifflin Harcourt Publishing Company: Boston, MA, USA, 2012.

56. Botsman, R.; Rogers, R. *What's Mine Is Yours: The Rise of Collaborative Consumption*; HarperCollins: New York, NY, USA, 2010.

57. Urbinati, A.; Chiaroni, D.; Chiesa, V. Towards a new taxonomy of circular economy business models. *J. Clean. Prod.* **2017**, *168*, 487–498. [CrossRef]

58. Mahajan, G. Value Dominant Logic. *J. Creat. Value* **2017**, *3*, 217–235. [CrossRef]

59. Duggad, G. *Value Migration: Picking Winners in Disruptive Times*; Motilal Oswal: Mumbai, India, 2017.

60. Eggerta, A.; Ulagab, W.; Frowc, P.; Payne, A. Conceptualizing and communicating value in business markets: From value in exchange to value in use. *Ind. Mark. Manag.* **2017**, *69*, 80–90. [CrossRef]

61. Hacklin, F.; Bjorkdahl, J.; Wallin, M.W. Strategies for business model innovation: How firms reel in migrating value. *Long Range Plan.* **2018**, *51*, 82–110. [CrossRef]

62. Jabłoński, M. Methods of evaluating the investment attractiveness of business models in the context of the performance management concept. In *Strategic Performance Management: New Concept and Contemporary Trends*; Jabłoński, M., Ed.; Nova Science Publishers, Inc.: New York, NY, USA, 2017; pp. 1–17.

63. Flick, U. *Managing Quality in Qualitative Research*; SAGE: London, UK, 2007.

64. Bocken, N.M.P.; Short, S.W.; Rana, P.; Evans, S. A literature and practice review to develop sustainable business model Archetypes. *J. Clean. Prod.* **2014**, *65*, 42–56. [CrossRef]

sustainability

MDPI

Article

Green Human Resource Management as a Tool for the Sustainable Development of Enterprises: Polish Young Company Experience

Edyta Bombiak * and Anna Marciniuk-Kluska

Faculty of Economic and Legal Sciences, Siedlce University of Natural Sciences and Humanities, Konarskiego 2, 08-110 Siedlce, Poland; anna.marciniuk-kluska@uph.edu.pl
* Correspondence: edyta.bombiak@uph.edu.pl; Tel.: +48-025-643-17-09

Received: 28 April 2018; Accepted: 20 May 2018; Published: 25 May 2018

Abstract: The growing role of sustainable development and, above all, its ecological aspect, in the development of modern company competitive edge leads to the popularization of the question of incorporating environmental practices into the area of human resource policy, referred to as Green HRM. The objective of the research was to identify pro-environmental HR practices embraced by young Polish enterprises and to prioritize them in accordance with their effect on company sustainable development. To attain these goals, a survey was conducted among a random, representative population of 150 young enterprises. The study revealed that the Green HRM concept in the Polish reality is relatively. However, there is a strong positive correlation between the evaluation of the impact of individual activities within Green HRM on sustainable company development and their practical implementation. Research demonstrated that the higher the evaluation of the impact of a given activity, the more frequent its implementation in the studied companies. This allowed the formulation of the following conclusion: in order to increase the scope of the implementation of the Green HRM concept in Polish young enterprises, it is necessary to raise awareness and disseminate knowledge concerning the impact Green HRM can have on sustainable development in organizations.

Keywords: green human resource management; sustainability development; young companies

---

1. Introduction

Progressive degradation of the natural environment due to human exploitation brought about the need to introduce the concept of sustainable development. Thereby, the natural environment and resource protection for the benefit of future generations have become global imperatives [1–3]. This emphasized the necessity to redefine the operating strategy of contemporary enterprises. The sustainable development paradigm not only deals with the attainment of economic goals but also the necessity to heed broadly understood social and ecological interests, laying foundations on which a sustainable business model based on the principles of value- and social responsibility-oriented management can be built [4].

Sustainable development is a concept responding to the global challenges related to human activity in both developed and developing countries. This new concept of civilizational development is the outcome of the need to mitigate and prevent the adverse effects of the economic development. It is a modern direction of the economic development, emphasising the introduction of the new methods of organisation and management, both on the national level and the levels of various economic entities, as well as on the replacement of the cumbersome technologies with the "environmentally-friendly" ones [5]. According to the World Commission on Environment and Development, sustainable development satisfies the needs of the present generation without jeopardising the ability of future generations to satisfy theirs [6]. Such development is intelligent, environmentally-friendly, based on the effective use of resources, knowledge and innovation [7].

There are three basic dimensions of sustainable development [8]:

- ecological (protection of the environment and its natural resources),
- economic (economic development that is not hindered, but stimulated by technological advancement andincreased effectiveness in the use of resources, materials and workforce),
- social (improvement inthe living conditions and safety of all people).

The concept of sustainable development is based on the so-called triple bottom Line [1,9]. Pursuant to the principles of sustainable development, the social, economic and environmental objectives are interdependent and mutually reinforcing [10]. Thus, the development strategy of the company should take into account the development of a balance between the economic, environmental and social dimensions of economic activity. This means the supported economic solutions should be socially responsible, environmentally friendly and economically valuable at the same time [11]. It has been emphasised that a sustainable enterprise fosters sustainable development simultaneously offering the economic, social and environmental benefits.

Theories of sustainable development have evolved over many years, however, there are still many controversies over the too narrowapproach to this concept, perceiving it only in terms ofenvironmental protection, as well as poor recognition on the microeconomic level, i.e., level of the organisation [12]. Moreover, sustainability issues involve complex interactions between social, economic and environmental factors, often perceived quite differently by different interest groups [13]. Different models, approaches and concepts presented inliterature make the idea of sustainability ambiguous and difficult to interpret. On the one hand, it mentions ensuring business sustainability, and, on the other hand, a multidimensional look at the organization considering the interests of various groups of stakeholders [14]. Numerous studies prove that corporate sustainability management focused on creating a harmonious relationship with various stakeholders brings a number of benefits to the organisation [15]. Among other things, the positive impact of socially responsible activities on the company's efficiency has been indicated [16]. The literature, however, also givesexamples of the unequivocal impact of social and environmental attitudes on a company's financial performance, based on cases where such an approach has not affected its economic success [17]. Despite these inconsistencies, a growing interest in the concept of sustainable development has been observed. More and more companies worldwide are implementing the principles of sustainable development in their business operations [15]. The factors stimulating social and environmental actions taken by enterprises include [18,19]:

- changes in the expectations of the stakeholders related to the increased level of their awareness,
- changes in the technological environment providing opportunities to implement innovations in the way the organisation operates and the products and services it offers;
- institutional and legal conditions defining the desired directions and framework for the development of the economy and itsparticular entities,
- searching fornew sources witha competitive edge.

The companies must take up the challenge of implementing the principles of sustainable development in such circumstances. This concept is motivation to undertake action aimed at increasing the welfare of the groups, regions and whole societies [20].The goal of sustainable development is toimprove the living standard of people, at the same time improving the access to natural resources and ecosystems for future generations [21]. Sustainable development is about the economic, social and environmental goals common to all people [10].

The resulting necessity to maintain symbiosis on the enterprise-society-environment axis means thatentrepreneurs are increasingly guided by the principles of corporate social responsibility (CSR) in a decision-making process. Socially-responsible business is a strategic and long-term approach based on the principles of social dialogue and search for the solutions beneficial to all the stakeholders [11]. It is a concept of conducting business activity that balances the profit and the needs of different groups of stakeholders [22,23]. The concept is reflected by the voluntary inclusion of the expectations of equal stakeholder groups into the company's strategy, which generates not only economic, but alsosocial effects.

CSR concentrates on the organisation, yet it is strictly connected to sustainable development [10]. The connection between CSR and sustainable development is emphasised by the definition formulated by the World Bank, stating that corporate social responsibility is the commitment of the business in contributing to the sustainable development through the cooperation of human employees, their families, local communities and society as a whole, aimed at improving the quality of life and thus both the business and social development [24]. The definition contained in the ISO 26000 Standard also indicates the relation between CSR and sustainable development, defining social responsibility as the responsibility of an organisation for the impact of its decisions and activities onsociety and the environment, through transparent and ethical behaviour which contributes to sustainable development, including the health and well-being of society [10]. Corporate social responsibility (CSR) is a component of a corporate policy to undertake the sustainability imperative [25]. This strategy, based on respecting the principles of accountability for the social, economic and environmental impact of the organisation, transparency of decisions and actions, ethical behaviour based on integrity and fairness, respect for human rights and observance of the law and international standards of conduct, constitute the foundation of sustainable development [10]. Implementing the concept of sustainable development at the enterprise level consists in the broadly understood ecology of the operating processes, while striving to meet the expectations of all stakeholders, both the financial expectations of owners and shareholders, as well as the needs for security and stability on the part of employees and other groups remaining in relations with the enterprise [26]. Business model sustainability is now one of the key determinants of doing business [14].

Irrespective of the fact that sustainable development has been at the center ofmanagement's attention for more than a dozen years now, whether at the macroeconomic or microeconomic level, it was not until recently that the relations between sustainable development and human resources in organizations were noted. However, it is the human factor which stimulates practices oriented at the improvement of organizations' environmental effectiveness. Eco-oriented management is performed exclusively by humans expressing a positive attitude towards the environment, competent in ecology, and bearing a sense of responsibility for the environmental implications of their actions. The key success factor with regards to sustainable development is understanding the nature and objectives of the Green economy [27–29]. Needless to say, Green Human Resource Management (GHRM) plays a significant role in the development of environmentally-friendly practices within organizations. Over recent years, there has been a growing interest in Green HRM. Source literature emphasizes the significant potential of HRM in the popularization of the sustainable balance concept [30–35] and indicates a number of implementable eco-practices [36–39]. Nevertheless, despite the significant progress made with respect to domain development over the last two decades, more research is required [40]. In Poland in particular, the issue has been raised somewhat infrequently. The low number of publications available on the Polish market addressing the issue of GHRM has allowed to formulate a thesis that the concept is relatively unknown in Poland. This fact inspired the authors to take the research route and concentrate on the implementation of GHRM practices in young Polish enterprises. The review of literature revealed a gap with respect to empirical studies in the field. There has been no attempt to evaluate the impact of pro-environmental human resource practices on the sustainable development of Polish organizations. What is more, there has been no assessment of the scope of the concept's practical implementation. The authors intended to bridge the identified gap, to some extent at least.

The objective of the research was to identify environment-friendly HR practices followed by young Polish enterprises and to prioritize them in accordance with their impact on the sustainable development of companies.The main research problem was to determine the correlation between the impact of individual pro-environmental human resource practices on the sustainable development of young enterprises and their practical implementation.

In the course of the analyses, the following research questions were addressed:

- Is the GHRM concept known to Polish managers?
- Which GHRM practices are most often implemented in young Polish enterprises?
- Which GHRM practices are key to the sustainable development of organizations in the Polish reality?
- Is there a relation between the impact of individual pro-environmental human resource practices and their practical implementation in the analyzed young Polish enterprises?

In order to solve the above presented problems, the study was based on a review of literature, a diagnostic survey, and statistical and comparative analyses.

The article is composed of five sections. The introductory part presents the nature of the idea of sustainable development, its relation to CSR, and the reasons for increased interest in GHRM topics. Moreover, it defines the purpose of research, provides a brief overview of research problems, methods applied, and the limitations of the study. In addition, the authors point at a research gap, which had motivated them to take up respectiveresearch, and present the structure of the article and its contribution to science.

Section two places the undertaken considerations in the wider perspective of the world's literature. It focuses on defining the term GHRM and presenting the benefits of practical implementation of the concept. Furthermore, it shows ecological practices that can be applied at each stage of HRM.

Section three outlines the subject of research and the population studies, formulates research hypotheses and describes the methods employed.

The fourth section contains the analysis of research results. It also includes an assessment of the impact of pro-environmental human resource practices on the sustainable development of young organizations and a diagnosis of the scope of Green HRM implementation in young Polish companies. The analysis of research outcome was performed in the context of studies conducted in other countries.

The last section refers to the degree of verification of research hypotheses, presents key conclusions, and indicates the barriers related to the implementation of the GHRM concept under Polish conditions. At the same time, the area of future research and the proposed course of improvement are presented. The authors believe that the requisite condition to expand the scope of GHRM implementation in Polish organizations is management education.

This study contributes to source literature by diagnosing a gap associated with human resource policy use as a tool for supporting corporate sustainable development under Polish conditions, which constitutes the foundation for taking up corrective actions by managers. In the opinion of the authors, the results of the cited studies may stimulate interest in the implementation of the GHRM concept in Polish organizations and the widening of the scope of its use as a tool for sustainable enterprise development. This is particularly vital from the point of view of young organizations' development, for the implementation of the GHRM idea at an early stage of development creates an opportunity to improve performance related to the shaping of green attitudes and corporate culture supporting sustainable development.

2. Literature Review

2.1. Nature and Importance of Green Human Resource Management

It is clear that sustainability concerns are vital to the operations of contemporary organizations [40–42]. Research demonstrates that environmental practices improve company performance and provide a competitive edge [43,44]. Therefore, more and more companies become interested in ecological issues, noting that environmental protection is in their best interest [45,46].

Green Human Resource Management may play an essential role in environmental management as it is an element of sustainable human resource management (SHRM) [47–49]. This is a new approach to the realization of the HR function, the nature of which is to include ecological objectives in all HRM sub-areas, from employment planning, through recruitment, selection, employee motivation and development, to their evaluation and influence on working conditions. This necessitates that the formulation of the HR function aims not only at the category of economic interest but also at ecological areas, so as to generate added value for stakeholders [50]. Hence, Green HRM reflects the level of the greening of human resource management practices [51], whereas its implementation requires individual stages of human resource management to be modified and adapted, to become green—i.e., environmentally-friendly [37,50,52]. The main focus of activities undertaken as part of Green HRM is the development of an ecological working environment and environmentally responsible worker attitudes which will subsequently penetrate—as a model of operation—private zones [53,54].

Green HRM is, therefore, part of a broader framework of corporate social responsibility [55] and means the application of HR policies to promote sustainable use of company resources and to support ecology [20,56]. Its primary objective is to develop ecological sensitivity in employees and to make them aware of how their own behaviour may affect the environment. This is about motivation and making one feel proud of participation in green initiatives. This way, Green HRM supports the creation of a green workforce, who understands, appreciates, and practices ecological initiatives [36]. At times, Green HRM is also defined as the use of personnel practices to improve environmental performance [28,40,57–60]. This is due to the fact that HR processes play a significant role in the practical application of sustainable development policies [61–63] and in the construction of a sustainable development culture [64,65]. Without a doubt, Green HRM enhances the role of HRM in making the sustainable development concept a reality [58]. It underscores the fact that HR departments play a key role in the practical implementation of environmental policies [63] and in the development of sustainable corporate culture [64]. In this context, it is a primary instrument allowing the implementation of sustainable development across an organization [29,66].

The implementation of Green HRM, promoting green organizational culture and stimulating environment-oriented employee behaviour, is beneficial to organizations for a number of reasons [67–69]. The first effect is image benefit [60]. The market success of contemporary enterprises is increasingly dependent on image. Given the above, taking up voluntary environmental initiatives, rather than merely conforming to the binding legal regulations regarding environmental protection, is becoming a means by which to gain a competitive advantage [70,71]. The increase in ecological awareness and the influence of various stakeholder groups are of primordial importance [72]. Consumers seek ecological products, whereas business partners pay attention to ecological attestations. Companies seeking to maintain their market share are forced to adopt an environment-friendly orientation. As a result of such an approach, companies are gradually developing a new philosophy of management, where expenditure on environmental protection is no longer only seen as a cost, but rather as an investment in an organization's development.

Authors providing an insight into Green HRM underpin that human resources may significantly contribute to the establishment of ecological organizations [31,45,73]. They argue that environmental policies with regards to recruitment, performance management, training, development, and remuneration are powerful tools for engaging employees in the practical implementation of environmental protection strategies [63]. Green HRM tools, processes, and practices may augment employee participation in the process of ecological innovations, reduce environmental waste, improve products, increase process efficiency, and cut costs [59]. Green HRM, therefore, constitutes a part of Green Management alongside greening operations, greening accounting and finance, greening retailing and greening marketing [28].

2.2. Green Human Resource Management Practices

Authors engaged in Green HRM issues draw attention to a number of environmental practices applicable to the field of human resource management at each stage of the HR process [28,36,37,52,55, 74,75].

The implementation of Green HRM concepts begins as early as during job analysis and design. It is important to have equivalent designfollowing the principles of environment-friendly jobs, and that each job role sets out tasks related to environment protection [52]. Many organizations have created a special position whose occupant is responsible for the coordination of various aspects of environmental management [37].

Green HRM implementation means that even during the recruitment process, candidates should be informed that as part of their roles within organizations, they are expected to adhere to an ecological attitude as standard, and environmental protection—of primordial importance.Companies with reputations for being green employers are able to attract talented specialists more effectively [28,40]. Research shows that even graduates, only just entering the market, tend to choose employers renowned for their corporate environmental responsibility [55]. Green recruitment, however, is not only about exposing environmental values with the intention of drawing candidates competent in ecology, but also about the very approach to the process of recruitment, i.e., through limiting the use of paper throughout the process. This is due to the fact that environmentally-friendly organizations ought to have a transparent set of rules and principles setting forth employee behaviour and encouraging employees to follow environmental protection requirements.

An important role in the effective implementation of Green HRM is played by motivating employees to undertake environmentally-friendly activities [28,52]. Studies confirm that Green Compensation is a vital tool for supporting environment management, which may help attain environmental goals [76–78]. Effective tools consist of awards and compensation for promoting environmental actions across organizations. Through the inclusion of elements of green management within the remuneration programme, managers may promote green attitudes amongst employees. Other non-financial incentives include, amongst other things, praise, diplomas of merit for the most active members, and grants for environmental projects [79]. Another crucial issue is the creation of a participative working environment, in which employees can freely present their ecological ideas, which may contribute to more efficient resource use. Employee participation results in the enhanced effectiveness of environmental management systems thanks to more efficient resource usage [76], limited wasteful practice [80], and reduced contamination [81].

Another key element of Green HRM is the expansion of employee rights with regards to the implementation of green initiatives, referred to as Green empowerment [82]. It involves encouraging staff to take ecological decisions as well as empowering them to take responsibility for their actions which translates into cost awareness, asense of belonging to the same community, better performance, and improved relations between team members thanks to the conviction that employees are afforded genuine, decision-making power. Hence, empowerment raises employees'engagement in ecological initiatives and the satisfaction they experience following their attainment of environmental goals [38,78,83–88].

In addition, Green HRM encompasses disciplining constraints, such as warnings, penalties or work suspensions, taken with respect to individuals who fail to conform to the environmental principles binding across organizations. This may prove necessary if a given organization aims to achieve environmental goals [52,63]. To implement Green HRM principles in large organizations, trade union support is required.

Yet another inherent part of the idea is an assessment of employee ecological performance. The inclusion of environmental management goals into the performance appraisal system is necessary, for it ensures regular feedback on employee progress in their attainment [28,37,52,63]. No organization would be capable of guaranteeing real, environmental effectiveness in the absence of such a policy.

One more integral element of Green HRM implementation is environmental protection, renewable energy, waste reduction and energy saving training [20]. Such training allows employees to gain ecological knowledge and raise environmental awareness. Research indicates that this is the most important element of the process of human resource management and facilitates the attainment of environmental objectives [83,89]. The role of environmental qualifications is also emphasized in strategic EU documents, inter alia in The Strategy for Education for Sustainable Development [90], as a low-emission economy and effective use of environmental resources is a priority for the EU. In the "Skills for Green Jobs European Synthesis Report", it is assumed that each job may potentially become more ecological; it also presents the primary needs with respect to green skill development [91].

In this context, another part of Green HRM is also the generation of green jobs defined as positions sensitive to the environment, resource-efficient, and socially responsible [92]. Persons occupying such positions are referred to as green collar workers [93–95]. The list of green jobs features not only occupations relating to farming or forestry, but also the following: ecological auditor, ecological campaign management specialist and energy efficiency advisor.

All in all, it needs to be emphasized that environmentally-friendly Green HRM practices result in the development of "green" human resources, i.e., highly-qualified employees who understand and follow the principles of ecological development.

3. Materials and Methods

The subject matter of the research were environment-friendly human resource practices implemented across young Polish enterprises. The list of activities included in the research is presented in Table 1. The diagnosis was conducted with reference to 28 activities regarding 7 areas of human resource policy:

-   Green job design and analysis (activities 1,2,3)
-   Green recruitment (activities 4,5,6,7,8,)
-   The shaping of green discipline at work (activities 9,10,11)
-   Green development (activities 12,13,14)
-   Green performance evaluation (activities 15,16,17,18)
-   Green motivation (activities 19,20,21,22,23)
-   Green HRM procedures (activities 24,25,26,27,28)

Table 1. A list of environmental practices in the field of Green HRM covered by the research [28,36,52,63,96].

Activity Number	Activities
1	Inclusion of tasks related to environmental protection (duties and responsibilities) in job descriptions
2	Inclusion of green competencies (such as ecological knowledge) as a part of competency requirements for each position
3	Creation of positions responsible for environmental management aspects across organizations
4	Communication of employer's commitment to ecology during recruitment
5	Exposure of environmental values in job vacancy advertising
6	Verification of candidate ecological knowledge and skills during recruitment process
7	Preference for candidates with competencies and experience in ecological projects
8	Introduction of new employees to environmental standards of organization during adaptation
9	Establishment of a clear set of rules and provisions regarding employee conduct in relation to environmental protection
10	Development of a disciplinary system to discipline employees breaching the principles of ecological conduct
11	Implementation of disciplinary actions (such as warning, penalty, suspension, dismissal) against employees breaching the provisions and rules of environmental protection
12	Analysis and identification of employee needs with regards to ecological training
13	Provisions of ecological training for employees and managers to develop ecological skills and knowledge

Table 1. *Cont.*

Activity Number	Activities
14	Incentives for workers to develop green competencies
15	Inclusion of ecological criteria in performance appraisals
16	Establishment of goals and responsibilities in relation to ecological initiative implementation
17	Conduct of environmental audits
18	Provision of regular feedback to employees on their progress in attaining ecological goals or improvement of their environmental effectiveness
19	Incentives for workers to submit ecological initiatives (e.g., Ecological project competitions)
20	Provision of advisory services and support to solve ecological problems
21	Sharing knowledge about environmental initiatives or programmes
22	Development of a rewards system for completion of ecological projects (awards, subsidies to wages)
23	Promoting environmentally-friendly attitudes when performing professional tasks (such as paper use reduction, waste sorting)
24	Inclusion of environmental goals of HRM in company strategy
25	Measurement of effectiveness of environmental actions in HRM
26	Provision for HRM environmental actions-related expenditure in the budget
27	HRM environmental action progress monitoring
28	Drafting reports on environmental actions in HRM

The list of practices covered by the research was identified pursuant to the analysis of source literature.

With a view to analyzing the effect of the above-listed HR practices on sustainable development, a (partial) survey was conducted among a random, representative population of 150 young enterprises with their seats in Poland. Young enterprises were defined as those operating on the market for no more than 3 years. The study was conducted in January 2018 with the application of the CATI technique. The study sample was selected on a layer basis. First, 25 entities from each of the six Polish regions were drawn: Central, South, East, North-West, South-West and North. The survey targeted individuals in charge of human resource policy development in the study enterprises. The characteristic features of the study population are shown in Table 2.

Table 2. Details of young enterprises included in the study.

Criterion	Number of Enterprises	Percentage
Employment number:		
50–249 employees	100	66.7
250–499 employees	42	28.0
More than 500 employees	8	5.3
Time on the market:		
up to 1 year	14	9.3
1–3 years	136	90.7
Type of ownership:		
limited liability company	86	57.3
joint-stock company	21	14.0
state-owned enterprise	43	28.7
Scope of operations		
international	49	32.7
national	44	29.3
regional	20	13.3
local	37	24.7
Main type of activity:		
services	99	66.0
production	43	28.7
trade	8	5.3
Respondent's position:		
CEO	12	8.0
HR Director	8	5.3
Head of HR Department	126	84.0
other	4	2.7

The enterprises which prevailed in the population studied were medium-sized, i.e., employing between 50 and 249 employees (66.7%), operating on the market for more than a year (90.7%). The most frequent type of ownership of young organizations was a limited liability company (57.3%). The geographical coverage of young enterprises was highly-diversified, with the most numerous operating within the country (29.3%). The prevailing type of business activity of the study entities was the provision of services (66%).Respondents were mainly heads of human resource departments (84%); others included deputy directors, coordinators, and department managers.

Research allows the following:

- determination of the impact of individual pro-environmental human resource practices on the sustainable development of young enterprises and identification of key practices as determined by respondents;
- identification of practices most frequently applied under Polish conditions;analysis of the correlation between the impact of individual pro-environmental human resource practices and their practical implementation in young Polish enterprises.

Over the course of research, attempts were made to verify the following research hypotheses:

Hypothesis 1. *Pro-environmental actions undertaken in the area of human resource management have an uneven impact on the sustainable development of young organizations, which allows one to highlight primary and secondary practices.*

Hypothesis 2. *There is a correlation between the impact of individual pro-environmental human resource practices from the point of view of sustainable development and their practical implementation within young Polish enterprises.*

To verify Hypothesis 1, measures of central tendency, both classic and location (in the case of impact asymmetry), and measures of dispersion, i.e., the extent to which a distribution is scattered, were applied.The dispersion measures revealed a mean deviation of individual actions from the average and aforce of activity variability.

In the process of verification of Hypothesis 2, Spearman's rank correlation coefficient was used, which allowed the authors to determine the strength and direction of correlations between the impact of Green HRM activities on the sustainable development of young companies, and their practical implementation. Furthermore, the parameters of the linear regression model were estimated, which allowed the modelling of the relationship between the two variables.

All of the above allowed an assessment of the extent of GHRM idea implementation under Polish conditions in the context of influencing sustainable development policy in young organizations, which is crucial due to the vital importance of sustainable development for improving the competitiveness of organizations (micro-economic level) and the Polish economic policy of sustainable development (macroeconomic level).

4. Results and Discussion

4.1. Assessment of the Impact of Pro-Environmental Human Resource Practices on the Sustainable Development of Organizations

The assessment of the impact of pro-environmental human resource practices on young organization development was conducted with the application of a five-level Likert scale, where 1 signified a very low impact and 5 a very high impact of a given practice. To analyze the impact, the structure of the group was described by the calculation of measures of central tendency, both classic and location (in the case of impact asymmetry), and measures of dispersion, specifying the extent to which a distribution is scattered (Table 3).

Table 3. Evaluation of the impact of activities on the sustainable development of young enterprises *.

Item	Activity No.	Aggregate Assessment of Impact (Points)	Mean Assessment of Impact (Points)	Median (Points)	Mode (Points)	Standard Deviation (Points)	Coefficient of Variation (%)
1	23	520	3.47	4	4	1.324	38.2
2	1	410	2.73	3	3	1.319	48.3
3	3	399	2.66	3	3	1.284	48.3
4	9	397	2.65	3	3	1.238	46.8
5	24	386	2.57	3	3	1.200	46.7
6	2	377	2.51	3	3	1.230	48.9
7	21	373	2.49	3	3	1.214	48.8
8	8	366	2.44	3	3	1.179	48.3
9	17	364	2.43	3	3	1.212	49.9
10	26	360	2.40	3	3	1.210	50.4
11	16	360	2.40	3	3	1.159	48.3
12	19	358	2.39	3	3	1.140	47.7
13	12	353	2.35	3	3	1.177	50.0
14	13	352	2.35	3	3	1.153	49.1
15	14	350	2.33	3	3	1.115	47.8
16	22	349	2.33	3	3	1.156	49.6
17	20	348	2.32	3	3	1.119	48.2
18	11	348	2.32	3	3	1.183	51.0
19	25	345	2.30	3	3	1.151	50.1
20	18	345	2.30	3	3	1.128	49.0
21	10	343	2.29	3	3	1.166	51.0
22	4	342	2.28	3	1	1.188	52.1
23	27	337	2.25	3	3	1.129	50.2
24	28	334	2.23	3	3	1.100	49.4
25	15	331	2.21	3	3	1.082	49.1
26	7	323	2.15	3	1	1.134	51.1
27	5	323	2.15	2	1	1.098	51.0
28	6	322	2.15	2	1	1.071	49.9

* Respondents made assessments whether or not a given activity was implemented within a given enterprise.

To identify environmental activities which, according to respondents, had the largest and the smallest impact on sustainable development across organizations, the study sample was divided into quartiles. The first quartile (7 activities) was composed of activities of primordial importance to the policy of sustainable development in organizations; whereas, the third quartile consisted of activities which did not contribute in any significant manner to policy implementation.

The coefficient of variation of the impact of activities on the sustainable development of young enterprises was highly diversified. The results oscillated around 50%, however, the average variability of the impact of environmental activities in relation to the average impact oscillated between 1.071 and 1.324. This means that respondents evaluated activities seen as key—higher and activities of lesser importance in terms of sustainable development—lower. The above analyses confirmed, therefore, the hypothesis which assumed that pro-ecological activities in the field of human resource management have a varied effect on the sustainable development of young organizations and allowed the identification of primary and secondary practices.

The analysis of data presented in Table 3 demonstrates that, in the opinion of respondents, it was activity No. 23, i.e., promoting environment-friendly attitudes when performing professional tasks (such as paper use reduction, waste sorting), which had the largest impact on sustainable development of young enterprises. Most frequently, respondents evaluated its impact as high (mode 4), and the average impact of the activity was 3.47. Other activities the respondents found crucial were:

— inclusion of tasks related to environmental protection (duties and responsibilities) in job descriptions (activity No. 1), with an impact average of 2.73;
— creation of positions responsible for environmental management aspects across organizations (activity No. 3), with an impact average of 2.66;

- establishment of a clear set of rules and provisions regarding employee conduct in relation to environmental protection (activity No. 9), with an impact average of 2.65;
- inclusion of environmental goals of HRM in company strategy (activity No. 24), with an impact average of 2.57;
- inclusion of green competencies (such as ecological knowledge) as a part of competency requirements at each position (activity No. 2), with an impact average of 2.51;
- sharing knowledge about environmental initiatives or programs (activity No. 21), with an impact average of 2.49.

On the contrary, a very small impact on sustainable development in organizations (mode 1) was associated by respondents with activities related to recruitment and the selection of employees, i.e.,

- verification of a candidate's ecological knowledge and skills during the recruitment process (activity No. 6), with an average impact of 2.15;
- exposure of environmental values in job vacancy advertising (activity No. 5), with an average impact of 2.15;
- communication of employer's commitment to ecology during recruitment (activity No. 7), with an average impact of 2.22;
- preference for candidates with competencies and experience in ecological projects (activity No. 15), with an average impact of 2.21.

In addition, the group of insignificant—from the point of view of sustainable development of young companies—activities comprised: HRM environmental action progress monitoring (activity No. 28) and drafting reports on environmental actions in HRM (activity No. 27), the average impacts of which were 2.23 and 2.25, correspondingly. The surveyed specialists opined that the sustainable development of organizations is not greatly affected by the communication of an employer's commitment to ecology during recruitment (activity No. 4), with an average impact of 2.24, and a mode of 1.

Here, let us recall the studies conducted in 376 Pakistani companies, whichdemonstrated the key role of educational practices in theattainment of environmental management goals [97]. Given the above, Green development practices, i.e., the identification of needs in respect of pro-environment-related training, the provisions of ecological training for employees and managers to develop green skills and knowledge, and the provision of incentives to employees to develop green competencies, appear to be undervalued in Poland. They were listed as No. 13, 14, and 15 in terms of their impact on the sustainable development of organizations.

Another surprising issue is little awareness of the importance of practices in the area of providing incentives for taking up environment-friendly actions. Encouraging employees to submit environmental initiatives ranked 12 in the opinion of the managers, whereas the provision of advisory services and support to solve ecological problems was found even less important (No. 17). This raises concerns in the view of studies conducted in Denmark, which showed that green motivation programs are an effective tool for increasing employee participation in pro-environmental initiatives [98]. It seems that the area of Green motivation should be treated as principal from the point of view of the effectiveness of pro-environmental human resource practices and the input of the HR function into the sustainable development of organizations. The lack of appreciation of the practices oriented at development of green competencies of employees as well as motivating them to get involved with green projects call into question the viability of GHRM concept development in the entities studies.

Another issue rated rather low by Polish managers is the role of recruiting candidates with green competencies. The verification of candidate's ecological knowledge and skills during the recruitment process was ranked 28—i.e., as the last position in the ranking of practices having an impact on the sustainable development of organizations. The preference for job applicants with competencies and experience in the performance of environmental projects was also ranked low—26.

The insignificant impact of green acquisition of employees was confirmed, however, by the studies conducted by Owino andKwasira [99] and Guerciet al. [100]. Research quoted demonstrated that green recruitment is perceived as an activity having no impact on the environmental performance of organizations. Given the average assessment of the impact of Green HRM, which was 2.3 in the 5-level scale, we can put forward the following conclusion: the importance of pro-environmental human resource practices is clearly underestimated in young Polish enterprises. Such an approach may be a consequence of the way the personnel function is perceived in organizations. Studies conducted by Harris and Tregidg [51] demonstrated that despite their personal interest in influencing environmental policy, managers of HR departments did not regard the HR function as the main driver in terms of achieving sustainable development. On the other hand, more and more often emphasis in source literature is placed on the importance of the human resource management practice as a mechanism driving innovation and environmental management effectiveness [32–34,40,53,96,101–104]. A number of models laying down theoretical foundations for the implementation of the strategy of sustainable development via Green HRM practices [33,40,53,104]. One published significant model is the LOS model of Buller and McEvoy [105], illustrating the relations between the strategy of sustainable development, practices of human resource management, and productivity. This model is based on the assumption that HRM practices, i.e., recruitment, selection, training, development, performance evaluation, and award system are key to the generation, reinforcement and maintenance of organizational skills and company effectiveness with reference to the performance of economic, environmental and social goals. The authors of the model underpin that organizational performance associated with the attainment of long-term goals increases whenever HRM practices are internally coherent and oriented at the reinforcement of environmental activities across all levels of management. Renwick et al. [28], in turn, presented an AMO model, wherein they identify concrete HRM practices that are potentially beneficial to the strategy of sustainable development. The authors claim that by attracting and shaping employees with "green" skills through HRM processes, companies improve their chances of successful environmental strategy performance. Next, we should mention Savitz and Weber [106], who applied a "workforce life-cycle" concept to present the manner in which a company may employ various HRM practices to transform traditional businesses into sustainable ones. Among HRM practices which, potentially, may enhance the results of sustainable development, the authors enumerated recruitment, selection, development, performance assessment, and rewarding.

Here, we can identify a gap between the theory and practice of human resource management. Despite the potential of Green HRM practices, greatly emphasized by a number of specialists, the function's contribution towards the attainment of sustainability under Polish conditions is not deemed sufficient. The underestimation of the role of HR in the building of sustainable organizations seems to be one of the more vital determinants of the limited scope in which the GHRM concept is implemented. A fact which may account for such a state of affairs is that many entities continue to perceive the HR function as a strategic partner that actively participates in key decision-making processes generating added value [92,106,107]. In view of the above, more and more frequently, source literature yields arguments highlighting the need to ensure that the HR function is employed, to a greater extent, for the benefit of sustainable companies [30,40,92,106,108,109].

4.2. Evaluation of the Scope of Green HRM Implementation in Poland

On the basis of data regarding the number of enterprises pursuing individual pro-ecological HR practices, characteristics of their structures were developed. The average number of enterprises performing a given activity was 38 (25.3%), whereas the average variability of the number of enterprises implementing ecological activities was 20. Most often a given activity was performed by 30 enterprises. Fifty percent of activities were accomplished by 33 enterprises at the most, and 50%—by a minimum of 33 enterprises. The range between the number of enterprises conducting an activity was 103, whereas the value of the coefficient of variation was 52.3%. This indicated a large variability of the number of enterprises carrying out ecological activities. The structure index (the frequency of occurrence of a given activity) oscillated between 10% and 78.68%. It should be emphasized that it exceeded 38% only in the case of activity No. 23. This means that only single activities were conducted more often than others. Research revealed therefore that the scope of Green HRM implementation under Polish conditions was limited. The research results revealed a small range of implementation of the GHRM concept in young Polish enterprises (Table 4).

Table 4. Performance of HRM pro-environmental activities in young Polish enterprises.

Activity No.	Number of Young Enterprises Performing the Activity	Percentage of Young Enterprises Performing the Activity (%)
1	65	43.33
2	44	29.33
3	48	32.00
4	31	20.67
5	15	10.00
6	19	12.67
7	17	11.33
8	49	32.67
9	56	37.33
10	27	18.00
11	30	20.00
12	38	25.33
13	35	23.33
14	29	19.33
15	21	14.00
16	34	22.67
17	38	25.33
18	28	18.67
19	39	26.00
20	30	20.00
21	42	28.00
22	30	20.00
23	118	78.67
24	53	35.33
25	28	18.67
26	34	22.67
27	30	20.00
28	26	17.33

The most popular activity turned out to be activity No. 23, i.e., promoting environment-friendly attitudes when performing professional tasks (such as paper use reduction, waste sorting). This practice was implemented relatively often—in as many as 118 of the entities studied (78.7% of the study population). Nevertheless, given its nature, we can presume that its implementation in enterprises was due to economic reasons than ecological attitudes. The remainder of practices were carried out by less than half of the study enterprises. The lowest frequency or practice application was recorded with regards to:

- activity No. 5—exposure of environmental values in job advertising, implemented in 15 enterprises;
- activity No. 7—preference for candidates with competencies and experience in ecological projects, carried out by 17 enterprises;
- activityNo. 6—verification of candidate ecological knowledge and skills during the recruitment process, applied in 19 enterprises.

The quoted results demonstrate significant omissions in the area of Green HRM implementation across young Polish organizations. The reason behind it could be, most notably, the deficit of knowledge concerning pro-environmental human resource practices. Such a competency gap was evidenced by the study. The Green HRM concept was familiar to as few as 29% of the study entities. A particularly underestimated area turned out to be green recruitment. Hence, we may formulate a conclusion that HR specialists in young Polish enterprises seem to underestimate the importance of recruiting environment-friendly staff and personnel with green competencies. Furthermore, it was quite rare for the entities covered by the study to prepare reports about pro-environmental HRM activities. This activity was pursued by a mere 26 companies. Needless to say, pro-environmental HR practice reporting is a great opportunity to systematize Green HRM activities. Data included in the reports show not only where a given organization is now, but also what it intends to achieve in the near future. This constitutes the basis for activity coordination and personnel process monitoring. Reports demonstrate the degree of involvement in environment-friendly HR practices, reveal key achievements in the field, and facilitate the drawing a roadmap for responding to new challenges. Therefore, they constituteextra support in the process of personnel-related decision-taking. Report development is, thus, an indication of Green HRM strategy maturity, as well as a tool for communicating information regarding a company's public involvement in ecological practices.

It was equally rare to find HRM pro-environmental action performance measurements, an activity that is worth contemplating. This practice was pursued by as few as 28 enterprises, which accounted for 18.67% of all study entities. It needs to be underpinned that the Green HRM subject literature lacks a definitive, commonly accepted method of measuring HR pro-environmental practices performance which may be a key obstacle to the implementation of the activity—on a par with the multifaceted nature of the issue. The authors assert that the following could be helpful:

— measurement of the level of Green HRM-related expenditure;
— Green HRM sub-indices (e.g., the extent of ecological training, the number of ecological initiatives, the number of awards given to employees for their environmental activity);
— surveys designed to evaluate the way in which the importance of Green HRM for the attainment of corporate goals is perceived by managers;
— determination of the number of Green HRM practices revealed in social reports.

It ought to be emphasized that when speaking of Green HRM we must refer to long-term, rather than short-term performance or productivity. This is because benefits of concept application are typically derived in a more distant future, multidimensional in nature and not always easy to quantify. GHRM should be approached as a long-term HR corporate strategy directed at using the instruments of personnel policy to build an environmentally-friendly organization.

4.3. Correlation between the Impact of Pro-Environmental Activities on Sustainable Development and Their Practical Implementation in Young Enterprises

In order to determine the strength and direction of correlations between the impact of pro-environmental human resource practices on the sustainable development of young companies and those activities which are actually implemented in practice, a Spearman's rank correlation coefficient was calculated (Table 5).

The rank correlation coefficient was 0.956 which means that there is a very strong positive relationship between the assessment of the impact of human resource activities on sustainable development and the implementation of those activities in individual companies. It means that only activities that, in the opinion of executives, were crucial in terms of the sustainable development policy were taken in the subject companies.

A regression analysis was applied to identify the relationship between the influence of environment-friendly activities and their actual implementation in companies using a mathematical model (Figure 1). The linear regression function (type II regression function) determines the relationship between the changes in one variable and the changes in the other variable in the sample. The calculated regression coefficients of $a_y = 0.5037$ inform us that a 1-point rise in the impact of an activity results in an average rise in the implementation of the activity in a given company of 0.5037 in the relevant sample. The coefficient of determination $R^2 = 0.9713$ indicates that in 97.13% of cases, the changeability of the number of companies taking environmentally-friendly activities in the scope of HRM is explained by the estimated regression function (elucidating the impact of environment-friendly activities).

Table 5. Correlation between the impact of pro-environmental human resource practices on thesustainable development and their practical implementation in young enterprises.

Activity No.	Aggregate Assessment of Impact of Activity X (Points)	Activity Pursued in Enterprises (Number of Entities)	Rank X	Rank Y	Di Distance	Square of Distance Di ^{2}
1	410	65	2	2	0	0
2	377	44	6	7	−1	1
3	399	48	3	6	−3	9
4	342	31	22	15	7	49
5	323	15	26.5	28	−1.5	2.25
6	322	19	28	26	2	4
7	323	17	27.5	27	0.5	0.25
8	366	49	8	5	3	9
9	397	56	4	3	1	1
10	343	27	21	23	−2	4
11	348	30	18	18.5	−0.5	0.25
12	353	38	13	10.5	2,5	6.25
13	352	35	14	12	2	4
14	350	29	15	20	−5	25
15	331	21	25	25	0	0
16	360	34	10.5	13.5	−3	9
17	364	38	9	11.5	−2.5	6.25
18	345	28	19.5	21	−1.5	2.25
19	358	39	12	9	3	9
20	348	30	17.5	17.5	0	0
21	373	42	7	8	−1	1
22	349	30	16	16.5	−0.5	0.25
23	520	118	1	1	0	0
24	386	53	5	4	1	1

$$r_s = 1 - (6 \times 161/28 \times (28^2 - 1)) = 0.956.$$

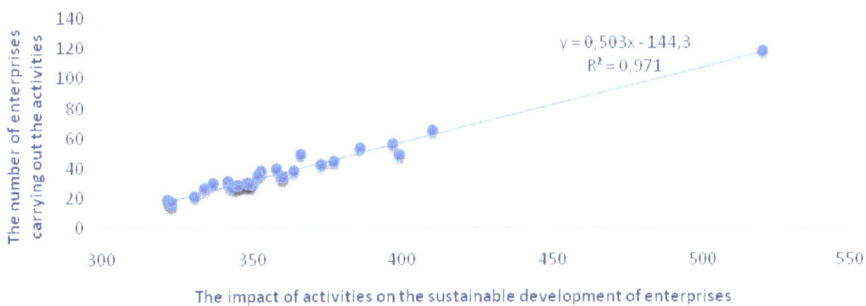

Figure 1. Correlation between the impact of activities and activity implementation in young enterprises.

The following two hypotheses were made in order to verify whether the taken sample of companies, which was to present how young companies truly operate, truly reflects the relationships developed in all young companies:

$$H_0 : \varrho_d = 0$$

$$H_1 : \varrho_d > 0$$

The null hypothesis assumes that there is no correlation in the population between the impact of eco-friendly actions on sustainable development and their implementation in companies. On the other hand, due to the positive result of the rank correlation coefficient in the sample, the alternative hypothesis permitsus to assume that there is correlation and that the correlation is positive.

It was the rank correlation coefficient calculated for the sample, denoted as ϱ_d, which tested the hypothesis $H_0 : \varrho_d = 0$. The null hypothesis was tested with the exact distribution of the critical values for Spearman's rank correlation coefficient at the significance level of $\alpha = 0.05$ using the relation P $(r_d \geq r_d^0) = \alpha$. The critical value for the Spearman's rank correlation coefficient was $r_d^0 = 0.317$, and the respective value in the sample was $r_d = 0.956$. Since it is true that $r_d \geq r_d^0$, in other words, $0.956 > 0.317$, the null hypothesis should be rejected in favour of the alternative hypothesis, which proves that there is a positive correlation between the impact of environmentally-friendly activities and their implementation in the whole population.

5. Conclusions

An overview of literature allows us to state that Green HRM is a human resource strategy supporting pro-environmental corporate management. Benefits resulting from its implementation may be due to an increase in the ecological awareness of the staff which translates into the sustainability of practices across organizations. It is also a tool for increasing competitivenessthanks to enhanced image, cost reduction, improved customer relations, acceptance by local authorities and communities, and increased employee satisfaction, loyalty and motivation.

To evaluate the extent to which Green HRM is implemented under Polish conditions, empirical research was conducted using a representative sample of young Polish enterprises. They allowed the following hypotheses to be positively verified:

Hypothesis 1. *Pro-environmental actions undertaken in the area of human resource management have an uneven impact on the sustainable development of young organizations which allows one to highlight primary and secondary practices.*

Hypothesis 2. *There is a correlation between the impact of individual pro-environmental human resource practices from the point of view of sustainable development and their practical implementation in young Polish enterprises.*

The analysis of correlations demonstrated a strong positive correlation between the evaluation of the impact of individual environmentally-friendly HR activities on sustainable company development and their practical implementation. Thus, research demonstrated that the higher the evaluation of the impact of a given activity, the more often it was implemented in the companies studied. Analysis of the regression function showed that a 1-point increase in the impact of any activity stimulated average growth in activity implementation in a company of 0.5037. This allowed the formulation of the following conclusion: in order to increase the scope of implementation of the Green HRM concept in Polish young enterprises, it is necessary to raise awareness of the importance of Green HRM activities to achieve company sustainability.

In addition, empirical research revealed that the Green HRM concept is relatively unknown and underestimated in Poland. It was determined that young Polish enterprises did not employ the whole range of HRM practices requisite for effective environmental management. Hence, we can state that Green HRM is in its initial phase of development in the study entities. The following shortcomings are evidence of the above conclusion:

- lack of familiarity with the concept among specialists responsible for human resources management, and related intuitive selection of practices to be implemented;

— lack of a systemic approach expressed by the execution of individual pro-environmental practices in HRM area;

— lack of developed measurement and reporting procedures regarding Green HRM.

The principal restriction encountered in the course of research was the shortage of studies conducted in the young enterprise population, which made it difficult to carry out a comparative analysis of the results of own research. The world's literature abounds in publications about GHRM practices implemented in mature enterprises with an established market position. Nonetheless, there are no analyses in the group of enterprises operating on the market for a period shorter than 3 years.

The authors assert that the reasons behind this limited scope of Green HRM concept implementation may be sought, above all, in the absence of knowledge about it across young Polish enterprises' management. A major role in overcoming the said barrier is played by dissemination of knowledge concerning the field in business circles. One requisite condition for the HR function to become a strategic partner in sustainable development is, therefore, manager qualification development.

In the opinion of the authors, activities vital for effective GHRM concept implementation are—although not appreciated by the study managers—also measurement and reporting of corporate activity in Green HRM. This is because there is no effective management in any area if no measurement or reporting is provided. The assessment of Green HRM performance is required to expand the scope of its practical implementation. This facilitates the impact of Green HRM activities on the sustainable development of organizations, which in turn lays foundations for changes to be introduced in the way the issue is approached and for the practices to be recognized. The implementation of the Green HRM measuring instrument may, therefore, pave the way for it to be recognized as an integral part of the sustainable development model in enterprises. Given the foregoing, there is a demand for enhanced measurement methods and reporting standards regarding pro-environmental HR practices, particularly in Poland. Enriched reporting in the CSR field by supplementing green personnel reports aimed at promoting enterprises as followers of good HR practices may be, according to the authors, a key tool in the popularization of the Green HRM idea.

Author Contributions: E.B. proposed research concept, reviewed source literature, and wrote the article. A.M.-K. designed the methodology of quantitative research, carried out the statistical analysis of study results, and wrote the article.

Acknowledgments: Research was funded by a MNiSW statutory grant as part of research topic No. 430/15/S "Preconditions of the effective operation of organizational units as part of sustainable development of the economy" carried out at the Department of Economy, Faculty of Economic and Legal Science, University of Natural Sciences and Humanities in Siedlce.

References

1. Dyllick, T.; Hockerts, K. Beyond the Business Case for Corporate Sustainability. *Bus. Strategy Environ.* **2002**, *11*, 130–141. [CrossRef]

2. Pinzone, M.; Guerci, M.; Lettieri, E.; Redman, T. Progressing in the change journey towards sustainability in healthcare: The role of "Green" HRM. *J. Clean. Prod.* **2016**, *122*, 201–211. [CrossRef]

3. Shaikh, M. Green HRM: A requirement of 21st century. *J. Res. Commer. Manag.* **2010**, *1*, 122–127.

4. Jabłoński, A. Scalability of Sustainable Business Models in Hybrid Organizations. *Sustainability* **2016**, *8*, 194. [CrossRef]

5. Poskrobko, B. Teoretyczne aspekty ekorozwoju. *Ekonomia i Środowisko* **1997**, *1*, 7–20. (In Polish)

6. Report of the World Commission on Environment and Development: Our Common Future. Available online: http://www.un-documents.net/our-common-future.pdf (accessed on 17 May 2018).

7. Kromer, B. Społecznaodpowiedzialnośćbiznesujakoczynnikkonkurencyjnościprzedsiębiorstw. *Studia Ekonomiczne* **2014**, *180*, 131–140. (In Polish)

8. Grapp, T. *Nachhaltigkeit und Kooperation*; Verlag Peter Lang: Frankfurt/M., Germany; Berlin, Germany; Bern, Switzerland; Bruxelles, Belgium; New York, NY, USA; Oxford, UK; Wien, Austria, 2001; ISBN 978-3-631-37379-8.

9. Elkington, J. *Cannibals with Forks: The Triple Bottom Line of Twenty-First Century Business*; Capstone: Mankato, MN, USA, 1997.

10. ISO 26000:2010 Guidance on Social Responsibility. Available online: http://www.cnis.gov.cn/wzgg/201405/P020140512224950899020.pdf (accessed on 17 May 2018).

11. Rok, B. *Odpowiedzialny biznes w nieodpowiedzialnym świecie*; Akademia Rozwoju Filantropii w Polsce, Forum Odpowiedzialnego Biznesu: Warszawa, Poland, 2001. (In Polish)

12. Borys, T. Zrównoważony rozwój organizacji—Co chcemy lub powinniśmy równoważyć? *Prace Naukowe Uniwersytetu Ekonomicznego we Wrocławiu* **2015**, *376*, 13–24. (In Polish) [CrossRef]

13. Gollagher, M.; Hartz-Karp, J. The role of deliberative collaborative governance in achieving sustainable cities. *Sustainability* **2013**, *5*, 2343–2366. [CrossRef]

14. Jabłoński, A.; Jabłoński, M. Research on Business Models in their Life Cycle. *Sustainability* **2016**, *8*, 430. [CrossRef]

15. Kim, J.; Kim, J. Corporate Sustainability Management and Its Market Benefits. *Sustainability* **2018**, *10*, 1455. [CrossRef]

16. Stubbs, W.; Cocklin, C. Conceptualizing a "sustainability business model". *Organ. Environ.* **2008**, *21*, 103–127. [CrossRef]

17. Schaltegger, S.; Burritt, R. Business cases and corporate engagement with sustainability: Differentiating ethical motivations. *J. Bus. Ethics* **2018**, *147*, 241–259. [CrossRef]

18. Munilla, L.S.; Miles, M.P. The corporate social responsibility continuum as a component of stakeholder theory. *Bus. Soc. Rev.* **2005**, *110*, 371–387. [CrossRef]

19. Przychodzeń, W. *Zrównoważone przedsiębiorstwo: Teoria, praktyka, wycena, kształcenie*; Poltext: Warszawa, Poland, 2013. (In Polish)

20. Zoogah, D. The dynamics of Green HRM behaviors: A cognitive social information processing approach. *Zeitschrift fur Personalforschung* **2011**, *25*, 117–139. [CrossRef]

21. Selier, G. *Sustainability in Manufacturing, Recovery of Resources in Product and Material Cycles*; Springer: Berlin/Heidelberg, Germany, 2007; ISBN 978-3-540-49871-1.

22. Gadomsk-Lila, K. Społeczna odpowiedzialność biznesu wobec pracowników. *Manag. Bus. Admin.* **2012**, *2*, 41–52. (In Polish) [CrossRef]

23. Porter, M.E.; Kramer, M.R. Tworzenie wartości dla biznesu i społeczeństwa. *Harv. Bus. Rev. Polska* **2011**, *5*, 80–87. (In Polish)

24. Szumiak-Samolej, J. *Odpowiedzialny biznes w gospodarce sieciowej*; Poltext: Warszawa, Poland, 2013; ISBN 978-83-7561-360-5. (In Polish)

25. Nicolăescu, E.; Alpopi, C.; Zaharia, C. Measuring Corporate Sustainability Performance. *Sustainability* **2015**, *7*, 851–865. [CrossRef]

26. Grudzewski, W.; Hejduk, I.; Sankowska, A.; Wańtuchowicz, M. *Sustainability w biznesie*; Poltex: Warszawa, Poland, 2010; ISBN 978-83-7561-257-8. (In Polish)

27. Gholami, G.; Rezaei, G.; Saman, M.Z.M.; Sharif, S.; Zakuan, N. State–of–the–Art Green HRM System: Sustainability in the Sports Center in Malaysia Using a Multi–Methods Approach and Opportunities for Future Research. *J. Clean. Prod.* **2016**, *124*, 142–163. [CrossRef]

28. Renwick, D.W.; Redman, T.; Maguire, S. Green human resource management: A review and research agenda. *Int. J. Manag. Rev.* **2013**, *15*, 1–14. [CrossRef]

29. Urbaniak, G. Colorful Human Resource Management: What Are We Talking About? *Hum. Resour. Manag.* **2017**, *6*, 9–20.

30. Cohen, E.; Taylor, S.; Muller-Camen, M. *HRM's Role in Corporate Social and Environmental Sustainability*; Research Report; SHRM: Alexandria, VA, USA, 2012.

31. Egri, C.P.; Hornal, R.C. Strategic environmental human resource management and perceived organizational performance: An exploratory study of the Canadian manufacturing sector. In *Research in Corporate Sustainability: The Evolving Theory and Practice of Organizations in the Natural Environment*; Sharma, S., Starik, M., Eds.; Edward Elgar Publishing: Northampton, UK, 2002; ISBN 978-1-84064-906-2.

32. Ehnert, I.; Harry, W.; Zink, K.J. Sustainability and HRM: An introduction to the field. In *Sustainability and Human Resource Management: Developing Sustainable Business Organizations*; Ehnert, L., Harry, W., Zink, K.J., Eds.; Springer: Heidelberg, Germany, 2014; pp. 3–32. ISBN 978-3-642-37524-8.

33. Ehnert, I.; Harry, W. Recent Developments and Future Prospects on Sustainable Human Resource Management: Introduction to the Special Issue. *Manag. Rev.* **2012**, *23*, 221–238. [CrossRef]

34. Jabbour, C.J.C.; Santos, F.C. A The central role of human resource management in the search for sustainable organizations. *Int. J. Hum. Resour. Manag.* **2008**, *19*, 2133–2154. [CrossRef]

35. Preuss, L.; Haunschild, A.; Matten, D. The rise of CSR: Implications for HRM and employee representation. *Int. J. Hum. Resour. Manag.* **2009**, *20*, 953–973. [CrossRef]

36. Ahmad, S. Green Human Resource Management: Policies and Practices. *Cogent Bus. Manag.* **2015**, *2*. [CrossRef]

37. Arulrajah, A.A.; Opatha, H.H.D.N.P.; Nawaratne, N.N.J. Green Human Resource Management Practices: A Review. *Sri Lankan J. Hum. Resour. Manag.* **2015**, *5*, 1–16. [CrossRef]

38. Davies, I.A.; Crane, A. Corporate social responsibility in small-and medium-size enterprises: Investigating employee engagement in fair trade companies. *Bus. Ethics Eur. Rev.* **2010**, *19*, 126–139. [CrossRef]

39. Leszczyńska, A. Conceptualization of Green Human Resource Management. In Proceedings of the International Scientific Conference on Economic and Social Development "The Legal Challenges of Modern World", Split, Croatia, 1–2 September 2016; pp. 431–441.

40. Jackson, S.E.; Seo, J. The greening of strategic HRM scholarship. *Organ. Manag. J.* **2010**, *7*, 278–290. [CrossRef]

41. Belal, A.R. Stakeholder accountability or stakeholder management: A review of UK firms' social and ethical accounting, auditing and reporting (SEAAR). *Corp. Soc. Responsib. Environ. Manag.* **2002**, *9*, 8–25. [CrossRef]

42. Jackson, S.E.; Renwick, D.W.; Jabbour, C.J.; Müller-Camen, M. State-of-the-art and future directions for green human resource management: Introduction to the special issue. *Zeitschrift für Personalforschung* **2011**, *25*, 99–116. [CrossRef]

43. Faleye, O.; Trahan, E.A. Labor-friendly corporate practices: Is what is good for employees good for shareholders? *J. Bus. Ethics* **2011**, *101*, 1–27. [CrossRef]

44. Li, S.; Fetscherin, M.; Alon, I.; Lattemann, C.; Yeh, K. Corporate social responsibility in emerging markets: The importance of the governance environment. *Manag. Int. Rev.* **2010**, *50*, 635–654. [CrossRef]

45. Norton, T.A.; Zacher, H.; Parker, S.L.; Ashkanasy, N.M. Bridging the gap between green behavioral intentions and employee green behavior: The role of green psychological climate. *J. Organ. Behav.* **2017**, *38*, 996–1015. [CrossRef]

46. Wiernik, B.M.; Dilchert, S.; Ones, D.S. Age and employee green behaviors: A meta-analysis'. *Front. Psychol.* **2016**, *7*, 1–15. [CrossRef] [PubMed]

47. Mazur, B. Sustainable Human Resource Management. The attempt of holistic approach. *Econ. Manag.* **2015**, *7*, 7–12. [CrossRef]

48. Pabian, A. Zrównoważone zarządzanie zasobami ludzkimi. *Zeszyty Naukowe Politechniki Częstochowskiej Zarządzanie* **2015**, *17*, 7–16. (In Polish)

49. Pocztowski, A. Zrównoważone zarządzanie zasobami ludzkimi w teorii i praktyce. *Zarządzanie i Finanse* **2016**, *2*, 303–314. (In Polish)

50. Ulrich, D.; Brockbank, W. *The HR Value Proposition*; Harvard Business School Press: Boston, MA, USA, 2005; ISBN 1-59139-707-3.

51. Harris, C.; Tregidga, H. HR managers and environmental sustainability: Strategic leaders or passive observers? *Int. J. Hum. Resour. Manag.* **2012**, *23*, 236–254. [CrossRef]

52. Opatha, H.H.D.N.P. Green Human Resource Management: A Simplified Introduction. In Proceedings of the HR Dialogue; Department of HRM, Faculty of Management Studies and Commerce, University of Sri Jayewardenepura: Nugegoda, Sri Lanka, 30 November, 2013; pp. 11–21.

53. Mohrman, S.A.; Worley, C.G. The organizational sustainability journey: Introduction to the special issue. *Organ. Dyn.* **2010**, *39*, 289–294. [CrossRef]

54. Whitmarsh, L.; O'Neill, S. Green identity, green living? The role of pro-environmental self-identity in determining consistency across diverse pro-environmental behaviors. *J. Environ. Psychol.* **2010**, *30*, 305–314. [CrossRef]

55. Mandip, G. Green HRM: People Management Commitment to Environmental Sustainability. *Res. J. Recent Sci.* **2012**, *1*, 244–252.

56. Mampra, M. Green HRM: Does it help to build a competitive service sector? A study. In Proceedings of the tenth AIMS International Conference on Management, Bangalore, India, 6–9 January 2013; pp. 1273–1281.
57. Kim, A.; Kim, Y.; Han, K.; Jackson, S.E.; Ployhart, R. Multilevel influences on voluntary workplace green behavior: Individual differences, leader behavior, and coworker advocacy. *J. Manag.* **2017**, *43*, 1335–1358. [CrossRef]
58. Kramar, R. Beyond strategic human resource management: Is sustainable human resource management the next approach? *Int. J. Oper. Prod. Manag.* **2014**, *25*, 1069–1089. [CrossRef]
59. Saifulina, N.; Carballo-Penela, A. Promoting sustainable development at an organizational level: An analysis of the drivers of workplace environmentally friendly behaviour of employees. *Sustain. Dev.* **2017**, *25*, 299–310. [CrossRef]
60. Shen, J.; Dumont, J.; Deng, X. Employees' perceptions of Green HRM and non-Green employee work outcomes: The social identity and stakeholder perspectives. *Group Organ. Manag.* **2016**, 1–29. [CrossRef]
61. Hersey, K. A close look at ISO 14000. *Prof. Saf.* **1998**, *43*, 26–29.
62. Pfeffer, J. Building sustainable organizations: The human factor. *Acad. Manag. Perspect.* **2010**, *24*, 34–45. [CrossRef]
63. Renwick, D.W.S.; Redman, T.; Maguire, S. Green HRM: A Review, Process Model, and Research Agenda. University of Sheffield Working Paper. 2008, Volume 1, pp. 1–46. Available online: https://www.sheffield.ac.uk/polopoly_fs/1.120337!/file/Green-HRM.pdf (accessed on 3 April 2018).
64. Harmon, J.; Fairfield, K.D.; Wirtenberg, J. Missing an opportunity: HR leadership and sustainability. *People Strategy* **2010**, *33*, 16–21.
65. Liebowitz, J. The role of HR in achieving a sustainability culture. *J. Sustain. Dev.* **2010**, *3*, 50–57. [CrossRef]
66. Dutta, S. Greening people: A strategic dimension. *Int. J. Bus. Econ. Manag. Res.* **2012**, *2*, 143–148.
67. Ehnert, I.; Parsa, S.; Roper, I.; Wagner, M.; Muller-Camen, M. Reporting on sustainability and HRM: A comparative study of sustainability reporting practices by the world's largest companies. *Int. J. Hum. Resour. Manag.* **2016**, *27*, 88–108. [CrossRef]
68. Jackson, S.E.; Ones, D.S.; Dilchert, S. *Managing Human Resources for Environmental Sustainability*; Jossey Boss: San Francisco, CA, USA, 2012.
69. Rayner, J.; Morgan, D. An empirical study of "green" workplace behaviours: Ability, motivation and opportunity. *Asia Pac. J. Hum. Resour.* **2018**, *56*, 56–78. [CrossRef]
70. Chodyński, A.; Jabłoński, A.; Jabłoński, M. ECSR—Koncepcja strategiczna oparta o ekologiczną i społeczną odpowiedzialność biznesu. In *W poszukiwaniu nowych paradygmatów zarządzania*; Grudzewski, W.M., Hejduk, I.K., Eds.; Oficyna Wydawnicza SGH: Warszawa, Poland, 2008; pp. 63–71. ISBN 978-83-7378-390-4.
71. Ziółko, M.; Mróz, J. Wpływ ekoinnowacji na wzrost konkurencyjności przedsiębiorstw. *Acta Universitatis Nicolai Copernici* **2015**, *42*, 73–84. [CrossRef]
72. Mazur-Wierzbicka, E. Uwarunkowania proekologicznych działań przedsiębiorstw. *Zeszyty Naukowe Wyższej Szkoły Ekonomiczno-Społecznej w Ostrołęce* **2014**, *13*, 83–93. (In Polish)
73. Cheema, S.; Javed, F. The effects of corporate social responsibility toward green human resource management: The mediating role of sustainable environment. *Cogent Bus. Manag.* **2017**, *4*, 1310012. [CrossRef]
74. Bangwal, D.; Tiwari, P. Green HRM—A way to greening the environment. *IOSR J. Bus. Manag.* **2015**, *17*, 45–53. [CrossRef]
75. Davies, G.; Smith, H. *Natural Resources*; People Management: London, UK, 8 March 2007; pp. 26–31.
76. Florida, R.; Davison, D. Gaining from Green Management: Environmental management systems inside and outside the factory. *Calif. Manag. Rev.* **2001**, *43*, 64–84. [CrossRef]
77. Milliman, J.; Clair, J. Best environmental HRM practices in the U.S. In *Greening People: Human Resources and Environmental Management*; Wehrmeyer, W., Ed.; Greenleaf Publishing: Sheffield, UK, 1996; pp. 49–73. ISBN 978-1351-283-021.
78. Ramus, C.; Steger, U. The roles of supervisory support behaviors and environmental policy in employee 'ecoinitiatives' at leading-edge European companies. *Acad. Manag. J.* **2000**, *43*, 605–626. [CrossRef]
79. Phillips, L. Go green to gain the edge over rivals. *People Manag.* **2007**, *13*, 9.
80. May, D.R.; Flannery, B.L. Cutting waste with employee involvement teams. *Bus. Horiz.* **1995**, *38*, 28–38. [CrossRef]
81. Kitazawa, S.; Sarkis, J. The relationship between ISO 14001 and continuous source reduction programs. *Int. J. Oper. Prod. Manag.* **2000**, *20*, 225–248. [CrossRef]

82. Tariq, S.; Jan, F.A.; Ahmad, M.S. Green employee empowerment: A systematic literature review on state-of-art in green human resource management. *Qual. Quant.* **2016**, *50*, 237–269. [CrossRef]
83. Daily, B.F.; Bishop, J.; Steiner, R. The mediating role of EMS teamwork as it pertains to HR factors and perceived environmental performance. *J. Appl. Bus. Res.* **2007**, *23*, 95–109. [CrossRef]
84. Govindarajulu, N.; Daily, B.F. Motivating employees for environmental improvement. *Ind. Manag. Data Syst.* **2004**, *104*, 364–372. [CrossRef]
85. Gutowski, T.; Murphy, C.; Allen, D.; Bauer, D.; Bras, B.; Piwonka, T.; Sheng, P.; Sutherland, J.; Thurston, D.; Wolff, E. Environmentally benign manufacturing: Observations from Japan, Europe and the United States. *J. Clean. Prod.* **2005**, *13*, 1–17. [CrossRef]
86. Matthews, R.A.; Diaz, W.M.; Cole, S.G. The organizational empowerment scale. *Pers. Rev.* **2003**, *32*, 297–318. [CrossRef]
87. Ramachandran, V. Strategic corporate social responsibility: A 'Dynamic Capabilities' perspective. *Corp. Soc. Responsib. Environ. Manag.* **2011**, *18*, 285–293. [CrossRef]
88. Rego, A.; Leal, S.; Cunha, M.P.; Faria, J.; Pinho, C. How the perceptions of five dimensions of corporate citizenship and their inter-inconsistencies predict affective commitment. *J. Bus. Ethics* **2010**, *94*, 107–127. [CrossRef]
89. Ramus, C.A. Encouraging innovative environmental actions: What companies and managers must do. *J. World Bus.* **2002**, *37*, 151–164. [CrossRef]
90. *Strategia Edukacji dla Zrównoważonego Rozwoju*; Europejska Komisja Gospodarcza ONZ: Warszawa, Poland, 2008.
91. *Skills for Green Jobs European Synthesis Report*; Publications Office of the European Union: Luxembourg, Luxembourg, 2010.
92. SHRM. *Advancing Sustainability: HR's Role*; A Research Report by the Society for Human Resource Management, BSR, and Aurosoorya; SHRM: Alexandria, VA, USA, 2011.
93. Green, G.P.; Dane, A. *Green-Collar Jobs*; Publication of University of Wisconsin's Department of Community and Environmental Sociology: Madison, WI, USA, 2010.
94. Kryk, B. Czas na zielone kołnierzyki. *Ekonomia i Środowisko* **2014**, *3*, 10–20.
95. Lewandowska, A. Zielone kołnierzyki. *Ecomanager* **2011**, *4*, 48–49.
96. Ambec, S.; Lanoie, P. Does it pay to be green? A systematic overview. *Acad. Manag. Perspect.* **2008**, *22*, 45–62. [CrossRef]
97. Bhutto, S.A. Effects of Green Human Resources Management on Firm Performance: An Empirical Study on Pakistani Firms. *Eur. J. Bus. Manag.* **2016**, *8*, 119–125.
98. Forman, M.; Joergensen, M.S. The Social Shaping of the Participation of Employees in Environmental Work within Enterprises—Experiences form the Danish Context. *Technol. Anal. Strateg. Manag.* **2011**, *13*, 71–90. [CrossRef]
99. Owino, W.A.; Kwasira, J. Influence of Selected Green Human Resource Management Practices on Environmental Sustainability at Menengai Oil Refinery Limited Nakuru, Kenya. *J. Hum. Resour. Manag.* **2016**, *4*, 19–27. [CrossRef]
100. Guerci, M.; Longoni, A.; Luzzini, D. Translating Stakeholder Pressures into Environmental Performance: The Mediating Role of Green HRM Practices. *Int. J. Hum. Resour. Manag.* **2016**, *27*, 262–289. [CrossRef]
101. Dubois, C.L.Z.; Dubois, D.A. Strategic HRM as social design for environmental sustainability in organization. *Hum. Resour. Manag.* **2012**, *51*, 799–826. [CrossRef]
102. Ehnert, I. Conceptual Model for Sustainable HRM and a Paradox Framework. In *Sustainable Human Resource Management*; Contributions to Management Science; Physica-Verlag HD: Heidelberg, Germany, 2009; pp. 163–181. ISBN 978-3-7908-2188-8.
103. Paille, P.; Chen, C.; Boiral, O.; Jin, J. The impact of human resource management on environmental performance: An employee-level study. *J. Bus. Ethics* **2014**, *121*, 451–466. [CrossRef]
104. Taylor, S.; Osland, J.; Egri, C.P. Introduction to HRM's role in sustainability: Systems, strategies, and practices. *Hum. Resour. Manag.* **2012**, *51*, 789–798. [CrossRef]
105. Buller, P.F.; Mcevoy, G.M. A Model for Implementing a Sustainability Strategy through HRM Practices. *Bus. Soc. Rev.* **2016**, *121*, 465–495. [CrossRef]

106. Savitz, A.W.; Weber, K. *Talent, Transformation, and the Triple Bottom Line: How Companies Can. Leverage Human Resources to Achieve Sustainable Growth*; John Wiley & Sons, Inc.: San Francisco, CA, USA, 2013; ISBN 978-1-118-14097-0.

107. Lawler, E.E.; Worley, C.G. *Management Reset: Organizing for Sustainable Effectiveness*; John Wiley & Sons Inc.: San Francisco, CA, USA, 2011.

108. Schmit, M.J.; Fegley, S.; Esen, E.; Schramm, S.; Tomassetti, A. Human resource management efforts for environmental sustainability: A survey of organizations. In *Managing Human Resources for Environmental Sustainability*; Jackson, S.E., Ones, D.S., Dilchert, S., Eds.; Wiley and Sons: San Francisco, CA, USA, 2012; pp. 61–63. ISBN 978-0-470-88720-2.

109. Stringer, L. *The Green Workplace. Sustainable Strategies That Benefit Employees, the Environment, and the Bottom Line*; Macmillan: New York, NY, USA, 2009; ISBN 978-0-230-10336-8.

sustainability

MDPI

Article

Value Creation Mechanism of Social Enterprises in Manufacturing Industry: Empirical Evidence from Korea

Hosung Son [1], Joosung Lee [2] and Yanghon Chung [1,*]

[1]   School of Business and Technology Management, College of Business, Korea Advanced Institute of Science and Technology, Gwahak-ro 335, Yuseong-gu, Daejeon 34141, Korea; hs_son@kaist.ac.kr
[2]   Management of Innovation Program, Daegu Gyeongbuk Institute of Science and Technology, Techno Jungang-daero 333, Hyeonpung-myeon, Dalseong-gun, Daegu 42988, Korea; jsl@dgist.ac.kr
*   Correspondence: coach@kaist.ac.kr; Tel.: +82-42-350-6321

Received: 9 November 2017; Accepted: 21 December 2017; Published: 25 December 2017

Abstract: A variety of social enterprises (SEs) have recently emerged in many different countries in an effort to resolve diverse social problems. However, the value creation mechanism of SEs has not yet been disclosed. The purpose of this study is to reveal the value creation mechanism of SEs in manufacturing industry. To do so, we verify the role of social entrepreneurship and examine the effects of product innovation attributes and social capital on social value creation and financial performance by using structural equation modelling. Then, we conduct interviews with six experts in SE fields. According to the results of empirical study, the social entrepreneurship works as an antecedent of product innovation and social capital in SEs and the degrees of products' simplicity, usability and standardization positively affect the social value creation of SEs. In addition, the social value creation works as a complete mediator between the product innovation of SEs and their financial performance. The interviews suggest policy implications for successful social value creation and sustainability of SEs. This research contributes towards further studies on innovation of SEs and provides social entrepreneurs with guidelines in planning their innovation strategy or developing their products.

Keywords: social enterprise; value creation; product innovation; social capital; social value

1. Introduction

Governments, non-profit organizations and for-profit companies have been making significant efforts to alleviate social problems such as unemployment, poverty and lack of education among people suffering from extreme poverty. However, there is still much work to be done [1–4]. As a result, a variety of social enterprises (SEs) have recently emerged in many different countries in an effort to resolve such problems and to secure the sustainability of society [5].

Many different definitions of SEs exist. According to Perrini and Vurro [6], a SE is an organization tasked with finding innovative solutions to social issues. Alter [7] defined a SE as a business that creates social benefits through financial management, innovative methods and decision-making processes similar to those of normal companies. There are several common elements of these definitions, as follows. First, the ultimate goal of a SE is to create social benefits and resolve social problems rather than maximize profits. Second, it creates and spearheads social innovation by using resources and engaging in business activities just as a regular company would. Finally, it also tries to maximize profits to survive in a given market. In other words, a SE is an innovative hybrid organization pursuing both social values and economic profit.

There are many kinds of SEs innovating to resolve different social problems. Some SEs improve social issues or create social values by product innovation. Examples include the 're-motion design', which provides affordable artificial knee joints for impoverished, disabled people in developing countries and Vestergaard Frandsen, which has created a portable water purifier for low-income people in water-scarce countries. This study especially focuses on the product innovation that SEs create, because SEs' products and services tend to bear distinctive marks of innovation, from the perspective of creating both economic profits and social value.

The prior studies on SEs mainly focused on social entrepreneurship, performance analysis and public policy. For example, Weerawardena and Mort [8] revealed key factors affecting social entrepreneurship. Bull [9] developed a balanced score card to analyze the performance of SEs. Kerlin [10] compared concepts and activities of SEs across seven regions and countries to provide practical implications for the development of such enterprises. However, although one of SEs' main characteristics is to create social values through innovative products, the value creation mechanism of SEs has not yet been uncovered. To address this gap, the purpose of this study is to reveal the value creation mechanism of SEs in manufacturing industry. Specifically, this study addresses the following questions: Does entrepreneurial orientation of social entrepreneurs affect product innovation implementation and social capital utilization to create social values? Do product innovation or social capital of SEs positively affect their social value creation or financial performance? Does the social value creation of SEs directly contribute to financial performance?

To do so, we verify the role of social entrepreneurship and examine the effects of product innovation attributes and social capital on social value creation and financial performance by using structural equation modelling (SEM). Then we conduct interviews with six experts in SE fields. This study employs survey data on Korean SEs in manufacturing industry. Because the Korean government has been nurturing SEs to alleviate social problems and create social benefits since 2007, data from Korean SEs is suitable to study on value creation mechanism of SEs. According to the results of empirical study, social entrepreneurship works as an antecedent of product innovation attributes and social capital in SEs and the degrees of product simplicity, usability and standardization positively affect the social value creation of SEs. In addition, the social value creation works as a complete mediator between the product innovation of SEs and their financial performance. The interviews suggest policy implications for successful social value creation and sustainability of SEs. This research contributes towards further studies on innovation of SEs and provides social entrepreneurs with guidelines in planning their innovation strategy or developing their products.

2. Korean Social Enterprises

The Korean government has enacted legislation to secure sustainable and stable jobs and to create more diverse social benefits by SEs. The legislation was published on 3 January 2007 and it came into effect on 1 July 2007. The legislation defines a SE in Korea as an enterprise that pursues social purposes, such as providing social services or creating jobs for vulnerable people, through business activities. Korean SEs should be approved by the committee for SEs promotion, under the auspices of the Ministry of Employment and Labor (MEL). The accredited SEs can receive diverse government supports.

Government supports for promoting SEs are also codified in legislation. First, consultation or information for the management of SEs can be supported by government institutions, or by private organizations appointed by the government. Second, central or local governments provide financial supports for equipment costs or establishment expenses. Third, products or services made by SEs are purchased preferentially by public agencies. Finally, the employment insurance, industrial accident insurance, health insurance and pensions as well as tax benefits are also supported by the government.

On account of these diverse government supports, Korean SEs have been growing rapidly. As Figure 1 shows, the number of accredited SEs has increased about 30-fold, from 50 in 2007 to 1506 in 2015 [11]. The number of vulnerable people hired by SEs increased from 1403 in 2007 to 15,815 in

2014. Meanwhile, the number of vulnerable customers who bought either the products or services of SEs also increased from 17,166 in 2007 to 2,400,706 in 2011 [11].

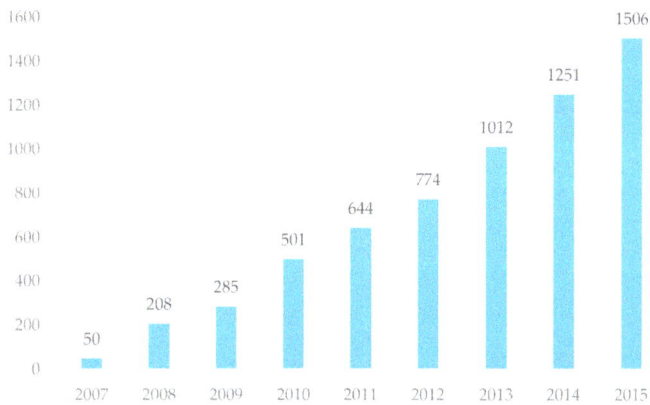

Figure 1. Number of accredited social enterprises in Korea (Source: MEL [11]).

However, the competitiveness and sustainability of each SE still remains in question. Although the average sales of Korean SEs has increased slightly from 0.91 billion Korean won in 2007 to 1.1 billion Korean won in 2013 (refer to the Figure 2), they are still considerably smaller than the average sales of for-profit small enterprises in Korea [11]. According to the Small Medium Business Administration, the average sales of small manufacturing enterprises in 2013 was 3.2 billion Korean won. In addition, the average number of paid employees per SE in Korea decreased from 50.8 in 2007 to 23.3 in 2013 [11]. According to the report analyzing the performance of Korean SEs, the total operating profits of SEs was in a deficit position in 2011 [12]. Nonetheless, Korean SEs have survived on account of non-operating income, such as that from government supports [13]. Thus, many Korean SEs would be in dire straits, if the government were to halt subsidies and tax benefits. This status shows that the research on value creation mechanism of SEs is necessary for growth and sustainability of SEs.

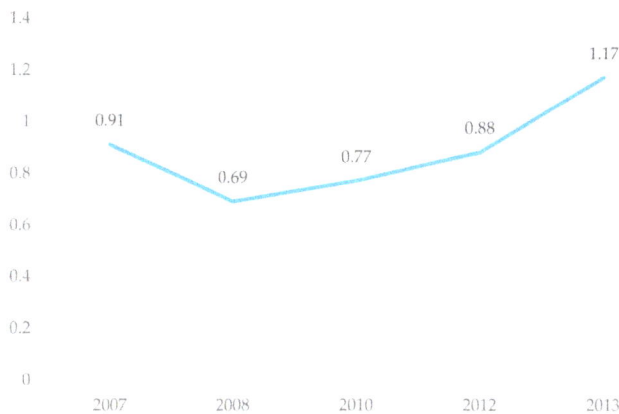

Figure 2. Average sales of Korean social enterprises (Unit: Billion Korean Won) (Source: MEL [11]).

3. Literature Review and Hypotheses Development

3.1. Entrepreneurial Orientation of Social Entrepreneurs

Entrepreneurship has been recognized as one of the key driving forces for success in business as well as in the social sector. The definitions of social entrepreneurship in prior studies are diverse. Liu, et al. [14] (p. 269) define the social entrepreneurship as 'the act of recognizing and pursuing opportunities to solve social problems through the creativity of the typical entrepreneurial process.' Dees and Anderson [15] remark that the social entrepreneurship is related to the innovative activities for social value creation and Thompson [16] insists that it is related to the business skill in non-profit organizations. The common elements of these definitions is that social entrepreneurship is an underlying factor for social value creation [17,18]. This is like the commercial entrepreneurship in for-profit companies which affects business activities for the maximization of firm performance.

Entrepreneurship builds an organizational process to explore business opportunities and to seize them through innovation [19]. Hitt, et al. [20] insists that the entrepreneurship anticipates changes of markets and develops products to meets the potential customers' needs. Similarly, social entrepreneurship is deeply involved in the activities and process for social value creation and survive of SEs. Social entrepreneurship starts with discovering entrepreneurial opportunities which arise from market failure [17]. In other words, social entrepreneurship has emerged because commercial enterprises cannot meet all social needs. Thus, social entrepreneurs seek innovative ways to overcome market failures and to create both social and economic values. Since SEs are hybrid organizations between commercial and non-profit organizations, social entrepreneurs have limitations to use the capital market that is fully utilized by commercial companies [17]. Thus, one of the important role of social entrepreneurs is to mobilize resources from external organizations.

Prior studies insist that entrepreneurial orientation which forms the basis of entrepreneurship reflects a company's strategic posture such as innovativeness, proactiveness and risk-taking [21–23]. Lumpkin and Dess [22] remark that entrepreneurial orientation affects a company's decision-making activities such as exploration and exploitation new opportunities in the markets. Thus, entrepreneurial orientation of a social entrepreneur can promote product innovation and active utilization of social capital for following reasons. First, because the innovativeness of an entrepreneur reflects a company's tendency to develop new products or services [22], a social entrepreneur with strong entrepreneurial orientation tends to emphasize product innovation to create social values. In addition, since the risk-taking attribute of an entrepreneur reflects a company's willingness to take uncertainty or failure in business [24], a social entrepreneur with higher degree of entrepreneurial orientation tends to invest more actively in developing new technologies or products to create social values. The proactiveness attribute of an entrepreneur may affect social capital utilization of SEs. Because the proactiveness reflects a company's tendency to anticipate and prepare for future demands or changes of business environments [22], a social entrepreneur with strong entrepreneurial orientation tends to actively accumulate and use social capital. Especially, since creating social value or solving social problems is difficult for one SE alone, cooperation with local communities, for-profit companies and diverse stakeholders is essential [25]. In other words, social entrepreneurs with strong entrepreneurial orientation can mobilize resources through relational networks to overcome lack of resources for social value creation. Consequently, we propose the following hypotheses.

Hypothesis 1 (H1). *A social entrepreneur with higher degree of entrepreneurial orientation implements product innovation more actively.*

Hypothesis 2 (H2). *A social entrepreneur with higher degree of entrepreneurial orientation accumulates and uses social capital more actively.*

3.2. Product Innovation Attributes in Low-End Markets

To determine the product innovation attributes of SEs, we first reviewed prior studies on product innovation in low-end markets, which constitute the targets of most SEs. Many researchers have identified certain patterns in product innovation and have found the characteristics of each innovation pattern [26–29]. Such categorization and analysis of product innovation helps business managers in planning strategies for their product innovation [30]. Although there is not much literature on product innovation in low-end markets, some of it tries to explain product innovation with notions of disruptive technology, architectural innovations or frugal innovation [31–33]. For example, Lettice and Parekh [25] adopted concepts of disruptive technology and architectural innovation in order to explain the product innovation generated by SEs.

Christensen [27] was the first to mention the notion of disruptive technology, which provides simpler and more modest versions of existing products. Although these simplified products are usually inferior compared to the existing ones in terms of performance, disruptive innovation offers different values such as low prices, product simplicity and convenience. Christenson also explained how enormous leading companies can be defeated by new emerging ones because of disruptive technology [27,34]. In focusing on satisfying their main customers and providing new and advanced features, leading companies sometimes make unnecessarily complicated products which overshoot customers' needs and expectations. Emerging companies using disruptive technology initially serve only niche markets. As time passes, however, they absorb most of the customers in the market, apart from the most-demanding customers. For this reason, Hart and Christensen [31] argued that it is important to develop products which focus on affordability and acceptability in low-end markets. In many cases of SEs' product innovation, products are developed from outside mainstream thinking because most of SEs' target customers are in the low end of the market. Thus, SEs need to transcend the boundaries or limitations of traditional product development in order to satisfy the demands imposed by these niche customers. In other words, SEs can meet the demands for affordability and acceptability in low-end markets which are their main target markets by improving the simplicity and usability of the product compared to existing products offered by for-profit companies [25,35,36].

The architectural innovation enables innovators to have different applications by using and reconfiguring existing technologies [37]. An architectural innovation can be created with relatively minor changes but bring about significant outcomes for low-end markets. Hellström [38] insists that the notion of architectural innovation can be extended into eco-innovation and be expanded further into social innovation. Because of the lack of technology competencies or financial resources, SEs may be better suited to reconfigure the existing systems in new ways instead of developing completely new systems or technologies in developing new products.

Prahalad [35] states that there is still a large and underserved low-end market and that individuals within that market cannot easily use the products or services offered by the mainstream market due to a harsh environment or a lack of financial resources. Therefore, new product innovation is required to meet the unique needs of low-end markets. Zeschky, Widenmayer and Gassmann [33] studied frugal innovation, a new form of product innovation in emerging countries. Many for-profit companies previously tried to sell outdated products in developing countries since these products were no longer competitive in developed countries [35]. However, given the fact that the products were originally developed for people in developed countries, there are still limitations such as environmental and maintenance costs. Therefore, companies need the frugal innovation, which involves modifying products using limited local resources. Frugal innovation has three distinct attributes: product localization is necessary to make it applicable to a local market; it is initiated by overcoming a limitation of resources and environmental conditions in developing new products; it is accompanied by lowering the cost of products, since most target customers are quite poor. Therefore, with the perspective of frugal innovation, SEs need to focus on standardizing their products to lower the maintenance cost of their main customers and to overcome limited local resources in the low-end market [25,35,36].

As previously discussed, in meeting the needs of the low-end market, product innovation by SEs usually needs to focus on product simplification, improved product usability, the reconfiguration of existing technologies and standardized products or components. Table 1 summarizes product innovation attributes in low-end markets based on prior studies and they can be applied to SEs due to the similarity of target market.

Table 1. Product innovation attributes in low-end markets.

Innovation	Attributes	Authors
Disruptive innovation	Simplifying products for improvement of affordability and accessibility	Hart and Christensen [31]
Architectural innovation	Reconfiguring existing technologies for saving organizations' resources	Lettice and Parekh [25]
Frugal innovation	Standardizing products or components for reducing customers' maintenance cost	Zeschky, Widenmayer and Gassmann [33]

Many prior researches have studied the relationship the product innovation and firm performance. Product innovation of SEs can positively contribute to a company's financial performance and non-financial performance for the following reasons. First, companies with high innovation competitiveness can achieve better firm performance by satisfying new customers' needs and actively responding to rapidly changing market conditions [39]. SEs with high competitiveness in product innovation attributes such as product simplicity, usability and standardization that are discussed above can create better firm performance by catching the new needs of the underprivileged and developing related products. Second, innovative products enhance firm performance by contributing to the superiority and the differentiation of products [40,41]. Product innovation of SEs can also secure differentiation advantage in the market through providing new social values and this can contribute to the company's financial performance. Third, in case of frugal innovation, new product development is highly relevant to the company's existing resources and previous experience and thus additional investments such as financial and human resources for product development are not much necessary [33]. These attributes improve a company's speed in time-to-market and shorten time to gain profits through new products [42,43]. Product innovation of SEs can also have positive impacts on improving profitability by reducing investment costs and contributing to fast product launch by focusing on product simplicity, usability and standardization rather than on developing new technologies that require huge investment costs.

Since the performance of a SE is mainly measured by non-financial performance such as social value creation and financial performance such as sales amount and operating income, we propose the following hypotheses regarding the relationship between the attributes of product innovation and firm performance in SEs.

Hypothesis 3 (H3). *The attributes of product innovation in low-end markets such as product simplicity, usability and standardization positively affect the social value creations of SEs.*

Hypothesis 4 (H4). *The attributes of product innovation in low-end markets such as product simplicity, usability and standardization positively affect the financial performance of SEs.*

3.3. Social Capital of Social Enterprises

There are some differences between the innovation undertaken by SEs and that by for-profit companies. Innovation by SEs emerges when they try to meet the unmet needs of individuals within the low-end market, or in solving societal problems; the innovation of for-profit companies, on the other hand, is driven by the existing mainstream market or the development of advanced technologies [25].

Bessant and Tidd [44] (p. 299) also insist that innovation by SEs is 'generating value rather than wealth' and that 'Wealth creation may be part of the process but it is not an end in itself.' In this context, Hall and Vredenburg [45] ascertain that the type of innovation undertaken by SEs is more vague and complicated than traditional innovation in the mainstream market. This is because SEs need to consider different types of market conditions and to satisfy a more diverse body of stakeholders. Hall and Vredenburg [45] also insist that the innovation undertaken by SEs bears greater uncertainty, which is ultimately absorbed into markets or communities. With respect to product innovation, they state that SEs should consider non-technical issues (such as public perceptions or social reactions), as well as technical problems.

Social capital is defined by institutional norms and relational networks of social bonds and behavior [46–50]. social capital enhances trust in the organization or community and acts as a bridge between internal norms and morality [48]. Social capital of SEs contributes to making relationship with various partners for social value creation and the sustainability of SEs [51,52]. In other words, social capital helps social entrepreneurs to create social values through cooperation with employees, NGOs, central government, local government and target users [53–56]. Because SEs mobilize resources through relational assets with external organizations and the relational assets create social value that exceeds transaction costs, social capital can have a positive impact on the social value creation and financial performance of SEs. Relational assets strengthen organizational competency and enhance cooperation in the community or region [57].

The relational networks in social capital are also one of the most important factors in value creation through product innovation. Many studies have also addressed the importance of information and knowledge sharing between organizations in improving corporate innovation capabilities [58–62]. In addition, Kogut [63] and Gulati [64] asserted that corporations secure diverse resource portfolios and improve their innovation capabilities by effectively combining and exploiting partners' resources. The relational networks also contribute to reducing costs, uncertainties and risks in developing new technologies or exploiting new markets [65–67].

Spear [68] says that networks with external organizations often hold a critical role in the entrepreneurial activities of SEs. Being part of a network with external organizations usually helps a SE promote its presence in the market, or to solve some legal or technical issue by providing pro bono advice or funding. Chell [69] remarks that SEs need to overcome their business-resource limitations, as well as any stress that comes with reconciling social benefits with financial profits. Johnstone and Lionais [70] reveal that successful social entrepreneurs usually build suitable relational networks with external organizations in order to overcome difficulties that arise in the course of entrepreneurial activities and to achieve innovation. For these reasons, SEs need to cooperate actively with external stakeholders to create social values effectively and efficiently.

In particular, it is more important to accumulate social capital with external stakeholders in manufacturing industry due to its complex supply chain. Krause, et al. [71] uncovered that close relationship with suppliers and accumulation of social capital with core suppliers contribute to improving buying firm performance. The accumulation of social capital with suppliers can improve buying firm performance for following reasons. First, inter-firm social capital promotes knowledge sharing and consequently contributes to value creation [72–74]. Knowledge sharing such as production schedules or technology development roadmaps can ensure that components are delivered in a timely manner from suppliers and can help to reduce costs and improve quality by improvement of suppliers' competence [75,76]. Second, inter-firm social capital accumulation improves firm performance efficiently through consistency of cognitive capital which is embodied in shared goals and visions [77,78]. If goals and visions among companies are aligned, efficient interactions and collaborations are promoted, while misinterpretation and conflict are reduced, resulting in improved productivity and performance of companies [79,80]. Consequently, social capital accumulation of SEs in manufacturing industry can positively affect social value creation and improve financial performance.

Hypothesis 5 (H5). *The social capital of SEs positively affects the social value creations of SEs.*

Hypothesis 6 (H6). *The social capital of SEs positively affects the financial performance of SEs.*

3.4. Social Value Creation and Financial Performance

Although there are some previous studies on methodology and measurement indicators for analyzing the performance of SEs, it is still difficult to compare the performance of SEs. Because the scope of the SEs is very wide, it is difficult to evaluate the performance uniformly. Some prior studies provide only a conceptual framework for the performance of SEs but do not disclose specific indicators and measurement tools [81]. On the other hand, other previous researches develop the measurement methods that are too specific for some fields and are difficult to apply to SEs in other fields. For example, Bellucci, et al. [82] studied the performance of Fairtrade stores in Italy but the measurement indicators tailored to the value chain of Fairtrade are difficult to apply to other SEs. Crucke and Decramer [83] also argue that it is not easy to develop performance measurement models that are appropriate for all types of SEs, because the performances of SEs are different with respect to the firm size, purpose, activity and stakeholders. Despite the diversity of performance measurement of SEs, prior studies have reached the consensus that the performance of SEs is multidimensional. In other words, non-financial performance such as social value as well as financial performance such as sales revenue or operating profits should be measured for the performance of SEs [81,84].

The social value creation is an ultimate goal of SEs. According to the prior studies, the main difference between for-profit companies and SEs is that the former pursues the maximization of financial performance, while the latter focuses on the social value creation [14]. This difference causes false assumption that financial performance is less critical than social value creation in SEs [14]. Many prior studies point out this erroneous assumption. The emphasizing financial performance may negatively impact on the legitimate status of SEs due to the conflicting priorities even though it is important to reduce financial dependency on external subsidies [85–87]. Dacin, et al. [88] insists that creating social value does not diminish the importance or necessity of financial performance in SEs. In fact, Liu, Eng and Takeda [14] present that SEs must develop strategies and implementation plans to secure a certain level of financial performance to sustainably create social value. Therefore, social entrepreneurs necessarily build their business model that links between social value creation and economic profits.

Consequently, we propose a following hypothesis regarding a relationship between social value creation of SEs and their financial performance.

Hypothesis 7 (H7). *The social value creation of SEs has a positive relationship with financial performance of SEs.*

The social entrepreneurship, attributes of product innovation, social capital of SEs and their effects on social value creation and firm performance, which our study focuses on, are summarized based on the seven hypotheses given. These relationships and hypotheses among all relevant variables are condensed in Figure 3.

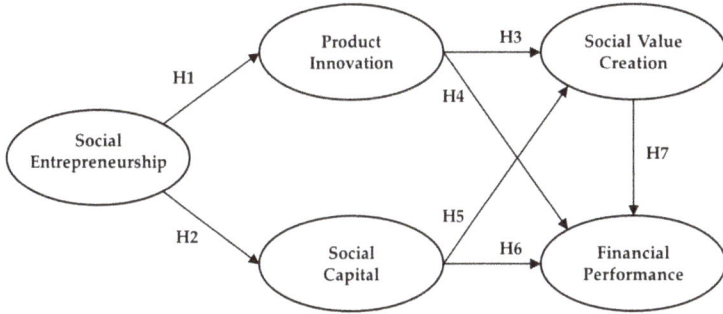

Figure 3. Research model.

4. Research Methodology

We employed a mixed methodology in conducting the research, first conducting an empirical study to verify the hypotheses. We then conducted in-depth interviews with social entrepreneurs and experts in SEs to supplement the results of empirical study and to draw implications for successful social value creation and sustainability of SEs.

According to Creswell [89], three types of mixed methods have been suggested. The first type is convergent designs, in which qualitative and quantitative data are collected at the same time and then the results are compared with each other. This method allows researchers to compare and contrast the results of research with two different perspectives to better explain the research topic. The second type is explanatory sequential designs, in which quantitative data is collected and analyzed in the first stage and then, qualitative research is conducted in the next stage. This method has the advantage to support the results of quantitative analysis or fill gaps of quantitative analysis through the qualitative research. The third type is exploratory sequential designs, in which qualitative research is conducted in the first stage and quantitative research is implemented in the next stage. In this type, the qualitative research contributes to theory building and the quantitative research provides an initial test of the insights of qualitative research. This study adopts the explanatory sequential designs in order to verify the hypotheses in the first stage and supplement the deficiencies of quantitative research through qualitative research in the next stage.

4.1. Empirical Study

4.1.1. Data for Empirical Study

In order to obtain contact information of SEs in manufacturing industry for the survey, we first contacted seven public institutes and one consulting firm that have relationships with Korean SEs. Next, we identified 121 SEs in manufacturing industry from the lists we received. To collect survey data, we called representatives of 121 SEs to briefly explain the purpose of the study and request participation. We then e-mailed and phoned representatives from each enterprise to provide the questionnaire and to request a response. If nobody was available to respond, we allowed a foundation member or a manager to do it. The questionnaire was developed as an Internet-based survey. An email with the survey URL was sent to CEOs or mangers. The survey was conducted from 6 March to 15 April 2014. We received total 68 responses and found that 59 responses were valid for result analysis. The total response rate was 56.2% and the valid response rate was 48.8%. The rest of responses were determined to be untrustworthy by detecting common methods bias (CMB).

4.1.2. Statistical Analysis Method

We verified the effects of product innovation and social capital on social value creation and financial performance in SEs by using survey data and structural equation modelling (SEM). In conducting SEM, we selected partial least squares (PLS) for data analysis, because PLS is a suitable tool to verify research models in an early stage of theoretical development. It also has several advantages. First, PLS is quite reliable in validating latent variable scores measured by one or more questions [90]. Second, a relatively small sample size can be analyzed by PLS [91]. Finally, PLS makes verifying complex models with several latent variables [92].

4.1.3. Measurement Indicators

Many scholars have measured social entrepreneurship with three components of entrepreneurial orientation: innovativeness, risk-taking and proactiveness [93–95]. Innovativeness of social entrepreneurship is a core element of social entrepreneurship. Innovativeness is defined as creating products with new methods or ideas, or promoting changes in organizations or businesses [22,96]. Risk-taking is a characteristic of operations of an organization. It is associated with the willingness to accept perceived risk by criteria such as time, human resources and financial resources in the process of creating or implementing new ideas or creative alternatives [97]. Proactiveness means to break the existing institutional norms or ideas and to try new business, programs, services, or policies [22,96]. These attributes are required when social entrepreneurs create social and economic value by business skills. In this study, social entrepreneurship is measured by three questions related to each attribute.

Most prior studies on innovation of for-profit companies measure the product innovation through the degree of product differentiation, new product introduction rates, or new product success rates [98,99]. However, since the target market and the purpose of innovation in SEs are different from those in for-profit companies, the measurement indicators for product innovation of SEs need to be modified. We developed the measurement indicators based on the attributes of product innovation in low-end markets found through literature review. The indicators measure how much a SE focuses on simplicity, usability and standardization to improve the affordability or accessibility of products when developing new products.

According to previous studies, social capital was measured based on the scale, intensity and diversity of the relationship network. Batjargal [100] measured the size of the relationship network through number of contacts between entrepreneurs and stakeholders. The size of the relationship network is able to limited to specific domains, such as managers in other companies or government officials [101]. Davidsson and Honig [102] measured social capital by investigating strong ties and weak ties. The intensity of the relationship is usually measured through interaction frequency or emotional intimacy. Finally, social capital can be measured through the heterogeneity in the entrepreneurs' personal network. Renzulli, et al. [103] measured diversity of the relationship network through demographic diversity, contacts with other industries and scope of international cooperation. In this study, social capital of SEs was measured by the respondents' subjective evaluation on the questions about the size, intensity and diversity of the relationship network.

The measurement indicators for social value creation were modified based on the extant literature. Liu, Eng and Takeda [14] assessed the social value creation of SEs through the respondents' subjective evaluation on comparison with the set goal in advance. They used a total of five indicators: bidding for public service contract, bidding government grants for enterprise activities, serves more beneficiaries in the community, provide more social service (different types), expand social service to different locations. We also measured the social value creation of SEs through the respondents' subjective evaluation with respect to the achievement of social value through product development, improvement in affordability of products and increase in the beneficiary. In this study, the indicators are adjusted in order to fit the product innovation of SEs in manufacturing industry. In addition, social value creation was measured based on the performance over the past 12 months with reference to prior researches [104–106].

To measure financial performance of companies, many researchers look at growth and profitability [107]. Baker and Sinkula [98] and Murat Ar and Baki [108] used three measurement indicators: change in sales revenue, market share and profits relative to large competitors. Wolff and Pett [107] used return and growth perspectives to assess financial performance, measuring return on total assets (ROA) and total sales growth compared to competitors. This study uses market share, sales revenue and operating profit compared to initial targets to measure financial performance in terms of market impact, growth and profitability. This study used subjective ratings for measuring financial performance. The subjective ratings are useful when the numerical data is difficult to obtain and the respondents are reluctant to share them [109–112].

A pilot test was conducted to increase the validity of the responses. The several participants in the pilot test pointed out that definitions and brief descriptions of the terms used in the survey are necessary because the definitions of terms recognized by respondents may be different. In accordance with the advice of participants, we have added definitions and brief descriptions of the terms which may be slightly vague. Table 2 presents measurement indicators for each latent variable. We used a seven-point Likert scale for measuring all indicators. One means "strongly disagree" and seven stands for "strongly agree". We attached the questionnaire to Appendix A.

Table 2. Measurement indicators for each latent variable.

Latent Variable	Indicator	Definition	Reference
Social entrepreneurship	SE1	Degree of innovativeness	Helm and Andersson [93]
	SE2	Degree of proactiveness	Sullivan Mort, Weerawardena and Carnegie [94]
	SE3	Degree of risk-taking	Giraud Voss, Voss and Moorman [95]
Product innovation	PI1	Degree of simplicity of product	Hart and Christensen [31]
	PI2	Degree of usability of product	Henderson and Clark [37]
	PI3	Degree of standardization	Zeschky, Widenmayer and Gassmann [33]
Social capital	SC1	Size of relationship networks	Batjargal [100]
	SC2	Diversity of relationship networks	Renzulli, Aldrich and Moody [103]
	SC3	Intensity of relationship networks	Davidsson and Honig [102]
Social value creation	SVC1	Achievements of social value through product development	Liu, Eng and Takeda [14]
	SVC2	Improvement in affordability of products	Crucke and Decramer [83]
	SVC3	Increase in the beneficiary	
Financial performance	FP1	Market impact	Baker and Sinkula [98]
	FP2	Growth	Wolff and Pett [107]
	FP3	Profitability	Murat Ar and Baki [108]

4.2. Qualitative Study

In order to reinforce and supplement the empirical study, we interviewed six experts from SEs field: two social entrepreneurs, one consultant for SEs and three researchers from non-profit organizations supporting SEs. At this stage, we tried to see how SEs in manufacturing industry implement product innovations such as product simplicity, usability and standardization and why social capital of SEs cannot significantly affect their social value creation or financial performance. The interviews were conducted between May and June 2014 and each interview took approximately two hours. Table 3 provides information about the interviewees and their affiliations.

Table 3. Information of interviewees and affiliations.

Name	Position	Affiliation	Location
Kim, Jung-hyun	CEO	Delight	Seoul
Kim, Nam-wook	Manager	Delight	Seoul
Kim, Hae-jin	Senior consultant	KMCCA	Daejeon
Moon, Jin-soo	Research manager	Hope institute	Seoul
Bae, Min-hae	Researcher	Hope institute	Seoul
Lee, Jae-heung	Researcher	Hope institute	Seoul

Delight was founded in 2009 to produce hearing aids at low prices for poor, hearing impaired people in Korea. Although Delight has a relatively short history compared to successful overseas SEs, it was featured several times in Korean media as one of the most promising SEs in the country. We investigated secondary sources such as press releases and online information and conducted an in-depth interview with a representative and manager of the company.

Hope institute is a policy research organization in Seoul, Korea. Their mission is to foster civic leadership based on sustainable values and to conduct policy research on important social issues. In order to achieve the mission, they analyze social phenomenon, form consensus and suggest of solutions on social issues. In addition, they hold seminars and conferences to reflect citizens' opinions and to enlarge their perspectives. We interviewed the research manager and two researchers who are studying the social economic field in order to draw policy implications for SEs. KMCCA (Korea Management Consulting Company Association) is a consulting corporation for management of corporation and start-up and supports consulting on the management and start-up of SEs in Daejeon city. We interviewed the senior consultant to learn about the attributes and management tendency of social entrepreneurs.

The questions were open-ended and semi-structured [113]; thus, the questions differed slightly for each organization. The interviewees were asked the following questions:

(1) What is the mission of your organization?
(2) How do SEs in manufacturing industry approach to solve social problems or to create social value?
(3) What are the main difficulties that SEs face in product development and social value creation? And how can SEs overcome these difficulties?
(4) What should Korean SEs do to increase their competitiveness and to secure their sustainability?
(5) Do Korean SEs actively cooperate with other organizations to create social value? If not, what are the difficulties of the cooperation?

In line with the methodology of Sekaran [114], we hold face-to-face meeting with interviewees; this is the best option when addressing a controversial topic. All interview contents were analyzed from three perspectives: data reduction, display and verification [113]. Two researchers coded and grouped the text by theme [115–117]. Next, another researcher checked for and compared discrepancies. Finally, all the researchers discussed the conflicting parts and made minor adjustments, until they were consistent [115,118,119].

5. Results

5.1. Results of Empirical Study

Assessments of PLS path model consists of a two-step process: outer model assessment and inner model assessment. Outer model assessment is composed of reliability and validity of reflective constructs and validity of formative constructs. Therefore, before the inner model is assessed, reliability and validity of each construct in the outer model should meet certain criteria [92].

5.1.1. Reliability Assessment of the Research Model

To evaluate reliability in the PLS model, composite reliability value or Cronbach's α can be a criterion for checking internal consistency reliability. However Cronbach's α tends to seriously underestimate internal consistency reliability of latent variables in the PLS model [120]. Therefore, we adopted composite reliability values for validation of internal consistency reliability. According to Bernstein and Nunnally [121], the reliability value should be above 0.7 in early stages of research and higher than 0.8 or 0.9 in advanced stages of research. Because this is the first exploratory study on product innovation of SEs, we follow the first criterion. Table 4 shows composite reliability values of each latent variable which meet the criterion suggested by Bernstein and Nunnally [121].

Table 4. Results of reliability test.

Latent Variable	Composite Reliability	Indicator	Outer Loading Values				
			SE	PI	SC	SVC	FP
SE	0.866	SE1	0.817				
		SE2	0.874				
		SE3	0.788				
PI	0.801	PI1		0.811			
		PI2		0.754			
		PI3		0.702			
SC	0.782	SC1			0.703		
		SC2			0.718		
		SC3			0.826		
SVC	0.779	SVC1				0.830	
		SVC2				0.767	
FP	0.934	FP1					0.840
		FP2					0.952
		FP3					0.929

For the reliability of indicators, Henseler, Ringle and Sinkovics [92] suggested that absolute standardized outer loadings should be above 0.7 if researchers postulate that each latent variable should explain at least 50% of each indicator's variance. Thus, among the indicators we designed, SVC3 were excluded because their outer loading scores are less than 0.7.

5.1.2. Validity Assessment of the Research Model

The assessment of validity in PLS consists of convergent validity and discriminant validity. Convergent validity indicates how well each set of indicators represents the same underlying construct. Discriminate validity states that two different concepts should show sufficient difference. Fornell and Larcker [122] said that average variance extracted (AVE) should be at least 0.5 for convergent validity and the square root of each latent variable' of AVE should be higher than the highest correlation coefficients for discriminate validity. Table 5 presents the AVE values and correlation coefficients of each latent variable. The AVE values of all latent variables exceed 0.5 and so we have determined that each latent variable achieved sufficient discrimination validity.

Table 5. Results of validity test.

Latent Variable	AVE Value	Discriminant Validity				
		FP	PI	SC	SE	SVC
FP	0.825	0.908				
PI	0.573	0.201	0.757			
SC	0.546	0.177	0.183	0.739		
SE	0.684	0.335	0.498	0.470	0.827	
SVC	0.638	0.402	0.356	0.206	0.241	0.799

5.1.3. Results of Path Model

The PLS model analysis results are shown in Table 6 and Figure 4. Based on path coefficients and measurement of *p*-value, we found that the social entrepreneurship positively affects the product innovation attributes and social capital of SEs and the product innovation has a positive relationship with social value creation of SEs. In addition, the social value creation of SEs is positively associated with financial performance of SEs. However, the effects of social capital on social value creation and financial performance of SEs are insignificant. Therefore, Hypotheses 1, 2, 3 and 7 are accepted while Hypotheses 4, 5 and 6 are rejected. The rejection of Hypothesis 4 implies that the social value creation works as a complete mediator between the product innovation and financial performance of SEs. In addition, the rejections of Hypotheses 5 and 6 mean that product innovation attributes of SEs such as product simplicity, usability and standardization rather than the social capital of SEs have critical influences on social value creation of SEs in the manufacturing industry.

Table 6. Results of research model.

Path	Original Sample	Sample Mean	Standard Deviation	*T*-Statistics	*p*-Value
SE→PI	0.498	0.510	0.116	4.292	0.000
SE→SC	0.470	0.484	0.113	4.150	0.000
PI→SVC	0.330	0.328	0.166	1.980	0.048
PI→FP	0.054	0.075	0.190	0.284	0.776
SC→SVC	0.146	0.161	0.135	1.084	0.278
SC→FP	0.092	0.091	0.130	0.707	0.480
SVC→FP	0.364	0.360	0.151	2.413	0.016

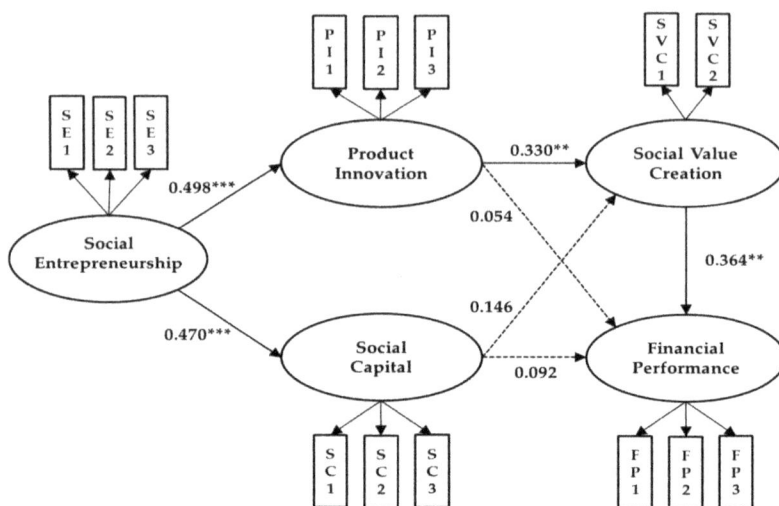

Figure 4. Results of research model. Notes: *** $p < 0.01$, ** $p < 0.05$.

5.2. Results of Qualitative Study

5.2.1. New Product Development and Social Value Creation of SEs

In this section, interviews with social entrepreneurs show how the SEs in the manufacturing industry have implemented product innovations such as product simplicity, usability and standardization.

Social entrepreneurs usually start from a tiny idea that can solve social problems or create social values. Junghyun Kim, a former CEO of Delight, founded a SE in 2010 to provide hearing aids to people who are vulnerable with hearing impairments. He said that:

> "We started our business after we found that there were many poor people with hearing impairments who could not purchase a hearing aid due to the price. The average price of a hearing aid in Korea is from $1500 to $2000. Meanwhile, the Korean government provides a subsidy of $340 for impoverished people with hearing impairments. As a result, we decided to develop a hearing aid priced at $340."

Since SEs should provide products or services to the vulnerable people at affordable prices, applied technologies should contribute to reducing product cost. SEs also try to make simpler and more modest versions of products for vulnerable people who are their main customer. To accomplish them, SEs focus on standardization of components. Junghyun Kim said that:

> "Most hearing aids are customized for each user's ear shape, leading to high costs. We studied Koreans' ear shapes in order to create 200 standardized sizes. It then mass produced them using an injection molding technology, dramatically reducing production costs. Making hearing aids consist of five steps: hearing tests, consulting with experts on selecting hearing aids, manufacturing products, customizing products for various ear types and delivering the products. We also notably reduced customers' costs and time for hearing tests by using doctor notes instead of in-house facilities. Moreover, we have an online system for users to choose a suitable hearing aid. This increases efficiency and convenience for customers. Finally, since we have a door-to-door delivery system, customers need not visit the store, again. Thanks to all of these approaches, Delight became the first company in Korea supplying low price hearing aids within just five days."

Namwook Kim, a manager of Delight, said that:

> "Actually, we tried to do away with stereotypes on current products. Otherwise, it was impossible to develop a totally new product for people at the low-end of markets. If we developed our products in the same way as for-profit companies, we would not have been able to lower prices and improve product usability and accessibility."

This argument is consistent with Lettice and Parekh [25] claim that destructive or architectural innovation is more appropriate than sustainable or incremental innovation in order to achieve social change. According to senior consultant Haejin Kim, one of the difficulties inherent in operating a SE is concurrently generating both social benefits and economic profits. He said that most SEs experience a conflict or tension between social objectives and economic objectives. Jaeheung Lee, a researcher at the Hope institute, also stated that:

> "Actually, SEs are not both for-profit companies and non-profit organizations. So, it is very difficult to be financially independent without any subsidies or funding, in normal situations. The social mission of a SE sometimes conflicts with its business, because most of its target customers do not have enough purchasing power. Therefore, some SEs adopt two pricing models: one is for customers in normal markets and the other is for poor customers in low-end markets."

These interviews confirm that it is important to improve the simplicity, accessibility and affordability of products in order to create social value by SEs in manufacturing industry, as demonstrated in the empirical study. In addition, the SEs need to innovate business models for overcome disadvantages of their target market.

5.2.2. Reinforcing Competitiveness of SEs

In this section, interviews with experts in SEs show how the SEs reinforce their competitiveness and why social capital of SEs cannot significantly affect their social value creation or financial performance. Furthermore, policy implications for enhancing competitiveness of SEs are drawn.

Chan Kim and Mauborgne [123] highlighted the importance of a well-developed relational network with external resources, given the fact that resources are usually insufficient when operations commence. It is important that companies use external resources to be effective and efficient. Most Korean SEs lack resources for business activities such as marketing, supply chain management, production and R&D. Therefore, SEs concentrate on the formation of relational network with external organizations to mobilize external resources. Minhae Bae, a researcher at the Hope institute, said that in order to solve social problems, it is important to establish relationships assets with various organizations such as for-profit companies, local government and civic groups for product development, distribution channels and promotions. Junghyun Kim also said that:

> "We actively collaborate with government agencies and non-profit organizations when we open medical camps on a large scale. They give financial supports and help in promotion activities . . . . We received external investments from Daewon, a large Korean pharmaceutical company, as well as technological support from KAIST, a prominent Korean university in order to develop the next version of our product."

Figure 5 shows Delight's mobilization of external resources for enhancing their competitiveness.

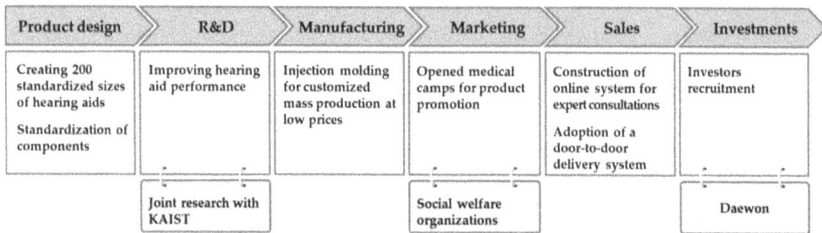

Figure 5. Delight's mobilization of external resources.

However, most Korean SEs do not actively cooperate with external organizations in technology development, securing distributors and marketing. Lee and Kim [124] report that in developing distribution channels, 10% of Korean SEs collaborate with local government or public agencies and 5% of Korean SEs collaborate with for-profit companies. As for technology development, 8.8% of Korean SEs received supports from central or local governments and 3.9% of Korean SEs received them from public institutions.

Haejin Kim also stated that:

> "Most SEs want to make business networks with external organizations (such as for-profit companies or public institutions), in order to secure their distribution channels or technological resources. However, it is difficult for SEs to find suitable partners, given a lack of information about external organizations who want to create relationships with SEs."

Consequently, most Korean SEs do not receive expert supports (like pro bono work), even when they lack business resources. Haejin Kim insisted that government needs to reduce information asymmetry between SEs and external organizations. These external organizations include for-profit companies that are interested in collaborating with SEs, as a part of their corporate social responsibility strategies. Jinsoo Moon said that:

> "Korean government supports such as subsidies and tax reduction benefits were really beneficial for SEs in the early stage of business. Now, the government needs to focus on efficient ways in which SEs can collaborate with other organizations. This approach would contribute to creating a more sustainable ecosystem for SEs."

Jaeheung Lee pointed out that SEs also need to develop their capability to enlarge their relational networks, if they want to grow their enterprises.

> "Most SEs depend on central or local government for their business. Only a few SEs try to enlarge their relational networks with external companies or institutions. In addition, only a few SEs create a department that promotes their business to external organizations and develop partnerships."

Although the interviewed experts have argued that social capital is an important factor for the business of SEs, the empirical study shows that there is no significant relationship between social capital and the social value creation or financial performance of SEs. As for this part, Jinsoo Moon mentioned as follows:

> "Although social capital is an important factor for the business of SEs, the quality of resources provided from the relational networks can also affect the social value creation of SEs. In other words, if external organizations do not actively support or cooperate with business of SEs, it may be difficult to create social value even if SEs accumulate the relational assets."

According to the results of interview, it is important to build relational assets in order for Korean SEs to secure competitiveness and contribute to social value creation more consistently. However, despite the fact that the majority of SEs want to collaborate with external organizations, it is difficult to find suitable partners. In order to build a sustainable social innovation system, the government needs to establish infrastructures for the formation of SEs' social capital. In addition, in order to effective social value creation of SEs, government also needs to prepare an incentive for external organizations formed social capital of SEs.

6. Discussion

6.1. Findings and Implications

This study explored the value creation mechanism of SEs in manufacturing industry. The results of the empirical study find that the social entrepreneurship works as an antecedent of product innovation and social capital in SEs and the degree of SEs' product innovation attributes such as simplicity, usability and standardization of products positively affect the social value creation of SEs. In addition, the social value creation works as a complete mediator between the product innovation of SEs and their financial performance. These results indicate that SEs in the manufacturing industry create social value through product innovation and that the social value created contributes to the financial performance that can secure the sustainability of the SEs. In addition, the product innovation of SEs can increase social value creation by focusing on simplicity, usability and standardization of products. The interviews with experts in the SE field also support the findings of empirical study. Junghyun Kim, founder of Delight recognized that poor, hearing-impaired people could not afford a hearing aid with a government subsidy. The Delight tried to develop a hearing aid improved in affordability and accessibility by securing simplicity, usability and standardization of products. In addition, they also tried to actively accumulate and use social capital for social value creation. They opened medical camps by collaborating with government agencies and nonprofit organizations and mobilized technical supports from the university for new product development.

Although the empirical study revealed that social entrepreneurship has a strongly positive effect on social capital of SEs, the significant effects of social capital on social value creation and financial performance of SEs were not found. This result implies that product innovation attributes of SEs such as product simplicity, usability and standardization rather than the social capital of SEs have critical influences on social value creation of SEs in the manufacturing industry. On the other hand, one of interviewee mentioned that if the external organizations do not actively support or cooperate with business of SEs, it may be difficult to create social value even if SEs accumulate the relational assets.

This study also suggests policy implications for successful social value creation and sustainability of SEs. Until now, Korean government has been focused on increasing the size and total numbers of SEs by providing subsidies and tax benefits. On account of these government supports, Korean SEs have grown rapidly in quantitative terms. The number of accredited SEs has increased about 30-fold, from 50 in 2007 to 1506 in 2015. In the future, the Korean government needs to focus on both improving the competitiveness of individual SEs and fostering a sustainable ecosystem of SEs.

To do so, this study proposes two policies as follow. First, government needs to support product innovation of SEs. For example, if the government allows SEs to use technologies that have not been transferred among technologies developed by public research institutes for free, innovative SEs will be more created. Some SEs misunderstand that product innovation requires a high level of technology, knowledge and investment. However, our study shows how these can be overcome in SEs. According to the results, the degree of products' simplicity, usability and standardization can improve social value creation. Moreover, the product innovation of SEs does not need huge investments and can be a resource-saving innovation [25]. The case of Delight shows that the product innovation of SEs is possible through reconfiguration of existing technologies without developing advanced technologies. Second, government needs to support the accumulation of SEs' social capital. For example, government can establish an online-platform to share information between SEs and external organizations such as for-profit companies, non-profit organizations, universities and public institutes. Currently, many SEs are trying to find external organizations for cooperation but it is difficult to find suitable partner due to the lack of relevant information. It is also not easy for external organizations that want to support SEs for social value creation to seek appropriate SEs. The government's online-platform reduces the information asymmetry and improves institutional-based trust among participants. The institutional-based trust is formed through a trustworthy third party organization and system, which is particularly important for cooperation between organizations that have no previous interaction [125]. In addition to building infrastructures for the social capital accumulation of SEs, the government also needs to draft incentive policies for external organizations that support SEs in order to create the positive effects of social capital on social value creation of SEs. This study has already shown that the social capital accumulation of SEs by itself has limitations to create positive effects on social value creation and financial performance of SEs. Therefore, the government needs to implement incentive policies so that many external organizations can support SEs and actively participate in social value creation.

6.2. Contribution and Limitations

We conducted an empirical study on the value creation mechanism of SEs in manufacturing industry and found the role of social entrepreneurship and the effects of product innovation on social value creation and financial performance in SEs. Although there have been some prior studies on product innovation in low-end markets, most studies have used only qualitative research methods (e.g., case studies). This study used both quantitative and qualitative research methods to complement the limitations of existing researches. In addition, the measurement indicators used in this study can contribute to future researches on social innovation or product innovation of non-profit organizations. Finally, this study can provide social entrepreneurs with guidelines in planning their innovation strategy or developing their products.

Although this study found the role of social entrepreneurship and the effects of SEs' product innovation attributes on social value creation and financial performance of SEs, this study has a few limitations which should be considered in future studies. First, we examined only Korean data to analyze the value creation mechanism of SEs. National differences such as political or economic environments can affect the value creation mechanism of SEs. Thus, it is necessary to research value creation mechanisms of SEs in diverse environments. Second, we only investigated SEs in manufacturing industry to focus on their product innovation. Therefore, in future research, it is necessary to analyze the innovation performance and the financial performance considering the characteristics of each industry. Finally, we propose comparative studies on SEs and for-profit companies that are similar size and same industry to compare product innovation paths and determine factors affecting product innovation and firm performance.

7. Conclusions

The purpose of this study is to uncover the value creation mechanism of SEs in manufacturing industry. In order to verify how SEs can effectively create social value and how SEs are sustainable despite focusing on social value creation rather than profit maximization, we have addressed several research questions: Does entrepreneurial orientation of social entrepreneurs affect product innovation implementation and social capital utilization to create social values? Do product innovation or social capital of SEs positively affect their social value creation or financial performance? Does the social value creation of SEs directly contribute to financial performance?

The results of this study confirm the following three points. First, social entrepreneurs with higher degree of entrepreneurial orientation implement product innovation and accumulate and use social capital more actively. Second, product innovation attributes such as product simplicity, usability and standardization positively affect the social value creations of SEs. Third, financial performance of SEs is improved only through social value creation and it is not directly affected by product innovation or social capital of SEs. Consequently, social entrepreneurs can achieve sustainable financial performance by creating social value through product innovation such as product simplicity, usability and standardization.

Acknowledgments: The authors would like to thank the editors and anonymous reviewers for their constructive comments and helpful suggestions.

Author Contributions: Hosung Son designed the research framework, analyzed the data and wrote the paper. Joosung Lee suggested research idea and designed the qualitative study. Yanghon Chung designed the overall conceptual framework of the study and guided the research methodology and writing of the paper.

Conflicts of Interest: The authors declare no conflict of interest.

Appendix A

Latent Variable	Indicator	Question
Social entrepreneurship	SE1	CEO emphasizes and implements R&D and innovation.
	SE2	CEO conducts active and bold business activities.
	SE3	CEO adopts a new management tool even if there is a risk.
Product innovation	PI1	We focused on simplification of the product when developing new products.
	PI2	We focused on improvement of the product usability when developing new products.
	PI3	We focused on standardization of components or products when developing new products.
Social capital	SC1	We make cooperative relationship with many external organizations.
	SC2	We build a cooperative channel with various external organizations.
	SC3	We continuously and frequently collaborate with external organizations.
Social value creation	SVC1	We created the social value we have aimed at.
	SVC2	We improved affordability of products.
	SVC3	We increased the number of beneficiaries of social benefit.
Financial performance	FP1	We achieved a higher market share than its target.
	FP2	We achieved higher sales than the target.
	FP3	We achieved a higher operating income than its target.

References

1. Borins, S. Loose cannons and rule breakers, or enterprising leaders? Some evidence about innovative public managers. *Public Adm. Rev.* **2000**, *60*, 498–507. [CrossRef]
2. Easterly, W.; Easterly, W.R. *The White Man's Burden: Why the West's Efforts to Aid the Rest Have Done So Much Ill and So Little Good*; Penguin Press: London, UK, 2006.
3. Collier, P. *The Bottom Billion: Why the Poorest Countries Are Failing and What Can Be Done about It*; Oxford University Press: Oxford, UK, 2008.
4. Yunus, M. *Creating a World without Poverty: Social Business and the Future of Capitalism*; PublicAffairs: New York, NY, USA, 2007.
5. Bornstein, D. *How to Change the World: Social Entrepreneurs and the Power of New Ideas*; Oxford University Press: Oxford, UK, 2007.

6. Perrini, F.; Vurro, C. Social entrepreneurship: Innovation and social change across theory and practice. In *Social Entrepreneurship*; Springer: Berlin, Germany, 2006; pp. 57–85.
7. Alter, K. *Social Enterprise Typology*; Virtue Ventures LLC: Wilmington, DE, USA, 2007; pp. 1–124.
8. Weerawardena, J.; Mort, G.S. Investigating social entrepreneurship: A multidimensional model. *J. World Bus.* **2006**, *41*, 21–35. [CrossRef]
9. Bull, M. "Balance": The development of a social enterprise business performance analysis tool. *Soc. Enterp. J.* **2007**, *3*, 49–66. [CrossRef]
10. Kerlin, J.A. A comparative analysis of the global emergence of social enterprise. *VOLUNTAS Int. J. Volunt. Nonprofit Organ.* **2010**, *21*, 162–179. [CrossRef]
11. Labor, M.M. *Direction of Social Enterprise Fostering Policy*; Ministry of Employment and Labor: Gwacheon, Korea, 2015.
12. *Hanshin Survey Report on Social Enterprise*; Hanshin University: Gyeonggi-do, Korea, 2012.
13. Kim, S.K. Issues of institutionalization of social economy and policies for fostering social enterprise. *Hum. Resour. Dev. Rev.* **2014**, *74*, 90–111.
14. Liu, G.; Eng, T.Y.; Takeda, S. An investigation of marketing capabilities and social enterprise performance in the UK and Japan. *Entrep. Theory Pract.* **2015**, *39*, 267–298. [CrossRef]
15. Dees, J.G.; Anderson, B.B. For-profit social ventures. *Int. J. Entrep. Educ.* **2003**, *2*, 1–26.
16. Thompson, J.L. The world of the social entrepreneur. *Int. J. Public Sect. Manag.* **2002**, *15*, 412–431. [CrossRef]
17. Austin, J.; Stevenson, H.; Wei-Skillern, J. Social and commercial entrepreneurship: Same, different, or both? *Entrep. Theory Pract.* **2006**, *30*, 1–22. [CrossRef]
18. Zadek, S.; Thake, S. Send in the social entrepreneurs. *New Statesman* **1997**, *126*, 31.
19. Covin, J.G.; Green, K.M.; Slevin, D.P. Strategic process effects on the entrepreneurial orientation-sales growth rate relationship. *Entrep. Theory Pract.* **2006**, *30*, 57–81. [CrossRef]
20. Hitt, M.A.; Nixon, R.D.; Hoskisson, R.E.; Kochhard, R. Corporate entrepreneurship and cross-functional fertilization: Activation, process and disintegration of a new product design team. *Entrep. Theory Pract.* **1999**, *23*, 145–145.
21. Covin, J.G.; Slevin, D.P. Strategic management of small firms in hostile and benign environments. *Strateg. Manag. J.* **1989**, *10*, 75–87. [CrossRef]
22. Lumpkin, G.T.; Dess, G.G. Clarifying the entrepreneurial orientation construct and linking it to performance. *Acad. Manag. Rev.* **1996**, *21*, 135–172.
23. Miller, D. The correlates of entrepreneurship in three types of firms. *Manag. Sci.* **1983**, *29*, 770–791. [CrossRef]
24. Rauch, A.; Wiklund, J.; Lumpkin, G.T.; Frese, M. Entrepreneurial orientation and business performance: An assessment of past research and suggestions for the future. *Entrep. Theory Pract.* **2009**, *33*, 761–787. [CrossRef]
25. Lettice, F.; Parekh, M. The social innovation process: Themes, challenges and implications for practice. *Int. J. Technol. Manag.* **2010**, *51*, 139–158. [CrossRef]
26. Abernathy, W.J.; Clark, K.B. Innovation: Mapping the winds of creative destruction. *Res. Policy* **1985**, *14*, 3–22. [CrossRef]
27. Christensen, C. *The Innovator's Dilemma: When New Technologies Cause Great Firms to Fail*; Harvard Business Review Press: Cambridge, MA, USA, 2013.
28. Kimberly, J.R.; Evanisko, M.J. Organizational innovation: The influence of individual, organizational and contextual factors on hospital adoption of technological and administrative innovations. *Acad. Manag. J.* **1981**, *24*, 689–713. [CrossRef]
29. Utterback, J.M.; Abernathy, W.J. A dynamic model of process and product innovation. *Omega* **1975**, *3*, 639–656. [CrossRef]
30. Saviotti, P.P. Technology mapping and the evaluation of technical change. *Int. J. Technol. Manag.* **1995**, *10*, 407–425.
31. Hart, S.L.; Christensen, C.M. The great leap: Driving innovation from the base of the pyramid. *MIT Sloan Manag. Rev.* **2002**, *44*, 51.
32. Ray, S.; Ray, P.K. Product innovation for the people's car in an emerging economy. *Technovation* **2011**, *31*, 216–227. [CrossRef]
33. Zeschky, M.; Widenmayer, B.; Gassmann, O. Frugal innovation in emerging markets. *Res. Technol. Manag.* **2011**, *54*, 38–45. [CrossRef]

34. Christensen, C.M.; Bohmer, R.; Kenagy, J. Will disruptive innovations cure health care? *Harv. Bus. Rev.* **2000**, *78*, 102–112. [PubMed]

35. Prahalad, C. *The Fortune at the Bottom of the Pyramid*; Wharton School Publishing: Philadelphia, PA, USA, 2005.

36. Rangan, V.K.; Thulasiraj, R. Making sight affordable (innovations case narrative: The Aravind eye care system). *Innov. Technol. Gov. Glob.* **2007**, *2*, 35–49. [CrossRef]

37. Henderson, R.M.; Clark, K.B. Architectural innovation: The reconfiguration of existing product technologies and the failure of established firms. *Adm. Sci. Q.* **1990**, *35*, 9–30. [CrossRef]

38. Hellström, T. Dimensions of environmentally sustainable innovation: The structure of eco-innovation concepts. *Sustain. Dev.* **2007**, *15*, 148–159. [CrossRef]

39. Lloréns Montes, F.J.; Ruiz Moreno, A.; Miguel Molina Fernández, L. Assessing the organizational climate and contractual relationship for perceptions of support for innovation. *Int. J. Manpower* **2004**, *25*, 167–180. [CrossRef]

40. Kim, N.; Shin, S.; Min, S. Strategic marketing capability: Mobilizing technological resources for new product advantage. *J. Bus. Res.* **2016**, *69*, 5644–5652. [CrossRef]

41. McNally, R.C.; Cavusgil, E.; Calantone, R.J. Product innovativeness dimensions and their relationships with product advantage, product financial performance and project protocol. *J. Prod. Innov. Manag.* **2010**, *27*, 991–1006. [CrossRef]

42. Chen, J.; Damanpour, F.; Reilly, R.R. Understanding antecedents of new product development speed: A meta-analysis. *J. Oper. Manag.* **2010**, *28*, 17–33. [CrossRef]

43. Langerak, F.; Jan Hultink, E. The impact of product innovativeness on the link between development speed and new product profitability. *J. Prod. Innov. Manag.* **2006**, *23*, 203–214. [CrossRef]

44. Bessant, J.; Tidd, J. *Innovation and Entrepreneurship*; John Wiley & Sons: Hoboken, NJ, USA, 2007.

45. Hall, J.; Vredenburg, H. The challenge of innovating for sustainable development. *MIT Sloan Manag. Rev.* **2003**, *45*, 61.

46. Bourdieu, P. *The Forms of Capital in Handbook of Theory and Research for the Sociology of Education*; Richardson, J., Ed.; Greenwood: New York, NY, USA, 1986.

47. Coleman, J.S. Social capital in the creation of human capital. *Am. J. Sociol.* **1988**, *94*, S95–S120. [CrossRef]

48. Coleman, J. *Foundations of Social Theory Harvard University*; Harvard University Press: Cambridge, MA, USA, 1990.

49. Putnam, R.D. The prosperous community. *Am. Prospect* **1993**, *4*, 35–42.

50. Putnam, R.D. Bowling alone: America's declining social capital. *J. Democr.* **1995**, *6*, 65–78. [CrossRef]

51. Bouchard, M.J.; Rousselière, D. Do Hybrid Organizational Forms of the Social Economy have a Greater Chance of Surviving? An Examination of the Case of Montreal. *VOLUNTAS Int. J. Volunt. Nonprofit Organ.* **2016**, *27*, 1894–1922. [CrossRef]

52. Sdrali, D.; Goussia-Rizou, M.; Giannouli, P.; Makris, K. What motivates employees to engage in the social economy sector? A case study of Greek cooperative enterprises. *Int. J. Soc. Econ.* **2016**, *43*, 1334–1350. [CrossRef]

53. Borzaga, C.; Tortia, E. Worker motivations, job satisfaction and loyalty in public and nonprofit social services. *Nonprofit Volunt. Sect. Q.* **2006**, *35*, 225–248. [CrossRef]

54. Doherty, B.; Foster, G.; Meehan, J.; Mason, C. *Management for Social Enterprise*; Sage Publications: Thousand Oaks, CA, USA, 2009.

55. Hansmann, H. *The Ownership of Enterprise*; Harvard University Press: Cambridge, MA, USA, 2009.

56. Jenner, P.; Oprescu, F. The sectorial trust of social enterprise: Friend or foe? *J. Soc. Entrep.* **2016**, *7*, 236–261. [CrossRef]

57. Kim, D.; Lim, U. Social Enterprise as a Catalyst for Sustainable Local and Regional Development. *Sustainability* **2017**, *9*, 1427. [CrossRef]

58. Anderson, E.; Weitz, B. Determinants of continuity in conventional industrial channel dyads. *Mark. Sci.* **1989**, *8*, 310–323. [CrossRef]

59. Bidault, F.; Despres, C.; Butler, C. The drivers of cooperation between buyers and suppliers for product innovation. *Res. Policy* **1998**, *26*, 719–732. [CrossRef]

60. Bolton, M.K. Organizational innovation and substandard performance: When is necessity the mother of innovation? *Organ. Sci.* **1993**, *4*, 57–75. [CrossRef]

61. Clark, K.B. Project scope and project performance: The effect of parts strategy and supplier involvement on product development. *Manag. Sci.* **1989**, *35*, 1247–1263. [CrossRef]

62. Sirilli, G.; Evangelista, R. Technological innovation in services and manufacturing: Results from Italian surveys. *Res. Policy* **1998**, *27*, 881–899. [CrossRef]

63. Kogut, B. Joint ventures: Theoretical and empirical perspectives. *Strateg. Manag. J.* **1988**, *9*, 319–332. [CrossRef]

64. Gulati, R. Social structure and alliance formation patterns: A longitudinal analysis. *Adm. Sci. Q.* **1995**, *40*, 619–652. [CrossRef]

65. De Man, A.-P.; Duysters, G. Collaboration and innovation: A review of the effects of mergers, acquisitions and alliances on innovation. *Technovation* **2005**, *25*, 1377–1387. [CrossRef]

66. Gulati, R. Alliances and networks. *Strateg. Manag. J.* **1998**, *19*, 293–317. [CrossRef]

67. Quinn, J.B. Outsourcing innovation: The new engine of growth. *Sloan Manag. Rev.* **2000**, *41*, 13.

68. Spear, R. Social entrepreneurship: A different model? *Int. J. Soc. Econ.* **2006**, *33*, 399–410. [CrossRef]

69. Chell, E. Social enterprise and entrepreneurship: Towards a convergent theory of the entrepreneurial process. *Int. Small Bus. J.* **2007**, *25*, 5–26. [CrossRef]

70. Johnstone, H.; Lionais, D. Depleted communities and community business entrepreneurship: Revaluing space through place. *Entrep. Reg. Dev.* **2004**, *16*, 217–233. [CrossRef]

71. Krause, D.R.; Handfield, R.B.; Tyler, B.B. The relationships between supplier development, commitment, social capital accumulation and performance improvement. *J. Oper. Manag.* **2007**, *25*, 528–545. [CrossRef]

72. Dyer, J.H.; Singh, H. The relational view: Cooperative strategy and sources of interorganizational competitive advantage. *Acad. Manag. Rev.* **1998**, *23*, 660–679.

73. Grant, R.M. Prospering in dynamically-competitive environments: Organizational capability as knowledge integration. *Organ. Sci.* **1996**, *7*, 375–387. [CrossRef]

74. Tyler, B.B. The complementarity of cooperative and technological competencies: A resource-based perspective. *J. Eng. Technol. Manag.* **2001**, *18*, 1–27. [CrossRef]

75. Kogut, B.; Zander, U. Knowledge of the firm, combinative capabilities and the replication of technology. *Organ. Sci.* **1992**, *3*, 383–397. [CrossRef]

76. Szulanski, G. Exploring internal stickiness: Impediments to the transfer of best practice within the firm. *Strateg. Manag. J.* **1996**, *17*, 27–43. [CrossRef]

77. Nahapiet, J.; Ghoshal, S. Social capital, intellectual capital and the organizational advantage. *Acad. Manag. Rev.* **1998**, *23*, 242–266.

78. Tsai, W.; Ghoshal, S. Social capital and value creation: The role of intrafirm networks. *Acad. Manag. J.* **1998**, *41*, 464–476. [CrossRef]

79. Inkpen, A.C.; Tsang, E.W. Social capital, networks and knowledge transfer. *Acad. Manag. Rev.* **2005**, *30*, 146–165. [CrossRef]

80. Schnake, M.E.; Cochran, D.S. Effect of two goal-setting dimensions on perceived intraorganizational conflict. *Group Organ. Stud.* **1985**, *10*, 168–183. [CrossRef]

81. Grieco, C.; Michelini, L.; Iasevoli, G. Measuring value creation in social enterprises: A cluster analysis of social impact assessment models. *Nonprofit Volunt. Sect. Q.* **2015**, *44*, 1173–1193. [CrossRef]

82. Bellucci, M.; Bagnoli, L.; Biggeri, M.; Rinaldi, V. Performance measurement in solidarity economy organizations: The case of fair trade shops in Italy. *Ann. Public Coop. Econ.* **2012**, *83*, 25–59. [CrossRef]

83. Crucke, S.; Decramer, A. The development of a measurement instrument for the organizational performance of social enterprises. *Sustainability* **2016**, *8*, 161. [CrossRef]

84. Arena, M.; Azzone, G.; Bengo, I. Performance measurement for social enterprises. *VOLUNTAS Int. J. Volunt. Nonprofit Organ.* **2015**, *26*, 649–672. [CrossRef]

85. Eikenberry, A.M.; Kluver, J.D. The marketization of the nonprofit sector: Civil society at risk? *Public Adm. Rev.* **2004**, *64*, 132–140. [CrossRef]

86. Foster, W.; Bradach, J. Should nonprofits seek profits. *Harv. Bus. Rev.* **2005**, *83*, 92–100. [PubMed]

87. Weisbrod, B.A. The pitfalls of profits. *Stanf. Soc. Innov. Rev.* **2004**, *2*, 40–47.

88. Dacin, M.T.; Dacin, P.A.; Tracey, P. Social entrepreneurship: A critique and future directions. *Organ. Sci.* **2011**, *22*, 1203–1213. [CrossRef]

89. Creswell, J.W. *A Concise Introduction to Mixed Methods Research*; Sage Publications: Thousand Oaks, CA, USA, 2014.

90. Haenlein, M.; Kaplan, A.M. A beginner's guide to partial least squares analysis. *Underst. Stat.* **2004**, *3*, 283–297. [CrossRef]

91. Yoo, Y.; Alavi, M. Media and group cohesion: Relative influences, on Social Presence, Task Participation, and Group Consensus. *MIS Q.* **2001**, *25*, 371–390. [CrossRef]

92. Henseler, J.; Ringle, C.M.; Sinkovics, R.R. The use of partial least squares path modeling in international marketing. In *New Challenges to International Marketing*; Emerald Group Publishing Ltd.: Bingley, UK, 2009; pp. 277–319.

93. Helm, S.T.; Andersson, F.O. Beyond taxonomy. In *Nonprofit Management and Leadership*; Wiley Periodicals: Indianapolis, IN, USA, 2010; Volume 20, pp. 259–276.

94. Sullivan Mort, G.; Weerawardena, J.; Carnegie, K. Social entrepreneurship: Towards conceptualisation. *Int. J. Nonprofit Volunt. Sect. Mark.* **2003**, *8*, 76–88. [CrossRef]

95. Giraud Voss, Z.; Voss, G.B.; Moorman, C. An empirical examination of the complex relationships between entrepreneurial orientation and stakeholder support. *Eur. J. Mark.* **2005**, *39*, 1132–1150. [CrossRef]

96. Schumpeter, J.A. The creative response in economic history. *J. Econ. Hist.* **1947**, *7*, 149–159. [CrossRef]

97. Kuratko, D.F. *Entrepreneurship: Theory, Process and Practice*; Cengage Learning: Boston, MA, USA, 2016.

98. Baker, W.E.; Sinkula, J.M. The synergistic effect of market orientation and learning orientation on organizational performance. *J. Acad. Mark. Sci.* **1999**, *27*, 411–427. [CrossRef]

99. Nieto, M.J.; Santamaría, L. The importance of diverse collaborative networks for the novelty of product innovation. *Technovation* **2007**, *27*, 367–377. [CrossRef]

100. Batjargal, B. Social capital and entrepreneurial performance in Russia: A longitudinal study. *Organ. Stud.* **2003**, *24*, 535–556. [CrossRef]

101. Peng, M.W.; Luo, Y. Managerial ties and firm performance in a transition economy: The nature of a micro-macro link. *Acad. Manag. J.* **2000**, *43*, 486–501. [CrossRef]

102. Davidsson, P.; Honig, B. The role of social and human capital among nascent entrepreneurs. *J. Bus. Ventur.* **2003**, *18*, 301–331. [CrossRef]

103. Renzulli, L.A.; Aldrich, H.; Moody, J. Family matters: Gender, networks and entrepreneurial outcomes. *Soc. Forces* **2000**, *79*, 523–546. [CrossRef]

104. Gainer, B.; Padanyi, P. The relationship between market-oriented activities and market-oriented culture: Implications for the development of market orientation in nonprofit service organizations. *J. Bus. Res.* **2005**, *58*, 854–862. [CrossRef]

105. Mottner, S.; Ford, J.B. Measuring nonprofit marketing strategy performance: The case of museum stores. *J. Bus. Res.* **2005**, *58*, 829–840. [CrossRef]

106. Nicholls, A. The legitimacy of social entrepreneurship: Reflexive isomorphism in a pre-paradigmatic field. *Entrep. Theory Pract.* **2010**, *34*, 611–633. [CrossRef]

107. Wolff, J.A.; Pett, T.L. Small-firm performance: Modeling the role of product and process improvements. *J. Small Bus. Manag.* **2006**, *44*, 268–284. [CrossRef]

108. Murat Ar, I.; Baki, B. Antecedents and performance impacts of product versus process innovation: Empirical evidence from SMEs located in Turkish science and technology parks. *Eur. J. Innov. Manag.* **2011**, *14*, 172–206. [CrossRef]

109. Narver, J.C.; Slater, S.F. The effect of a market orientation on business profitability. *J. Mark.* **1990**, *54*, 20–35. [CrossRef]

110. Slater, S.F.; Narver, J.C. Does competitive environment moderate the market orientation-performance relationship? *J. Mark.* **1994**, *58*, 46–55. [CrossRef]

111. Vickery, S.K.; Jayaram, J.; Droge, C.; Calantone, R. The effects of an integrative supply chain strategy on customer service and financial performance: An analysis of direct versus indirect relationships. *J. Oper. Manag.* **2003**, *21*, 523–539. [CrossRef]

112. Ward, P.T.; Leong, G.K.; Boyer, K.K. Manufacturing proactiveness and performance. *Decis. Sci.* **1994**, *25*, 337–358. [CrossRef]

113. Miles, M.B.; Huberman, A.M. *Qualitative Data Analysis: An Expanded Sourcebook*; Sage Group: Newcastle, UK, 1994.

114. Sekaran, U. *Research Methods for Managers: A Skill Building Approach*; John Wiley & Sons: New York, NY, USA, 1984; p. 352.

115. Lee, T.W. *Using Qualitative Methods in Organizational Research*; Sage Group: Newcastle, UK, 1999.

116. Corbin, J.; Strauss, A. *Basics of Qualitative Research: Techniques and Procedures for Developing Grounded Theory*; Sage Group: Newcastle, UK, 2008.
117. Silverman, D. *Doing Qualitative Research: A Practical Handbook*; Sage Publications Ltd.: Thousand Oaks, CA, USA, 2013.
118. Eisenhardt, K.M. Building theories from case study research. *Acad. Manag. Rev.* **1989**, *14*, 532–550.
119. Robson, C. *Real World Research: A Resource for Social Scientists and Practitioners-Researchers*; John Wiley & Sons: Hoboken, NJ, USA, 1993.
120. Werts, C.E.; Linn, R.L.; Jöreskog, K.G. Intraclass reliability estimates: Testing structural assumptions. *Educ. Psychol. Meas.* **1974**, *34*, 25–33. [CrossRef]
121. Bernstein, I.H.; Nunnally, J. *Psychometric Theory*; McGraw-Hill: New York, NY, USA, 1994.
122. Fornell, C.; Larcker, D.F. Structural equation models with unobservable variables and measurement error: Algebra and statistics. *J. Mark. Res.* **1981**, *18*, 382–388. [CrossRef]
123. Chan Kim, W.; Mauborgne, R. *Blue Ocean Strategy: How to Create Uncontested Market Space and Make the Competition Irrelevant*; Harvard Business School Press: Boston, MA, USA, 2005.
124. Lee, Y.-J.; Kim, B.-H. Resources Linkage and Activation Plan in Social Enterprise. *J. Korea Contents Assoc.* **2013**, *13*, 227–235. [CrossRef]
125. Zucker, L.G. Production of trust: Institutional sources of economic structure, 1840–1920. *Res. Organ. Behav.* **1986**, *8*, 53–111.

sustainability

MDPI

Article

Directions for Social Enterprise from an Efficiency Perspective

Pyoungsoo Lee [1] and Yong Won Seo [2,*]

[1]   Korea E-Trade Research Institute, Chung-Ang University 221 Heukseok, Dongjak, Seoul 06974, Korea;
      pyoungsoo@cau.ac.kr
[2]   College of Business and Economics, Chung-Ang University 221 Heukseok, Dongjak, Seoul 06974, Korea
*   Correspondence: seoyw@cau.ac.kr; Tel.: +82-2-820-5580

Received: 22 September 2017; Accepted: 21 October 2017; Published: 23 October 2017

Abstract: Social enterprise is recognized as an alternative for sustainable development, as it balances social aspects with economic prosperity. Evaluating social enterprises is very important for both the enterprises themselves and the government, since grants from the government or institutions highly depend on their performance. While relatively significant attention is paid to the social value that these enterprises create, there is a lack of interest in assessing the operational performance directly linked to the sustainable operation of social enterprises. Therefore, this research analyzes the performance of social enterprises from the efficiency perspective, incorporating both operational (economic) and social performance measures. To this end, we apply data envelopment analysis to assess the performance of social enterprises when considering the dual-role factor—the grants. To facilitate clarity for readers, a dataset of Korean social enterprises is used. Through this analysis, we show that the grants can be used for performance evaluation in different ways for each enterprise. Furthermore, an industry-specific analysis provides more realistic and feasible benchmarking information to which inefficient social enterprises should refer. We expect that these findings will complement existing methods of social enterprise evaluation.

Keywords: social enterprises; performance evaluation; efficiency; data envelopment analysis

1. Introduction

Many business organizations now recognize social responsibility as key to a sustainable business environment and society. Although there is still a debate and argumentation on whether it is appropriate for corporations to expand their value creation beyond shareholders, many companies have actively committed to greater social challenges [1]. For more than half a century, many academic researchers and practitioners have studied the issues concerning corporate social responsibility to cope with these challenges. With a growing awareness of the social economy, recently, social enterprise has become more glaring as a new business model. Undoubtedly, it is recognized as an alternative for sustainable development, as it balances social aspects with economic prosperity.

Although there is no universal definition of social enterprise, there are various definitions from researchers and state institutions [2–10]. Therefore, clarifying the definition is an important research topic, but it is not the main purpose of this study, so it is not to be introduced further. However, most scholars and practitioners agree that social enterprise is an organization or venture that combines a social purpose with the pursuit of financial success in the private marketplace [11]. Thus, although somewhat less specific, here, we define social enterprise as an organization that tries to achieve its social purpose in a financially sustainable way. In addition, social purpose refers to the social contribution that provides the activities for a wide array of marginalized and disadvantaged people, such as the disabled, long-term unemployed, ex-offenders, and homeless.

Among the various definitions from other scholars, Grassl [12] stated that social enterprise falls into the space between for-profit and nonprofit organizations. Moreover, Doherty et al. [13] underlined two characteristics of social enterprises—commercial activities to generate revenue and the pursuit of social goals. As the above two studies described, it is worth noting that social enterprise pursues both social value and the economic mission. In this regard, want to emphasize the economic aspects rather than the social value generated by social enterprises. For any social enterprise, it is difficult to survive if financial performance is not guaranteed. Generally, financial performance would result from operational excellence, and economic prosperity should be a prerequisite for further social contribution. Therefore, a social enterprise can reinvest its profits back into the business or directly into the community only if its survival is assured. In other words, the performance of business operations should be evaluated in order to maintain the sustainability of social activities.

Roughly speaking, the efficiency is the concept of how productively resources are being used to achieve organizational goals. Because the goals of an organization, such as social contribution or creation of social value, are often considered abstract, it is difficult to find the concept of efficiency when evaluating organizations that create social value. However, social enterprise is not a nonprofit organization. Thus, social enterprises must secure the operational efficiency for sustainable management. In other words, a social enterprise that operate inefficiently will fail to achieve its ultimate goal of creating social value. Because social enterprises compete with mainstream corporations, they cannot afford to offer better products and services than their competitors, in order to competitively survive. Of course, sometimes they have the right to take advantage of the competition. For example, social enterprises can be considered a priority in public procurement in South Korea. Beyond these exceptional circumstances, social enterprises should closely follow their business models by assuring operational excellence in terms of the efficient use of resources. To highlight economic and financial concern, Bagnoli and Megali [14] suggested a performance measurement system for social enterprises, but their research is limited in that it only presents a framework, without further empirical investigation.

Social enterprises are highly dependent upon the grants, typically provided by the government or institutions. Consequently, it often leads to poor financial independence. In particular, young social enterprises are likely to make efforts to secure grants. On the other hand, enterprises with stabilized operations tend to seek financial independence from the grants. Therefore, the variable of grants must be utilized to measure their efficiency, and researchers should be cautious about how they will use this variable. In this study, we analyze the efficiency by providing a flexible model that considers the grants as a variable that can be selectively served as an input or output role.

The current study analyzes the performance evaluation of social enterprises by using data on Korean social enterprises. Specifically, this research attempts to make three primary contributions to the field of social enterprises. First, it presents a model that can evaluate social enterprises with both operational and social indicators, which can be quantified, and shows that the grants can be used for performance evaluation in different ways for each enterprise. Second, it attempts to examine the differences in efficiency according to industry, and suggests that an industry-specific analysis may be helpful in creating a set of benchmarks that can be realistically achieved. Lastly, it confirms that grants play a different role in evaluating the performance of social enterprises according to their age.

The remainder of the paper is structured as follows. In Section 2, the research background and literature review are presented. In Section 3, the methodology and empirical analysis, including the research design, are presented. In Section 4, we present the results. Finally, in Section 5, the conclusions, limitations, and future research opportunities of this study are discussed.

2. Background and Literature Review

2.1. Performance Evaluation for Social Enterprises

Performance evaluation is critical to any organization in managing operations because it provides a way to improve the operations for business sustainability. While some studies have simultaneously considered financial and non-financial measures (e.g., the Balanced Scorecard), most studies have mainly focused on economic performance evaluation. The selection of evaluation methods depends on the purpose of the business organization. Accordingly, it is very important to clarify the main objectives of the business organization prior to performing the performance assessment. Social enterprises aim to create not only economic value, but also social value, ultimately creating social changes for sustainability. In this sense, measuring such value has become a major challenge for both social entrepreneurs and investors (government and private investors).

Since measuring social value involves subjective judgement, it is far more difficult than measuring economic value, which can be done objectively using financial statements. One of the most prominent techniques to overcome this difficulty is social return on investment (SROI), proposed by the Roberts Enterprise Development Fund [15]. SROI measures the performance of a social enterprise by quantitatively calculating the social performance created in a certain period of time. It is widely used because it offers an advantage, in that it can be flexibly applied by considering the unique characteristics of a social enterprise, including the type of business, social purpose, and context of the management environment. In addition, this technique is based on due diligence, so the result is recognized as highly reliable. However, in order to obtain accurate results, all of the elements related to the organization's social activities need to be logically and carefully examined, which is a time-consuming task; the greater the number of social enterprises to be evaluated, the more time and expenses involved in the evaluation.

This research utilizes a data envelopment analysis (DEA) model to analyze the performance of social enterprises. In contrast to SROI, extra-financial value as social performance is not considered in this study. In other words, only the measurable economic and social measures are taken into account. We believe that it is much more useful to evaluate many social enterprises simultaneously rather than making excessive efforts to convert extra-financial values into monetary values.

The first study to analyze the efficiency of social enterprises using a DEA model was conducted by Jang [16]. In the study, the inputs are the total number of employees and government funds and the output is the service provided. However, this study was difficult to generalize the applicability of the proposed evaluation model, since an empirical analysis was performed on the healthcare service industry in a certain region. In addition, it has been criticized for not dealing with the variables that reflect the characteristics of social enterprises. Lee and Lee [17] attempted to estimate the efficiency score of 158 social enterprises by using a DEA model, and tried to find the factors that exert the greatest influence on the that score. In the study, the input factors were selected as the number of employees, the labor cost, and the total assets, while the output factors were used as the number of services provided, sales, and vulnerable employment. Although it seems to use a well-designed output variable, the vulnerable employment, the types of social enterprises are not considered in this research. Accordingly, the "homogeneity of decision making units" which is the condition of the DEA was not secured. More recently, Natesan et al. [18] provides a DEA-based efficiency evaluation model that takes into account social economic factors. In this study, the social economic impacts were evaluated using employment related variables and funds. But, this study is somewhat weaker in relation to our study in that it evaluates the policy efficiency for the regions in India, while our research is aimed at evaluating the efficiency of social enterprises. Lee et al. [19] suggested an evaluation framework for measuring social enterprises' efficiency, including both the financial performance and social impacts simultaneously. The authors defined the grants as an important input of social enterprise and analyzed its efficiency. Our study also provides a DEA-based model that takes into account the operational and social aspects for social enterprises. However, the present study does not limit the grants to the input factor in social enterprise evaluation.

2.2. Data Envelopment Analysis

DEA, first proposed by Charnes et al. [20], is a methodology for evaluating the efficiency of a set of decision making units (DMUs), which use multiple inputs to produce multiple outputs. Basically, in DEA, efficiency is defined as the ratio of the weighted sum of outputs to that of inputs. Moreover, DEA does not require the parametric specifications of a particular function nor the predetermined weights to be attached to each input and output. A major advantage of DEA is that it allows the user to evaluate the economic performance of individual DMUs depending on the profitability perspective. Because of this merit, DEA has also been widely applied in various fields, such as air transportation management [21], supply chain management [22], hospitality management [23], research and development [24], environmental management [25], healthcare management [26], and government services [27].

In the conventional application of DEA, the decision maker has to clearly specify the inputs and outputs, given a set of measures available. However, there are some measures that cannot be clearly defined as inputs or outputs, and they are referred to as dual-role factors. For example, research funding was treated as a dual-role factor for evaluating university performance [28,29], and the research and development cost was considered as a dual-role factor in the supplier selection problem [30,31].

In this study, we deal with grants as a performance measure of social enterprises, which can be regarded as a dual-role factor, and analyze the efficiency of social enterprises by using this factor in the DEA model. Furthermore, the benchmarking information resulting from the DEA model allows social enterprises with inefficient operations to set the direction for sustainable business.

2.3. Social Enterprises in South Korea

The concept of social enterprise is attracting increasing interest worldwide, especially in European countries, the United States, South Korea, Japan, Taiwan, and some Latin American countries. In most cases, to be referred to as a social enterprise in a particular country, an organization must be certified by the government. In South Korea, about 10 years ago, the law related to social enterprises—the Social Enterprise Promotion Act—was enacted and went into effect. Under this act, social enterprise is defined as "an organization which is engaged in business activities of producing and selling goods and services while pursuing a social purpose of enhancing the quality of local residents' life by means of providing social services and creating jobs for the disadvantaged". Moreover, to support and promote social enterprises, the Korea Social Enterprise Promotion Agency was established. According to each organization's social purposes, Korean social enterprises are classified into five types: job-creation, social service provision, mixed (job-creation while providing social service), local community contribution, and other. Recently, more than 1700 entities have been recognized as social enterprises. The majority of Korean social enterprises are primarily concerned with job-creation, as presented in Table 1.

Table 1. Current status of Korean social enterprises.

Types	Number of Social Enterprises	Percentage
Job-creation	1229	69.2%
Social service provision	115	6.5%
Mixed	173	9.7%
Local community contribution	76	4.3%
Others	183	10.3%
Total	1776	100.0%

Sources: Korea Social Enterprise Promotion Agency (reported in June 2017).

The main purpose of the job-creation type of social enterprise is to offer jobs to vulnerable social groups. The following two key conditions must be met in order for organizations to be certified as such. (1) The vulnerable employment rate is 30% or more of all workers; (2) the total number of employees must be five or more. Further, the jobs provided to vulnerable groups should be full-time, with at least 20 h of work per week, and the wages paid must be above the minimum wage set by the government.

3. Methodology

In this section, we apply the DEA model to investigate operational and social performance in the efficiency context.

3.1. Job-Creation Social Enterprises

We perform an efficiency evaluation that is mainly focused on the job-creation type of social enterprises. The data are collected from the information disclosure system, managed by the Korea Social Enterprise Promotion Agency. Through this system, social enterprises can report their performance. Since public disclosure of management performance is not mandatory, not all social enterprise data are available through this system. A total of 228 out of 1661 enterprises certified by 2016 voluntarily released their business performance, based on their business operations in 2015. It should be noted that social enterprises might have differences in their business operations, depending on their management purpose. If one ignores the type of goal orientation and evaluates the efficiency, the results would be unrealistic. In other words, it is necessary to analyze, by category, according to the types of goal orientation. From the perspective of DEA theory, in addition, since it assumes the homogeneity of DMUs under evaluation, we need to check that all of the social enterprises perform their activities in a similar manner. Unfortunately, the aforementioned 228 social enterprises do not share the goal for social contributions. Therefore, we believe that it is desirable to analyze the efficiency by categorizing companies into the types defined by the Korea Social Enterprise Promotion Agency, in order to avoid a distortion of the evaluation results. Now, we focus on the job-creation social enterprises, which, as we have mentioned, make up the majority.

3.2. Performance Measures

There is no clear agreement on how to specify the inputs and outputs of social enterprises. It is necessary to apply different performance measurements depending on the characteristics of the evaluation subject, that is, the social-purpose orientation in this study. Reinvestment for social purpose can be an output regardless of the type. Moreover, the rate of social service provision may be one of the critical outputs for the social-service provision type, while the vulnerable employment rate is a key output for evaluating the job-creation type. Regarding the job-creation social enterprises, we specify the inputs and outputs for the performance evaluation, as shown in Table 2.

Table 2. Performance measures.

Categories		Variables
Inputs		Labor, Assets
Outputs	Operational Outputs	Revenue, Operating Profit
	Social Outputs	Vulnerable employment rate, Reinvestment for social purpose
Dual-Role Factor		Grants

A social enterprise is a business unit engaged in the production of one of more economic goods or services. Thus, we set labor and assets as two inputs for the performance evaluation of social enterprises. Labor is considered the most important traditional input in the process of any business unit. The total labor cost is the sum of salaries, incentives, and contributions for benefit plans.

In this study, salaries are computed by multiplying the wage per week by the number of employees. The second input is assets, which are resources that not only present the results of past events, but also allow the companies to look forward to future economic benefits. All the data of assets are collected from the balance sheet as the sum of liabilities and shareholders' equity.

We decompose the outputs into two types—operational and social. Operational outputs consist of revenue and operating profit. Revenue is one of the most frequently used performance measures and is presented on the income statement. Operating profit is a key indicator in that it shows the ability to operate a company that can run independently without government support. Moreover, we present two components of social outputs. The first is the vulnerable employment rate, defined as the proportion of vulnerable employees in total employment. This output would be the most critical factor in assessing social contribution, especially for the job-creation type of social enterprise. The second factor is reinvestment for social purpose. According to the Social Enterprise Promotion Act, at least two-thirds of the profit available for dividends has to be reinvested for social purposes, the scope of which includes community social service, expansion of facilities, additional employment, salary increases, improvement of working conditions, and donations for public interest.

Grants are the most powerful means for supporting social enterprises, and are typically provided by the government or institutions. Grants received by social enterprises take the form of government, corporate, and parent institution grants, as well as general donations. In addition, grants can be viewed as an input to a company's growth engine, but at the same time, they can be seen as an output, in that outstanding operational and social performance may lead to an increase in grants. As introduced in Section 2.2, such types of variables are referred to as dual-role factors in the DEA methodology. To incorporate grants into the DEA model, we consider the framework to deal with the dual-role factors proposed by Cook et al. [32].

3.3. Data Envelopment Analysis Model

In this study, the traditional DEA model is used as the basis for dealing with the dual-role factor. This model implicitly assumes that all DMUs transform inputs to outputs at a constant returns to scale (CRS). Suppose that there are m inputs x_{ik} ($i = 1, 2, \ldots, m$), s outputs y_{rj} ($r = 1, 2, \ldots, s$), and a dual-role factor w for each DMU k ($k = 1, 2, \ldots, K$). An envelopment model for deriving the efficiency of a particular DMU o can be formulated as follows.

If w plays a role of an input,

$$\min \theta_1$$
$$\text{s.t.}$$
$$\sum_{k=1}^{K} \lambda_k x_{ik} \leq \theta_1 x_{ik}$$
$$\sum_{k=1}^{K} \lambda_k y_{rk} \geq y_{ro} \tag{1}$$
$$\sum_{k=1}^{K} \lambda_k w_k \leq w_o$$
$$\lambda_k \geq 0$$

Model (1) is input-oriented because it considers the possible radial reductions of all inputs when the outputs are maintained at their current levels. θ_1^* is the optimal objective function value of Model (1) and represents the efficiency score of DMU o. If $\theta_1^* = 1$, then the current input levels cannot be proportionally reduced, indicating that DMU o is on the efficient frontier. Otherwise, if $\theta_1^* < 1$, then DMU o is dominated by the frontier.

As Ruggiero [33] asserted, socio-economic factors are not controllable by management, but are important in determining efficiency variations. Thus, in Model (1), we assume, that a dual role factor w is a non-discretionary variable when it is treated as an input. Since, in an input-oriented DEA model, it considers the possible radial reductions of all inputs when the outputs are fixed at their current level [32].

Likewise, if w plays a role of an output, a DEA model can be formulated as follows:

$$\min\theta_2$$
$$\text{s.t.}$$
$$\sum_{k=1}^{K} \lambda_k x_{ik} \leq \theta_2 x_{ik}$$
$$\sum_{k=1}^{K} \lambda_k y_{rk} \geq y_{ro} \qquad (2)$$
$$\sum_{k=1}^{K} \lambda_k w_k \geq w_o$$
$$\lambda_k \geq 0$$

In Model (2), θ_2^* represents the efficiency of DMU o when w is considered an output. Mahdiloo et al. [30] proposed the method for deriving efficiency by comparing two efficiency scores obtained from Models (1) and (2). However, it requires much computational efforts, since $2k$ linear programming models must be solved. Thus, we follow the unified and simplified model proposed by Toloo and Barat [34]. The formulation is presented in Model (3) as follows:

$$\min\theta$$
$$\text{s.t.}$$
$$\sum_{k=1}^{K} \lambda_k x_{ik} \leq \theta x_{ik}$$
$$\sum_{k=1}^{K} \lambda_k y_{rk} \geq y_{ro}$$
$$\sum_{k=1}^{K} \lambda_k w_k \leq w_o + M(1-d) \qquad (3)$$
$$\sum_{k=1}^{K} \lambda_k w_k \geq w_o - Md$$
$$d \in \{0,1\}$$
$$\lambda_k \geq 0$$

In order to reflect the behavior of the dual-role factor, we construct the constraints by setting a binary variable d, where M is a sufficiently large number. If w is considered an input, d is set to 1; then, the third constraint of Model (3) is active, and the fourth one becomes redundant. Therefore, Model (3) is considered a mixed-integer linear program. Though this programming, each DMU verifies the status of a dual-role factor in the most favorable way.

4. Results

As described in Section 3.1, we analyze the job-creation social enterprises in Korea. Since the disclosure of business performance is not necessarily required for social enterprises, available data is limited. Based on their business operations in 2015, 228 social enterprises released their business performance through the official website of Korea Social Enterprise Promotion Agency. From this database, we extracted 167 enterprises that share the common goal of job-creation. Some inappropriate and missing values were found in this web-based dataset. Thus, we supplement the recording and typographical errors through the official financial statements published on the corporate homepages. It is worth noting that a non-homogenous DMU may cause outliers in DEA. Because each enterprise belongs to different industries and operates in different ways, there is concern about the possibility of the occurrence of inherent outliers. In this study, we attempt to reduce the risk of outlier occurrence through the industry specific analysis and secure the homogeneity of DMUs on the premise that it has a common purpose of job-creation. Therefore, all 167 data were used for the analysis. The descriptive statistics for their inputs and outputs as well as the dual-role factor are presented in Table 3.

Table 3. Descriptive statistics of 167 social enterprises.

Variables	Mean	Std. Dev.	Min	Max
Labor (1000 KRW)	61,151	281,770	3666	3,518,760
Assets (1000 KRW)	693,896	1,311,817	14,541	10,989,393
Revenue (1000 KRW)	1,394,634	3,044,868	32,775	32,051,162
OP (1000 KRW)	934,540	158,611	56,318	1,437,694
VER	0.63	0.16	0.29	1.00
RSP (1000 KRW)	73,290	139,915	0	843,793
Grants (1000 KRW)	140,141	159,285	56	948,729

OP: Operating profit, VER: Vulnerable employment rate, RSP: Reinvestment for social purpose.

The correlation matrix of inputs and outputs is analyzed to see if there is a significant relationship between the variables. From the results in Table 4, we can see that there is a positive correlation between input variables. The obtained coefficient of 0.629 shows relatively strong correlation, but it is not large enough to require further manipulation such as variable reduction or dimension reduction techniques (The correlation is unacceptable when the correlation coefficient exceeds 0.9). Also, most of output variables are correlated positively, but the vulnerable employment rate is negatively correlated with other output variables, although it does seem small in magnitude. In general, the correlation between input and output variables should be positive in DEA. However, the results show that the vulnerable employment rate is negatively correlated with the two input variables. Nonetheless, the vulnerable employment rate is considered an output in this application, since the correlation coefficients are not statistically significant at the 0.05 level.

Table 4. Correlation matrix for all variables.

	Labor	Assets	Revenue	OP	VER	RSP	Grants
Labor	1.000						
Assets	0.629 ***	1.000					
Revenue	0.873 ***	0.825 ***	1.000				
OP	0.227 ***	0.097	0.233 **	1.000			
VER	−0.023	−0.061	−0.043	−0.121	1.000		
RSP	0.382 ***	0.502 ***	0.436 ***	0.244 **	0.078	1.000	
Grants	0.372 ***	0.348 ***	0.365 ***	−0.592 ***	0.148	0.338 ***	1.000

OP: Operating profit, VER: Vulnerable employment rate, RSP: Reinvestment for social purpose. * indicate significance level at $p < 0.05$. ** indicate significance level at $p < 0.01$. *** indicate significance level at $p < 0.001$.

Table 5 presents the efficiency scores of 167 social enterprises calculated by Model (3). Among them, 27 social enterprises (DMU 7, 19, 21, 36, 39, 44, 47, 51, 77, 78, 80, 84, 94, 96, 107, 119, 121, 123, 130, 131, 135, 136, 137, 151, 157, 163 and 166) are identified as being efficient with a relative efficiency score of 1. The amount of grants is considered an input in 56 DMUs with $d = 0$, and it is considered an output in 95 DMUs with $d = 1$. Since each DMU evaluates itself by assigning the dual-role factor to either the input or output side in the most favorable way, the 56 DMUs consider that setting the amount of grants as an input is highly valued for their efficiency. Similarly, 95 DMUs perceived that setting it as an output is more favorable for this self-evaluation. Consequently, such DMUs can improve their efficiency if there are decreases or increases in the amount of grants. Moreover, there are 16 social enterprises in which the amount of grants can play the role of both an input and output. This phenomenon typically occurs in efficient DMUs, although not in all cases. In other words, the efficiency scores of 16 DMUs out of the 27 efficient DMUs do not change with respect to the behavior of the dual-role factor. Accordingly, for these DMUs, it is unnecessary to consider the behavior determination on the amount of grants.

Table 5. Results of data envelopment analysis.

DMU	Efficiency	d	DMU	Efficiency	d	DMU	Efficiency	d
1	0.2948	0	58	0.5750	0	115	0.6293	0
2	0.5408	0	59	0.5621	0	116	0.6226	0
3	0.6224	0	60	0.4327	0	117	0.6393	1
4	0.9336	0	61	0.4067	0	118	0.6182	1
5	0.5263	1	62	0.5628	0	119	1.0000	0 or 1
6	0.7797	1	63	0.4526	0	120	0.5735	0
7	1.0000	0 or 1	64	0.5848	0	121	1.0000	0 or 1
8	0.8051	0	65	0.2708	1	122	0.4050	0
9	0.5373	0	66	0.3414	0	123	1.0000	0 or 1
10	0.7620	1	67	0.2818	0	124	0.8855	0
11	0.7086	0	68	0.7210	0	125	0.1812	0
12	0.4131	1	69	0.8270	0	126	0.4107	0
13	0.6737	0	70	0.6717	0	127	0.5397	0
14	0.6433	1	71	0.4971	0	128	0.6545	0
15	0.9093	1	72	0.3585	0	129	0.8622	1
16	0.3000	0	73	0.4097	0	130	1.0000	1
17	0.8200	0	74	0.6737	1	131	1.0000	0 or 1
18	0.5025	0	75	0.4178	1	132	0.8004	0
19	1.0000	0 or 1	76	0.4393	0	133	0.7291	1
20	0.5847	0	77	1.0000	0	134	0.2913	1
21	1.0000	1	78	1.0000	0	135	1.0000	0 or 1
22	0.3145	0	79	0.3836	0	136	1.0000	0 or 1
23	0.5700	1	80	1.0000	0 or 1	137	1.0000	0
24	0.7282	0	81	0.4586	1	138	0.4824	1
25	0.6319	0	82	0.2583	0	139	0.4443	1
26	0.4567	0	83	0.7370	0	140	0.2725	0
27	0.5398	1	84	1.0000	1	141	0.2601	0
28	0.8299	1	85	0.8408	0	142	0.4276	0
29	0.7257	0	86	0.6682	0	143	0.3889	1
30	0.5585	1	87	0.7095	0	144	0.2821	0
31	0.3205	0	88	0.5852	1	145	0.7017	1
32	0.5400	1	89	0.8668	1	146	0.3021	1
33	0.9865	0	90	0.5716	0	147	0.3600	1
34	0.3994	1	91	0.6724	0	148	0.5062	0
35	0.6608	0	92	0.6275	0	149	0.3955	0
36	1.0000	0 or 1	93	0.6861	0	150	0.1764	0
37	0.7468	0	94	1.0000	0 or 1	151	1.0000	0 or 1
38	0.5255	0	95	0.7382	0	152	0.7214	1
39	1.0000	1	96	1.0000	0 or 1	153	0.5024	0
40	0.6170	0	97	0.8159	0	154	0.9751	1
41	0.4196	0	98	0.4785	1	155	0.7876	1
42	0.7172	0	99	0.3332	0	156	0.1599	1
43	0.8778	0	100	0.9841	1	157	1.0000	0 or 1
44	1.0000	1	101	0.3675	0	158	0.4732	1
45	0.1869	1	102	0.4462	0	159	0.4618	0
46	0.2964	1	103	0.2875	0	160	0.6326	1
47	1.0000	0 or 1	104	0.9601	1	161	0.7562	1
48	0.6002	1	105	0.9320	0	162	0.3405	0
49	0.5947	0	106	0.7495	0	163	1.0000	1
50	0.9943	0	107	1.0000	0	164	0.3749	0
51	1.0000	1	108	0.9243	0	165	0.3575	0
52	0.6566	0	109	0.5166	0	166	1.0000	0 or 1
53	0.8287	1	110	0.4397	0	167	0.3513	1
54	0.4207	1	111	0.9166	0			
55	0.5936	1	112	0.6861	0			
56	0.7464	1	113	0.6678	0			
57	0.3017	1	114	0.8738	1			

We perform a non-parametric Kruskal–Wallis test that assumes there is no difference between the efficiency of three groups. We denote the groups as follows: G1 (the amount of grants is considered an input), G2 (the amount of grants is considered an output), and G3 (the amount of grants is considered both an input and output). In this statistical test, the null hypothesis is that there are no differences in the mean ranks of the groups, and the test statistic indicated that at least one of the groups is significantly different from the other two. The results indicated that the null hypothesis is rejected at a significance level of 0.01 (test statistic H = 41.77, degree of freedom = 2, p-value = 8.50×10^{-10}). Accordingly, we conduct Wilcoxon rank-sum tests for pairwise comparisons. The results indicated that the null hypothesis, that is, G1 and G3 had same distribution of efficiency scores, was rejected at a significance level of 0.01 (test statistic W = 840, p-value = 6.99×10^{-8}); therefore G3 outperforms G1. Similarly, Group 3 outperforms Group 1 (test statistic W = 1488, p-value = 9.02×10^{-10}). However, we cannot see a significant difference between G1 and G2 (test statistic W = 3817, p-value = 0.1696).

DEA identifies a reference set as benchmarks for improvement. The inefficient social enterprises can identify their reference units through the DEA results. These reference sets also refer to the benchmarks, which can guide the inefficient DMUs in improving their efficiency by suggesting realistic targets. See the Appendix A for the benchmarking information for the inefficient DMUs. Using this benchmarking information, an inefficient DMU can refer to the efficient DMUs it must follow to improve its efficiency. For example, DMU 7 and 19 represent the benchmarking partners of DMU 2 and 6, respectively, while DMU 1 should be guided by the business strategies of DMU 47, 123, 136, and 157 to improve the efficiency of its business processes.

In this study, to mitigate the impact of heterogeneity, we limit the analysis to social enterprises certified for the primary purpose of job-creation. Strictly speaking, DEA results might be inappropriately interpreted if the homogeneity assumption of the DMUs does not hold. In this regard, all of the samples that we consider may seem to be against this assumption. Yet, we agree with Samoilenko and Osei-Bryson [35] that the "heterogeneity of the DMUs is a matter of a degree". Consequently, we note that the decision on the similarity of the operating systems of DMUs depends on the decision maker's subjective judgement. Therefore, it seems reasonable to suppose that the concept of homogeneity coincides with the purpose orientation of social enterprises.

In addition, if a homogeneous group with high efficiency is discovered after the efficiency assessment, it can be seen that this group is relatively efficient as a social enterprise with the primary purpose of job-creation. As shown in Table 6, among 27 efficient DMUs, 14 were manufacturing firms (51.9%), followed by education (14.8%) and the social service sector (14.8%), which yielded four efficient DMUs. A large proportion of manufacturing and education-service firms shows relatively better performance. These results show that entrepreneurs preparing a new social enterprise are more likely to gain benefits by initiating manufacturing, education, and social-service organizations. Further, this provides policy implication for the government in terms of supporting social enterprises; government agencies should understand the characteristics of each industry and consider these characteristics when evaluating social enterprises.

A total of 167 social enterprises with the primary purpose of job-creation belong to different industries, such as manufacturing, agriculture, construction, social service, food and beverage, education, and welfare (see Table 6). In relation to the issue of homogeneity, the DEA results may be problematic when an inefficient DMU tries to resemble the benchmarks for efficiency improvement. For example, DMU 25 is a graphic design company, categorized in the culture and arts industry. Its efficiency score is 0.6319 and its identified benchmarks are DMU 36, 94, 135, 136, 137, and 157. Among the six benchmarks, only four DMUs can be considered to operate similar business activities because they are social-service-providing companies. For DMU 25, the λ values corresponding to the benchmarks are 0.1806, 0.1782, 0.3650, 0.0019, 0.0513, and 0.2508. These values provide information on the importance of each benchmark for a specific inefficient social enterprise. Therefore, the entrepreneur of DMU 25 can try to catch up or resemble DMU 135 and 157, corresponding to relatively larger λ values. However, this interpretation may be difficult to apply when the entrepreneur does not agree that the operating activities of the graphic design company are similar to those of the benchmarks. In fact, DMU 157, with the second largest λ value, is a wholesale distributor of agricultural products.

Table 6. Proportion of efficient decision making units.

Industry	DMUs		Efficient DMUs		Efficient DMUs/DMUs
	No.	Percentage	No.	Percentage	Percentage
Manufacturing	64	38.3	14	51.9	21.9
Agriculture	4	2.4	1	3.7	25.1
Distribution	12	7.2	1	3.7	8.3
Construction	8	4.8	1	3.7	12.5
Social service	33	19.8	4	14.8	12.1
Culture & Arts	11	6.6	0	0	0
Food & Beverage	5	3.0	0	0	0
Education	9	5.4	4	14.8	44.4
Welfare	5	3.0	0	0	0
The others (IT, Transportation, Publication, Broadcasting, Eco, etc.)	14	8.4	2	7.4	14.3
Mixed					
Manufacturing, distribution, and publication service	1	0.6	0	0	0
Manufacturing, construction, and social service	1	0.6	0	0	0
Total	167	100.0	27	100.0	

Sometimes, researchers overlook checking the homogeneity of DMUs beforehand. When DMUs with different technologies are evaluated by referring to the homogenous frontier, the difference in technologies is ignored. Dyson et al. [36] highlighted the heterogeneity of DMUs as a pitfall of DEA applications, and suggested several protocols to guide the applications. One of the protocols is to cluster the DMUs into homogeneous sets. Following this guideline, we perform an additional analysis for an industry-specific assessment with a focus on the manufacturing sector, with a set of 64 social enterprises.

Table 7 presents a comparison of the results. The efficiency scores in the third column are larger than or equal to those in the second column because the data of the non-manufacturing sector is excluded. Twenty-three manufacturing social enterprises are derived as efficient DMUs, nine of which were classified as inefficient DMUs in the evaluation that did not consider the characteristics of each industry. For example, a manufacturing social enterprise, DMU 17, is inefficient, with an efficiency score of 0.82, and its benchmarks are DMU 123 (λ = 0.6104) and 135 (λ = 0.4489); DMU 123 is a manufacturing firm, while DMU 135 is a social-service provider. In such situations, DMU 17 may think that it is very difficult or almost impossible to follow the way in which DMU 135 operates if the organizational structures of the two enterprises fall apart. Therefore, an industry-specific analysis may be desirable to provide references with an achievable performance level for social enterprises, in order to practically improve their performance.

As seen in the fourth column of Table 7, the amount of grants is used as an input for 32 DMUs and as an output for 16 DMUs. In addition, 16 DMUs consider it either an input or output. We conduct an additional analysis to confirm that perceptions of grants may vary according to the age of the social enterprises. The average age of 64 manufacturing social enterprises is 4.2 years and the median is 3 years. Thus, we classify them into two groups based on the age of the enterprises: Group 1 (<4 years) and Group 2 (≥4 years). Social enterprises in Group 2 are more likely to rate grants as an input than are those in Group 1. Specifically, 15 out of the 36 enterprises in Group 1 and 17 out of the 28 in Group 2 are manufacturing social enterprises that perceive the grants as an input. It can be seen that relatively old companies that are certified as social enterprises want to increase their independence by minimizing grants. On the other hand, the start-up social enterprises tend to regard the securing of grants as the output of enterprises.

Table 7. Comparisons of results.

DMU	DMUs under Evaluation		Grants
	Total 167 SEs	64 Manufacturing SEs	
2	0.5408	0.6079	Input
4	0.9336	**1.0000**	Input
7	1.0000	1.0000	Input or Output
8	0.8051	**1.0000**	Input or Output
16	0.3000	0.4106	Input
17	0.8200	**1.0000**	Input or Output
19	1.0000	1.0000	Input or Output
20	0.5847	0.7025	Input
21	1.0000	1.0000	Output
24	0.7282	0.9974	Output
32	0.5400	0.6720	Output
33	0.9865	**1.0000**	Input or Output
35	0.6608	0.9423	Output
40	0.6170	0.9573	Output
43	0.8778	**1.0000**	Input or Output
44	1.0000	1.0000	Output
52	0.6566	0.8331	Output
59	0.5621	0.5997	Input
61	0.4067	0.5569	Input
63	0.4526	0.5794	Input
64	0.5848	0.6796	Output
66	0.3414	0.4323	Input
68	0.7210	0.7307	Input
69	0.8270	**1.0000**	Input
71	0.4971	0.6883	Input
75	0.4178	0.4216	Output
76	0.4393	0.4542	Input
78	1.0000	1.0000	Input or Output
80	1.0000	1.0000	Input or Output
82	0.2583	0.3772	Input
83	0.7370	0.7772	Input
84	1.0000	1.0000	Input or Output
85	0.8408	**1.0000**	Input or Output
87	0.7095	0.8882	Input
88	0.5852	0.6247	Output
97	0.8159	0.8250	Input
101	0.3675	0.4434	Input
102	0.4462	0.5280	Output
106	0.7495	0.9534	Input
107	1.0000	1.0000	Input
108	0.9243	**1.0000**	Input
110	0.4397	0.4414	Input
113	0.6678	0.7525	Input
117	0.6393	0.8357	Output
120	0.5735	0.7355	Input
121	1.0000	1.0000	Input or Output
123	1.0000	1.0000	Input or Output
127	0.5397	0.7231	Input
128	0.6545	0.7076	Input
130	1.0000	1.0000	Input or Output
132	0.8004	0.8013	Input
136	1.0000	1.0000	Input or Output
140	0.2725	0.3136	Input
148	0.5062	0.5837	Output
149	0.3955	0.6718	Input
151	1.0000	1.0000	Input or Output
153	0.5024	0.6384	Output
159	0.4618	0.6243	Input
160	0.6326	0.7928	Output
161	0.7562	**1.0000**	Output
162	0.3405	0.3706	Input
164	0.3749	0.3913	Input
165	0.3575	0.3602	Input
166	1.0000	1.0000	Input or Output

5. Conclusions

Social enterprise pursues both social and economic goals. Economic performance should be emphasized in the operation of a company to achieve social goals. Nonetheless, there is less interest in operational excellence than social values in the evaluation of social enterprises. Therefore, in this study, the efficiency of social enterprise was analyzed by applying a social-enterprise evaluation model that simultaneously considers economic and social measures. In this study, since the enterprises to be evaluated have a similar operating system, we focus on analyzing the social enterprises that share a common purpose. Based on the classification system of the Korea Social Enterprise Promotion Agency, we analyzed social enterprises with the primary purpose of job-creation.

The contribution of this research can be summarized in four dimensions. First, it presents a social enterprise evaluation model that takes into account both the economic and social measures that can be quantified. Measuring the social value created by social enterprises is very difficult and time-consuming. Therefore, when evaluating a large number of social enterprises, it is necessary to objectively use a measurable index and develop an evaluation model that is simple to use. Moreover, a DEA application for responding to such a demand is as meaningful as the model itself, and it can be very helpful if it is used prior to a detailed analysis using qualitative factors like SROI. Second, this research provides clues as to how each social enterprise perceives the amount of grants. If a social enterprise perceives the grants as a financial resource, it will try to improve its efficiency in the direction of increasing independence by minimizing the grants. On the contrary, the grants could be used as a measure of output, since it is possible that a large amount of grants are provided to social enterprises with high social value-creation. In this study, we analyzed efficiency by setting grants as a dual-role factor, and showed that they can be used for performance evaluation in different ways for each enterprise. Third, the industry-specific analysis provides a realistic way for the inefficient manufacturing social enterprises to improve their efficiency with benchmarks in the same industry sector. Methodologically, this enhances the reliability of the study by securing a reasonable degree of homogeneity of the DMUs. Lastly, this research confirms that grants play a different role in evaluating the performance of social enterprises according to the age of such enterprises. From the results, it can be interpreted that older companies operate their businesses to reduce grants for their sustainable business. On the other hand, younger social enterprises tend to perceive grants as an output that has to be increased. Thus, this study shows that it may be helpful to use different variable settings depending on the age of the social enterprises.

However, this study does have some limitations. First, it has been applied to Korean social enterprises only. Because each country has a different social enterprise classification system, it is difficult to say that the model applied to social enterprises in Korea may be applied to those in other countries. Yet, any classification system might be based on the similarity of the entities being classified. Therefore, this evaluation model is applicable to a system where the classification is made according to the homogeneity assumption of DEA. We leave it to future research to investigate the performance of social enterprises in different countries. Second, we performed an industry-specific assessment with only focus on the manufacturing sector. Although the application in the manufacturing sector is intended to provide an example of how to apply the proposed evaluation model, there is a limitation in that only one technology is considered. Therefore, we expect that future work should perform an analysis for suggesting the detailed and realistic improving directions in different industry sectors, by applying different technologies. Third, the qualitative factors are not reflected in the evaluation model, although they are very important in measuring the level of social contribution. Quantifying the qualitative elements of social contribution is very difficult and time-consuming. This study does not suggest, though, that only measurable factors should be incorporated in the performance evaluation; we feel that the evaluation of qualitative factors, such as SROI, is essential. However, it is worth emphasizing the importance of assessment using quantitative factors, as a preliminary investigation prior to such an investigation. Nevertheless, the evaluation model presented in this study is meaningful in terms of its simplicity and efficiency. We believe that the advanced DEA model considering qualitative factors is very beneficial for evaluating the social value of social enterprises.

Acknowledgments: This work was supported by the Ministry of Education of the Republic of Korea and the National Research Foundation of Korea (NRF-2015S1A5B8046893).

Author Contributions: Pyoungsoo Lee conceived, designed, and performed the numerical analysis, wrote and revised the paper. Yong Won Seo supervised the whole process and revised the paper.

Conflicts of Interest: The authors declare no conflict of interest.

Appendix A. Benchmarking Information

Table A1. Benchmarking information.

DMU	Grants	No. of Benchmarks	DMU	Grants	No. of Benchmarks	DMU	Grants	No. of Benchmarks
1	Output	4	61	Output	4	121	I/O	-
2	Output	3	62	Output	4	122	Output	5
3	Output	5	63	Output	4	123	I/O	-
4	Output	3	64	Output	5	124	Output	4
5	Input	3	65	Input	3	125	Output	5
6	Input	3	66	Output	5	126	Output	4
7	I/O	-	67	Output	4	127	Output	4
8	Output	5	68	Output	3	128	Output	4
9	Output	5	69	Output	4	129	Input	4
10	Input	3	70	Output	5	130	Input	-
11	Output	5	71	Output	4	131	I/O	-
12	Input	3	72	Output	5	132	Output	3
13	Output	4	73	Output	4	133	Input	4
14	Input	2	74	Input	5	134	Input	4
15	Input	3	75	Input	5	135	I/O	-
16	Output	4	76	Output	4	136	I/O	-
17	Output	3	77	Output	-	137	Output	-
18	Output	4	78	Output	-	138	Input	4
19	I/O	-	79	Output	5	139	Input	4
20	Output	4	80	I/O	-	140	Output	4
21	Input	-	81	Input	4	141	Output	3
22	Output	5	82	Output	5	142	Output	4
23	Input	3	83	Output	5	143	Input	3
24	Output	4	84	Input	-	144	Output	4
25	Output	6	85	Output	4	145	Input	5
26	Output	5	86	Output	4	146	Input	4
27	Input	3	87	Output	4	147	Input	3
28	Input	2	88	Input	4	148	Output	4
29	Output	5	89	Input	3	149	Output	3
30	Input	3	90	Output	6	150	Output	5
31	Output	4	91	Output	5	151	I/O	-
32	Input	2	92	Output	4	152	Input	3
33	Output	4	93	Output	4	153	Output	4
34	Input	3	94	I/O	-	154	Input	3
35	Output	4	95	Output	5	155	Input	3
36	I/O	-	96	I/O	-	156	Input	4
37	Output	4	97	Output	4	157	I/O	-
38	Output	5	98	Input	4	158	Input	3
39	Input		99	Output	5	159	Output	4
40	Output	5	100	Input	3	160	Input	4
41	Output	5	101	Output	4	161	Input	4
42	Output	5	102	Output	6	162	Output	4
43	Output	6	103	Output	5	163	Input	-
44	Input	-	104	Input	3	164	Output	4
45	Input	4	105	Output	4	165	Output	5
46	Input	3	106	Output	3	166	I/O	-
47	I/O	-	107	Output	-	167	Input	6
48	Input	2	108	Output	4			
49	Output	4	109	Output	4			
50	Output	3	110	Output	3			
51	Input	-	111	Output	4			
52	Output	4	112	Output	4			
53	Input	4	113	Output	6			
54	Input	4	114	Input	5			
55	Input	4	115	Output	3			
56	Input	3	116	Output	5			
57	Input	3	117	Input	4			
58	Output	3	118	Input	5			
59	Output	4	119	I/O				
60	Output	4	120	Output	3			

I/O: Input or output.

References

1.   Wang, H.; Tong, L.; Takeuchi, R.; George, G. Corporate social responsibility: An overview and new research directions thematic issue on corporate social responsibility. *Acad. Manag. J.* **2016**, *59*, 534–544. [CrossRef]
2.   Borzaga, C.; Galera, G.; Nogales, R. *Social Enterprise: A New Model for Poverty Reduction and Employment Generation*; United Nations Development Programme Regional Bureau for Europe and the Commonwealth of Independent States: Bratislava, Slovakia, 2008.
3.   Defourny, J.; Borzaga, C. *From Third Sector to Social Enterprise*; Routledge: London, UK, 2001.
4.   Defourny, J.; Nyssens, M. Social enterprise in Europe: Recent trends and developments. *Soc. Enterp. J.* **2008**, *4*, 202–228. [CrossRef]
5.   Kerlin, J.A. Defining social enterprise across different contexts: A conceptual framework based on institutional factors. *Nonprofit Volunt. Sec. Q.* **2013**, *42*, 84–108. [CrossRef]
6.   Kim, Y. Can social enterprise stand for persons with disabilities? The case of South Korean social enterprises, 2007–2008. *J. Asian Public Policy* **2009**, *2*, 293–308. [CrossRef]
7.   Parkinson, C.; Howorth, C. The language of social entrepreneurs. *Entrep. Reg. Dev.* **2008**, *20*, 285–309. [CrossRef]
8.   Pharoah, C.; Fisher, A.; Scott, D. *Social Enterprise in the Balance: Challenges for the Voluntary Sector*; Charities Aid Foundation: West Malling, UK, 2004.
9.   Ridley-Duff, R. Communitarian perspectives on social enterprise. *Corp. Gov.* **2007**, *15*, 382–392. [CrossRef]
10.   Teasdale, S. What's in a name? Making sense of social enterprise discourses. *Public Policy Adm.* **2012**, *27*, 99–119. [CrossRef]
11.   Young, D.R.; Lecy, J.D. Defining the universe of social enterprise: Competing metaphors. *Int. J. Volunt. Nonprofit Organ.* **2014**, *25*, 1307–1332. [CrossRef]
12.   Grassl, W. Business models of social enterprise: A design approach to hybridity. *ACRN J. Entrep. Perspect.* **2012**, *1*, 37–60.
13.   Doherty, B.; Haugh, H.; Lyon, F. Social enterprises as hybrid organizations: A review and research agenda. *Int. J. Manag. Rev.* **2014**, *16*, 417–436. [CrossRef]
14.   Bagnoli, L.; Megali, C. Measuring performance in social enterprises. *Nonprofit Volunt. Sec. Q.* **2011**, *40*, 149–165. [CrossRef]
15.   Emerson, J.; Twersky, F. *New Social Entrepreneurs: The Success, Challenge and Lessons of Non-Profit Enterprise Creation*; The Homeless Economic Fund, the Roberts Foundation: San Francisco, CA, USA, 1996.
16.   Jang, J.J. A Study on the use of DEA models for evaluating managerial efficiency of the social enterprises—Focus on nursing and healthe-care firms in H area. *Korean Corp. Manag. Rev.* **2010**, *34*, 179–191.
17.   Lee, J.-M.; Lee, W.-Y. Measuring relative efficiency of social enterprises in Korean using data envelopment analysis and Tobit regression analysis. *Soc. Enterp. Stud.* **2016**, *9*, 3–30.
18.   Natesan, S.D.; Natesan, S.D.; Marathe, R.R.; Marathe, R.R. Evaluation of MGNREGA: Data envelopment analysis approach. *Int. J. Soc. Econ.* **2017**, *44*, 181–194. [CrossRef]
19.   Lee, S.-Y.; Lim, S.; Chae, M. Management efficiency estimation of social enterprises with data envelopment analysis. *J. Soc. Korea Ind. Syst. Eng.* **2017**, *40*, 121–128. [CrossRef]
20.   Charnes, A.; Cooper, W.W.; Rhodes, E. Measuring the efficiency of decision making units. *Eur. J. Oper. Res.* **1978**, *2*, 429–444. [CrossRef]
21.   Feng, C.-M.; Wang, R.-T. Performance evaluation for airlines including the consideration of financial ratios. *J. Air Transp. Manag.* **2000**, *6*, 133–142. [CrossRef]
22.   Liang, L.; Yang, F.; Cook, W.D.; Zhu, J. DEA models for supply chain efficiency evaluation. *Ann. Oper. Res.* **2006**, *145*, 35–49. [CrossRef]
23.   Hsieh, L.-F.; Lin, L.-H. A performance evaluation model for international tourist hotels in Taiwan—An application of the relational network DEA. *Int. J. Hosp. Manag.* **2010**, *29*, 14–24. [CrossRef]
24.   Lee, H.; Park, Y.; Choi, H. Comparative evaluation of performance of national R&D programs with heterogeneous objectives: A DEA approach. *Eur. J. Oper. Res.* **2009**, *196*, 847–855.
25.   Lee, P.; Park, Y.-J. Eco-efficiency evaluation considering environmental stringency. *Sustainability* **2017**, *9*, 661. [CrossRef]
26.   Hollingsworth, B. The measurement of efficiency and productivity of health care delivery. *Health Econ.* **2008**, *17*, 1107–1128. [CrossRef] [PubMed]

27. Narasimhan, R.; Talluri, S.; Sarkis, J.; Ross, A. Efficient service location design in government services: A decision support system framework. *J. Oper. Manag.* **2005**, *23*, 163–178. [CrossRef]
28. Beasley, J.E. Comparing university departments. *Omega* **1990**, *18*, 171–183. [CrossRef]
29. Beasley, J.E. Determining teaching and research efficiencies. *J. Oper. Res. Soc.* **1995**, *46*, 441–452. [CrossRef]
30. Mahdiloo, M.; Noorizadeh, A.; Saen, R.F. A new approach for considering a dual-role factor in supplier selection problem. *Int. J. Acad. Res.* **2011**, *3*, 261–266.
31. Saen, R.F. Restricting weights in supplier selection decisions in the presence of dual-role factors. *Appl. Math. Model.* **2010**, *34*, 2820–2830. [CrossRef]
32. Cook, W.D.; Green, R.H.; Zhu, J. Dual-role factors in data envelopment analysis. *IIE Trans.* **2006**, *38*, 105–115. [CrossRef]
33. Ruggiero, J. Performance evaluation when non-discretionary factors correlate with technical efficiency. *Eur. J. Oper. Res.* **2004**, *159*, 250–257. [CrossRef]
34. Toloo, M.; Barat, M. On considering dual-role factor in supplier selection problem. *Math. Methods Oper. Res.* **2015**, *82*, 107–122. [CrossRef]
35. Samoilenko, S.; Osei-Bryson, K.-M. Increasing the discriminatory power of DEA in the presence of the sample heterogeneity with cluster analysis and decision trees. *Expert Syst. Appl.* **2008**, *34*, 1568–1581. [CrossRef]
36. Dyson, R.G.; Allen, R.; Camanho, A.S.; Podinovski, V.V.; Sarrico, C.S.; Shale, E.A. Pitfalls and protocols in DEA. *Eur. J. Oper. Res.* **2001**, *132*, 245–259. [CrossRef]

MDPI

St. Alban-Anlage 66

4052 Basel

Switzerland

Tel. +41 61 683 77 34

Fax +41 61 302 89 18

www.mdpi.com

Sustainability Editorial Office

E-mail: sustainability@mdpi.com

www.mdpi.com/journal/sustainability

www.ingramcontent.com/pod-product-compliance
Lightning Source LLC
Chambersburg PA
CBHW051729210326
41597CB00032B/5660